C++ Programming 101

C++ PROGRAMMING 101

Greg Perry

SAMS
PUBLISHING

This book is for Dr. Roger Wainwright, my first and only "real" computer teacher.

Copyright© 1992 by Sams Publishing

International Standard Book Number: 0-672-30200-4

Library of Congress Catalog Card Number: 92-62272

95   94   4   3   2

Interpretation of the printing code: the rightmost double-digit number is the year of the book's printing; the rightmost single-digit, the number of the book's printing. For example, a printing code of 92-1 shows that the first printing of the book occurred in 1992.

Trademarks

Composed in New Century Schoolbook and MCPdigital by Prentice Hall Computer Publishing

Printed in the United States of America

Publisher
Richard K. Swadley

Acquisitions Manager
Jordan Gold

Acquisitions Editor
Stacy Hiquet

Development Editor
Rosemarie Graham

Editors
Gayle L. Johnson
Keith Davenport
Mary Corder
Tad Ringo

Editorial Coordinators
Rebecca S. Freeman
Bill Whitmer

Editorial Assistant
Lori Kelley

Technical Editor
Timothy C. Moore

Cover Designer
Jean Bisesi

**Director of Production and
Manufacturing**
Jeff Valler

Production Manager
Corinne Walls

Imprint Manager
Matthew Morrill

Book Designer
Michele Laseau

Production Analyst
Mary Beth Wakefield

**Proofreading/Indexing
Coordinator**
Joelynn Gifford

Graphics Image Specialists
Dennis Sheehan
Sue VandeWalle
Jerry Ellis

Production
Katy Bodenmiller
Christine Cook
Lisa Daugherty
Carla Hall-Batton
Howard Jones
John Kane
Sean Medlock
Linda Quigley
Michelle Self
Susan Shepard
Greg Simsic
Angie Trzepacz
Alyssa Yesh

Indexer
Loren Malloy

Overview

Classroom 8   Structures, Files, and OOP

Lessons

Appendixes

Classroom 2   Working with Data

Lessons

Classroom 3   Operators

Lessons

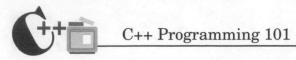

Classroom 4   Controlling Program Flow

Lessons

Classroom 6   Supplied Functions

Lessons

Classroom 7   Arrays and Pointers

Lessons

Classroom 8   Structures, Files, and OOP

Lessons

Acknowledgments

My thanks go to all the readers of my other programming books and to my students for keeping me on track and helping me present my material even more clearly in this book.

I want to thank the wonderful editors and production department at Sams Publishing for producing this book. Their hearts are huge, and their desire to reach the reader at any level is obvious. The books that Sams publishes are some of the most respected in the industry. Both beginners and experts can find the help they need. This is because of the people at Sams, not because of my or any other author's writing.

My beautiful bride, Jayne, my friends Michael Stapp and Diane Moore, co-workers and students at Tulsa Junior College, and my parents, Glen and Bettye Perry, continue to support my efforts. It is all of them I hope I never let down. This book's effort was due to them.

About the Author

Greg Perry is quickly becoming one of the most sought-after speakers and writers in the programming field. He is known for being able to take programming topics and bring them down to the beginner's level. Perry has been a programmer and trainer for the past 15 years. He received his first degree in computer science, then he received a master's degree in corporate finance. He currently is a professor of computer science at Tulsa Junior College, as well as a computer consultant and lecturer. Perry is the author of 14 other computer books, including *Moving from C to C++* (Sams Publishing, 1992). In addition, he has published articles in several publications, including *PC World, Data Training,* and *Inside First Publisher.*

Introduction

Get ready to learn C++! Every day, more and more people learn and use the C++ programming language. C++ is quickly becoming the most widely used programming language. As soon as you master C++, you will be ready to join the ranks of today's programmers in writing C++ programs that do what you want them to do.

C++ Programming 101 offers a brand-new approach to computer-book learning. This book brings you into the learning process by letting you become active while you read. Scattered throughout the text are examples of code, questions for you to ponder, and brief exercises for you to try. Command descriptions, format syntax, and language references are not enough to teach a newcomer a programming language.

By the time you finish this book, you will be writing powerful C++ programs, even if you have never programmed a computer before. This book marks an innovation not tried by other computer books. From teaching about variables to providing an introduction to object-oriented programming, this book is perfect for beginning programmers and for programmers who want to know more about C++.

Who Should Use This Book

C++ Programming 101 is aimed primarily toward beginning programmers who either have never programmed or who have never seen a C++ program. Text, questions, exercises, and numerous programs are aimed at both beginning programmers and those new to C++.

If you already program computers but have never had the time to tackle C++, this book is right for you because it teaches more than just the language. This book attempts to teach you how to program correctly, concentrating on proper coding techniques as well as the C++ language itself.

A Note to the Instructor

If you are an instructor using this book for your class, you will find that it promotes active learning more than other books do. The questions and exercises offer a foundation for classroom discussions. Not all of the questions and programming assignments are included on the enclosed disk, so there is lots of room for you to assign homework directly from this book.

Because *C++ Programming 101* becomes a part-time teacher, questioning and guiding the student as he or she reads and learns, you can spend more time in the classroom looking at complete program examples and exploring the theory of C++ instead of taking time to cover all the petty details you normally would have to cover.

During the writing and production of this book, you, the C++ instructor, were kept in the forefront. This book will not disappoint you. It takes much of the classroom burden from you, letting you teach the importance of C++ and letting you act more as the students' mentor instead of as a "verbal textbook" that instructors sometimes become.

This Book's Philosophy

C++ Programming 101 takes the workbook approach to learning. This book contains all the text and language syntax needed for newcomers to C++, yet it is full of complete program examples, exercises, questions, tips, and side notes.

The primary goal of this book is to make you, the reader, more active in the learning process. So many books require the reader to read an entire chapter before seeing any questions or before trying any examples. This book continually breaks up the reading with questions and quizzes designed to give you immediate feedback on the material you just read.

C++ Programming 101 focuses on programming *correctly* in C++ by teaching structured programming techniques and proper program design. Emphasis is placed on a program's readability rather than on "tricks of the trade" code examples. In this changing world, programs should be clear, properly structured, and well-documented, and this book does not waver from this philosophy.

This book contains more than 100 sample program listings. These programs show ways that you can use C++ for personal finance, school and business record keeping, math and science, and general-purpose applications that almost everybody with a computer can use. This wide variety of programs shows you that C++ is a very powerful language that is easy to learn and use.

Overview

C++ Programming 101 is divided into eight sections called *classrooms*. Each classroom contains two to five chapters, appropriately called *lessons*. Classroom 1 introduces you to the C++ environment and introductory programming concepts. Starting with Classroom 2, this book presents the C++ programming language commands and built-in functions. After mastering the language, you can use this book as a handy reference. When you need help with a specific C++ programming problem, turn to the appropriate area that describes that part of the language to see numerous examples of code.

To get an idea of this book's layout, read the following descriptions of each section:

Classroom 1: Looking at C++

This classroom explains what C++ is by describing a brief history of the C++ programming language and presenting an overview of C++'s advantages over other languages. You learn how to develop C++ programs and the steps you follow to write and run programs. You dive right into C++ beginning in Lesson 2, "The C++ Program."

Classroom 2: Working with Data

This classroom teaches you all about C++ variables and data. You must understand the various data types possible in C++ before you can work with data. You begin to write programs and see results. You also learn all about printing to the screen and getting data from the keyboard.

Classroom 3: Operators

This classroom teaches the entire set of C++ operators. The rich assortment of operators (more than are contained in any other programming language except APL) makes up for the fact that the C++ programming language is very small. The operators and their order of precedence are more important to C++ than to most other programming languages.

Classroom 4: Controlling Program Flow

C++ data processing is powerful due to the looping, comparison, and selection constructs that C++ offers. The lessons in this classroom show you how to write programs that make decisions that execute certain parts of the program.

Classroom 5: Scope and Functions

To support true structured programming techniques, C++ must allow for local and global variables, as well as offer several ways to pass and return variables between functions. C++ is a very strong structured language that attempts, if the programmer is willing, to "listen to the language" by protecting local variables by making them visible only to the parts of the program that need them.

Classroom 6: Supplied Functions

C++ contains no commands that perform input or output. To make up for this apparent oversight, C++ compiler writers supply several useful input and output functions. By separating input and output functions from the language, C++ achieves better portability between computers. If your program runs on one computer, it will work on any other.

This classroom also describes several of the other built-in math, character, and string functions available with C++. These functions keep you from having to write your own routines to perform common tasks.

Classroom 7: Arrays and Pointers

C++ offers single and multidimensional arrays that hold multiple occurrences of repeating data but that do not require much effort on your part to process. Unlike many other programming languages, C++ also uses pointer variables a great deal. Pointer variables and arrays work together to give you flexible data storage that allows for easy sorting and searching of data.

Classroom 8: Structures, Files, and OOP

Variables, arrays, and pointers are not enough to hold the types of data that your programs require. Structures allow for more powerful grouping of many different kinds of data into manageable units.

Your computer would be too limiting if you could not store data to the disk and retrieve that data back in your programs. Disk files are required by most "real-world" applications. The lessons in this classroom describe how C++ processes sequential and random-access files and teaches the fundamental principles needed to effectively save data to disk.

The most dramatic difference in C++ over many other programming languages is its object-oriented programming (*OOP*) allowance. Through *classes,* C++ implements data-hiding and smart data objects. The concepts of OOP take time to master, but this short section introduces you to the initial structure of an OOP program.

Conventions Used in This Book

The following typographic conventions are used in this book:

- Code lines, variables, and any text you see on-screen appear in `monospace`.

- Placeholders in statement syntax explanations appear in *`italic monospace`*.

- Filenames are in regular text, all uppercase (CDATA.CPP).

- Optional parameters in statement syntax explanations are enclosed in flat brackets ([ ]). You do *not* type the brackets when you include these parameters.

- New terms appear in *italic*.

- Pseudocode, a way of explaining in English what a program does, appears in *italic*.

Index to the Icons

Unlike many computer books, this book contains several items in the text that promote the *workbook* approach. You will run across many icons that bring specific items to your attention and that offer questions and exercises that you might want to answer. After each of the questions and exercises are gray-screened blank lines where you can finish the problem before moving to the next topic. In addition, several blank pages for notes are provided at the end of this book.

The following icons appear throughout this book:

The *Lesson Objective* icon appears at the beginning of each lesson. The goal of the lesson is stated so that you have a good idea of where the lesson is headed.

 This is the *Think About...* icon. When further thought is needed on a particular topic, the *Think About...* icon brings extra information to your attention.

 When a topic becomes particularly difficult, the *Still Confused?* icon offers some help. The *Still Confused?* paragraphs are meant to further explain a concept that was taught earlier in the text.

The *Try This* icon marks a question or offers a small exercise for you to finish. After each *Try This* exercise is ample blank space so that you can answer the exercise before moving on to the next topic. The *Try This* icon gives you instant feedback that tests your knowledge of what you just read about.

 Next to the *Find the Bug* icon you find a program listing that contains one or more errors. After the program is room for you to correct the error.

 This is the *Finish the Program* icon. A section of a program is left unfinished, with ample space for you to fill in the missing code. The *Finish the Program* icon tests your ability to write programming statements that you just learned about.

In addition, tips and notes appear as boxed text.

TIP: A tip shows you an extra shortcut or advantage possible with the command you just learned.

NOTE: A note brings a particular side effect or useful topic to your attention.

This Book's Disk

The disk supplied with this book is an integral part of your learning C++ with the *C++ Programming 101* workbook approach. The disk contains all of the code in all of the programs in this book. The disk is divided into a separate directory for each lesson. Within that directory is a listing of each program from that lesson. In the first line of every program in this book is a comment with the program's disk filename. For example, if you want to try the program named CH1.CPP from Lesson 23, you would find it in the directory named L23 on the disk.

The disk also contains answers to many of the review questions and exercises at the end of each lesson. Also, you will find answers to many of the Try This, Find the Bug, and Finish the Program exercises throughout each lesson. All of the answers supplied are in files named ANSWERS.TXT within each directory on the disk.

Each directory also contains one or two suggested exercises and extra questions that you might want to consider. These extra exercises and questions are located in the file named EXTRAQS.TXT in each directory on the disk.

All of the files on the disk are ASCII text files that any PC editor can read.

C++ CLASSROOM One

Looking at C++

Introduction to C++

OBJECTIVE *To introduce you to the C++ programming language and its environment.*

This book is all you need to learn the fundamentals of C++, even if you have never programmed a computer. Writing computer programs is different from using them. Most of today's word processors are fairly easy to learn to use, but lots of work goes into creating them. Word processors are just an example of the results of programming efforts. Many programmers spend many hours, days, and weeks writing the programs that people use.

The C++ programming language is one of the newest programming languages in existence. Based on the C programming language, C++ is an improved version of C that takes the C language to the next level of evolution of programming languages.

This lesson introduces you to the C++ programming language and to programming concepts in general. You will learn about the history of C++, and see how C++ compares to the C programming language.

Introduction to Programming

A *program* is simply a list of instructions that tells the computer what to do. Computers are only dumb machines. They cannot think; they can only execute your orders within the programs that you write.

A program is to a computer what a recipe is to a cook. A recipe is nothing more than a program (a list of instructions) that tells the cook exactly what to do. The recipe's end result is a finished dish, and the end result of a computer program is an application, such as a word processor or a payroll program. By itself, your computer does not know how to be a word processor. By following a list of detailed programming instructions written by a programmer, however, the computer performs the actions necessary to do word processing.

If you want your computer to help you with your household budget, keep track of names and addresses, or play an electronic game of solitaire, you have to supply a program so that it knows how to do those things. You can either buy the program or write one yourself.

There are several advantages to writing your own programs. When you write your own programs, they do exactly what you want them to. Although it would be foolish to try to write *every* program that you need to use (there is not enough time and there are many good programs on the market), some applications are so specific that you simply cannot find a program that does exactly what you want.

> Companies generally hire a staff of programmers to write all the programs used within the company. When a company acquires a computer system, that company does not want to change the way it does business. Therefore, the programmers design and write programs that are exactly right for the company.

The Programming Process

To give C++ programming instructions to your computer, you need an *editor* and a C++ *compiler*. An editor is similar to a word processor. It is a program that enables you to type a C++ program into memory, make changes to the program (such as moving, copying, and inserting text), and save the program permanently to a disk file. After you use the editor to type the program, you must compile it with a C++ compiler before you run the program.

4

The C++ programming language is a *compiled* language. The compiler (the C++ programming language that you must have before running C++ programs) takes your C++ language instructions and translates them into a form that your computer can read. A C++ compiler is a tool that your computer uses to understand the C++ language instructions in your programs. Many compilers come with their own editor. (The two most popular PC C++ compilers, Borland's Turbo C++ and Microsoft's C++ compilers, both come with their own editors and integrated programming environments.) If your compiler includes an editor, you probably will feel that your programming environment is more integrated.

Because this book teaches the generic AT&T C++ standard programming language, no attempt is made to tie in any editor- or compiler-specific commands. There are too many different versions of C++ compilers on the market to cover each one of their specifics in a single book. AT&T was the first company to produce a C++ language, so AT&T has been the de facto language standard for the last few years.

As long as you write programs that conform to the AT&T specification (all programs in this book do), they will work on almost any C++ compiler on the market. (You deviate from the AT&T standard by putting lots of compiler-specific built-in functions into your program code.) Most compiler companies tell you which version of AT&T C++ is compatible with what compiler. As long as your compiler conforms to AT&T 2.1 or higher, all programs in this book work fine.

A program is also known as *code*. After you write C++ code, you run it through the C++ compiler, issue the proper compiling instructions, and run the program. The program's *output* is the result of the program. The *user* of the program is the person (sometimes the programmer) who uses the program but cares little (or not at all) about the underlying program that produces the output. Figure 1.1 shows a diagram of the steps necessary to write and execute a C++ program.

Notice that your C++ program must be routed through a *preprocessor* before it is compiled. The preprocessor reads *preprocessor directives* that you enter in the program to control the program's compilation. Your C++ compiler automatically performs the preprocessor step, so it requires no additional learning on your part except for the preprocessor directives that you put inside your programs. This book teaches you about the two primary preprocessor directives in Lesson 7, "Preprocessor Directives."

Turn to your compiler's reference manuals now, or ask your company's data processing personnel, to learn how to compile programs with your own C++ programming environment. The compiler's manual often

includes a short tutorial that teaches you how to use the editor and compile a program. Learning your compiler's entire programming environment, including all the ins and outs of your editor and compiler's options, is not as critical as learning the C++ language. The compiler is just a way to transform your program from a *source program* (the C++ instructions you write) to an executable file.

Figure 1.1. The steps necessary to make a C++ program produce results.

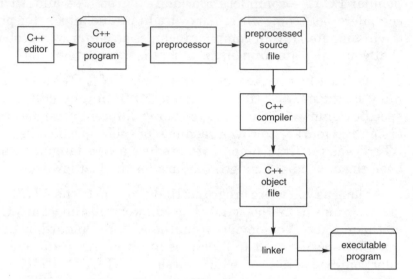

As Figure 1.1 shows, your program must go through one last stage after compiling and before running. It is called the *linking,* or the *link editing,* stage. When your program is linked, a program called the *linker* supplies needed runtime information to the compiled program. You also can combine several compiled programs into one executable program by linking them. Most of the time, however, your compiler does all the link editing (both Borland's and Microsoft's C++ compilers automatically take care of the link editing for you). You rarely have to concern yourself with the linking stage until you write advanced applications.

Exterminating Pests

Because you are typing instructions for a machine, you must be very accurate. If you misspell a word, leave out a quotation mark, or make another mistake, your C++ compiler informs you with an error message. The most common error is a *syntax error,* which generally means that you misspelled a word.

When you compile your program and it has mistakes, your compiler tells you what those mistakes are. The compiler will not send your program through the link editor if you made typing mistakes. Therefore, you must read the compiler's error message, figure out what the problem is, and correct the error by returning to the editor and fixing the mistake.

A program error is commonly known as a *bug*. If you don't understand the error message, you might have to check your compiler's reference manual or scour your program's source code until you find the offending code line. The process of locating and correcting program errors is called *debugging*.

> **NOTE:** Your compiler does not catch all program bugs. Sometimes *logic errors* creep into your code. Logic errors are more difficult to find than typing errors because your compiler does not tell you about them. For instance, if you wrote a program that prints payroll checks, but you told the computer to print all checks for a negative amount, the computer would obey your instructions. Of course, the instructions themselves would be incorrect because they were the result of an error in your logic.

Throughout this book you are given a chance to find bugs in programs. Once or twice a lesson you will see an incorrect program next to a Find the Bug icon. This is your chance to hone your debugging skills.

C++ Compared with Other Languages

If you have programmed before, you should understand a little about how C++ differs from other programming languages. C++ is efficient and has much stronger typing than its C predecessor. C is known as a *weakly typed* language; in other words, variable data types do not necessarily have to hold the same type of data. (Function prototyping and typecasting help to alleviate this problem.)

For example, if you declare an integer variable and decide to put a character value in it, C enables you to do so. The data might not be in the format you expect, but C does its best. This is much different from stronger-typed languages such as COBOL and Pascal.

 If this discussion seems a little over your head at this point, relax. The upcoming lessons elaborate on these topics and provide many examples.

C++ is a small, block-structured programming language with only 48 commands (called *keywords*). To compensate for its small vocabulary, C++ has one of the largest assortment of *operators* (second only to the APL programming language), such as +, -, and &&. The large number of operators in C++ might tempt programmers to write cryptic programs that have only a small amount of code. You will see throughout this book, however, that making the program more readable is more important than saving some bytes. This book teaches you how to use the C++ operators to their fullest extent while maintaining readable programs.

C++'s large number of operators (almost equal to the number of keywords) requires a more judicious use of an *operator precedence* table. Appendix D includes the complete C++ operator table. Unlike most other languages that have only four or five levels of precedence, C++ has 17 (some books combine a few to produce only 15). As you learn C++, you must master each of these 17 levels. This is not as difficult as it sounds, but its importance cannot be overstated.

C++ also has no input or output statements. (You might want to read that sentence again!) C++ has no commands that perform input or output. This is one of the most important reasons why C++ is available on so many different computers. The I/O (input/output) statements of most languages tie those languages to specific hardware. BASIC, for instance, has almost 20 I/O commands—some of which write to the screen, to the printer, to a modem, and so forth. If you write a BASIC program for a microcomputer, chances are good that it cannot run on a mainframe without considerable modification.

C++'s input and output is performed through the abundant use of operators and function calls. With every C++ compiler comes a library of standard I/O functions. I/O functions are *hardware-independent,* meaning that they work on any device and on any computer that conforms to the AT&T C++ standard.

To master C++ completely, you must be more aware of your computer's hardware than most other languages require. You certainly do not have to be a hardware expert, but understanding the internal data representation makes C++ much more usable and meaningful.

It also helps if you can become familiar with binary and hexadecimal numbers. You might want to read Appendix B for a tutorial on these topics before you start to learn C++. If you do not want to learn these topics, you can still become a good C++ programmer, but knowing what goes on "under the hood" might make C++ more meaningful to you as you learn it.

C++ and Microcomputers

C was a relatively unknown language until it was placed on the microcomputer. With the invention and growth of the microcomputer, C blossomed into a worldwide computer language. C++ extends that use on smaller computers. Most readers of *C++ Programming 101* probably are working on a microcomputer-based C++ system.

Microcomputers typically are called *PCs,* from the widespread use of the original IBM PC. The early PCs did not have the memory capacity of the large computers used by government and big business. Nevertheless, PC owners still needed a way to program these machines. BASIC was the first programming language used for PCs. Over the years, many other languages were ported from larger computers to the PC. However, no language was as successful as C in becoming the worldwide standard programming language. C++ seems to be the next standard. AT&T introduced C++ in 1981, and over the last three years, C++ has become one of the most popular programming languages in use.

Get on board and hang on as best you can! Lesson 2, "The C++ Program," takes you directly into the C++ programming language so that you can begin writing programs as soon as possible.

The C++ Program

 OBJECTIVE   *To acquaint you with C++ programs.*

This lesson shows you a few C++ programs. You will learn to familiarize yourself with the look and feel of simple C++ programs. Do not be too concerned about understanding every line in every program. As a matter of fact, the less you worry about each program's specifics, the better off you will be for this lesson.

Your First C++ Program

Here is a C++ program. Although it is extremely simple, it contains all the elements necessary to be a valid C++ program.

```
// Filename: CFIRST.CPP
// Program displays a message on-screen
#include <iostream.h>
void main()
{
    cout << "I will be a C++ expert!";
}
```

Even a simple C++ program might intimidate a beginning programmer. Do not let it intimidate you! C++ has a bark that is often worse than its bite. If you were to type this program into your C++ compiler's editor, compile it, and run it (usually by selecting Run from a pull-down menu), you would see the following output on your screen:

```
I will be a C++ expert!
```

At this point, do not concern yourself with the specifics of the code in this program. The rest of this book explains things like that. Only one line in the entire seven-line program does anything noticeable (the one that begins with cout), and the rest of the program exists to set up the program properly.

The preceding program contains a total of seven lines, and only one really produces something you can see. More advanced C++ programs might consist of 500 lines or more. That 7-to-1 setup-to-work ratio does *not* exist for every C++ program. That would cause too much work on your part! The amount of code that sets up the program diminishes as a program grows.

C++ Special Characters

C++ is one of the few programming languages that uses almost every key on your keyboard. C++ is picky about the keys you press. Notice that the program in the preceding section contains a left and a right brace, { and }. If you were to use parentheses, (and), or square brackets, [and], in place of the braces, C++ would complain.

Be extremely careful to use the characters you are supposed to use. Computers are precise machines without as much tolerance for typing ambiguities as people have. Throughout *C++ Programming 101*, you will learn when to use each of the characters and what they mean. Until then, be very careful to type the correct characters.

C++ distinguishes between a capital letter O and a number 0 (zero). Also, a lowercase letter l will not substitute for a number 1. Because you're dealing with a machine, you should type numbers when C++ wants numbers, letters when C++ wants letters, and exact special characters (characters that are neither letters nor numbers, such as brackets and the plus sign) when C++ wants them.

Draw a line from the special character on the left to the special character's description on the right.

Special Character	Description
[	Backslash
<	Left bracket
}	Right angled bracket
¦	Right parenthesis
\	Forward slash (or just "slash")
]	Left angled bracket
{	Left parenthesis
)	Right brace
(	Vertical line
>	Left brace
/	Right bracket

Freeform Style

Most of the time, you can put lots of spacing in a C++ program and C++ will not complain. C++ programmers often put extra spaces and blank lines in programs to make the programs more readable. The extra spacing is called *white space*. With white space, C++ programmers make C++ programs more readable to *people,* not to the C++ compiler.

To your C++ compiler, the following program is *exactly the same program* as the previous one you saw:

```
//Filename:CFIRST.CPP//Program displays a message on-screen
#include <iostream.h>
void main(){cout<<"I will be a C++ expert!";}
```

Which is easier for *you* to read, the first or the second version of the program? Obviously, the first version is. C++ is called a *freeform* compiler. *Freeform* means that the compiler lets you put blanks and extra lines just about anywhere you want. You can indent lines of the program, or leave all the lines flush left.

Because your computer is a machine, it does not require extra white space to understand a program. As long as you follow all the coding rules of C++, the compiler will be happy with the code you supply. In spite of the C++ *compiler's* lack of concern for how nice a program looks, *you* should be concerned about the program's look. Add extra white space to group similar lines of code together and make the program easier to understand for people who read the program.

> **NOTE:** As you see other programs throughout this book, you will begin to pick up some C++ whitespace conventions and develop some of your own.

While you write C++ programs, consider that someday you might have to change those programs—or somebody you work with will have to. You could squeeze as much space out of a program as possible, but you will gain nothing from doing so. (You might save a few characters of computer memory, but not enough to make up for a messy program.)

If you add extra white space to make the program more readable to people, the program will be easy to modify in the future. In this ever-changing world, programs have to be modified to reflect those changes, and the person who writes more readable code gets hired for programming jobs faster than one who does not care about program readability. Updating and changing programs is called *maintaining* programs. A maintainable program is a readable program.

If you are confused now, you are right on track! You still do not have to understand any specifics about the two program listings seen so far. This lesson is getting you used to the look and feel of C++ programs, not their particulars. If you understand that C++ is picky about the characters you type, and if you realize that a program should be readable to people, you deserve an A+ for the lesson so far.

Uppercase and Lowercase

Although C++ cares little about white space, it does know the difference between uppercase and lowercase letters. Most of the time, C++ prefers

14

lowercase letters. C++'s preference for lowercase letters sets it apart from most other programming languages. To many programming languages, the following statements are identical:

```
if (netpay > grosspay)


If (NetPay > GrossPay)


IF (NETPAY > GROSSPAY)
```

To C++, the three lines are extremely different. As you learn the C++ language, you will see when to use lowercase and when to use uppercase. Again, most of the time, you will program in lowercase letters.

C++ contains a fixed vocabulary of commands, sometimes called *keywords* (and also referred to as *reserved words*). Appendix A contains a complete list of C++ commands. A command is part of the limited vocabulary that C++ recognizes. For example, the command that transmits a value from one place in the program to another is return. You *must* use lowercase letters for return, as well as for all the other commands in C++.

TIP: Refer to Appendix A often as you learn the commands of C++, especially the specific commands beginning in Classroom 2, "Working with Data."

If you want to print messages to the screen or to your printer, you can use uppercase, lowercase, or a mixture of both for the message itself. For example, recall that the program shown earlier printed this message to the screen:

```
I will be a C++ expert!
```

Because this is a message for the user of the program to read, you would want C++ to print it using regular uppercase and lowercase characters. Because the message is not a keyword, it does not have to be all lowercase.

Before you go any further, a short review of the previous sections is warranted. C++ is picky about lowercase commands and about making sure that you type special characters exactly right. White space, however, is another thing entirely. C++ does not care how much white space you add to a program for readability.

Longer Programs

The sample program shown earlier is extremely simple. Some C++ programs require several hundred thousand lines of code. Budding authors would not tackle a sequel to *War and Peace*; likewise, brand-new C++ programmers should stay away from huge programming projects. Most of the programs you write for a while will be relatively small, maybe only 10 to 100 lines of code.

Even a large program usually is not one big program stored in one file on the disk. Programmers often break up large programs into a set of smaller programs. The smaller programs work like building blocks, fitting together as needed to handle some kind of programming application.

Just to give you another early view of a C++ program, here is a program longer than the one you saw earlier. Don't sweat the specifics yet. Glance over the program and start getting used to the variety of special characters that C++ understands.

```cpp
// Filename: 1STLONG.CPP
// Longer C++ program that demonstrates comments,
// variables, constants, and simple input/output
#include <iostream.h>
void main()
{
   int i, j;   // These three lines declare four variables
   char c;
   float x;

   i = 4;   // i is assigned an integer literal
   j = i + 7;   // j is assigned the result of a computation
   c = 'A';   // Enclose all character literals
              // in single quotation marks

   x = 9.087;   // x is a floating-point value

   x = x * 12.3;   // Overwrites what was in x
                   // with something else

   // Sends the values of the four variables to the screen
   cout << i << ", " << j << ", " << c << ", " << x << "\n";

   return;   // Not required, but helpful
}
```

The next few lessons discuss the commands in this program in depth. Again, just to give you an idea of the importance of readability, here is the same program to the C++ compiler, but a very different one indeed to someone who must maintain the program later:

```
//Filename: 1STLONG.CPP//Longer C++ program that demonstrates
//comments, variables, constants, and simple input/output
#include <iostream.h>
void main(){int i,j;//These three lines declare four variables
char c;float x;i=4;// i is assigned an integer literal
j=i+7;//j is assigned the result of a computation
c='A';//Enclose all character literals//in single quotation marks
x=9.087;//x is a floating-point value
x=x*12.3;//Overwrites what was in x with something else
//Sends the values of the four variables to the screen
cout<<i<<", "<<j<<", "<<c<<", "<<x<<"\n";return;
//Not required, but helpful
}
```

Review Questions

1. What is meant by program *maintenance*?

2. Some lines in C++ programs do not produce results, but are needed for something else. What are they needed for?

3. Does C++ care how much white space you put in (or leave out of) a program?

4. Does C++ care whether you type programs mixing uppercase and lowercase letters? Are there times when C++ cares and times when it does not?

C++ Comments

OBJECTIVE ***To teach you how to comment
C++ programs.***

Lesson 2, "The C++ Program," explained why white space is so important. Not only do you write programs for the computer, but you also write programs that you or other people might have to change someday. No matter how much white space you put in a C++ program, C++ still is not as readable as English, and some programs get complicated.

Through ample use of *comments,* messages you can scatter throughout a program, you improve a program's maintainability even more. The best place to start commenting is with the first few programs you write. Good habits are best learned early.

The Importance of Comments

Suppose that your car breaks down in the middle of nowhere with no other cars in sight. The problem is not tools or parts; they are in the trunk. The problem is that you know absolutely nothing about the car, and when you open the trunk, you have no clue as to where the parts go or how to fix the problem.

Just about to despair, you glance down and see two car repair books in the trunk. You pick up the first one and realize that it is a book written by advanced, expert mechanics *for* advanced, expert mechanics. The book uses technical jargon you've never heard. You toss the worthless repair book over your shoulder and pick up the next book. The title is *Car Repair for the Un-Mechanic.* Glancing through the opening pages, you begin to smile. The second book assumes that you don't know a rotor widget #4 from a tactile stem #3B-7. The second book explains, in uncluttered, non-mechanic language and with a friendly style, exactly how to fix your problem.

You find that the second book contains the very same facts that the first one does. Of course, the first book does not help your plight one bit. It teaches you nothing and explains nothing. It assumes that you know enough to write the book yourself. The second book explains every concept in easy-to-understand language, and in 10 minutes, you fix the car just in time to drive to the cafe across the street for dinner. (You thought you were in the middle of a desert or something?)

A Program's Comments

That car story either:

1. Has a point to it.

2. Mistakenly got mixed in with this book at the printer.

3. Proves that this book's author cannot focus on one subject for very long.

Obviously, the story has a point (and also hints at #3). The point is that people react much better to material that is not technically above their heads. Of course, any subject is easy if it is explained well enough. If thermonuclear space transportation were explained in a simple manner, you could understand it.

By their very nature, C++ programs are cryptic, even to established C++ programmers. As Lesson 2, "The C++ Program," explained, programs rarely remain in one form. The life of a programmer includes not only writing new programs, but updating programs written earlier. As you write a C++ program, add white space so that the program is easier to read. Even more important, add comments as well.

Comments are *not* C++ commands. As a matter of fact, C++ ignores any and all comments in your programs. Comments are nothing more than messages that explain what the program does. Comments are for people, not for the computer.

If your C++ programs contain only C++ code and no comments, they will be virtually impossible to figure out later. Remember that C++ is cryptic and extremely difficult to read. Many companies that employ programmers *require* that their programmers put comments throughout every program they write. Why do you think these companies require comments? It is because people change, jobs change, and companies must ensure that a program written by one person can be understood by the next.

The Syntax of C++ Comments

In computer lingo, *syntax* refers to the spelling of commands, the ordering of special characters, and the placing of the language elements. When you learn the syntax for a C++ command or operation, you learn the exact format required so that C++ knows what you want it to do.

Comments are so important that you are now going to learn the syntax of comments (how to write comments so that C++ knows that they are comments) before you learn any C++ commands. Use comments abundantly so that someone reading your program later has a clear guide to the program's contents. A C++ programmer *might* be able to trace through your C++ code and figure out what the program does, but comments speed the process. The faster someone understands your code, the faster he or she can make any needed changes and move on to other projects.

A comment begins with two forward slashes, sometimes called a *double slash*. Comments extend to the end of the line. In other words, you cannot have a command, a comment, then another command all on the same line. Here is an example of a C++ line with a comment:

```
return ((a > b)?a:b);  // Grabs the larger of two values
```

Here is the same line without the comment:

```
return ((a > b)?a:b);
```

With a comment, you don't even have to know C++ in order to know what the statement is doing. Without a comment, as you can see, the statement looks like garbage characters that make no sense.

The double slash is vital: without it, C++ would refuse to accept the line. Even though `return ((a > b)?a:b);` is a valid C++ command, if you left off the double slash comment signal, C++ would see the words `Grabs the larger of two values` and not know what to do with them. After all, C++ does not know English; it knows only C++. The comment is there not for C++ but for a person looking through your program.

Comments can reside on lines all by themselves. Sometimes you use comments for more than one program statement. Comments are useful for describing a section of several lines in a program and for putting in program notes about the programmer and the program. For example, the following small C++ program contains two lines of comments that extend the entire line length, as well as three additional comments to the right of C++ code.

```cpp
// Filename: COMAVGE.CPP
// Program to compute the average of three values
#include <iostream.h>
void main()
{
    float g1, g2, g3;    // Variables to hold student grades

    cout << "What grade did the first student get? ";
    cin >> g1;

    cout << "What grade did the second student get? ";
    cin >> g2;

    cout << "What grade did the third student get? ";
    cin >> g3;

    float avg = (g1 + g2 + g3) / 3.0;    // Computes average

    cout << "The student average is " << avg;  // Prints average
    return;
}
```

All the programs on this book's program disk are stored under a separate filename. You must tell your C++ compiler the program's filename before it can load the program into memory and run it. To help you quickly try the examples throughout this book, a comment on the first line of every program contains the name of the program as it is stored on the disk. For instance, you can load the preceding program from the book's program disk by retrieving the file named COMAVGE.CPP.

Many companies require their programmers to put their names in comments at the top of programs they write. If someone later has a question about the program, the original programmer can be traced. If several people make changes to a program, they often put their names too, with a brief comment about the changes they made. Because all these types of lines are commented, C++ skips over them, as it should.

Scatter comments throughout a program as well. If you write some tricky code that needs explanation, spend a few lines of comments, if needed, explaining what the next few lines of code do.

Be proud of yourself! You do not yet know one bit of C++ code, yet you understand exactly what the preceding program does. That's the purpose of comments! They document a program so that you don't have to go through tedious code to learn what parts of the program are doing.

The following program contains three comment bugs. See whether you can determine what is wrong.

```
// This program computes taxes
#include <iostream.h>
void main()
{
   The next few lines calculate payroll taxes
   // Computes the gross pay    float gross = 40 * 5.25;

   float taxes = gross * .40;    / Just computed the taxes
   cout "The taxes are " << taxes;
   return;
}
```

Because you do not yet know C++, you might not know exactly what the problems are in this program, but you should have a feeling that something is wrong in three places. The first problem occurs in the fifth line, which begins The next few lines. A double slash should appear before the line. The line is an explanation in English, not in C++ code, so it should be made into a comment.

The second problem appears on the sixth line. A comment always begins with a double slash and extends to *the end of the line.* C++ will ignore the calculation to the right of the comment because C++ thinks that the entire line is an English message for people. If you transpose the calculation and the comment, C++ will perform the calculation as it should.

The last problem is easy. On the eighth line, the one that begins `float taxes = gross`, the comment does not start properly. According to the ancients, "One slash does not a comment make."

A C++ programmer usually can understand what a C++ program is supposed to do, even if the program has no comments at all. As soon as you learn the C++ language, you will be able to look through straight C++ code, with no comments, and make changes that need to be made. The comments simply help describe what the program is doing.

Comments Are For You Too

Suppose that you write programs for your own use and amusement. Nobody but you will ever see the C++ code you write. Can you think of why you should take the time to add comments to your own programs? There are plenty of reasons.

Suppose that you write a C++ program to track your bank records. A year later, your bank allows for automatic transfers of utility bill payments straight from your savings account. Your old program no longer suffices for the new banking system, so you get the C++ code out and begin making changes. However, you can't remember what you did before, and the code is so succinct that it is difficult to follow. Luckily, you put comments in the code, so you read through the program until you get to the place you need to change. As soon as you are there, you know what is going on in the code, and you quickly make the changes.

Get into the habit of commenting *as you write programs*. Many people write programs without commenting as they go, thinking that they will add comments later. More often than not, the comments never get added. When program maintenance is required, it takes twice as long to change the code than it would if the programmer had added comments during the original programming phase.

Here is the same program you saw near the end of the preceding lesson, with one difference: the programmer forgot to precede the comments with double slashes. After trying to compile the program, the programmer looked at the 20 or so error messages and realized what was left out. See if you can help the programmer correct the program by inserting the proper commenting symbols everywhere they go.

```
Filename: 1STLONG.CPP
Longer C++ program that demonstrates comments,
variables, constants, and simple input/output
#include <iostream.h>
```

```
void main()
{
    int i, j;          These three lines declare four variables
    char c;
    float x;

    i = 4;             i is assigned an integer literal
    j = i + 7;         j is assigned the result of a computation
    c = 'A';           Enclose all character literals
                       in single quotation marks

    x = 9.087;         x is a floating-point value

    x = x * 12.3;      Overwrites what was in x with something else

       Sends the values of the four variables to the screen
    cout << i << ", " << j << ", " << c << ", " << x << "\n";

    return;            Not required, but helpful
}
```

Before peeking at the correct program in Lesson 2, "The C++ Program," count the number of double slashes you put in this program. If you did not add 12 double slashes (or if you added more than 12), try again.

Use Good Judgment

As important as comments are, you can over-comment a program. Add comments to lines only when the program's code warrants it. You see many more comments in the first few programs in this book than you see later. As you learn the simple commands, this book attempts to clarify them through extra comments in the program listings.

Nevertheless, redundant comments are as bad as no comments at all. For example, even though you know nothing about C++ commands, you might agree that the following code contains worthless comments:

```
totalsales = oldsales + newsales;    // Adds the old sales and
                                     // the new sales to get
                                     // total sales

cout << "Happy Birthday";    // Sends the Happy Birthday
                             // message to the cout
return;    // Return
```

Each of these comments is redundant, and they really do not explain what is going on any more than the C++ code itself. However, consider this statement:

```
for (int ctr = 10; ctr > 0; ctr--) {    // Prints the numbers
    cout << ctr << endl; }               // from 10 to 1
                                         // on-screen
```

Although you don't know C++ (and even if you did), you can see that the purpose of these two lines of code is hidden in the cryptic C++ language. A C++ programmer could figure out this code, but the comment makes it effortless. As you saw in the previous three code fragments, comments often span more than one line. The comment can continue on the next line if it is too long to place on a single line.

Of the following five lines, which contain useful comments and which contain redundant ones?

```
clog << '\n';    // Sends an end-of-line to the error log
radius3 = radius1 + radius2;    // Calculates radius3
// The following code contains a C++ program
// The following code tracks your investments
clog << '\n';    // Sends '\n' to clog
```

C-Style Comments

C++ supports another kind of comment that you might see occasionally. C++ is based on the C language, but C++'s comment syntax differs from C's. The designers of C++ decided to keep the old C-style comment syntax so that C programs would work with little or no change with C++ compilers. Nevertheless, the double slash comments are considered superior. You should learn C comments just in case you see them.

A comment in C begins with the characters /* and ends with the characters */. Unlike with C++ comments, you *must* end a C comment. If you do not put the ending */, C assumes that the next line (or the next hundred lines) is still a comment until it finally finds another */. The following line contains a C-style comment:

```
char name[25];    /* Reserves space for a 25-character name */
```

Because a C comment ends only when the */ is reached, the following three lines make up a single comment:

```
/* The following program calculates stock statistics
   using the most modern technical analysis techniques
   available. */
```

Of course, the three lines could also be commented like this:

```
/* The following program calculates stock statistics */
/* using the most modern technical analysis techniques */
/* available. */
```

Although you should become familiar with C comments, true C++ programmers tend to avoid using them. The double slash is easier because you don't have to remember to end the comment. The C-style comments can be error-prone as well. If you embed one C-style comment within another, C++ gets confused. Stay with C++ comments as much as possible, and both you and your C++ compiler will lead healthier and more productive lives.

Review Questions

1. What is a comment?

2. Do comments help the C++ compiler, the C++ programmer, or both?

3. TRUE or FALSE: A C++ comment begins with a double slash and ends with the next C++ command.

4. Why are C++ comments superior to C comments?

5. Why should you not comment every line in a program?

Review Exercises

1. Write a C++ comment spanning two lines that explains a checkbook program's job.

2. Convert the comment in Exercise 1 to a C-style comment.

The C++ Program's Format

OBJECTIVE *To explain the parts of a C++ program.*

C++ programs can be very different from one another, but they all share a similar structure. As Lesson 2, "The C++ Program," explained, part of a C++ program only sets up the rest of the program. Whether you write a checkbook program, a payroll program, or a chemical analysis program, you need to understand the overall structure of C++ programs. This lesson provides some explanation of a C++ program's pieces so that you will be comfortable with the format of a program before getting to the specifics in Lesson 5, "C++ Numeric Data."

The Format of Every C++ Program

All C++ programs ever written have one thing in common: all have a `main()` function. The previous lessons showed you some C++ programs. If

you look them over, you will see the word `main()` in every one of them. Looking further still, you will see an opening brace after `main()` and a closing brace a little later. You never find an opening brace (a left brace) without a closing brace (a right brace).

C++ programs also share another trait: almost all have one or more lines that begin with the # (pound sign) character, followed by `include`. Figure 4.1 shows a simple outline of a C++ program.

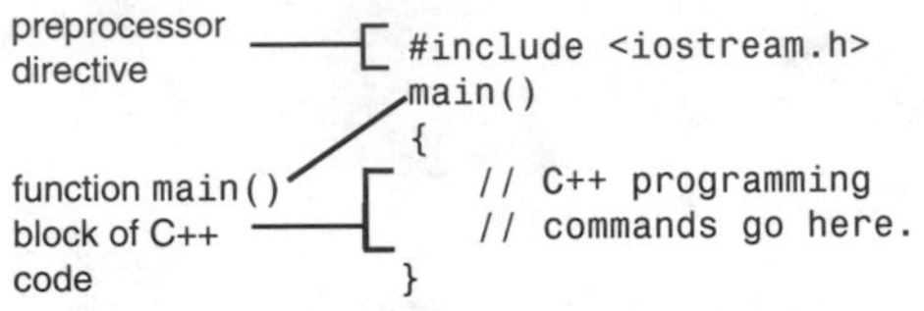

Figure 4.1.
An outline of a
simple C++
program.

```
preprocessor ──────┌ #include <iostream.h>
directive           main()
                    {
function main() ──┌     // C++ programming
block of C++             // commands go here.
code                }
```

Why do you think there is a closing brace for every opening brace? There is also a closing parenthesis for every opening parenthesis and a closing bracket for every opening bracket that appears in a program. The parentheses, braces, and brackets enclose language elements within the C++ program. As with parentheses in written languages, these C++ symbols enclose pieces of a program, and you must indicate, with the closing character, where the piece ends.

Before you know it, you will be comfortable with `main()`, `#include`, braces, and all the other parts of a C++ program. The next section looks at a longer C++ program and dissects pieces of it to ease you into C++.

Dissecting a Program

The next few pages provide a closer examination of the following program. The idea is to give you a look at the "big picture" before getting into the specific language elements starting in Lesson 5, "C++ Numeric Data."

```
// Filename: DISSECT.CPP
// Simple program for you to analyze

#include <iostream.h>

void main()
{
    int age, weight;   // These lines define four variables
```

```
    char initial;
    float salary;

    age = 13;    // Assigns an integer literal to age
    weight = age * 6;    // Assigns a weight based on a formula
    initial = 'D';    // All character literals are
                      // enclosed in single quotes
    salary = 200.50;    // salary requires a floating-point
                        // value because it was defined to
                        // be a floating-point
    salary = salary * 2.5;    // Changes what was in salary

    // Next line sends the values of the variables to the screen
    cout << age << ", " << weight << ", " << initial
        << ", " << salary;

    return;    // Good habit to end programs
               // and functions with return
}
```

Keep in mind that this program is simple and does not actually perform a lot of valuable work. Despite its simplicity, you might not fully understand it all even after the explanation that comes next, but it is a good place to begin.

While looking through the program, see whether you can understand any or all of it. If you are new to programming, you should know that the computer reads each line of the program, starting with the first line and working its way down, until it has completed all the instructions (the statements on each line) in the program. (Of course, first you have to compile and link the program, as described in Lesson 1, "Introduction to C++," before seeing the output from the program on your computer.)

Here is the output that results when you run this program:

```
13, 78, D, 501.25
```

The Program

After Lesson 3, "C++ Comments," you know all about the first two lines in the program. They contain comments that describe the filename and a little about the program. Comments also are scattered throughout the code to explain what happens along the way.

The next line is called a *preprocessor directive*. It is repeated here:

```
#include <iostream.h>
```

This strange-looking statement is not actually a C++ command, but it is a directive to the C++ compiler. The directive *directs* the compiler (that is easy to remember). #include tells C++ to take the filename located inside the angled brackets and load that file into the C++ program at that point. In other words, the program grows to become the size of DISSECT.CPP (the program shown in the preceding section) plus iostream.h. Most files included with #include end in the .h filename extension because these files are *header files*.

The header file named iostream.h comes with your C++ compiler. It helps ensure that the output, generated a little later with cout, works properly. Lesson 7, "Preprocessor Directives," explains #include in much more detail.

You might see other header files included, either in addition to iostream.h or in place of it. Sometimes, C++ programmers use a C program that includes the header file named stdio.h instead of iostream.h. Notice in Appendix A that #include is not listed with all the other C++ commands. #include is not a C++ command; it is simply a pre-command (hence its name, *preprocessor directive*) that directs the compiler to do something *before* it compiles the actual commands. In this case, #include tells C++ to include a file from disk at that point in the program.

Braces and main()

You see these two lines in every C++ program:

```
main()
{
```

main() does not always appear toward the top of the program, as it does here. Sometimes main() appears farther down into the code. Wherever main() is, however, it begins the most critical section of any C++ program. When you run the program, the program *always* begins executing at main(). No matter where main() is located in the program, it is the starting point for the program's execution. Therefore, it makes sense to put main() toward the top of a program. Sometimes, however, a lot of other stuff has to go before main(). No matter what appears before main(), main() begins the program's execution when you run the program.

`main()` is called a *function*. A function is not a command. It is a named section of a program, and its name always ends with a pair of parentheses. A program can have one function or many functions, but every program contains the `main()` function because the program has to begin somewhere. You can always tell where a function begins because functions always have names that end with parentheses. The parentheses tell C++ that `main()` is a function and not a command or something else.

None of the commands in Appendix A contain parentheses. Parentheses are part of function names, but they are never part of command names.

Glance through the program listing and see whether you can figure out where `main()` ends. In other words, if there were more functions in this program, where would the next one go?

Because an opening brace follows `main()`, you can look for the matching closing brace (they always appear in pairs) and find out where `main()` ends. Every pair of braces in a C++ program encloses something known as a *block*. In this case, a *block* is almost as long as the `main()` function. The next function, if there were one, could go after `main()`'s closing brace. You can never define a function inside another one. `main()` must finish before another function can begin being listed in the program.

Before you get too sidetracked, you are going to become extremely comfortable with the fact that `main()` is a function and that braces enclose blocks in a program. Read on to learn more about the rest of this sample program named DISSECT.CPP. There are more important aspects to the program at this stage in the game than fully understanding `main()`.

NOTE: The `void` before `main()` is required in simple C++ programs that do not return values to the operating system. You will learn more about `void` in Lesson 21, "Return Values and Prototypes."

What is missing from this short program? Add the missing line of code.

```
// Program to calculate swimming pool floor area
main()
```

```
{
    int width, length, area;
    width = 16;
    length = 32;
    area = width * length;
    cout << "The area is " << area;
```

Data

Here are the three lines that follow main()'s opening brace:

```
int age, weight;    // These lines define four variables
char initial;
float salary;
```

These three lines define four *variables*. A variable is a place in memory that has a name and holds some data. A *variable definition* tells C++ exactly what variables will be used in the lines that follow. This variable definition tells the compiler to make room in memory for four values, label them with names, and get ready to use them. Later in the program, values will be stored in those variables.

All C++ programs contain both commands and data. The data is always made up of one or more variables, one or more *literals,* or a combination of both. A *literal* is sometimes called a *constant,* but in C++, the word *constant* actually has another meaning (in most languages, *literal* and *constant* are synonymous).

As the name implies, a variable is data that can change (become variable) as the program runs. A literal remains the same. In real life, a variable might be your net worth. It increases over time (you hope). A literal would be something such as your first name or social security number, because each remains constant throughout life and (usually) does not change.

A variable is like a box inside your computer that holds something. That something might be a number or a character, a value of another variable, or the result of a calculation. Every variable within the same block is distinguished from others by its unique name. No two variables within the same block can have the same name. You can have as many variables as needed to hold changing data. After you define a variable and give it a value, the variable keeps its value until you change the value or define the variable with something else by putting some other data value into it. Lesson 5, "C++ Numeric Data," more fully explains these concepts.

The three lines of code that follow the opening brace define four variables. The variable definition informs the rest of the program that two *integer* variables named age and weight, as well as a *character* variable named initial and a *floating-point* variable named salary, appear throughout the program. The terms *integer, character,* and *floating-point* basically refer to different types of data. Integers are whole numbers, and floating-point numbers contain decimal places.

Just as there are different types of variables, there are different types of literals. For now, you simply have to understand that a C++ literal is any number, character, word, or phrase whose value does not change as the program runs. The following are all valid C++ literals:

```
5.6
-34
'W'
"Mary"
18.293345
0.0
```

As you can see, some literals are numeric and some are character-based. The single and double quotation marks around two of the literals, however, are not part of the actual literals. A single-character literal requires single quotation marks around it, and a string of characters, such as "Mary", requires double quotation marks (often called just quotation marks).

Find all the literals in the DISSECT.CPP program and list them below. *Hint:* There are eight if you count the ones embedded in the cout statement.

The body of the DISSECT.CPP program assigns values to the defined variables.

```
age = 13;    // Assigns an integer literal to age
weight = age * 6;    // Assigns a weight based on a formula
```

35

```
initial = 'D';    // All character literals are
                  // enclosed in single quotes
salary = 200.50;  // salary requires a floating-point
                  // value because it was defined to
                  // be a floating-point
salary = salary * 2.5;   // Changes what was in salary
```

The first line puts 13 in the integer variable, age. The second line multiplies 6 by the variable age's value to produce the value 78 stored in weight. The multiplication sign (*) in C++ works just as it does in mathematics. The other primary math operators are shown in Table 4.1.

Table 4.1. The primary math operators.

Operator	Meaning	Example
+	Addition	4 + 5
-	Subtraction	7 - 2
*	Multiplication	12 * 6
/	Division	48 / 12

Computer designers use an asterisk (*) for multiplication and not a lowercase x as people generally do. The computer would confuse the variable name x with the multiplication symbol x if both were allowed.

When mathematical operators appear on the right side of an equal sign, the program completes the math before assigning the result to a variable. In the following statement:

```
salary = salary * 2.5;    // Changes what was in salary
```

the multiplication of salary and 2.5 is performed, then the result is stored in salary.

Which of the following are variables and which are literals? *Hint:* A variable name cannot have quotation marks around it. If it did, C++ would think it were a character literal (if single quotations were used) or a string literal (if double quotation marks were used).

```
'1.2'
Payroll
4543.23
name
47
"Diane"
```

> **NOTE:** C++ follows math rules by calculating multiplication and division before it calculates any addition and subtraction if a combination appears within the same expression. Therefore, the following produces a result of 8, not 10, because C++ multiplies first, even though addition appears to the left. Lesson 9, "Math Operators and Precedence," explains math ordering in more detail.
>
> ```
> result = 2 + 3 * 2;    // Stores an 8 in result
> ```

Assigning Values to Variables

You use an equal sign, =, called the *assignment operator,* to put values into variables. The following statement:

```
age = 13;    // Assigns an integer literal to age
```

puts the literal 13 into the variable named age.

> **TIP:** Think of an equal sign as working exactly as a left-pointing arrow would. The value on the right of the equal sign moves left into the variable on the left of the equal sign. If there is a formula on the right, C++ computes the answer and moves the answer into the variable on the left side of the equal sign.

In the DISSECT.CPP sample program shown earlier, you find the following variables:

```
age
weight
initial
salary
```

Because age is an integer, you should put only integers into it.

> **NOTE:** A variable must hold a value that matches the variable's type.

Output to the Screen

The line that begins with cout at first looks very confusing:

```
cout << age << ", " << weight << ", " << initial
    << ", " << salary;
```

When the program reaches this line, it prints the contents of the four variables on-screen.

The output from the line is

```
13, 78, D, 501.25
```

Because there are no other output statements in the program, this line is the only line that produces something you can see when you run the program. The rest of the program either sets up the code (such as main() and the braces) or performs internal data manipulations (such as assigning values to variables).

cout is not a C++ command, but it acts a lot like one. You will not see cout (pronounced "see-out") in Appendix A. cout has no built-in input or output commands. cout is an operator, just as + and * are operators, described in the header file iostream.h. cout sends output to an output device, usually the screen.

> You can guess at cout's purpose just by looking at the line with cout. The data values are being sent, via the double angled brackets, <<, to the cout device. The list of values following cout goes to the screen in the left-to-right order that they appear. The opposite of cout is cin. cin gets keystrokes from the keyboard. Can you see that the following statement gets a number from the keyboard and stores it in the location called Amount?
>
> ```
> cin >> Amount;
> ```

Returning to the Operating System

As soon as your C++ program finishes executing, it should return to the operating system so that another program can be run. The return statement at the end of main() ensures that the program returns to the operating system. Because return is optional, you do not have to use it for simple returns from functions such as main(). Nevertheless, get into the habit of putting a return at the end of each function so that when one *is* required, you will have it.

TIP: Put a return at the end of each function.

The closing brace after the return does two things in this program. It signals the end of a block (begun earlier with the opening brace), which is the end of the main() function, and it signals the end of the program.

Program Structure

Figure 4.2 repeats the entire program listing with some callouts that label the various parts of the program.

```
comments ————[ // Filename: DISSECT.CPP
              [ // Simple program for you to analyze

preprocessor ——[ #include <iostream.h>     Does not return values
directive                                  to the O.S.
function name ——( void main() )
                {
variable ————[   int age, weight;    // These lines define four variables
definition   [   char initial;
             [   float salary;

                 age = 13;           // Assign an integer literal to age
                 weight = age * 6;   // Assign a weight based on a formula
                 initial = 'D';      // All character literals are
                                     // enclosed in single quotes
                 salary = 200.50;    // salary requires a floating-point value
                                     // because it was defined to be a floating
                 salary = salary * 2.5;  // Change what was in salary

                 // The next line sends the values of the variables to the scr
                 cout << age << "," << weight << "," << initial << "," << s

                 return;             // Good habit to end programs
                                     // and functions with return
end of main() ——[ }
                                              comments
```

*Figure 4.2.
The structure of
the simple C++
program.*

Familiarize yourself with the overall look and feel of this program. It helps to see an overview before diving straight into the specifics of the commands. Now that you have a general understanding of the format of

C++ programs, you are ready to tackle the language elements. Good luck with your venture into the world of the C++ language particulars, beginning in the next lesson, "C++ Numeric Data."

Review Questions

1. What preprocessor directive almost always includes header files?

2. TRUE or FALSE: cout is a C++ command.

3. What are the characters that enclose a C++ block?

4. What kind of data must be enclosed in single quotation marks?

5. What kind of data must be enclosed in double quotation marks?

6. What non-command in C++ sends output to the screen?

7. What kind of numeric data contains no decimal points?

8. What kind of numeric data contains decimal points?

9. Write the four arithmetic symbols:

10. Is return ever optional? If so, why is it a good idea to learn to always use return?

Review Exercises

1. Write a preprocessor directive that includes the header file named string.h.

   ```
   #include <string.h>
   ```

2. Write the statement that stores the result of a sales variable multiplied by a profit variable into a third variable named netsales.

   ```
   netsales = sales * profit
   ```

3. Write the statement that outputs your name to the screen. *Hint:* Because your name is a string of more than one character, enclose it in double quotation marks.

```
cout << "Dave";
```

C++ CLASSROOM Two

Working with Data

C++ Numeric Data

OBJECTIVE ***To explain C++ numeric constants, variables, and their types.***

Computers can store data in many different formats. C++ works with that data and, through programs you write, processes it into information the user needs. In Lesson 4, "The C++ Program's Format," you learned that programs consist of data and commands. You must learn to store that data properly so that your programs can manage it properly. C++ uses constants and variables to hold data your programs need.

The term *data* is plural for *datum*. As is common in many texts these days, this book uses the word *data* to mean both the plural and the singular. Accuracy in English is as important as accuracy in programming, but moving between the terms *datum* and *data* often results in more confusion than clarity.

Data and Information

Is there a difference between data and information? Maybe you have not thought too much about the two words and their meanings. Although

most people think they have a good idea of what data and information mean, when asked to define them, people often use one to define the other, saying "Data is information" or "Information is data." As this section points out, there is a difference.

You might have heard the term *data processing*. Data processing is simply the processing of data into meaningful information by a computer. At its simplest level, that's what the computer does best and does quickly. Figure 5.1 shows the basic model of every computer program ever written. The computer takes data as input, processes the data, and produces meaningful information as output.

Figure 5.1. The basic input-process-output model.

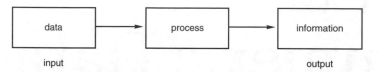

Think of a corporate president's information needs. Does the president want to get a daily list of the salaries of each of the company's 5,000 employees, down to the lowest-paid part-time clerk? Of course not. A list of every employee would be just raw facts and figures that the president does not have time to deal with. To the president, the list would be a waste of time.

The president certainly is concerned with payroll, but he or she needs meaningful information, not a bunch of raw facts and figures (data). The president might prefer a computerized graphic that shows such things as the payroll trends over the past year, how the company's payroll figures match those of the competitors, and how one department's payroll compares to another's. Data organized in such a fashion is information for the president—something he or she can use to make a decision. Computers are the perfect tools for processing all the data and producing meaningful information used by people who make decisions based on that information.

What is data to one person might be information to another. Would the part-time clerk care about the detailed payroll figure for his or her job? If so, wouldn't the salary for part-time clerks be important information to the clerk?

Data in a C++ Program

Representing data properly should be the goal of every C++ programmer. An adage says that "Garbage in produces garbage out (GIGO)." A computer is not magic. It simply follows your program instructions and processes data with the commands you give it. If you give it bad data, it will produce bad results.

A C++ program can process many kinds of data, but all C++ data falls into these two broad categories:

- numeric data

- character data

This lesson explains the numeric data types. Lesson 6, "Characters, Strings, and Character Arrays," explains the character data types. You do not have to be a mathematician to understand numeric data in a C++ program. Let the computer do all the math! You want meaningful results, and it is the computer's job to take your data and produce meaningful results based on the instructions you supply.

In Lesson 4, "The C++ Program's Format," you learned about variables. You also saw programs that contain several *literals* (sometimes called *constants*). A variable is a storage location that holds a value. The contents of variables can change. Literals are numbers or character data that do not change.

If you were writing a program that tracked your financial records, which of the following generally are variable and which usually are constant?

Description	Variable or Literal?
Your social security number	_____
Your age	_____
Your salary	_____
Your first name	_____
Your date of birth	_____

Characteristics of Variables

Whenever your program needs to store some data temporarily, you store that data in a variable. You also can store data in a file for long-term storage, but during a program's execution, variables are the primary place you put data until you are ready to use it. You, the programmer, are responsible for telling the program when it needs a variable. Before you use a variable, you must *define* it. When you define a variable, you tell C++ to reserve some storage for that variable and give it a name. Any time after a variable is defined, you can place values into that variable.

In C++, you can place variable definitions anywhere in the program, as long as the program does not use the variables until after they are defined. To define a variable, you must understand the characteristics of variables:

- Each variable has a name.
- Each variable has a type.
- Each variable holds a value that you stored in it.

The following sections explain each of these characteristics in detail.

Naming Variables

Because you can have many variables in a single program, you must assign them names to keep track of them. Variable names are unique, just as house addresses are unique. If two variables had the same name, C++ would not know which you were referring to when you requested one of them.

Variable names can be as short as a single letter or as long as 31 characters. Their names must begin with a letter of the alphabet, but after the first letter they can contain letters, numbers, and the underscore (_) character. (C++ compilers enable you to start variable names with an underscore, but this practice is not recommended.)

> **TIP:** Because spaces are not allowed in a variable name, use the underscore character to separate parts of the name.

The following variable names are all valid:

```
salary      aug93_sales      i      AgeLimit      Amount
```

It is traditional to use lowercase letters for C++ variable names, or uppercase for only the first letter. When a variable name is a combination of two or more words, such as NumOfEmps, it is common to uppercase each subname. Never uppercase every letter in a variable name.

Circle the following *valid* variable names:

```
93Sales      Sales#93      Sales93      Sales_93      SALES_93
Sales(93)    93_Sales      Sales93LastQtr      Sales()
```

Some programs have variables on 95 percent of their code lines. Because of the importance and abundance of variables, take the time to learn what makes a valid variable name and what makes an invalid variable name. You must know the naming rules of a variable before moving on. By the way, one of the variables in the preceding Try This section is technically valid, but is not recommended. Which one is it?

You do not have to follow the uppercase/lowercase tradition, but you should know that uppercase letters in variable names are different from lowercase letters. For example, each of the following four variables is viewed differently by your C++ compiler.

```
sales      Sales      SALES      sALES
```

Be very careful with the Shift key when you type a variable name. Do not inadvertently change the case of a variable name throughout a program. If you do, C++ interprets the names as distinct and separate variables.

Never give a variable the same name as a C++ command. Appendix A is a list of all the C++ command names. If you inadvertently give a variable the same name as a command, such as while, the C++ compiler will become confused and will not compile your program correctly.

Although you can call a variable any name that fits the naming rules (as long as it is not being used by another variable in the program), you should always use meaningful variable names. Give your variables names that help describe the values that they hold. For example, keeping track of total payroll in a variable called total_payroll is much more descriptive than using the variable name XYZ34. Even though both names are valid, total_payroll is easier to remember, and you get a good idea of what the variable holds by looking at its name.

Variable Types

Variables can hold different types of numeric data. Table 5.1 lists the different types of C++ variables. For instance, if a variable holds an integer, C++ assumes that no decimal point or fractional part (the part to the right of the decimal point) exists for the variable's value.

Table 5.1. The C++ variable types.

Declaration Name	Data Type Description
char	Character
unsigned char	Unsigned character
signed char	Signed character (same as char)
int	Integer
unsigned int	Unsigned integer
signed int	Signed integer (same as int)
short int	Short integer
unsigned short int	Unsigned short integer
signed short int	Signed short integer (same as short_int)
long	Long integer
long int	Long integer (same as long)
signed long int	Signed long integer (same as long_int)
unsigned long int	Unsigned long integer
float	Floating-point (real)
double	Double floating-point (real)
long double	Long double floating-point (real)

The next sections more fully describe these types. For now, you need to concentrate on the importance of defining variables before using them.

Defining Variables

You can define a variable in two places:

- before the code that uses the variable
- before a function name (such as before main())

The first of these is the most common, and it is used throughout much of this book. (If you define a variable that precedes a function name, it is called a *global* variable. Many of the lessons later in this book address the pros and cons of global variables.) To declare a variable, you must state its type, followed by its name. In Lesson 4, "The C++ Program's Format," you saw a program that defined four variables in the following way:

```
main()
{
    int age, weight;    // These lines define four variables
    char initial;
    float salary;
    // Rest of program follows
```

These lines define two integer variables named `age` and `weight`, a character variable named `initial`, and a floating-point variable named `salary`. You have no idea what is inside these variables, however. Generally you cannot assume that a variable holds zero, or any other number, until you assign it a value. The first line after the opening brace basically tells C++ the following:

"I am going to use two integer variables somewhere in this program. Reserve memory for them and expect them. I want them named `age` and `weight`. When I put a value into `age` or `weight`, I ensure that the value will be an integer, or something that will fit within an integer's memory space."

Without such definitions, you could not assign `age` or `weight` a value later. All variables must be defined before you use them. This does not necessarily hold true in other programming languages, such as BASIC, but it does in C++. You could define each of these two variables on its own line, as in the following code:

```
main()
{
    int age;
    int weight;
    // Rest of program follows
```

You do not gain any readability by doing this, however. Most C++ programmers prefer to define variables of the same type on the same line.

The second line in the example of variables declares a character variable called `initial`. Put only single characters in character variables. Next, a floating-point variable called `salary` is defined.

Rewrite the following lines of variable definitions so that the data types are grouped in a more orderly fashion:

```
main()
{
    float height;
    int num1;
    char answer;
    float salary;
    int num2;
        // Rest of program follows
```

Suppose that you were taking three classes at a local community college and you wanted to write a program to keep track of your letter grade and your numeric average in each class. To the following code fragment add the variable definition lines that define the six variable names and their types.

```
main()
{
```

Looking at Data Types

You might be asking why it is important to have so many variable types. There are many different types of data, and C++ wants to have a data type available to hold any data you might need to store. C++ has more data

52

types than almost any other programming language. The variable's type is critical, but choosing the type among the many offerings is not as difficult as it might seem at first.

The character variable is easy to understand. A character variable can hold only a single character. You cannot put more than a single character into a character variable.

> Unlike many other programming languages, C++ does not have a string variable. As you know, you cannot hold more than a single character in a C++ character variable. To store a string of characters, you must use an *aggregate* variable type that combines other fundamental types, such as an array. Lesson 6, "Characters, Strings, and Character Arrays," explains this more fully.

Integers hold whole numbers. Although mathematicians might cringe at this loose definition, an integer is any number that does not contain a decimal point. All the following expressions are integers:

```
45      -932     0     12     5421
```

Floating-point numbers contain decimal points. They are known as *real* numbers to mathematicians. Any time you have to store a salary, a temperature, or any other number that might have a fractional part (a decimal portion), you must store it in a floating-point variable. All the following expressions are floating-point numbers, and any floating-point variable can hold them:

```
45.12    -2344.5432    0.00    .04594
```

Circle any of the following that are floating-point values:

```
-0       -12      34.      04.0      31.4444444      -0.00001
```

Sometimes you need to keep track of large numbers, and sometimes you need to keep track of smaller numbers. Table 5.2 shows a list of typical ranges that each C++ variable type can hold.

Table 5.2. Typical ranges that C++ variables can hold.

Type	Range*
char	−128 to 127
unsigned char	0 to 255

continues

53

Lesson 5

Table 5.2. continued

Type	Range*
signed char	−128 to 127
int	−32768 to 32767
unsigned int	0 to 65535
signed int	−32768 to 32767
short int	−32768 to 32767
unsigned short int	0 to 65535
signed short int	−32768 to 32767
long int	−2147483648 to 2147483647
signed long int	−2147483648 to 2147483647
unsigned long	0 to 4294967296
float	−3.4E−38 to 3.4E+38
double	−1.7E−308 to 1.7E+308
long double	−3.4E−4932 to 1.1E+4932

*Use this table only as a guide. Different compilers and different computers can have different ranges.

All good AT&T C++ programmers know that they cannot count on using the exact values in Table 5.2 on every computer that uses C++. These ranges are typical on a PC, but they might be much different on another computer. Use this table only as a guide. Do not spend any time memorizing these ranges. As you begin to write C++ programs using one of the many C++ compilers, check your compiler manual for its specific data ranges.

The unsigned variable types can hold only positive numbers, but they can hold larger positive values than the signed ones.

At first, it might seem strange that the character variables shown in Table 5.2 can hold numeric values. In C++, integers and character variables frequently can be used interchangeably. As explained in Appendix B, each ASCII table character has a unique number that

54

corresponds to its location in the table. If you store a number in a character variable, C++ treats the data as if it were the ASCII character that matches that number in the table. Conversely, you can store character data in an integer variable. C++ finds that character's ASCII number and stores that number rather than the character. Examples that help illustrate this point appear later in this lesson.

The floating-point ranges in Table 5.2 are shown in scientific notation. To determine the actual range, take the number before the E (meaning *Exponent*) and multiply it by 10 raised to the power after the plus sign. For instance, a floating-point number (type `float`) can contain a number as small as -3.4^{38}.

Rewrite the following three numbers so that they do not use scientific notation:

```
2.3221E+4      2.3221E-4      -1.789E+2
```

Notice that long integers and long doubles tend to hold larger numbers (and therefore, have a higher precision) than regular integers and regular double floating-point variables. This is due to the larger number of memory locations used by many of the C++ compilers for these data types.

Every time your computer has to access more storage for a single variable (as is usually the case for `long` variables), it takes the computer much longer to access it, perform calculations, and store it. Use the `long` variables only if you suspect your data might overflow the typical data type ranges. Although the ranges differ between computers, you should have an idea of whether your numbers might exceed the computer's storage ranges. If you are working with extremely large (or extremely small and fractional) numbers, you should consider using the `long` and `double` variables.

Generally, all numeric variables should be signed (the default) unless you know for certain that your data contains only positive numbers. (Some values, such as age and distances, are always positive.) By making a variable unsigned, you gain a little extra storage range. That range of values, however, must always be positive. Obviously, you must be aware

of what kinds of data your variables hold. You certainly do not always know exactly what each variable is holding, but you can have a general idea. For example, in storing a person's age, you should realize that a long integer variable would be a waste of space, because nobody can yet live longer than the largest value a regular integer can hold.

Literals

As with variables, there are several types of C++ literals. Remember that a literal does not change. Integer literals are whole numbers that do not contain decimal points. Floating-point literals are numbers that contain a fractional portion (a decimal point with an optional value to the right of the decimal point).

Assigning Integer Literals

You already know that an integer is any whole number without a decimal point. C++ enables you to assign integer literals to variables, use integer literals for calculations, and print integer literals using the cout operator.

A regular integer literal cannot begin with a leading 0. To C++, the number 012 is not the number twelve. If you precede an integer literal with a 0, C++ interprets it as an *octal* literal. An octal literal is a base-8 number. The octal numbering system is not used much in today's computer systems. The newer versions of C++ retain octal capabilities for compatibility with previous versions.

A special integer in C++ that is still greatly used today is the base-16, or *hexadecimal,* literal. Appendix B describes the hexadecimal numbering system. If you want to represent a hexadecimal integer literal, add the 0x prefix to it. The following numbers are hexadecimal numbers:

```
0x10      0x2C4      0xFFFF      0X9
```

Notice that it does not matter whether you use a lowercase or upper-case letter x after the leading zero, or a lowercase or uppercase hexadecimal digit (for hex numbers A through F). If you write business-application programs in C++, you might think that you will never have the need for hexadecimal, and you might be correct. For a complete understanding of C++ and your computer in general, however, you should become familiar with the fundamentals of hexadecimal numbers.

Table 5.3 shows a few integer literals represented in their regular decimal, hexadecimal, and octal notations. Each row contains the same number in all three bases.

Table 5.3. Integer literals represented in three different bases.

Decimal (Base 10)	Hexadecimal (Base 16)	Octal (Base 8)
16	0x10	020
65536	0x10000	0200000
25	0x19	031

Which of the following integers are decimal, which are hexadecimal, and which are octal?

| 0 | 05 | 0x15 | 250 | 0250 | 0x250 |

> **NOTE:** You can begin floating-point literals with a leading zero—for example, 0.7. They are properly interpreted by C++. Only integers can be hexadecimal or octal literals.

Long, Unsigned, and Floating-Point Literals

When you use a number in a program, C++ interprets its data type as the smallest type that can hold that number. For example, if you type 13, C++ knows that this number fits into a signed integer memory location. It does not treat the number as a long integer, because 13 is not large enough to warrant a long integer literal size.

However, you can append a suffix character to numeric literals to override the default type. If you put an L at the end of an integer, C++ interprets that integer as a long integer. The number 13 is an integer literal, but the number 13L is a long integer literal. For example, you might want to add the L if you were adding a number to a long integer variable.

Assign the U suffix to designate an unsigned integer literal. The number 13 is, by default, a signed integer literal. If you type 13U, C++ treats it as an unsigned integer. The suffix UL indicates an unsigned long literal.

C++ interprets all floating-point literals (numbers that contain decimal points) as double floating-point literals (double floating-point literals
hold larger numbers than floating-point literals). This process ensures
the maximum accuracy for such numbers. If you use the literal 6.82, C++
treats it as a double floating-point data type, even though it would fit in
a regular float. You can append the floating-point suffix (F) or the long
double floating-point suffix (L) to literals that contain decimal points to
represent a floating-point literal or a long double floating-point literal.

What are the data types of each of these numbers?

5   5.55   5L   5.55L

You might only rarely use these suffixes, but if you have to assign a
literal value to an extended or unsigned variable, your literals might be
a little more accurate if you append a U, L, UL, or F (their lowercase
equivalents also work).

Putting Values in Variables

Now that you know about the C++ variable types, you are ready to learn
the specifics of putting values into those variables. You learned in Lesson
4, "The C++ Program's Format," that you do this with the *assignment*
operator. The equal sign (=) is used for assigning values to variables. The
format of an assignment is

variable = *expression*;

The *variable* is any variable name that you defined earlier in the
program. The *expression* is any variable, literal, expression, or combination that produces a resulting data type that is the same as the *variable*'s
data type.

> **TIP:** Putting spaces around the equal sign makes it more readable,
> but the C++ compiler does not require them.

> Think of the equal sign as a left-pointing arrow. Loosely, the equal
> sign means that you want to take the number, variable, or expres-
> sion on the right side of the equal sign and put it into the variable on
> the left side of the equal sign.

Consider a program that tracks your current age, salary, and dependents. You could store these values in three C++ variables. You first would define the variables by deciding on correct types and choosing descriptive names for them. You would then assign them values. Later in the program, these values might change (for example, if the program were to calculate a new pay increase for you).

Here is the code that defines these variables:

```
// Defines and stores three values
main()
{
   int age, dependents;
   float salary;
```

The next three statements assign values to the variables:

```
   age = 32;
   salary = 25000.00;
   dependents = 2;
   // Rest of program follows
```

You don't need to assign variables in the same order that you defined them. This example is not very long and it doesn't do much, but it illustrates how to use and assign values to variables.

> **NOTE:** Never put commas in values that you assign to variables. Numeric literals should never contain commas. The following statement is invalid:
>
> ```
> salary = 25,000.00;
> ```

You can assign variables or mathematical expressions to other variables. Suppose that earlier in a program you stored your tax rate in a variable called `tax_rate`, then decided to use your tax rate for your spouse's rate as well. At the proper point in the program, you would code the following:

```
spouse_tax_rate = tax_rate;
```

At this point in the program, the value in `tax_rate` is copied to a new variable named `spouse_tax_rate`. The value in `tax_rate` is still there after this line finishes. The variables were declared earlier in the program.

If your spouse's tax rate is 40 percent of yours, you can assign an expression to the spouse's variable, as in:

```
spouse_tax_rate = tax_rate * .40;
```

Any of the four mathematical symbols you learned in Lesson 4, "The C++ Program's Format," as well as the additional ones you will learn later in this book, can be part of the expression you assign to a variable.

If you want to assign character data to a character variable, you must enclose the character in single quotation marks. All C++ character literals must be enclosed in single quotation marks. The following section of a program declares three variables, then assigns three initials to them.

```
main()
{
    char first, middle, last;
    first = 'G';
    middle = 'M';
    last = 'P';
    // Rest of program follows
```

C++ allows a shortcut for defining variables and then placing values in them. The following program both defines and initializes three variables at the same time.

```
main()
{
    char initial = 'G';    // Defines and initializes
                           // at the same time

    int books = 230;
    float price = 23.95;
    // Rest of program follows
```

> **TIP:** C++ prefers that you store matching data values in the proper variables. Although you can assign a character literal to a floating-point variable, you should not do so. Sometimes C++ will not allow it. There are ways that you can safely mix types, and this book explains when you can.

What is wrong with the following program?

```
// Program that stores values in variables
main()
{
    int age;
    char letter = 45.43;
    age = 12.5;
    // Rest of program follows
```

Constant Variables

The term *constant variable* might seem like a contradiction. After all, a constant never changes, and a variable holds values that change. C++ constant variables, often called just *constants,* are different from the term *constant* used in other programming languages. In most programming languages, a constant is the same thing as a *literal*. Although some C++ programmers use the words interchangeably, a literal is, technically speaking, reserved for data values that are typed directly into a program and that do not change. Constants are the special variables described as follows.

In C++ terminology, you can declare variables to be constants with the const keyword. Throughout your program, the constants act like variables; you can use a constant variable anywhere you can use a variable, but you cannot change constant variables. To declare a constant, put the keyword const in front of the variable declaration. For instance:

```
const int days_of_week = 7;
```

You *must* put an initial value into the constant variable. If you don't, C++ will never let you assign it a value later because you cannot do anything to change the value of a constant.

Any type of variable can be made a constant. C++ offers the const keyword as an improvement of the #define preprocessor directive that C uses. Although C++ supports #define as well, const enables you to specify constant values with specific data types.

61

> **TIP:** If you omit the data type of a constant variable, C++ assumes that it is an integer. Therefore, the following two lines are equivalent:
>
> ```
> const int days_of_week = 7;
> ```
>
> and
>
> ```
> const days_of_week = 7;
> ```

The const keyword is appropriate when you have data that does not change. For example, the mathematical pi is a good candidate for a constant. If you accidentally attempt to store a value in a constant, C++ will let you know. Most C++ programmers choose to type their constant names in uppercase characters to distinguish them from regular variables. This is the one time when uppercase reigns in C++.

 A variable holds literals. Literals are also called constants. In the following line of code, age is a variable and 27 is a literal:

```
age = 27;
```

 Suppose that you were to write a program for a driver's license agency and needed to store the driving age limit of 16 in a constant integer variable. How would you define it?

 There are two errors in the first few lines of this program. What are they?

```
// Program that uses a constant variable
main()
{
    const salary = 234.54;
    const int age;
    age = 21;
    // Rest of program follows
```

Review Questions

1. What are the two broad types of data?

2. TRUE or FALSE: A variable can be a literal.

3. What is another name for a literal?

4. What are the numeric literal suffixes and what do they mean?

5. What does C++ do when you define a variable?

6. What is the C++ difference between a variable and a constant?

7. What is the C++ difference between a constant and a literal?

8. What is the C++ difference between a variable and a literal?

9. Why can you never assign a value to a constant variable after you define it?

10. Why should you use the smallest variable data type available that holds the data you need to hold?

Review Exercises

1. Write the first few lines in a program that stores your lucky number, your favorite television channel, and the price you paid for your car. Because you are such a big spender, be sure to use a large enough floating-point variable to hold a very expensive vintage auto.

2. Enter and compile a complete program that stores a value and prints each type of variable you learned in this lesson. Use the cout operator that you saw in Lesson 4, "The C++ Program's Format," to print the results.

Characters, Strings, and Character Arrays

OBJECTIVE *To explain C++ character variables and to demonstrate how you store strings of characters in memory.*

C++ differs from many other programming languages in that there is no such thing as a character string variable. There are character variables, but they hold only a single character of data. There are character string literals, but no character string variables. A string is simply a list of characters such as a word, phrase, sentence, or any set of characters strung together. If you have never programmed before, you will not miss string variables. If you have programmed in other languages, you might question C++'s usefulness because it does not support string variables.

The designers of the C++ language decided against using string variables, but C++ offers alternatives to them that are almost as easy to use and much more efficient. After all, C++ must offer a way for you to store people's names and addresses. This lesson shows you how to designate string literals and how to store them in memory.

Character Literals and Variables

All character literals must appear between two single quotation marks. All of the following are character literals:

```
'A'      'x'      '.'      '*'      '&'      '1'
```

As you can see, a character is any character, whether a letter, number, space, or special character enclosed in single quotes. Never put single quotation marks around something other than a single character of data.

In Lesson 5, "C++ Numeric Data," you learned how to define a character variable with the char keyword. The following statement defines a character variable:

```
char MyGrade;    // Defines a character variable
```

The following section of a program declares three variables, then assigns three initials to them. The initials are character literals because they are enclosed in single quotation marks.

```
main()
{
   char first, middle, last;
   first = 'G';
   middle = 'M';
   last = 'P';
   // Rest of program follows
```

What if the character literals in this partial program did not have single quotation marks? What would C++ do with the G, M, and P? C++ would think that G, M, and P were three variables! Because it would not have seen any definition for those variables, C++ would issue an error message. The quotation marks are vital to let C++ know that you are assigning character literals and not other variables.

String Literals

One type of C++ literal, called the *string literal,* does not have a matching variable. A string literal is always enclosed in double quotation marks, often called just *quotation marks.* The following are examples of string literals:

```
"C++ Programming"   "123"   "."   "4323 E. Oak Road"   "x"
```

Any string of characters between double quotation marks—even a single character—is considered to be a string literal. A single space, a word, or a group of words between double quotation marks are all C++ string literals.

If the string literal contains only numeric digits, it is *not* a number; it is a string of numeric digits that cannot be used to perform mathematical calculations. You can perform calculations on numbers only, not on string literals.

A string literal is *any* character, digit, or group of characters enclosed in double quotation marks. A character literal is any character enclosed in single quotation marks. That is how you determine whether a literal is a character or a string. If the literal has no quotation marks, it is a numeric constant.

Which of the following are string literals, which are character literals, which are numeric literals, and which are variable names?

```
Hi     _____

'H'    _____

"56"   _____

'2'    _____

"hi"   _____

'1'    _____

1      _____
```

The double quotation marks are never considered part of the string. The double quotation marks surround the string and simply inform your C++ compiler that the code is a string literal and not another type of literal.

It is easy to print string literals. Simply put the string literals in a cout statement. The following code prints a string literal to the screen:

```
cout << ."C++ Programming 101";
```

You can just as easily print character literals like this:

```
cout << 'A' << 'B' << 'C';
```

 The following cout attempts to rewrite the preceding one more efficiently. It comes close, but there is a problem. What is it?

```
cout << 'ABC';    // Almost works
```

String-Literal Endings

One additional aspect of string literals sometimes confuses beginning C++ programmers. All string literals end with a zero. You do not see the zero, but C++ stores it at the end of the string in memory. Figure 6.1 shows what the string "C++ Lesson" looks like in memory.

Figure 6.1.
In memory, a
string literal
always ends
with 0.

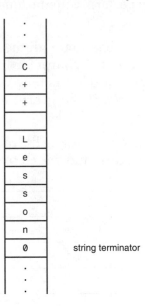

You do not have to worry about putting the zero at the end of a string literal. C++ does it for you every time it stores a string. If your program contained the string "C++ Lesson", for example, the compiler would recognize it as a string literal (from the double quotation marks) and store the zero at the end.

The zero is important to C++. It is called the *string terminator*. C++ uses the string terminator to know where the string literal ended in memory. (Remember that the double quotation marks are not stored as part of the string, so C++ cannot use them to determine where the string ends.)

The string-delimiting zero is not the same as the character zero. If you look in Appendix C, you see that the first entry, ASCII number 0, is the *null* character. This string-delimiting zero is different from the character '0', which has an ASCII value of 48.

As explained in Appendix B, all memory locations in your computer actually hold bit patterns of characters. If the letter A is stored in memory, an A is not actually there; the binary bit pattern for the ASCII A (01000001) is stored there. Because the binary bit pattern for the null zero is 00000000, the string-delimiting zero is also called a *binary zero.*

To illustrate this further, Figure 6.2 shows the bit patterns for the following string literal when stored in memory:

```
"I am 30"
```

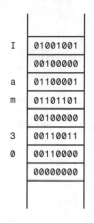

Figure 6.2.
The bit pattern showing that a null zero and a character zero are different.

Figure 6.2 shows how a string is stored in your computer's memory at the binary level. It is important for you to recognize that the character 0 inside the number 30 is not the same zero (at the bit level) as the string-terminating null zero. If it were, C++ would think that this string ended after the 3, which is incorrect.

Using the ASCII table in Appendix C, what do the bit patterns of the following string look like? Fill in the blanks of Figure 6.3 with the answer. *Hint:* The two special characters each take one memory location.

```
"I'll take 10."
```

String Lengths

Your program often has to know the length of a string. This becomes critical when you learn how to accept string input from the keyboard. The length of a string is the number of characters up to, but not including, the

string terminator. Do *not* include the string terminator in the count, even though you know that C++ adds it to the end of the string.

Figure 6.3.
The bit patterns
for "I'll take 10."

Table 6.1 shows some string literals and their corresponding string ·lengths.

Table 6.1. String literals and their lengths.

String	Length
"C"	1
"0"	1
"Hello"	5
" "	0
"30 oranges"	10

What is the length of this string? *Hint:* There is a difference between a character 0 and the string-terminating zero.

`"That costs 50"`

All character literals have a length of one, with no exception. There is no string terminator for character literals. The double quotation marks signal to C++ that a string terminator is needed, so C++ adds one to the end of every string inside double quotes.

You should know that the following are different to C++:

`'R'` and `"R"`

'R' is a single character literal. It is one character long, because *all* character literals (and variables) are one character long. "R" is a string literal because it is delimited by double quotation marks. Its length is also one, but it includes a null zero in memory so that C++ knows where the string ends. Due to this difference, you cannot mix character literals and character strings. Figure 6.4 shows how these two literals are stored in memory.

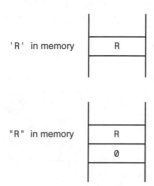

Figure 6.4.
The difference in memory between 'R' *as a character literal and* "R" *as a string literal.*

Special Character Literals

All the alphabetic, numeric, and special characters on your keyboard can be character literals. Some characters, however, cannot be represented by using your keyboard. They include some of the higher ASCII characters (such as the Spanish Ñ). Because you do not have keys for every character in the ASCII table, C++ enables you to represent these characters by typing their ASCII hexadecimal number inside single quotation marks.

For example, to store the Spanish Ñ in a variable, look up its hexadecimal ASCII number in Appendix C. You find that it is A5. Add the prefix \x to it and enclose it in single quotation marks so that C++ will know to use the special character. You could do that with the following code:

```
char sn='\xA5';   // Puts the Spanish Ñ into
                  // a variable called sn
```

This is the way to store (or print) any character from the ASCII table, even if that character does not have a key on your keyboard.

Looking at the '\xA5', you might wonder how a *single character* can reside between those quotes. Earlier it was stated that single quotes always enclose a single character. Even though '\xA5' contains four

characters inside the quotation marks, those four characters represent a single character, not a character string. If you were to include those four characters inside a string *literal,* C++ would treat \xA5 as a single character in the string. The following string literal

```
"An accented a is \xA0"
```

is a C++ string that is 18 characters, not 21 characters. C++ interprets the \xA0 character as the á, just as it should. The backslash (\) signals to C++ that it should treat the next characters in a special way, not as a three-character string.

 Using the ASCII table in Appendix C, write a line that assigns an upside-down question mark to a character variable named q.

Any character preceded by a backslash (such as the ones you have been seeing) is called an *escape sequence* or an *escape character.* In addition to the hexadecimal ASCII code you just read about, C++ defines some special escape sequences that come in handy when you want to print special characters. Table 6.2 shows you what these special escape sequences are.

Table 6.2. Special C++ escape sequence characters.

Escape Sequence	Meaning
\a	Alarm (the terminal's bell)
\b	Backspace
\f	Form feed (for the printer)
\n	Newline (carriage return and line feed)
\r	Carriage return
\t	Tab
\v	Vertical tab
\\	Backslash (\)
\?	Question mark
\'	Single quotation mark
\"	Double quotation mark
\000	Octal number

Escape Sequence	Meaning
\xhh	Hexadecimal number
\0	Null zero (or binary zero)

The "\n" is useful for cout statements. What is the output of the following program?

```
// Program that uses \n
#include <iostream.h>
void main()
{
   cout << "Line #1";
   cout << "Line #2";

   cout << "\n\n";
   cout << "Line #3\n";
   cout << "Line #4";
}
```

Write a cout statement in the middle of this program that rings the bell when the program runs.

```
// Rings the computer's bell
#include <iostream.h>
void main()
{



}
```

The following cout statement attempts to send a single quotation mark to the screen. It tries to specify the single quotation mark as a character literal, but C++ balks at '''. What is another way to designate and output a single quotation mark? Write the correction beneath the incorrect cout.

```
cout << '''';    // Attempts to output a single quotation mark
```

Math with C++ Characters

Because C++ associates characters so closely with their ASCII numbers, you can perform arithmetic on character data. This is one of the few places where it is okay to mix data types. C++ integers and characters work together well thanks to the ASCII table in Appendix C. The following section of code

```
char c;
c = 'T' + .5;    // Adds 5 to the ASCII character
```

actually stores a Y in the character variable c. The ASCII value of the letter T is 84. Adding 5 to 84 produces 89. Because the variable c is not an integer variable, but a character variable, C++ adds the ASCII character value for 89, not the actual number.

Conversely, you can store character literals in integer variables. If you do, C++ stores the matching ASCII number for that character. The following section of code

```
int i = 'P';
```

does not put a letter P in i because i is not a character variable. C++ assigns the number 80 in the variable because 80 is the ASCII number for the letter P.

 What value is in c when these two lines finish executing?

```
int c;
c = 'A' + 5;    // Adds 5 to the ASCII character
```

Character Array Variables

A *character array* is the C++ vehicle that holds character strings. As mentioned earlier, although C++ has no string variables, character arrays work well for holding strings. The concept of an array might be new to you. As you will see in the rest of this lesson, arrays are not difficult to understand. There are several kinds of arrays—integer arrays, floating-point arrays, and so on. As soon as you have mastered character arrays, the remaining array types (discussed in Lesson 25, "Array Processing") will be easy for you.

An array is a list (sometimes called a *table*) of variables. Most programming languages allow the use of such lists. Suppose that you had to keep track of the sales records of 100 salespeople. You could make up 100 variable names and assign a different salesperson's sales record to each one.

All those different variable names, however, are difficult to track. If you were to put them in an array of floating-point variables, you would have to keep track of only a single name (the array name) and reference each of the 100 values by a numeric subscript.

Later lessons in this book cover array processing in more detail. Because a string is simply a list of one or more characters, a character array is the perfect place to hold strings of information. Suppose that you want to keep track of a person's full name, age, and salary in variables. The age and salary are easy because there are variable types that can hold such data. The following code declares those two variables:

```
int age;
float salary;
```

You have no string variable to hold the name, but you can create an appropriate array of characters (which is actually one or more character variables in a row in memory) with the following definition:

```
char name[10];
```

This reserves a character array. An array declaration always includes brackets ([]) that declare the space for the array. This array is 10 characters long. The array name is name. You also can assign a value to the character array at the time you define the array. The following definition statement not only defines the character array, but it also assigns the name "Ted Jones" at the same time:

```
char name[10] = "Ted Jones";
```

Figure 6.5 shows what this array looks like in memory. Each of the 10 boxes of the array is called an *element*. Notice the null zero (the string-terminating character) at the end of the string. Notice also that the last character of the array contains no data. You filled only the first nine elements of the array with the data and the data's null zero. The tenth element does have a value in it, but whatever follows the string's null zero is not a concern.

 How many elements are reserved in the following character array?

```
char MyAddress[25];    // Defines room for an address
```

You can access individual elements in an array, or you can access the array as a whole. This is the primary advantage of using an array rather than using many differently named variables. You can assign values to the individual array elements by putting the elements' location, called a *subscript,* in brackets, as follows:

```
name[1] = 'a';
```

This overwrites the e in the name Ted with an a. The character array now holds "Tad Jones".

Figure 6.5.
A character array
after being
declared and
assigned a
string value.

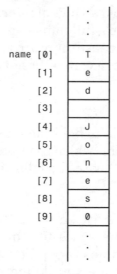

All array subscripts start at zero. Therefore, to overwrite the first element, you must use 0 as the subscript. Assigning name[1] (as done earlier) changes the value of the second element in the array, not the first.

 How would you define and initialize a character array that is 20 characters long and that holds a company named "Widgets, Inc."?

You can print individual elements of an array as well. The following statement:

```
cout << name[0] << '. ' << name[4] << ".\n";
```

prints this:

```
T. J.
```

What does the following print, assuming that name still holds the "Tad Jones" name?

```
cout << name[4] << name[5] << name[6]
     << name[7] << name[8] << ".\n";
```

You can print the entire string—or, more accurately, the entire array—with a single cout statement, as follows:

```
cout << name;
```

Notice that when you print an array, you do not include brackets after the array name. You must be sure to reserve enough characters in the array to hold the entire string. The following line

```
char name[5]="Michael Jones";
```

is incorrect because it reserves only five characters for the array, whereas the name and its null zero require 14 characters. C++ issues the error message illegal initialization if you do not reserve enough characters.

> **NOTE:** Always reserve enough array elements to hold the string and its null-terminating character. It is easy to forget the extra place for the null character, but don't!

If your string contains 13 characters, it also must have a 14th location for the null zero or it will never be treated like a string. To help eliminate this error, C++ gives you a shortcut. The following two character array statements are the same:

```
char horse[9] = "Stallion";
```

and

```
char horse[] = "Stallion";
```

If you assign a value to a character array at the same time you declare the array, C++ counts the string's length, adds one for the null zero, and reserves the array space for you.

 How many characters will C++ reserve in the following array definition?

```
char movie[] = "Cinema Fantastico";
```

If you do not assign a value to an array at the time it is declared, you cannot declare it with empty brackets. The following statement:

```
char people[];
```

does not reserve any space for the array called `people`. Because you did not assign a value to the array when you declared it, C++ assumes that this array contains zero elements. Therefore, you have no room to put values in this array later. Most compilers generate an error if you attempt this.

 An array is not a single variable. It is a list of variables. A character variable holds a single character, and a character array holds a bunch of character variables. Instead of that bunch of variables having different names, they all have the same name (the name of the array). To distinguish one array element (variable) from another, use subscripts that always begin at 0.

Character Arrays Versus Strings

In the preceding section you saw how to put a string in a character array. Strings can exist in C++ only as string *literals,* or as stored information in character arrays. At this point, you need to understand only that strings must be stored in character arrays. As you read through this book and become more familiar with arrays and strings, however, you should become more comfortable with their use.

> **NOTE:** Strings must be stored in character arrays, but not all character arrays contain strings.

Look at the two arrays shown in Figure 6.6. The first one, called `cara1`, is a character array, but it does not contain a string. Rather than a string, it contains a list of several characters. The second array, called `cara2`, contains a string because it has a null zero at its end.

You could initialize these arrays with the following assignment statements:

```
char cara1[10]={'a', 'b', 'c', 'd', 'e', 'f', 'g', 'h',
                'i', 'j'};

char cara2[10]="Excellent";
```

If you want to put only individual characters in an array, you must enclose the list of characters in braces, as shown. You could initialize cara1 later in the program, using assignment statements, as the following code section does:

```
char cara1[10];
cara1[0]='a';
cara1[1]='b';
cara1[2]='c';
cara1[3]='d';
cara1[4]='e';
cara1[5]='f';
cara1[6]='g';
cara1[7]='h';
cara1[8]='i';
cara1[9]='j';    // Last element possible with subscript of 9
```

cara1 [0]	a
[1]	b
[2]	c
[3]	d
[4]	e
[5]	f
[6]	g
[7]	h
[8]	i
[9]	j

no null zero

cara2 [0]	E
[1]	x
[2]	c
[3]	e
[4]	l
[5]	l
[6]	e
[7]	n
[8]	t
[9]	0

null zero

Figure 6.6.
Two character arrays: cara1 *contains characters, and* cara2 *contains a character string.*

Because the cara1 character array does not contain a null zero, it does not contain a *string* of characters. It does contain characters that can be stored in the array—and used individually—but they cannot be treated in a program as if they were a string.

CAUTION: You cannot assign string values to character arrays in a regular assignment statement, except when you first declare the character arrays.

Because a character array is not a string variable (it can be used only to hold a string), it cannot go on the left side of an equal (=) sign. The program that follows is invalid:

```
#include <iostream.h>
main()
{
   char petname[20];    //  Reserves space for the pet's name
   petname = "Luke";    // INVALID!
   cout << petname;     // The program will never get here
   return;
}
```

Because the pet's name was not assigned *at the time the character array was declared,* it cannot be assigned a value later. The following is allowed, however, because you can assign values individually to a character array:

```
#include <iostream.h>
main()
{
   char petname[20];  // Reserves space for the pet's name
   petname[0]='L';  // Assigns values one element at a time
   petname[1]='u';
   petname[2]='k';
   petname[3]='e';
   petname[4]='\0';  // Needed to ensure that this is a string!
   cout << petname;  // Now the pet's name prints properly
   return;
}
```

The petname character array now holds a string because the last character is a null zero.

How long is the string in petname? *Hint:* The length of a string never includes the null zero.

The length of the string is always the number of characters in the character array up to, but not including, the string-terminating null zero. The number of elements reserved for an array can be, and usually is, different from the string length. The character array in the preceding code contains 20 elements. This remains true whether those elements contain a string or just some character data.

You cannot assign more than 20 characters to this array because its reserved space is only 20 characters. However, you can store any string of 19 (leaving one for the null zero) or fewer characters to the array. If you assign the "Luke" string in the array as shown, and then assign a null zero to petname[3] as in

```
petname[3]='\0';
```

the string in petname is now only three characters long. You have, in effect, shortened the string. There are still 20 characters reserved for petname, but the data inside it is the string "Luk" ending with a null zero.

There are many other ways to assign a value to a string. You can use the strcpy() function, for example. This is a built-in function that enables you to copy a string literal in a string. To copy the "Benji" pet name into the petname array, type:

```
strcpy(petname, "Benji");   // Copies Benji into the array
```

The strcpy() ("string copy") function assumes that the first value in the parentheses is a character array name and that the second value is a valid string literal or another character array that holds a string. You must be sure that the first character array in the parentheses is long enough (in number of reserved elements) to hold whatever string you copy into it.

Other methods of initializing arrays are explored throughout the rest of this book.

> **NOTE:** Place an #include <string.h> line before the main() function in programs that use strcpy() or any other built-in string functions mentioned in this book. Your compiler supplies the string.h file to help the strcpy() function work properly. The #include files such as iostream.h and string.h are explained in more detail in later lessons.

What is wrong with the following program?

```cpp
#include <iostream.h>
void main()
{
   char addr[25];
   strcpy(addr, "35 W. Hazelnut");
   cout << "My address is " << addr;
}
```

Write the output of the following program in the blank lines following the program. This program takes three friends' character arrays and assigns them string values by using the three methods shown in this lesson. Notice the extra #include file used with the string function strcpy().

```cpp
// Filename: STR.CPP
// Stores and initializes three character
// arrays for three friends

#include <iostream.h>
#include <string.h>
void main()
{
   // Declares all arrays and initializes the first one
   char friend1[20]="Jackie Paul Johnson";
   char friend2[20];
   char friend3[20];

// Uses a function to initialize the second array
   strcpy(friend2, "Julie L. Roberts");

   friend3[0]='A';    // Initializes the last,
   friend3[1]='d';    // an element at a time
   friend3[2]='a';
   friend3[3]='m';
   friend3[4]=' ';
   friend3[5]='G';
   friend3[6]='.';
   friend3[7]=' ';
```

```
friend3[8]='S';
friend3[9]='m';
friend3[10]='i';
friend3[11]='t';
friend3[12]='h';
friend3[13]='\0';

// Prints all three names
cout << friend1 << "\n";
cout << friend2 << "\n";
cout << friend3 << "\n";
}
```

The method just shown of initializing a character array with a string—one element at a time—is not used as often as the other methods. It is too tedious.

Review Questions

1. TRUE or FALSE: A character literal is a letter of the alphabet.

2. What is another name for a string terminator?

3. Where is the string terminator in this string?

   `"000000000"`

4. TRUE or FALSE: These are exactly the same thing in C++:

   `"C"` and `'C'`

5. If you want to assign data to a 15-element character array named MyStr, why will this not work?

   `MyStr = "A string";`

6. Given the conditions of Question 5, will this work?

   `MyStr[] = "A string";`

7. Will this?

    ```
    MyStr[15] = "A string";
    ```

8. Will this?

    ```
    strcpy(MyStr, "A string");
    ```

9. Can you assign `MyStr[]` the string when you define it like this?

    ```
    char MyStr[15] = "A string";   // At definition time
    ```

10. Does a character array always hold a string? Why or why not?

Review Exercise

1. Write a program that defines two arrays, one called `first` and one called `last`, and that asks the user for a first and last name. Use the `cin` operator (the opposite of `cout`) to retrieve data from the keyboard. The program should then print the user's initials on-screen by printing the first character of each name in the array. The program must print each array's 0 subscript because the first subscript of any array begins at 0, not at 1.

Lesson

7

Preprocessor Directives

To explain the two most common uses for the preprocessor: the #include and #define directives.

Lesson 1, "Introduction to C++," explained that your compiler does not get your source code as soon as you compile it. Instead, a precompiler, called the *preprocessor,* looks at your source code and modifies it before giving it to the compiler. The preprocessor is important in C++ (more so than in C). Almost every C++ program contains *preprocessor directives.* The preprocessor interprets the preprocessor directives in your program.

Looking at Preprocessor Directives

Preprocessor directives are not C++ commands or functions. A C++ command, such as int i;, or a function, such as printf(Age);, is compiled by the compiler. A preprocessor directive always begins with a pound sign (#). Because preprocessor directives are not commands, they should not

have semicolons at the end of their lines. Typically, preprocessor directives begin in column 1 (in other words, flush-left, not indented). Because C++ is freeform, it does not matter in which column you begin preprocessor directives, but the standard convention is to begin them in column 1.

Here is a preprocessor directive:

```
#include <iostream.h>
```

The following line is an attempt at a preprocessor directive. It has two problems. What are they?

```
define AGE 21;
```

Preprocessor directives cause your C++ preprocessor to change your source code, but these changes last only as long as the compilation. When you look at your source code again, the preprocessor is finished with your file, and its changes are no longer in the file. Your preprocessor does not in any way compile your program or change your actual C++ commands. This concept confuses some beginning C++ students, but just remember that your program has yet to be compiled when your preprocessor directives execute. It is a precompiler.

It has been said that a preprocessor does nothing more than text edit your program. This analogy holds true throughout this lesson, and you will see why.

The #include Directive

The #include preprocessor directive merges a disk file with your source program. In other words, #include tells the compiler to go out to disk, find a file, and insert it into the location of the #include. Remember that a preprocessor directive does nothing more than a text-editing command does to your program; text editors are capable of file merging.

The format of #include is

```
#include <filename>
```

or

```
#include "filename"
```

The *filename* is a text file called a *header file* that is stored on disk. Header files almost always have an .h filename extension. The header must be a text file (as must your source file) located somewhere on the disk. If you put the filename inside the angled brackets, C++ looks in a special directory called the *include directory*. You do not have to do anything special with this directory. When you install C++, the installation program sets up the include directory and stores many header files there.

If you write your own header files and store those files somewhere other than the default C++ include directory, you must put the directory path and filename inside the quotation marks. You do not need to specify the directory path if the file resides in the same directory as the source file.

> **NOTE:** Never put spaces inside the < and >, or C++ will incorrectly think that there are spaces in your filename.

Given the following #include, where would the file named string.h be located on the disk?

```
#include <string.h>
```

Given the following #include, where would the file named address.h be located on the disk?

```
#include "d:\files\address.h"
```

The more you learn about C++, the more header files you will learn about. The primary header file that you must include in almost every C++ program is named iostream.h. All programs that perform input and output using cin and cout need the iostream.h header file for some setup commands. Because almost every C++ program uses cin or cout, almost every C++ program includes iostream.h. The iostream.h header file comes with every C++ compiler.

To better understand how #include works, you might want to leave C++ for a moment. Suppose that there are two files on disk. One is called OUTSIDE and the other is called INSIDE.

87

Here are the contents of the OUTSIDE file:

```
Now is the time for all good men

#include <INSIDE>

to come to the aid of their country.
```

The INSIDE file contains the following:

```
A quick brown fox jumped
over the lazy dog.
```

Assume that you can run the OUTSIDE file through the C++ preprocessor, which finds the #include directive and replaces it with the entire file called INSIDE. In other words, the C++ preprocessor directive merges the INSIDE file into the OUTSIDE file—at the #include location—and OUTSIDE expands to include the merged text. After the preprocessing ends, OUTSIDE looks like this:

```
Now is the time for all good men

A quick brown fox jumped
over the lazy dog.

to come to the aid of their country.
```

The INSIDE file remains on disk in its original form. Only the file containing the #include directive is changed. This change is only temporary; that is, OUTSIDE is expanded by the included file only for as long as it takes to compile the program.

A few real-life examples might help, because the OUTSIDE and INSIDE files are not C++ programs. You might want to include a file containing common code that you frequently use. Suppose that you print your name and address quite often. You can type the following few lines of code in every program that prints your name and address:

```
cout << "Kelly Jane Peterson\n";
cout << "Apartment #217\n";
cout << "4323 East Skelly Drive\n";
cout << "New York, New York\n";
cout << "              10012\n";
```

Instead of having to retype the same five lines again and again, you type them once and save them in a file called myadd.h. From then on, you have to type only a single line:

```
#include <myadd.h>
```

This not only saves typing, but it also maintains consistency and accuracy. (Sometimes this kind of repeated text is known as a *boilerplate*.)

When the preprocessor sees the #include <myadd.h>, it replaces the line with the entire contents of the file named myadd.h. Do you see that your source code grows to contain the number of lines of the header file *and* the original source file as you typed it?

The compiler actually thinks that *you typed the included text* when it compiles your program. The preprocessor changes your source file from the way you originally typed it. As soon as the program finishes compiling and you look at the source file, it looks the same as it looked earlier, with the #include just the way it was before the include took place. You must admit that including a file where you need it is easier than typing all the text that is in the file—and more accurate as well.

In Lesson 6, "Characters, Strings, and Character Arrays," you saw the strcpy() function. Its header file is called string.h. Therefore, if you write a program that contains strcpy(), include its string.h header file at the same time you include <iostream.h>. These appear on separate lines, such as:

```
#include <iostream.h>
#include <string.h>
```

The order of your include files does not matter, as long as you include the files before the functions that need them. Most C++ programmers include all their needed header files before main().

The following program copies a message into a character array and prints it to the screen. Because cout and the strcpy() built-in function are used, both of their header files are included.

```
// Filename: INC.CPP
// Uses two header files

#include <iostream.h>
#include <string.h>

main()
{
```

```
    char message[20];
    strcpy(message, "This is fun!");
    cout << message;
    return 0;
}
```

The #define Directive

The #define preprocessor directive is used in C++ programming, although not nearly as frequently as it is in C. Due to the const keyword (in C++) that enables you to define variables as constants, #define is not used as much in C++. Nevertheless, #define is useful for compatibility with C programs that you are converting to C++. The #define directive might seem strange at first, but it is similar to a search-and-replace command in a word processor. The format of #define is

#define ARGUMENT1 argument2

where ARGUMENT1 is a single word containing no spaces. Use the same naming rules for the #define statement's first argument as for variables. For the first argument, it is traditional to use uppercase letters—one of the only uses of uppercase in the entire C++ language. At least one space separates ARGUMENT1 from argument2. argument2 can be any character, word, or phrase, and it can contain spaces or anything else you can type on the keyboard. Because #define is a preprocessor directive and not a C++ executable command, do not put a semicolon at the end of its expression.

The #define preprocessor directive replaces the occurrence of ARGUMENT1 everywhere in your program with the contents of argument2. In most cases, the #define directive should go before main() (along with any #include directives). Look at the following #define directive:

#define AGELIMIT 21

If your program includes one or more occurrences of the term AGELIMIT, the preprocessor replaces every one of them with the number 21. The compiler then reacts as if you actually had typed 21 rather than AGELIMIT, because the preprocessor changes all occurrences of AGELIMIT to 21 before your compiler reads the source code. Again, the change is only temporary. After your program is compiled, you see it as you originally typed it, with #define and AGELIMIT still intact.

> **NOTE:** AGELIMIT is not a variable, because variables are declared and assigned values only at the time your program is compiled and run. The preprocessor changes your source file before the time it is compiled.

You might wonder why you would ever have to go to this much trouble. If you want 21 everywhere AGELIMIT occurs, you could type 21 to begin with! But the advantage of using #define rather than literals is that if the age limit ever changes (perhaps to 18), you have to change only one line in the program, not every single occurrence of the literal 21.

Because #define enables you to easily define and change literals, the replaced arguments of the #define directive are sometimes called *defined literals*. (C programmers say that #define "defines constants," but C++ programmers rarely use the word *constant* unless they are discussing the use of const.) You can define any type of literal, including string literals. The following program contains a defined string literal that replaces a string in two places.

```
// Filename: DEF1.CPP
// Defines a string literal and uses it twice

#include <iostream.h>
#define MYNAME "Phil Ward"

void main()
{
   char name[] = MYNAME;
   cout << "My name is " << name << "\n";  // Prints the array
   cout << "My name is " << MYNAME << "\n";  // Prints the
                                              // defined literal
   return;
}
```

The first argument of #define is in uppercase to distinguish it from variable names in the program. Variables usually are typed in lowercase. Although your preprocessor and compiler will not confuse the two, other users who look at your program can more quickly scan through and tell which items are defined literals and which are not. They will know when

they see an uppercase word (if you follow the recommended standard for this first #define argument) to look at the top of the program for its actual defined value.

On the line provided after the following program, write every variable you find. *Hint:* There are only three.

```
// Filename: FINDV.CPP
#include <iostream.h>

#define A 25
#define B 35
#define C 45

void main()
{
   int a = 100;
   int b = 200;
   int c = 300;

   cout << "A is " << A << "\n";
   cout << "B is " << B << "\n";
   cout << "C is " << C << "\n";
   cout << "a is " << a << "\n";
   cout << "b is " << b << "\n";
   cout << "c is " << c << "\n";
}
```

The fact that defined literals are not variables is even more clear in the following program. This program prints three values. Try to guess what those three values are before you look at the answer following the program.

```
// Filename: DEF2.CPP
// Illustrates that #define literals are not variables

#include <iostream.h>

#define X1 a + b
#define X2 X1 * X1

void main()
{
```

```
   int a = 2;    // Declares and initializes two variables
   int b = 3;

   // Prints some values
   cout << a << ", " << b << ", " << X2 << "\n";
}
```

The output from this program is

```
2, 3, 11
```

If you treated X1 and X2 as variables, you would not receive the correct answer. You probably assumed that the third number would be 25, but if you did, you assumed that X1 and X2 are variables. However, they are defined literals, *not* variables. Before your program is compiled, the preprocessor reads the first line and changes every occurrence of X1 to a + b. This occurs before the next #define is processed. Therefore, after the first #define, the source code looks like this:

```
// Filename: DEF2.CPP
// Illustrates that #define literals are not variables

#include <iostream.h>

#define X2 a + b * a + b

void main()
{
   int a = 2;    // Declares and initializes two variables
   int b = 3;

   // Prints some values
   cout << a << ", " << b << ", " << X2 << "\n";
}
```

After the first #define finishes, the second one takes over and changes every occurrence of X2 to a + b * a + b. Your source code at that point becomes:

```
// Filename: DEF2.CPP
// Illustrates that #define literals are not variables

#include <iostream.h>

#define X2 a + b * a + b
```

```
void main()
{
   int a = 2;    // Declares and initializes two variables
   int b = 3;

   // Prints some values
   cout << a << ", " << b << ", " << a + b * a + b << "\n";
}
```

The #define makes the source code grow rapidly. After the preprocessor finishes with the second #define, the cout prints a rather long expression. Because multiplication is performed before addition, the b is multiplied by a, then the result is added to the remaining a and b. The compiler thinks that you typed the full, expanded version. You did not type the expanded version; you typed the original listing (shown first). The preprocessor expanded your source code into this longer form, just as if you had typed it this way.

This is an extreme example, but it serves to illustrate how #define works on your source code. #define does not define any variables.

Really Change Things

The #define behaves like a text editor's search-and-replace command. Due to #define's behavior, you can even rewrite the C++ language itself!

If you are used to BASIC, you might be more comfortable typing PRINT rather than C++'s cout when you want to print on-screen. If so, the following #define statement:

```
#define PRINT cout
```

enables you to print in C++ with these statements:

```
PRINT << "This is a new printing technique\n";
PRINT << "I could have used cout instead."\n;
```

This works because by the time your compiler reads the program, it thinks that you typed the following:

```
cout << "This is a new printing technique\n";
cout << "I could have used cout instead."\n;
```

 What does the compiler think you really typed when it sees the following few lines of code?

```
#define PI 3.14159
#define INTEGER int
```

```
void main()
{
    INTEGER i;
    float x = PI;
    // Rest of program follows
```

> **NOTE:** You cannot replace a defined literal if it resides inside another string literal. For example, you cannot use the following #define statement:
>
> ```
> #define AGE 21
> ```
>
> to replace information in this cout:
>
> ```
> cout << "AGE";
> ```
>
> because "AGE" is a string literal, and it prints literally just as it appears inside the double quotation marks. The preprocessor can replace only defined literals that do not appear in quotation marks.

Do Not Overdo #define

Many early C programmers enjoyed redefining parts of the language to suit whatever they were used to in another language. The cout to PRINT example is only one example of this. You can redefine virtually any C++ statement or function to "look" any way you like.

There is a danger to this, however, so be wary of using #define for this purpose. Your redefining the language becomes confusing to others who modify your program later. Also, as you become more familiar with C++, you naturally will use the true C++ language more and more. When you are comfortable with C++, older programming statements that you redefined will be confusing—even to you!

If you are programming in C++, use the language conventions that C++ provides. Don't try to redefine commands in the language. Think of the #define directive as a way to define numeric and string literals. If those literals ever change, you have to change only one line in your program. "Just say no" to any temptation to redefine commands and built-in functions. Better yet, modify any older C code that uses #define, and replace the #define preprocessor directive with the more useful const command.

Many C++ programmers define a list of error messages. As soon as they have defined the messages with an easy-to-remember name, they can print those literals if an error occurs and still maintain consistency in their programs. The following error messages (or similar ones) often appear at the beginning of C++ programs.

```
#define DISKERR "Your disk drive seems not to be working"
#define PRNTERR "Your printer is not responding"
#define AGEERR  "You cannot enter an age that small"
#define NAMEERR "You must enter a full name"
```

You then could put these error message definitions in a header file and include them at the top of any program that needs them.

Review Questions

1. TRUE or FALSE: You can define variables with the preprocessor directives.

2. Which preprocessor directive merges another file with your program?

3. Which preprocessor directive defines literals throughout your program?

4. TRUE or FALSE: You can define character, string, integer, and floating-point literals with the #define directive.

5. Which happens first: your program is compiled or your program is preprocessed?

6. What C++ keyword is used to replace the #define preprocessor directive?

7. When do you use the angled brackets in an #include, and when do you use double quotation marks?

8. Which are easier to change: defined literals or literals that you type throughout a program? Why?

9. TRUE or FALSE: The #define in the following:

```
#define MESSAGE "Please press Enter to continue..."
```

changes this statement:

```
cout << "MESSAGE";
```

10. What is the output of the following program?

```
// Filename: EXER.CPP

#include <iostream.h>
#define AMT1 a + a + a
#define AMT2 AMT1 - AMT1

void main()
{
   int a=1;
   cout << "Amount is " << AMT2 << "\n";
}
```

Review Exercises

1. Write a program that prints your name to the screen. Use a defined literal for the name. Do not use a character array, and don't type your actual name inside the cout.

2. Suppose that your boss wanted you to write a program that produced an "exception report." If the company's sales are less

than $100,000.00 or more than $750,000.00, your boss wants your program to print the appropriate message. You learn how to produce these types of reports later in the book, but for now just write the #define statements that define these two floating-point values with easy-to-remember defined labels.

3. Write a program that defines the 10 digits, 0 through 9, as literals ZERO through NINE. Add these 10 defined digits and store the sum in a variable named total and print the result.

I/O with cout and cin

 To teach the proper use of cout and cin.

Performing input and output (often referred to as just *I/O*) is extremely easy with C++. You need a way to get data and results of calculations to the screen and to get input from the user at the keyboard. This book has already used cout and cin for simple input and output. This lesson reviews cout and cin and then explains how to make them work exactly the way you want.

Comparing cout and cin

cout and cin are defined in iostream.h. As long as you include this header file, as explained in Lesson 7, "Preprocessor Directives," you can perform I/O with cout and cin. cout and cin are called *objects*. In C++ terminology, an object is just another name for a variable. You will never treat cin and cout as variables, however. As far as you are concerned, you can think of cin as being the keyboard and cout as being the screen.

Use cout with the << operator and use cin with the >> operator. << is called the *inserter* operator because you are inserting to the screen

(putting data there). >> is called the *extractor* operator because you are extracting from the keyboard (getting data from it). To get a number from the keyboard, you do only this:

```
cin >> Salary;    // Lets the user type a value for Salary
```

To send a string and a floating-point variable to the screen, you do only this:

```
cout << "I am now making $" << Salary;
```

You often see cout and cin in pairs. For example, before asking the user for a value, you should prompt the user with a cout description of what you want. The following two lines tell the user what he or she is expected to type, and then waits for the user to type a number:

```
cout << "How much do you make? ";
cin >> Salary;    // Waits for the user to type a number
```

Can you see the flow of data in the >> and << operators? The direction of the arrows tells you which way the data is flowing: either to the screen or from the keyboard.

Figure 8.1 shows you how cout and cin work. Notice how cout and cin perform mirror-image actions.

Figure 8.1. Looking at the flow of data with cout *and* cin.

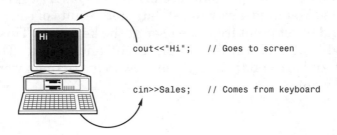

```
cout<<"Hi";    // Goes to screen

cin>>Sales;    // Comes from keyboard
```

The following program is supposed to ask for a user's age and then display that age in dog years (to make the user feel younger). Something is wrong. Can you spot it?

```
#include <iostream.h>
void main()
{
    int age, dogage;

    cout >> "How old are you? ";
    cin << age;
```

100

```
    dogage = age / 7;    // Converts to a dog's age
    cout >> "In dog years, you are " >> dogage >> "years old.";
}
```

Output Options

The cout operator guesses how you want data printed. Sometimes, C++ makes an incorrect guess as to how cout should produce a value, but most of the time, cout suffices for any output you require. cout can output integers:

```
cout << 45;    // Prints a 45
cout can output floating-point values:
cout << 1.234567;    // Prints 1.234567
cout can output string values:
cout << "I am learning C++";    // Prints I am learning C++
```

At the end of a cout, you might want a newline character printed so that the cursor moves down to the next line.

```
cout << "I am learning C++";
cout << "\n";    // Moves the cursor down
```

cout can output more than one value at any one time. The preceding cout is better combined into a single one, like this:

```
cout << "I am learning C++" << "\n";    // Moves the cursor down
```

Because the newline can be part of a string, this is even better:

```
cout << "I am learning C++\n";    // Moves the cursor down
```

The following statement outputs two integers with a space between them, then sends a newline to the screen:

```
cout << 5 << " " << 7 << "\n";
```

Write the output of the following program in the spaces provided.

```
// Filename: COUT1.CPP
#include <iostream.h>
void main()
```

```
{
    int age = 21;
    float weight = 165.5;
    char initial = 'S';

    cout << "My age is " << age;
    cout << "\n";

    cout << "My ";
    cout << "weight is ";
    cout << weight << "\n";

    cout << "My initial is " << initial << "\n";
}
```

You also can print any of the escape sequences that you learned in Table 6.2 of Lesson 6, "Characters, Strings, and Character Arrays." For example, if you want to ring the bell on your computer, you can put this line in your program:

```
cout << '\a';   // Rings the alarm
```

Output Manipulators

Because C++ cannot always guess properly at how you want your data printed, you should learn a few of the *I/O manipulators*. An I/O manipulator modifies the way cout works. Most of the time, you need a manipulator when you output numeric values. For instance, a float variable always contains six digits of precision. Therefore, when you print a float value, whether it is a literal or a floating-point variable, C++ prints six digits. When you print a 4.5 like this:

```
cout << 4.5;
```

C++ prints a 4.500000. The extra digits of precision often get in your way. You need a way to tell C++ that you want only two digits of precision if you are printing a dollar value.

An output manipulator called setprecision() limits the precision of output printed with cout. Inside the setprecision() parentheses, you specify by integer literal or variable how many digits of precision you want to see in the output. To ensure trailing zeros, you must also set a cout flag. For instance, the following cout:

```
cout.setf(ios::showpoint);   // Sets the cout flag for
                             // trailing zeros
cout << setprecision(2) << 4.5;
```

prints 4.50 on the screen.

> **TIP:** All subsequent couts retain the precision set with the last setprecision(). Think of setprecision() as being "sticky." Whatever precision you set sticks with the cout device until you change it with a subsequent setprecision() later in the program.

What will the following three couts print?

```
cout << 4.5 << " ";
cout << setprecision(1) << 4.5 << " ";
cout << 4.5 << "\n";
```

If you have changed the precision with setprecision() and want to revert the precision to its default number of six places, either of the following statements works:

```
cout << setprecision(0);   // Resets to the default six places
```

or

```
cout << setprecision(6);   // Sets to the default six places
```

One important requirement of the manipulators is that you must include a header file named iomanip.h in addition to the iostream.h header file you already included. Therefore, in a program that performs lots of output, you often see the following two lines toward the top of the program:

```
#include <iostream.h>
#include <iomanip.h>
```

C++ uses as much space as needed to print your numbers. For instance, it uses two output spaces to print a two-digit number, three

output spaces for a three-digit number, and so on. You can use the setw() manipulator to add spacing to your output. The following cout statements show you what is possible with setw():

```
cout.setf(ios::showpoint);
cout << 4.56 << "\n";
cout << setw(12) << 4.56 << "\n";
cout << setw(8) << "xyz" << "\n";
cout << setw(6) << 12 << "\n";
```

These four output commands produce this output:

```
4.560000
  4.56000000
xyz
    12
```

Notice that each value prints within the width you specified.

When you set a wide width and print numeric data within that width, the numeric data is *right-justified*. In other words, it prints jutted up against the right side of the width. When you set a wide width and print character data within that width, the character data is *left-justified*. In other words, it begins at the far-left column of the width.

NOTE: The setw() is the only manipulator that does not stick from one command to the next. Therefore, if you wanted to right-justify three numbers with a 10-space output width, you would have to repeat setw(), like this:

```
cout << setw(10) << 123 << "\n";
cout << setw(10) << 12345 << "\n";
cout << setw(10) << 1234567 << "\n";
```

These three couts produce this:

```
       123
     12345
   1234567
```

Using cout, a programmer wants to print three people's names, each stored in character array variables. The programmer wants the names to start printing every 15 columns. The following cout will *not* do it. Why?

104

```
cout << setw(15) << name1 << name2 << name3;    // Invalid
```

The setw() is nice for aligning output. You can print data in tables where the all rows line up even if the data takes varying widths. What is the output of the following program? *Hint:* This program prints a table of wins from a season of a local kids' soccer team. The numbers fall nicely beneath each team's name.

```cpp
// Filename: TEAMMD.CPP
// Prints a table of team names and wins for three weeks
// using width-modifying conversion characters

#include <iostream.h>
#include <iomanip.h>

void main()
{
  cout << setw(10) << "Parrots" << setw(10) <<
       "Rams" << setw(10) << "Kings" << setw(10) <<
       "Titans" << setw(10) << "Chargers" << "\n";
  cout << setw(10) << 3 << setw(10) << 5 <<
         setw(10) << 2 << setw(10) << 1 <<
         setw(10) << 0 << "\n";
  cout << setw(10) << 2 << setw(10) << 5 <<
         setw(10) << 1 << setw(10) << 0 <<
         setw(10) << 1 << "\n";
  cout << setw(10) << 2 << setw(10) << 6 <<
         setw(10) << 4 << setw(10) << 3 <<
         setw(10) << 0 << "\n";
}
```

> **TIP:** If you are an advanced programmer and you want to print a number in hexadecimal or octal, insert the hex or oct manipulator in the cout output. The result will appear in base-16 or base-8, respectively. To revert to decimal, insert the dec manipulator in the output before the decimal value prints.

Another I/O manipulator that C++ often uses is endl. endl sends a newline to the output device. There is absolutely no difference between "\n" and '\n' and endl when you are writing to the screen. All three send the newline character to the screen, which forces the cursor to the next line. The following lines are equivalent:

```
cout <<  "C++ Programming 101" << "\n";
cout <<  "C++ Programming 101" << '\n';
cout <<  "C++ Programming 101" << endl;
```

Input Options

The cin acts like your keyboard, and combined with the >> operator, cin pauses your program and waits for the user at the keyboard to enter data. With a single cin, you can get one or more values (just as with cout you can display one or more values), as long as you separate the values in the cin with extra >> operators.

The following statement gets input from the user into a variable named Result:

```
cin >> Result;    // Lets the user type a value into Result
```

Will the user always type exactly what he or she is supposed to type? Think of the times you have visited an automatic teller. Did you ever press the wrong button? Most people do at one time or another. Usually, you can correct your mistake or cancel the operation and start over. When you write programs that require user input, you must be aware that the user, either intentionally or unintentionally, might not follow directions. When you want an integer, the user might type a floating-point value. With simple cin statements, there is little you can do except check the data that the user entered to see whether it is reasonable and whether it falls within certain expected ranges.

The problem of getting multiple values with `cin` is further hindered by the fact that the user must type a *whitespace character* between the values. In C++ terminology, a whitespace character is any space, Tab keystroke, or Enter keystroke. Therefore, in response to the following statement:

```
cin >> a >> b >> c;    // Gets three values from the keyboard
```

the user can enter three values separated by a space:

```
5 7 9
```

or the user can press the Tab key:

```
5     7      9
```

or the user can press Enter at the end of each value:

```
5
7
9
```

and in all three cases, the program will store a 5 in a, a 7 in b, and a 9 in c.

It might seem that with all those choices, the user has as much freedom to do whatever seems most comfortable. The only problem is that there are many typing choices that the user might make that do *not* work. For example, what do you think will happen if the user types this:

```
5, 7, 9
```

The C++ program does not consider a comma to be a whitespace character. Therefore, only the 5 is correctly put in a, and the other two variables will have garbage in them.

There is little you can do to control the user, but you can tell the user exactly what you want to see input with a prompt message before each `cin`:

```
cout << "Please type three numbers.  Separate the three\n";
cout << "values with a space and do not use a period in ";
cout << "the numbers.\n";

cin >> a >> b >> c;
```

It is even safer to stay away from multiple variables with `cin`. Instead of getting all three in one input, it might be better to get them one at a time, prompting the user along the way:

```
cout << "What is the first value?  (Please, no decimal ";
cout << "points)\n";
```

```
cin >> a;
cout << "What is the second value? ";
cin >> b;
cout << "What is the last value? ";
cin >> c;
```

In typical programming, you would be asking for input that the user understands, such as "What is your result?" or "How old are you?"

NOTE: cin gets only a single word at a time. If you need to get more than one word into a character array, you must use getline, shown later in this lesson.

The following program asks the user for his or her first and last name. Finish the program so that it prints the names as they would appear in a phone book. In other words, if the user enters Mary Freeman for the first and last name, finish the program so that it prints this:

```
In a phone book, your name would look like this:
Freeman, Mary
```

```
#include <iostream.h>
void main()
{
   char first[15], last[15];

   cout << "What is your first name? ";
   cin >> first;
   cout << "What is your last name? ";
   cin >> last;
   cout << "\n\n";   // Prints two blank lines
```

Getting Lines of Data

If you need to get a line of input, the `getline()` function is the right choice. `getline()` is useful when you want the user to enter a string of data into a character array. Whereas `cin` stops reading input when it gets to the first space, `getline()` ends only after the user presses the Enter key. Whatever the user typed up to that point goes to the character array.

There are several forms of `getline()`, but the most common one looks like this:

```
cin.getline(chararray, num);
```

The *chararray* is any character array you defined earlier that holds the input string. The *num* is the maximum number of characters you want to read with `getline()`. The `cin.` in front of `getline()` might look strange to you. `cin.` is not part of the `getline()` name. Rather, you are telling the `cin` object to go get a line from the keyboard. You do not have to understand object-oriented programming to understand `getline()`, but as soon as you have learned object-oriented concepts (explained in Lesson 34, "Introduction to OOP"), you will see why `cin` and `getline()` are separated by a period.

Why do you think the designers of C++ put the *num* value inside `getline()`? Suppose that you defined a character array that holds 20 characters, but the user types 25. There is no room in the array for the last few characters. If you put 20 in the `getline()` instead, you ensure that even if the user types 25 characters, only the first 20 will be input. Of course, if the user enters only 12 characters, the input string will consist of the 12 characters, plus a 13th for the string-terminating zero.

`getline()` always stops reading the user's input when the maximum number of characters is entered. `getline()` also ensures that there is always room for a string-terminating zero. Therefore, if the user types *exactly* the same number of characters as the maximum number `getline()` allows, C++ replaces the last character with a string terminator, thereby ensuring that the input is made into a string. (The newline keystroke is never stored in the string). Given this explanation, what output do you think the following program produces, assuming that the user types the word `Carmel` in response to the city request?

```
// Filename: GETL.CPP
#include <iostream.h>
```

```
void main()
{
   char city[6];
   cin.getline(city, 6);
   cout << "\n" << city << "\n";
}
```

Review Questions

1. TRUE or FALSE: `cin` and `cout` are objects.

2. What symbol is used for the extractor operator, and which object, `cin` or `cout`, does it go with?

3. What symbol is used for the inserter operator, and which object, `cin` or `cout`, does it go with?

4. TRUE or FALSE: `cout` is useful for inputting lines of input, such as a user's street address.

5. Which I/O manipulator limits the number of decimal places printing when you output floating-point data?

6. What header file must you include when you use the I/O manipulators?

7. What is the advantage of using `getline()` rather than `cin` when getting strings of user input?

8. What does the number in `getline()` do?

9. What is the output of the following program? (Assume that the user enters `The Italian Riviera` for the title.)

```
#include <iostream.h>

void main()
{
   char title[12];
   cin.getline(title, 6);
   cout << title << "\n";
}
```

Review Exercises

1. Write a program that prompts the user for his or her full name and weight. Store these values in variables and print them to the screen. *Hint:* Use `getline()` for the name.

2. Assume that you are a college professor who has to average grades for 10 students. Write a program that prompts you for 10 different grades, then displays the average of them.

3. Write a program that tests your seven-year-old daughter in arithmetic. Ask her to type two numbers, then ask her for the sum of the first number added to the second. Print the result when she is ready (wait for her to press Enter after telling her to do so) so that she can check her answer.

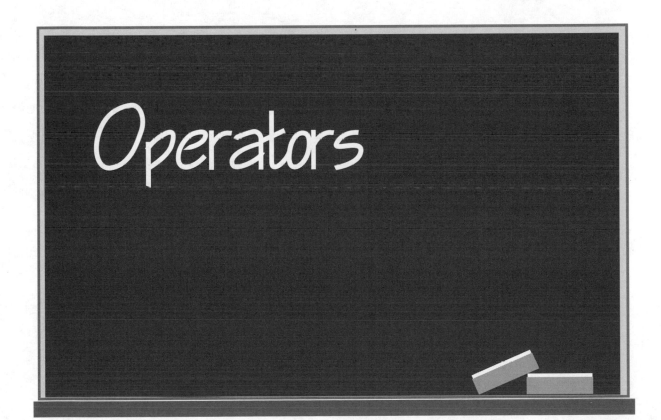

Operators

Math Operators and Precedence

 OBJECTIVE ***To explain the primary math operators and describe their order of operation.***

This lesson teaches you how to make the computer perform all your math for you. You do not have to be good in math to be an expert computer programmer. You need to know only how to formulate your requests so that the computer produces the results you need. C++ contains numerous math operators. Not only do you need to understand the math operators, but you also must understand how C++ executes them. Some operators operate before others in the same expression.

Primary Math Operators

A *math operator* is a symbol used for addition, subtraction, multiplication, division, and other math operations.

In Lesson 4, "The C++ Program's Format," you saw the four basic math operators. They are repeated in Table 9.1, which also includes a new operator called the *modulus* operator.

Table 9.1. C++ primary math operators.

Symbol	Description
*	Multiplication
/	Division and integer division
%	Modulus (or remainder)
+	Addition
-	Subtraction

Most of these operators work just as you would expect them to. Generally, you have to assign expressions containing math operators to variables, although you also can print the results of calculations. For instance, here are two statements that illustrate addition and subtraction:

```
Result1 = 34 + 8;    // Addition
Result2 = 59 - 2;    // Subtraction
```

Here is an example of printing a math operation:

```
cout << 34 + 13;    // Displays answer on-screen
```

Most C++ compilers properly output expressions, but they might warn you about trying to display the result of a calculation that does not have parentheses around it. Therefore, most C++ compilers prefer the following cout to the preceding one:

```
cout << (34 + 13);    // Displays answer on-screen
```

Parentheses have special meaning in many math expressions. They are discussed in more detail later in this lesson.

C++ does not care whether you put spaces around the math symbols. To C++, both of the following expressions are identical:

```
Sales = Quant * Price;
```

and

```
Sales=Quant*Price;
```

116

> **TIP:** Get used to putting spaces in expressions to make them more readable.

> When you use a math operator between two values, whether those values are numbers, variables, or a combination of both, they are known as *binary operators*. Do not confuse binary operators with *binary numbers* (Appendix B explains binary numbers). A binary operator simply means that the operator operates on both values, one on each side of the operator, to produce a result.

Some of the following statements contain bugs, and others simply can be improved. Write the correction to the right of each statement:

```
Result = 34+1;         _____
Result = + 34 1;       _____
cout << 3 + 3;         _____
Pay = Rate x Hours;    _____
```

Unary Operators

The nice thing about *unary operators* is that they work exactly the way you would think they do. A unary operator works on a single value or variable. You can assign a variable a positive or negative value by using the unary + or -. Unary operators do not change the value or variable they are operating on, but they might change the sign. A few examples that follow explain unary operators.

The following four statements demonstrate the use of unary positive and negative in assigning values to the variables on the left of the equal sign:

```
a = -25;  // Puts -25 in a
b = -a;  // Negates a. Positive 25 goes in b. a still holds -25
c = +25;  // Puts 25 in c
d = +c;  // Puts 25 in d
```

> **NOTE:** You do not have to use the unary positive. C++ always assumes a number or variable is positive unless you negate it.

The unary negative prints the negative of values or negates an entire expression enclosed in parentheses:

```
cout << -b;    // Displays the negative of b
Result = -(a + b + c);    // Assigns the negative of the answer
```

> **TIP:** When subtracting the negative of a value, put a space between the binary subtraction symbol and the unary negation symbol, like this:
>
> ```
> temp = temp - -factor;    // Leave space between minus
>                           // signs
> ```

Write the output of the following program in the space provided.

```
// Filename: TRYMATH1.CPP
#include <iostream.h>
void main()
{
   int a, b, c, d;
   a = -10;
   b = -a;
   c = -(a + b + a);
   d = b - -a;
   cout << "a is " << a << "\n";
   cout << "b is " << b << "\n";
   cout << "c is " << c << "\n";
   cout << "d is " << d << "\n";
}
```

Division and Modulus

Division behaves differently from the other math operators because the division symbol, the forward slash (/), performs integer division if it sees an integer value on both sides. Integer division is rounded down to the nearest integer. If a floating-point value is on either side of a division symbol, real floating-point division occurs.

The following program illustrates the difference between division and integer division. The average pay per department is accurate for dollars and cents (the result is a floating-point value) because one side of the division (pay) is a floating-point value. The average employees per department is rounded to the nearest integer because both sides of that division are integers.

```
// Filename: DIV.CPP
#include <iostream.h>
#include <iomanip.h>
void main()
{
    int num_dept, total_emp, avg_dept;
    float avg_pay, pay;

    cout << "How many departments are there in the company? ";
    cin >> num_dept;
    cout << "How many employees are in the company? ";
    cin >> total_emp;
    cout << "What is the company's total payroll? ";
    cin >> pay;
    avg_dept = total_emp / num_dept;   // Integer division
    avg_pay = pay / num_dept;   // Floating-point division
    cout << "\nThe average number of per department employees "
            "is " << avg_dept << "\n";
    cout << "The average payroll per department is $"
         << setprecision(2) << avg_pay;
}
```

Here is the output from this program:

```
How many departments are there in the company? 7
How many employees are in the company? 45
What is the company's total payroll? 7645.32

The average number of employees per department is 6
The average payroll per department is $1092.19
```

NOTE: Depending on the design of your compiler's cout, you might get a somewhat different answer for average payroll. Some compilers output the value in scientific notation unless you declare avg_pay as double.

119

The percent sign (%) produces a *modulus,* or a *remainder,* of an integer division. The modulus requires that integers be on both sides of the symbol, or it does not work. The following program shows you how the modulus produces remainder results.

```cpp
// Filename: MOD.CPP
#include <iostream.h>
void main()
{
   int n;

   n = 25 % 5;
   cout << "25 % 5 : " << n << endl;
   n = 25 % 6;
   cout << "25 % 6 : " << n << endl;
   n = 25 % 7;
   cout << "25 % 7 : " << n << endl;
   n = 25 % 8;
   cout << "25 % 8 : " << n << endl;
   n = 25 % 9;
   cout << "25 % 9 : " << n << endl;
   n = 25 % 10;
   cout << "25 % 10 : " << n << endl;
}
```

Here is the output:

```
25 % 5 : 0
25 % 6 : 1
25 % 7 : 4
25 % 8 : 1
25 % 9 : 7
25 % 10 : 5
```

 Write the answers to these different types of division to the right of each statement.

```
4 / 2          _____
4 % 2          _____
25 / 4.0       _____
25.0 / 4       _____
25.0 / 4.0     _____
25 % 6         _____
```

You now know how to perform three types of division. You can get a true division result if at least one of the division values is a floating-point value. You can get the whole-number answer of division with integer division. You can get the remainder of division by using the modulus operator.

As a review, write the math symbols to the right of their corresponding descriptions:

Description	*Symbol*
Floating-point division	_____
Integer division	_____
Multiplication	_____
Modulus	_____
Subtraction	_____
Addition	_____
Unary negation	_____
Unary positive	_____

Order of Precedence

Understanding the math operators is the first of two steps toward understanding C++ calculations. You must also understand the *order of precedence.* The order of precedence (sometimes called the *math hierarchy* or the *order of operators*) determines exactly how C++ computes formulas. The precedence of operators is exactly the same concept you learned in high school algebra courses. (Don't worry, this is the easy part of algebra!) To see how the order of precedence works, try to determine the result of the following simple calculation:

```
2 + 3 * 2
```

If you said 10, you are not alone; many people say that. However, 10 is correct only if you interpret the formula from left to right. What if you calculated the multiplication first? If you took the value of 3 * 2 and got an answer of 6, then added the 2, you would receive an answer of 8—which

is the same answer that C++ computes (and which happens to be the correct way). Lesson 4, "The C++ Program's Format," mentioned that C++ computes multiplication before addition. This lesson helps drive that fact home.

C++ always performs multiplication, division, and modulus first, then addition and subtraction. Table 9.2 shows the order of the operators you have seen so far. There are many more levels to C++'s precedence table of operators than the ones shown in Table 9.2. Unlike most computer languages, C++ has 17 levels of precedence. Appendix D contains the complete precedence table. Notice in this appendix that multiplication, division, and modulus reside on level 5, one level higher than level 6's addition and subtraction. In the next few lessons, you will learn how to use the remainder of this precedence table in your C++ programs.

Table 9.2. Order of precedence for the primary math operators.

Order	Operator
First	Multiplication, division, modulus remainder (*, /, %)
Second	Addition, subtraction (+, -)

Although the designers of C++ could have let C++ perform math from left to right, too much ambiguity can result in long calculations, especially when many other operators are involved. By following the strict rules of the operator precedence table, you have to learn a little more up front, but you have more programming freedom. You do not have to worry about structuring your formulas from left to right.

It is easy to follow C++'s order of operators if you follow the intermediate results one at a time. The three calculations in Figure 9.1 show you how to do this.

C++ calculates each part of an expression in the order dictated by the operator precedence table. It does not matter where addition or subtraction appear in the equation. If any multiplication, division, or modulus also appear, they are calculated first, leaving the addition and subtraction for last.

122

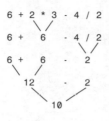

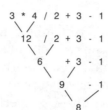

Figure 9.1. C++'s order of operators, with lines indicating precedence.

Compute the answers to each of the following expressions, drawing lines that connect each subequation as C++ would evaluate it (as seen in Figure 9.1).

25 / 5 * 2 % 2

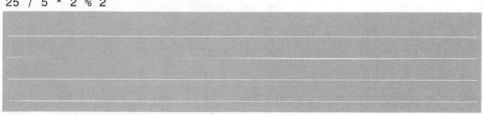

25 + 20 / 5 * 2 - 10

```
35 / 7 * 2 - 5 + 10
```

Looking back at Table 9.2, you might notice that multiplication, division, and modulus are on the same level of precedence. This implies that there is no hierarchy on that level. If more than one of these operators appear in a calculation, C++ performs the math from the left. The same is true of addition and subtraction—C++ performs the operation on the far left first.

Figure 9.2 shows this left-to-right ordering. The order of evaluation just happens to be from left to right in the entire expression. The first subexpression to evaluate is the integer division. Even though multiplication also appears in the equation, the integer division calculates first because it appears to the left of the multiplication. If addition or subtraction appeared first, they would have to wait until all the multiplication and division were finished.

Figure 9.2. C++'s order of operators from the left, with lines indicating precedence.

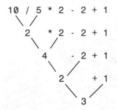

You don't have to worry about the math because C++ does the actual work. However, you should understand this order of operators so that you know how to structure your calculations.

Using Parentheses

If you want to override the order of precedence, you can add parentheses to the calculation. The parentheses actually reside on a level above the multiplication, division, and modulus in the precedence table. In other words, any calculation in parentheses—whether addition, subtraction, division, or whatever—is always calculated before the rest of the line. The other calculations are then performed in their normal operator order.

The first formula in this lesson, 2 + 3 * 2, produced an 8 because the multiplication was performed before addition. However, by adding parentheses around the addition, as in (2 + 3) * 2, the answer becomes 10.

In the precedence table shown in Appendix D, the parentheses reside on level 4. Because they are on a higher level than the other mathematical operators, the parentheses take precedence over multiplication, division, and most other operators.

The calculations shown in Figure 9.3 illustrate how parentheses override the regular order of operators. These are the same three formulas as shown in the preceding section, but their results are calculated differently because the parentheses override the normal order of operators.

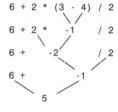

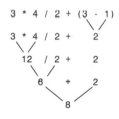

Figure 9.3.
Example of parentheses as the highest precedence level, with lines indicating precedence.

TIP: Use plenty of parentheses in your C++ programs to clarify the order of operators, even when you don't have to override their default order. Parentheses make the calculations easier to understand if you must modify the program later.

If an expression contains parentheses within parentheses, C++ evaluates the innermost parentheses first. The expressions in Figure 9.4 illustrate this.

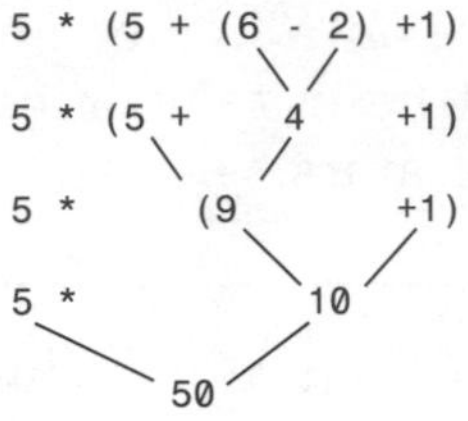

Figure 9.4.
Precedence
example of paren-
theses within
parentheses, with
lines indicating
precedence.

```
5 * (5 + (6 - 2) +1)

5 * (5 +    4    +1)

5 *      (9      +1)

5 *          10

           50
```

The following program produces an incorrect result, even though it looks as if it will work. It attempts to compute an average, but something is wrong. See whether you can spot the error.

```cpp
// Filename: AVG.CPP
// Computes the average of three grades
#include <iostream.h>
void main()
{
    float avg, grade1, grade2, grade3;

    grade1 = 87.5;
    grade2 = 92.4;
    grade3 = 79.6;

    avg = grade1 + grade2 + grade3 / 3.0;
    cout << "The average is " << avg << "\n";
}
```

Convert each of the following formulas into its C++ assignment equivalent.

Original	Answer
(a) $a = \dfrac{3+3}{4+4}$	_____
(b) $x = (a - b)*(a - c)*2$	_____
(c) $f = \dfrac{a2}{b3}$	_____
(d) $d = \dfrac{(8 - x2)}{(x - 9)} \quad \dfrac{(4 * 2 - 1)}{x3}$	_____

126

Assignment Statements

In C++, the assignment operator, =, behaves differently from what you might be used to in other languages. So far, you have used it to assign values to variables, which is consistent with its use in most other programming languages.

However, the assignment operator also can be used in other ways, such as in multiple assignment statements and compound assignments, as the following sections illustrate.

Multiple Assignments

If two or more equal signs appear in an expression, each performs an assignment. Multiple assignments introduce a new aspect of the precedence order that you should understand. Consider the following expression:

```
a = b = c = d = e = 100;
```

This might seem confusing at first, especially if you know other computer languages. To C++, the equal sign always means: assign the value on the right to the variable on the left. This right-to-left order is described in Appendix D. The third column in the table is labeled *Associativity,* and it describes the direction of the operation. The assignment operator associates from the right, whereas some of the other C++ operators associate from the left.

Because the assignment associates from the right, the preceding expression assigns 100 to the variable named e. This assignment produces a value, 100, for the expression. In C++, all expressions produce values, typically the result of assignments. Therefore, 100 is assigned to the variable d. The value 100 is assigned to c, then to b, and finally to a. The old values of these variables are replaced by 100 after the statement finishes.

Because C++ does not automatically set variables to zero before you use them, you might want to do so before you use the variables with a single assignment statement. The following section of variable declarations and initializations is performed using multiple assignment statements.

```
main()
{
    int ctr, num_emp, num_dep;
    float sales, salary, amount;
```

```
ctr = num_emp = num_dep = 0;
sales = salary = amount = 0;
// Rest of program follows
```

In C++, you can include the assignment statement almost anywhere in a program, even in another calculation. For example, consider this statement:

```
value = 5 + (r = 9 - c);
```

This is a perfectly legal C++ statement. The assignment operator resides on the first level of the precedence table, and always produces a value. Because of the parentheses, the r is assigned 9 - c because the equal sign on the far right is evaluated first. The subexpression (r = 9 - c) produces a value (and places that value in r), which is then added to 5 before the answer is stored in value.

Write the value of r1 and r2 after each of the following assignment statements executes:

Assignment Statement	r1	r2
r1 = r2 = 33;	_____	_____
r1 = (r2 = 33);	_____	_____
r1 = 3 + (r2 = 12 / 2);	_____	_____

Compound Assignments

Some equations in C++ do not make sense to beginning programmers. Consider the following assignment statement.

```
total = total + 1;
```

In math, no value is equal to itself plus one. In C++, however, the equal sign means assignment, not necessarily equality as it does in math. This statement means that you want to add one to total and update total's original value with the incremented total.

Many times in programming, you might want to update the value of a variable. Computers are great tools for keeping track of totals and for counting. To keep track of totals, you have to add some value to a variable holding the running total. When your program counts, it always adds one to the total count. In other words, you have to take a variable's current value, add or multiply that value by an expression, then reassign it to the original variable. The following assignment statement demonstrates this process:

```
salary = salary * 1.2;
```

This expression multiplies the old value of `salary` by 1.2 (in effect, raising the value in `salary` by 20 percent), then reassigns it to `salary`. C++ provides several operators, called *compound operators,* that you can use whenever the same variable appears on both sides of the equal sign. The compound operators are shown in Table 9.3.

Table 9.3. C++'s compound operators.

Operator	Example	Equivalent
+=	bonus += 500;	bonus = bonus + 500;
-=	budget -= 50;	budget = budget - 50;
*=	salary *= 1.2;	salary = salary * 1.2;
/=	factor /= .50;	factor = factor / .50;
%=	daynum %= 7;	daynum = daynum % 7;

The compound operators are low in the C++ operator precedence table. They typically are evaluated last or near-last.

Here is a good example to explain why updating variables is important. Suppose that you have been storing your factory's production amount in a variable called `prod_amt`, and your supervisor has just informed you that a new addition has to be applied to the production value. You could code this update in a statement:

```
prod_amt = prod_amt + 2.6;    // Adds 2.6 to current production
```

Instead of using this formula, use C++'s compound addition operator by coding the statement like this:

```
prod_amt += 2.6;    // Adds 2.6 to current production
```

Associativity of Compound Assignments

The precedence of the compound operators requires important consideration when you decide how to code compound assignments. Notice in Appendix D that the compound operators are on level 16, much lower than the regular math operators. This means that you must be careful how you interpret them.

For example, suppose that you want to update the value of a sales variable with this formula:

```
4 - factor + bonus
```

You can update the sales variable with the following statement:

```
sales *= 4 - factor + bonus;
```

This statement adds the quantity 4 - factor + bonus to sales. Due to operator precedence, this statement is not the same as the following one:

```
sales = sales * 4 - factor + bonus;
```

Because the *= operator is much lower in the precedence table than * or -, it is performed last, and with right-to-left associativity. Therefore, the following are equivalent, from a precedence viewpoint:

```
sales *= 4 - factor + bonus;
```

and

```
sales = sales * (4 - factor + bonus);
```

 Write the values of the Result variable to the right of each statement. Assume that each statement operates independently of the other ones. Also, assume that Result has the value of 10 before each statement executes.

Statement	*Result*
Result += 1;	_____
Result *= 2;	_____
Result /= 2;	_____
Result *= 1 + 2 * 3;	_____

Mixing Data Types in Calculations

You can mix data types in C++, although not always with as much freedom as regular C allows. Adding an integer and a floating-point value is mixing data types. C++ generally converts the smaller of the two types into the other. For instance, if you add a double floating-point to an integer, C++ first converts the integer into a double value, then performs the calculation. This method produces the most accurate result possible.

The automatic conversion of data types is only temporary; the converted value is back in its original data type as soon as the expression is finished.

Table 9.4 shows how most C++ compilers convert data types when you mix them. The term *promotion* refers to the compiler's converting small data types into larger data types in an attempt to end up with expressions of uniform data types.

Table 9.4. Type promotions.

Data type	Promotes to*
char	int (if int is the largest data type in the expression)
short	int (if int is the largest data type in the expression)
unsigned short	unsigned int (if unsigned int is the largest data type in the expression)
float	double (if double is the largest data type in the expression)
double	long double (if a long double appears in the expression)

*C++ converts all numeric literals—such as 87.3, –91., and 23.2111—to float, except when float will not hold the literal, such as for 823223.4556544333. In this case, C++ promotes the value to double. If you do not want certain literals promoted, use the numeric suffix explained in Lesson 5, "C++ Numeric Data," in the section entitled "Long, Unsigned, and Floating-Point Literals."

If C++ converts two different data types to the smaller value's type, the higher-precision value is *truncated,* or shortened, and accuracy is lost. For example, in the following short program, the floating-point value of sales is added to an integer called bonus. Before C++ computes the answer, it converts bonus to floating-point, which results in a floating-point answer. If the reverse were true—that is, if C++ converted the floating-point value to an integer before calculating the answer—all precision to the right of the decimal point would be lost.

```
// Filename: DATA.CPP
// Demonstrates mixed data type in an expression
#include <iostream.h>
void main()
```

```
{
   int bonus = 50;
   float salary = 1400.50;
   float total;

   total = salary + bonus;    // bonus becomes floating-point,
                              // but only temporarily
   cout << "The total is " << total;
}
```

TIP: Try not to mix data types. For example, it is not good form to add an int variable to a float variable and assign both of them to double. If you have to mix data types, use a typecast (discussed in the next section) to clarify your intentions.

 What is the resulting data type of the following statements? Assume that a is double, b is float, c is int, and d is char.

Statement	Promoted Data Type
a + b	_____
a + c	_____
d + c	_____
a * d	_____
a + b + c + d	_____

Suppose that you want to verify the interest calculation used by your bank on a loan. The interest rate is 15.5 percent, stored as .155 in a floating-point variable. The amount of interest you owe is computed by multiplying the interest rate by the amount of the loan balance, then multiplying that by the number of days in the year since the loan originated. The following program finds the daily interest rate by dividing the annual interest rate by 365, the number of days in a year. C++ must convert the integer 365 to a floating-point literal automatically, because it is used in combination with a floating-point variable.

```
// Filename: INTEREST.CPP
// Calculates interest on a loan
#include <iostream.h>
#include <iomanip.h>
void main()
{
```

```
int days = 45;    // Days since loan origination
float principal = 3500.00;    // Original loan amount
float interest_rate = 0.155;    // Annual interest rate
float daily_interest;    // Daily interest rate

daily_interest=interest_rate/365;    // Computes floating-
                                     // point value


// Because days is int, it too is converted to float
daily_interest = principal * daily_interest * days;
principal += daily_interest;    // Updates principal
                                // with interest
cout << "The balance you owe is $" << setprecision(2)
     << principal;
}
```

Here is the program's output:

```
The balance you owe is $3566.88
```

> **TIP:** If your dollar amount prints in scientific notation and not in a fixed decimal format, you can add the following line to your program before the first cout:
>
> ```
> cout.setf(ios::fixed);    // Forces decimals to print
> ```

Typecasting

Problems can occur if you mix unsigned variables with variables of other data types. Due to differences in computer architecture, unsigned variables do not always convert to the larger data type. This can result in loss of accuracy, and even incorrect results. There are other times when you might want to fully control the type conversions instead of letting C++ make its best bet.

You can override C++'s default conversions by specifying your own temporary type change. This process is called *typecasting*. When you typecast, you temporarily change a variable's data type from its declared data type to a new one. The two formats of the typecast are

(data type) expression

and

data type(expression)

where *data type* can be any valid C++ data type, such as int or float, and the *expression* can be a variable, literal, or an expression that combines both. The following code temporarily typecasts the integer variable age into a double floating-point variable, so that it can be multiplied by the double floating-point factor. Both formats of the typecast are illustrated.

```
age_factor = (double)age * factor;    // Temporarily changes age
                                      // to double
```

The second way of typecasting puts the parentheses around the variable rather than the data type:

```
age_factor = double(age) * factor;    // Temporarily changes age
                                      // to double
```

> **NOTE:** Typecasting by putting parentheses around the expression and not the data type is new to C++. C programmers do not have this option—they must put the data type in parentheses. The second method just shown "feels" like a function call and seems more natural for the C++ language. Therefore, becoming familiar with the second method will help you clarify your code.

 Instead of having C++ perform the conversion, you might want to typecast all mixed expressions to ensure that they convert the way you want them to. Here is the same program as in the preceding section, except that typecasts are used to convert the integer literals to floating-points before they are used.

```
// Filename: INT2.CPP
// Uses typecasting to calculate interest on a loan
#include <iostream.h>
#include <iomanip.h>
void main()
{
   int days = 45;   // Days since loan origination
   float principal = 3500.00;   // Original loan amount
   float interest_rate = 0.155;   // Annual interest rate
   float daily_interest;   // Daily interest rate

   daily_interest = interest_rate/float(365);  // Typecasts
                                               // days to float

   // Because days is integer, convert it to float also
```

134

```
    daily_interest = principal * daily_interest * float(days);
    principal += daily_interest;    // Updates principal
                                    // with interest
    cout << "The balance you owe is $" << setprecision(2)
        << principal;
}
```

The output from this program is exactly the same as the preceding program's output.

Rewrite the following statements using typecast to promote the statement values that need promoting. Assume that a is double, b is float, c is int, and d is char. The first one is done for you.

Original Statement	Rewritten with Typecasts
Answer = c * 4.5;	Answer = float(c) * 4.5;
Answer = c * a;	_____
Answer = d + c + b;	_____
Answer = a + d;	_____
Answer = d + c + 2;	_____

> **TIP:** You can typecast an entire expression. Suppose that in the following expression Total is defined as a double, and the rest are defined as ints and floats. You can typecast the entire right side of the equal sign, like this:
>
> ```
> Total = double(a + b + 25 / 5 * 2);    // Typecasts entire
>                                        // expression
> ```

Review Questions

1. What is the difference between a unary and binary operator?

2. Which of the two unary operators is usually optional?

3. Which operator described in this lesson has two uses?

4. How do you find the remainder of integer division?

5. What is the result of each of the following expressions?

   (a) `1 + 2 * 4 / 2`
   (b) `(1 + 2) * 4 / 2`
   (c) `1 + 2 * (4 % 2)`

6. What is the result of each of the following expressions?

   (a) `9 % 2 + 1`
   (b) `(1 + (10 - (2 + 2)))`

7. Convert the following formula into its C++ assignment equivalent.

$$c = \frac{r * 2 + 3}{14 - 4 / 2}$$

Review Exercises

1. Write the assignment and `cout` statements that print the remainder of 100/3.

2. Write a short program that prints the area of a circle when its radius equals 4 and pi equals 3.14159. (*Hint:* The area of a circle is computed by `pi * radius2`.)

3. Write a program that prints each of the first 8 powers of 2 (2^1, 2^2, 2^3,...2^8). Write comments and include your name at the top of the program. Print string literals that describe each answer printed. The first two lines of your output should look like this:

   ```
   2 raised to the first power is 2
   2 raised to the second power is 4
   ```

4. Assume that a video store employee works 50 hours. He is paid $4.50 for the first 40 hours, time-and-a-half (1.5 times the regular pay rate) for the first five hours over 40, and double-time for all hours over 45. Assuming a 28 percent tax rate, write a program that prints his gross pay, taxes, and net pay to the screen. Label each amount with appropriate titles (using string literals) and add appropriate comments in the program.

Relational Logic and Operators

OBJECTIVE ***To explore relational logic and teach the relational operators of C++.***

Computers are finite machines. That is, given the same input and the same program instructions, the same output will result. Rarely, however, does a computer get the same input. Input comes from many different sources representing many different aspects of input. The computer needs to be taught how to deal with different types of data, and how to handle each. When you write a payroll program, for instance, you don't want the computer printing the same check for each employee. When you enter an hourly employee, you want the program to deal with that employee differently than if that employee were salaried.

Sometimes you want every statement in your C++ program to execute every time the program runs. So far, every program in this book has executed from the top and has continued, line-by-line, until the last statement completes. Depending on your application, you might not always want this to happen.

> Programs that don't always execute by rote are known as *data-driven* programs. In data-driven programs, the data dictates what the program does.

This lesson shows you how to create data-driven programs. These programs do not execute the same way every time. This is possible through the use of *relational* operators that *conditionally* control other statements. Relational operators first "look" at the literals and variables in the program, then operate according to what they "find." This might sound like difficult programming, but it is actually straightforward and intuitive.

Defining Relational Operators

You must use relational operators in any program that needs *relational logic.* Relational logic is nothing more than the computer's comparing two different values and making a decision based on how the values compare. You use relational logic in everyday life. Consider the following statements:

"The generic butter costs less than the name brand."
"My child is younger than Johnny."
"Our salaries are equal."
"The dogs are not the same age."

Relational logic always returns a True or False value. Each of these statements can be either true or false. There is no other possible answer.

> When you were growing up, did you ever play the game in which someone thinks of a word, and the others must try to guess the word by asking only yes-or-no questions? There is nothing more to relational logic than yes-or-no questions. Instead of yes and no, however, programmers use the terms True and False. With enough True and False comparisons, your computer can decide which path in the program logic is best executed next.

In addition to the math operators you learned in Lesson 9, "Math Operators and Precedence," there are also operators that you use for data comparisons. They are called *relational operators,* and their task is to

138

compare data. They enable you to determine whether two variables are equal or not equal, and which one is less than the other. Table 10.1 lists each relational operator and its meaning.

Table 10.1. The relational operators.

Operator	Description
==	Equal to
>	Greater than
<	Less than
>=	Greater than or equal to
<=	Less than or equal to
!=	Not equal to

The six relational operators form the foundation of data comparison in C++ programming. They always appear with two literals, variables, or expressions (or some combination of these), one on each side of the operator. These relational operators are useful. You should know them as well as you know the +, -, *, /, and % mathematical operators.

> **NOTE:** Unlike many programming languages, C++ uses a double equal sign (==) as a test for equality. The single equal sign (=) is reserved for the assignment of values.

Assume that a program initializes four variables as follows:

```
int a = 5;
int b = 10;
int c = 15;
int d = 5;
```

The following statements are then True:

> a is equal to d, so a == d
> b is less than c, so b < c
> c is greater than a, so c > a

Which of the following relations result in a True or False? (Assume that the variables have the values just shown.)

139

Description	Result
b is more than or equal to a, so b >= a	_____
d is more than or equal to b, so d >= b	_____
b is not equal to c, so b != c	_____

These are not C++ statements; they are statements of comparison between the values of the variables. Relational logic is easy.

Relational logic always produces a True or False result. In C++, unlike with some other programming languages, you can directly use the True or False result of relational operators inside other expressions. Soon you will learn how to do this, but for now, you have to understand only that the following True and False evaluations are correct:

- A True relational result evaluates to 1.

- A False relational result evaluates to 0.

Assuming the same values as stated for the preceding example's four variables, each of the value's statements is False (0):

```
a == b
b > c
d < a
d > a
```

What 1 (True) or 0 (False) result occurs with each of these relational comparisons of the data?

Description	Result
a == d	_____
b >= c	_____
c >= b	_____

Look over this section before going further. Review all the relational statements to see why each is True or False and why some evaluate to 0 and some to 1. The variables a and d, for example, are equal to the same value (5), so neither is greater or less than the other.

Many people say they are not "math-inclined" or not "logical," and you might be one of them. But, as mentioned in Lesson 9, "Math Operators and Precedence," you do not have to be good in math to be a good computer programmer. Neither should you be frightened by the term *relational*

logic, because you just saw how you use it in everyday life. The two primary relational operators, *less than* (<) and *greater than* (>), are easy to remember. You probably learned this concept in school, but you might have forgotten it: the relational operators' signs tell you what they mean. Notice in the previous examples that the arrow (the point of the < or >) always points to the lesser value. The larger, open part of the arrow points to the larger value.

The relation is False if the arrow points the wrong way. In other words, 4 > 9 is False because the operator symbol is pointing to the 9, which is not the lesser number. In English this statement says, "4 is greater than 9," which clearly is false.

The `if` Statement

The `if` statement is the command that most often uses the relational operators in C++ programs. The `if` expression is called a *decision statement* because it tests a relationship—using the relational operators—and, based on the test's result, makes a decision about which statement to execute next.

The format of the `if` statement appears as follows:

```
if (condition)
   { block of one or more C++ statements }
```

The `condition` includes any relational comparison, and it must be enclosed in parentheses. You saw several relational comparisons earlier, such as a == d, c < d, and so on. The `block of one or more C++ statements` is any C++ statement, such as an assignment or cout, enclosed in braces. The block of the `if`, sometimes called the *body* of the `if` statement, usually is indented a few spaces for readability. This enables you to see, at a glance, exactly what executes if the `condition` is True.

> **NOTE:** If only one statement follows the `if`, the braces are not required (but it is always good to include them).

The block executes only if `condition` is True. If `condition` is False, C++ ignores the block and simply executes the next appropriate statement in the program that follows the `if` statement.

The following is an example of a valid C++ `if` statement:

```
if (sales > 5000)
   { bonus = 500; }
```

The value inside the variable `sales` determines what happens next. If `sales` contains more than 5,000, the next statement that executes is the one inside the block that initializes `bonus`. If, however, `sales` contains 5,000 or less, the block does not execute, and the line following the `if`'s block executes.

Basically, you can read an `if` statement in the following way: "If the condition is True, perform the block of statements inside the braces. Otherwise, the condition must be False, so do not execute that block, but continue executing the remainder of the program as though this `if` statement did not exist."

NOTE: Do not type a semicolon after the parentheses of the `if` relational test. Semicolons appear after each statement inside the block.

The `if` statement is used to make a decision. The block of statements following the `if` executes if the decision (the result of the relation) is True, but the block does not execute otherwise. As with relational logic, you use `if` logic in everyday life. Consider the following statements:

"If the day is warm, I will go swimming."
"If I make enough money, we will build a new house."
"If the light is green, go."
"If the light is red, stop."

Each of these statements is *conditional*. That is, *if and only if* the condition is true do you perform the activity.

What is wrong with the following `if` statement?

```
if Initial == 'A'
   { cout << "Early in the alphabet."; }
```

Write three of your own daily-life conditional statements based on True and False conditions such as the ones you just saw.

Expressions as the Condition

C++ interprets any nonzero value as True, and zero always as False. This enables you to insert regular nonconditional expressions in the if logic. To understand this concept, consider the following section of code:

```
main()
{
   int age = 21;    // Declares and assigns age as 21

   if (age = 85)
   {  cout << "You have lived through a lot!"; }


   // Remaining program code goes here
```

At first, it might seem as though the cout does not execute, but it does! Because the code line uses a regular assignment operator (=), not a relational operator (==), C++ performs the assignment of 85 to age. This, as with all the assignments you saw in Lesson 9, "Math Operators and Precedence," produces a value for the expression of 85. Because 85 is nonzero, C++ interprets the if condition as True and then performs the body of the if statement.

Confusing the relational equality test (==) with the regular assignment operator (=) is a common error in C++ programs, and the nonzero True test makes this bug even more difficult to find.

The designers of C++ didn't intend for this to confuse you. They want you to take advantage of this feature whenever you can. Instead of putting an assignment before an if and testing the result of that assignment, you can combine the assignment and if into a single statement.

143

The following program has two bugs. See whether you can spot them. *Hint:* The programmer obviously does not consider all things equal!

```cpp
#include <iostream.h>
void main()
{
    int age1, age2, yrs_apt;
    cout << "What is your oldest child's age? ";
    cin >> age1;
    cout << "How many years apart are your children? ";
    cin >> yrs_apt;

    age2 == age1 - yrs_apt;
    if (age2 = 19)
        { cout << "Your youngest can vote already? \n"; }
}
```

TIP: Most C++ compilers issue a warning message if you enclose an assignment inside an `if` relational test. Although you might need to do that, most of the time you probably will want to type an equality comparison (==) operator.

 Would C++ interpret the following condition as True or False?

```cpp
if (10 == 10 == 10)...   // Rest of the if statement follows
```

Be careful! At first glance the condition seems True, but C++ "thinks" that the expression is False! Because the == operator associates from the left, the program compares the first 10 to the second. Because they are equal, the result is 1 (for True), and the 1 is then compared to the third 10, which results in a 0 (for False)!

 Write a description in English that explains what the following `if` does with age:

```cpp
if (age <= 21)
    { cout << "You are a minor.\n";
      cout << "What is your grade? ";
      cin >> grade; }
```

144

```
if (balance > low_balance)
   {cout << "Past due!\n"; }
```

In this if, if the value in balance is more than that in low_balance, execution of the program continues at the block, and the message Past due! prints on-screen. You can compare two variables to each other (as in this example), a variable to a literal (as in the previous examples), a literal to a literal (although this is rarely done), or a literal to any expression in place of any variable or literal. The following if statement shows an expression included in the if.

```
if (pay * tax_rate == minimum)
   { low_salary = 1400.60; }
```

The precedence table of operators in Appendix D includes the relational operators. They are at levels 8 and 9, lower than the other primary math operators. When you use expressions such as the one shown in this example, you can make these expressions much more readable by enclosing them in parentheses (even though C++ does not require it). Here is a rewrite of the previous if statement, with ample parentheses:

```
if ((pay * tax_rate) == minimum)
   { low_salary = 1400.60; }
```

The following is a simple program that computes a salesperson's pay. The salesperson receives a flat rate of $4.10 per hour. In addition, if sales are more than $8,500, the salesperson also receives an additional $500 as a bonus. This is an introductory example of conditional logic, which depends on a relation between two values, sales and $8500.

```
// Filename: PAY1.CPP
// Calculates a salesperson's pay based on his or her sales
#include <iostream.h>
#include <iomanip.h>
void main()
{
   char sal_name[20];
   int hours;
```

```
    float total_sales, bonus, pay;

    cout << "\n\n";    // Prints two blank lines
    cout << "Payroll Calculation\n";
    cout << "-------------------\n";

    // Asks the user for needed values
    cout << "What is salesperson's last name? ";
    cin >> sal_name;
    cout << "How many hours did the salesperson work? ";
    cin >> hours;
    cout << "What were the total sales? ";
    cin >> total_sales;

    bonus = 0;    // Initially, there is no bonus

    // Computes the base pay
    pay = 4.10 * (float)hours;    // Typecasts the hours

    // Adds bonus only if sales were high
    if (total_sales > 8500.00)
       { bonus = 500.00; }

    cout.setf(ios::fixed);
    cout << sal_name << " made $" << setprecision(2)
         << pay << "\n";
    cout << "and got a bonus of $" << bonus << "\n";
}
```

The following output shows the result of running this program twice, each time with different input values. Notice that the program does two different things: it computes a bonus for one employee but not for the other. The $500 bonus is a direct result of the `if` statement. The assignment of `$500` to `bonus` executes only if the value in `total_sales` is more than $8500.

```
Payroll Calculation
-------------------
What is salesperson's last name? Harrison
How many hours did the salesperson work? 40
What were the total sales? 6050.64
Harrison made $164.00
and got a bonus of $0.00
```

```
Payroll Calculation
-------------------
What is salesperson's last name? Robertson
How many hours did the salesperson work? 40
What were the total sales? 9800
Robertson made $164.00
and got a bonus of $500.00
```

Write the output of each of these code fragments in the space provided.

```
num = 5;
if (num >= 5)
   { cout << "Yes \n"; }
cout << "Done.";
```

```
num = 5;
if (num <= 5)
   { cout << "Yes \n";
     cout << "Done."; }
```

```
num = 5;
if (num <= 5)
   { cout << "Yes \n";
     cout << "Done."; }
cout << "Abc";
```

Data Validation

When programming for user input, it is wise to perform *data validation* on the values the user types. If the user enters a bad value (for instance, a negative number when the input cannot be negative), you can inform the user of the problem and ask him or her to reenter the data.

Not all data can be validated, of course, but most of it can be checked for reasonability. For example, if you write a student record-keeping program to track each student's name, address, age, and other pertinent data, you can check whether the age falls in a reasonable range. If the user enters 213 for the age, you know that the value is incorrect. If the user enters -4 for the age, you know that this value is also incorrect. Not all erroneous input for age can be checked, however. If the user is 21, for instance, and types 22, your program has no way of knowing whether this is correct, because 22 falls in a reasonable age range for students.

The following program is a routine that requests an age and makes sure that it is more than 10. This certainly is not a foolproof test (because the user can still enter incorrect ages), but it takes care of extremely low values. If the user enters a bad age, the program asks for the age again inside the if statement.

```
// Filename: AGECHK.CPP
// Program that ensures age values are reasonable
#include <iostream.h>
void main()
{
   int age;

   cout << "\nWhat is the student's age? ";
   cin >> age;

   if (age < 10)
     { cout << '\a';    // BEEP
       cout << "*** The age cannot be less than 10 ***\n";
       cout << "Try again...\n\n";
       cout << "What is the student's age? ";
       cin >> age;
     }

   cout << "Thank you. You entered a valid age.\n";
}
```

This routine also can be a section of a longer program. You learn later in this book how to prompt repeatedly for a value until a valid input is given. This program takes advantage of the bell (ASCII 7) to warn the user that a bad age was entered. The \a character is an escape sequence for the alarm. (See Lesson 6, "Characters, Strings, and Character Arrays," for more information on escape sequences.)

If the entered age is less than 10, the user receives an error message. The program beeps and warns the user about the bad age before asking for the age again.

The following shows the result of running this program. Notice that the program "knows," due to the if statement, whether age is more than 10.

```
What is the student's age? 3
*** The age cannot be less than 10 ***
Try again...


What is the student's age? 21
Thank you. You entered a valid age.
```

Suppose that you were writing a program that requested payroll information. Before calculating the gross pay, you want to validate the hours worked. Write the lines of code needed to request the hours worked in a variable named hrs_wrkd that ensure that the user typed a positive number of hours (nobody works a negative number of hours).

TIP: The values of 1 and 0 for True and False, respectively, can help save you an extra programming step that you might not be able to save in other languages. To understand this, examine the following section of code:

```
commission = 0;   // Initializes commission

if (sales > 10000)
   { commission = 500.00; }

pay = net_pay + commission;   // Commission is 0 unless
                              // high sales
```

You can make this program more efficient by combining the `if`'s relational test because you know that the test returns 1 or 0:

```
pay = net_pay + (commission = (sales > 10000) * 500.00);
```

This single line does what the preceding four lines did. Because the assignment on the far right has parentheses, it is computed first. The program compares the variable `sales` to `10000`. If it is more than `10000`, a True result of 1 returns. The program then multiplies 1 by `500.00` and stores the result in `commission`. If, however, the `sales` were not more than `10000`, a 0 results and the program receives 0 from multiplying 0 by `500.00`.

Whichever value (`500.00` or `0`) the program assigns to `commission` is then added to `net_pay` and stored in `pay`.

The user usually does not mean to enter incorrect data, but hands slip and accidents happen. Therefore, you must help ensure that the user types reasonable answers to the questions you ask. You can improve the programs from this section with the `else` statement, which you learn about in the next section. Some of the code you have seen includes a redundant check of the user's input.

The `else` Statement

The `else` statement never appears in a program without an `if` statement. This section introduces the `else` statement by showing you the popular `if-else` combination statement. Its format is

```
if (condition)
   { A block of one or more C++ statements }
else
   { A block of one or more C++ statements }
```

The first part of the `if-else` is identical to the `if` statement. If `condition` is True, the block of C++ statements following the `if` executes. If `condition` is False, however, the block of C++ statements following the `else` executes instead. Whereas the simple `if` statement determines what happens only when the `condition` is True, the `if-else` also determines what happens when the `condition` is False. No matter what the outcome is, the statement following the `if-else` executes next.

The following statements describe the nature of the if-else:

- If the *condition* test is True, the entire block of statements following the if executes.

- If the *condition* test is False, the entire block of statements following the else executes.

You use if-else logic in everyday life. Almost any time you use the word "otherwise," you are stating an if-else conditional statement. Consider these sentences:

"If I make a bonus we will go to Italy; otherwise, we will go to Arkansas."

"If you make straight A's you can have a car; otherwise, you can take the bus."

NOTE: You also can compare characters in addition to numbers in if-else tests. When you compare characters, C++ uses the ASCII table to determine which character is "less than" the other (lower in the ASCII table). But you cannot compare character strings or arrays of character strings directly with relational operators.

The following program asks the user for a number. It then prints whether or not the number is greater than zero, using the if-else statement.

```
// Filename: IFEL1.CPP
// Demonstrates if-else by printing whether or
// not an input value is greater than zero
#include <iostream.h>
void main()
{
   int num;

   cout << "What is your number? ";
   cin >> num;    // Gets the user's number

   if (num > 0)
      { cout << "More than 0\n"; }
   else
      { cout << "Less than or equal to 0\n"; }
```

```
   // No matter what the number was, the following executes
   cout << "\n\nThanks for your time!\n";
}
```

There is no need to test for both possibilities when you use an else. The if tests whether the number is greater than zero, and the else automatically handles all other possibilities.

The following program is a more complete payroll routine than the one seen earlier in this lesson. It uses the if statement to illustrate how to compute overtime pay. The logic goes something like this:

If employees work 40 hours or less, they are paid regular pay (their hourly rate times the number of hours worked). If employees work between 40 and 50 hours, they receive one-and-a-half times their hourly rate for the hours over 40, in addition to their regular pay for the first 40. All hours over 50 are paid at double the regular rate.

```
// Filename: PAY2.CPP
// Computes the full overtime pay possibilities
#include <iomanip.h>
#include <iostream.h>
void main()
{
   int hours;
   float dt, ht, rp, rate, pay;

   cout << "\n\nHow many hours were worked? ";
   cin >> hours;
   cout << "\nWhat is the regular hourly pay? ";
   cin >> rate;

   // Computes pay here
   // Double-time possibility
   if (hours > 50)
     { dt = 2.0 * rate * (float)(hours - 50);
       ht = 1.5 * rate * 10.0;}    // Time + 1/2 for 10 hours
   else
     { dt = 0.0; }    // Either none or double for hours over 50

   // Time-and-a-half
   if (hours > 40)
     { ht = 1.5 * rate * (float)(hours - 40); }
```

152

```
    // Regular pay
    if (hours >= 40)
      { rp = 40 * rate; }
    else
      { rp = (float)hours * rate; }

    pay = dt + ht + rp;    // Adds three components of payroll

    cout << setprecision(2) << "\nThe pay is $" << pay << "\n";
}
```

The block of statements following the if can contain any valid C++ statement—even another if statement! This sometimes comes in handy, as the following example shows.

You can even use this program to award employees for their years of service to your company. In this example, you are giving a gold watch to those with more than 20 years of service, a paperweight to those with more than 10 years, and a pat on the back to everyone else!

```
// Filename: SERV.CPP
// Prints a message depending on years of service
#include <iostream.h>
void main()
{
    int yrs;
    cout << "How many years of service? ";
    cin >> yrs;    // Determines the years the person has worked

    if (yrs > 20)
        { cout << "Give a gold watch\n"; }
    else
        { if (yrs > 10)
            { cout << "Give a paperweight\n"; }
          else
            { cout << "Give a pat on the back\n"; }
        }
}
```

> **NOTE:** Don't rely on the if within an if to handle too many conditions, because more than three or four conditions can cause confusion. You might mess up your logic, such as: "If this is True, and this is also True, then do something; but if not that, but something

else is True, then..." (and so on). The `switch` statement that you learn about in Lesson 17, "Controlling with `switch`," handles these types of multiple `if` selections much better than a long `if` within an `if` statement does.

The `if` and `if-else` statements provide the tools you need to write powerful data-checking programs. This lesson shows you how to compare literals, variables, and combinations of both by using the relational operators. The `if` and `if-else` statements rely on such data comparisons to determine which code to execute next. You can now *conditionally execute* statements in your programs. Therefore, your programs produce different results by traversing different paths of code, depending on the user's input.

Convert the following sentence into an `if-else` statement:

"If the sales are more than $5,000.00, your bonus will be $75; otherwise, your bonus will be only $25."

The modulus operator is useful for testing odd or even conditions. Suppose that you needed to know whether the user typed an odd or even number. After you divide by 2, the remainder is 0 if the number is even and 1 if the number is odd. Finish the following program and print either `The number is odd` or `The number is even`, depending on the result of a modulus calculation. *Hint:* Use an `if-else` to print the proper message.

```cpp
#include <iostream.h>
void main()
{
    int num;
    cout << "Please type a number ";
    cin >> num;
    if ((num % 2) == 0)    // Finish the program
```

Review Questions

1. Which operator tests for equality?

2. State whether each of these relational tests is True or False:

   (a) `4 >= 5`
   (b) `4 == 4`
   (c) `165 >= 165`
   (d) `0 != 25`

3. TRUE or FALSE: `C++ is fun` prints on-screen when the following statement executes:

   ```
   if (54 <= 54)
       { cout << "C++ is fun\n"; }
   ```

4. TRUE or FALSE: `C++ is fun` prints on-screen when the following statement executes:

   ```
   temp = 0;
   if (temp = 0)
       { cout << "C++ is fun\n"; }
   ```

5. What is the difference between an `if` and an `if-else` statement?

6. Does the following `cout` execute?

   ```
   if (3 != 4 != 1)
       { cout << "This will print"; }
   ```

155

7. Using the ASCII table (see Appendix C), state whether these character relational tests are True or False:

   (a) `'C' < 'c'`
   (b) `'0' > '0'`
   (c) `'?' > ')'`

Review Exercises

1. Write a weather-calculator program that asks for a list of the previous five days' temperatures, then prints `Brrrr!` every time a temperature falls below freezing.

2. Write a program that asks for a number and then prints the square and the cube (the number multiplied by itself three times) of the number you input, if that number is more than 1. Otherwise, the program does not print anything.

3. In a program, ask the user for two numbers. Print a message telling how the first one relates to the second. In other words, if the user enters 5 and 7, your program prints `5 is less than 7`.

4. Write a program that prompts the user for an employee's pre-tax salary and prints the appropriate taxes. The taxes are 10 percent if the employee makes less than $10,000; 15 percent if the employee earns $10,000 up to, but not including, $20,000; and 20 percent if the employee earns $20,000 or more.

Logical Operators: Combining Relational Operators

To teach the logical operators and how they enable you to combine the multiple relational operators you learned in the preceding lesson.

Often, the simple relational operators you learned in Lesson 10, "Relational Logic and Operators," are not enough. Sometimes it is helpful to combine several relational tests into a single, compound test. C++'s *logical operators* enable you to combine relational operators into more

powerful data-testing statements. The logical operators are sometimes used to produce *compound relational operators* (the combination of relational operations). As C++'s precedence table shows, relational operators take precedence over logical operators when you combine them. The precedence table plays an important role in these types of operators, as this lesson emphasizes.

The Logical Operators

There might be times when you have to test more than one set of variables. You can combine more than one relational test into a *compound relational test* by using C++'s logical operators, shown in Table 11.1.

Table 11.1. Logical operators.

Operator	Meaning
&&	AND
¦¦	OR
!	NOT

The first two logical operators, && and ¦¦, never appear by themselves. They typically go between two or more relational tests.

Table 11.2 shows how each logical operator works. These tables are called *truth tables* because they show you how to achieve True results from an if statement that uses these operators. Take some time to study these tables.

Table 11.2. Truth tables.

The AND (&&) Truth Table
(Both sides must be True.)

True	&&	True	= True
True	&&	False	= False
False	&&	True	= False
False	&&	False	= False

The OR (¦¦) Truth Table
(One side or the other must be True.)

True	¦¦	True	= True
True	¦¦	False	= True
False	¦¦	True	= True
False	¦¦	False	= False

The NOT (!) Truth Table
(Causes an opposite relation.)

!True	=	False
!False	=	True

The True and False conditions shown in these tables are the result of C++ relational tests. A relational test that uses > or < or any of the other relational operators you saw in Lesson 10 always produces a True or False value. The logical operators combine more than one relational test into a single compound relational test so that you can test more than one condition with a single `if` statement.

Without looking at the truth tables, what is the result of each of the following logical statements?

Statement	True or False
True && False	_____
False && True	_____
!True	_____
True ¦¦ False	_____
True ¦¦ True	_____

Using the Logical Operators

The True and False on each side of the operators represent a relational `if` test. The following statements, for example, are valid `if` tests that use logical operators (sometimes called *compound relational operators*).

```
if ((a < b) && (c > d))
    { cout << "Results are invalid."; }
```

This statement says the following: "If a is less than b and c is greater than d, then and only then display Results are invalid. If either side of the && condition is False, the entire expression will be False, and the message will not print."

The variable a must be less than b and, at the same time, c must be greater than d for the cout to execute. You must remember that the if statement requires parentheses around its complete conditional test. Consider this portion of a program:

```
if ((sales > 5000) || (hrs_worked > 81))
    { bonus = 500; }
```

The sales must be more than 5,000 or the hrs_worked must be more than 81 before the assignment executes. The || is sometimes called *inclusive OR,* meaning that one side of the || must be True for the result to be True.

 Explain in English the behavior of the following compound relational test.

```
if ((age < 18) || (native_status == 1))
    { cout << "You don't need a passport to enter."; }
```

Here is a program segment that includes the NOT (!) operator:

```
if (!(sales < 2500))
    { bonus = 500; }
```

If sales is greater than or equal to 2,500, bonus is initialized. This illustrates an important programming tip: use ! sparingly. It is much clearer to rewrite the preceding example by turning it into a positive relational test:

```
if (sales >= 2500)
    { bonus 500; }
```

But the ! operator is sometimes helpful, especially when testing for end-of-file conditions for disk files, as you will learn in Lesson 32, "Sequential Files." Most of the time, however, you can avoid using ! by using the reverse logic shown in the following:

```
!(var1 == var2) is the same as (var1 != var2)
!(var1 <= var2) is the same as (var1 > var2)
!(var1 >= var2) is the same as (var1 < var2)
!(var1 != var2) is the same as (var1 == var2)
!(var1 > var2) is the same as (var1 <= var2)
!(var1 < var2) is the same as (var1 >= var2)
```

Notice that the overall format of the if statement is retained when you use logical operators, but the relational test expands to include more than one relation.

Rewrite the following if statement so that it uses positive relational logic by getting rid of the ! operator.

```
if (!(a > b) && (c < d))
    // Rest of program follows
```

You even can have three or more relational conditions in the same if test, as shown in the following statement:

```
if ((a == B) && (d == f) ¦¦ (l = m) ¦¦ !(k <> 2)) ...
```

This is a little too much, however, and good programming practice dictates using *at most* two relational tests inside a single if statement. If you have to combine more than two relational tests, use more than one if statement to do so.

What is the result of the following logical expressions?

```
(TRUE ¦¦ (FALSE && TRUE))     _____
(FALSE ¦¦ (FALSE ¦¦ FALSE))   _____
(TRUE ¦¦ TRUE ¦¦ TRUE)        _____
```

As with relational operators, you use logical operators in everyday conversation:

"If my pay is high and my vacation time is long, we can go to Italy this summer."

161

"If you take the trash out or clean your room, you can watch TV tonight."

"If you aren't good, you'll be punished."

To see the logical operators in action, consider the following program. The summer Olympics are held every four years, during each year that is evenly divisible by 4. The U.S. Census is taken every 10 years, during each year that is evenly divisible by 10. The following short program asks for a year, then tells the user whether it is a year of the summer Olympics, a year of the census, or both. If it is neither, such as the year 1993, nothing is printed. It uses relational operators, logical operators, and the modulus operator to determine this output.

```cpp
// Filename: YEARTEST.CPP
// Determines whether it is summer Olympics year,
// U.S. Census year, or both
#include <iostream.h>
void main()
{
    int year;
    // Asks for a year
    cout << "What is a year for the test? ";
    cin >> year;

    // Tests the year
    if (((year % 4)==0) && ((year % 10)==0))
      { cout << "Both Olympics and U.S. Census!";
        return; }   // Quits program and returns
                    // to operating system
    if ((year % 4)==0)
      { cout << "Summer Olympics only"; }
    else
       { if ((year % 10)==0)
          { cout << "U.S. Census only"; }
       }
}
```

Here is the program's output:

```
What is a year for the test? 2000
Both Olympics and U.S. Census!
```

Logical operators offer another way to validate input for reasonability. The following program includes a logical operator in its `if` statement to determine whether the age is greater than 10 and less than 100. If the age is less than 10 or greater than 100, the program concludes that the user did not enter a valid age.

```
// Filename: AGETEST.CPP
// Program that helps ensure that age values are reasonable
#include <iostream.h>
void main()
{
   int age;

   cout << "What is your age? ";
   cin >> age;
   if ((age < 10) || (age > 100))
     { cout << " \a \a \n";    // Beeps twice
       cout << "*** The age must be from 10 to 100 ***\n"; }
   else
     { cout << "You entered a valid age."; }
}
```

Here is the program's output after the program has been run twice. In the first execution, the user enters an age that does not pass the validity check. The second time, the user enters an age that is reasonable.

```
What is your age? 2

*** The age must be between 10 and 100 ***

What is your age? 21
You entered a valid age.
```

One final logical operator program explains things even further. The following program could be used by a video store to calculate a discount, based on the number of rentals people transact as well as their customer status. Customers are classified as either R for *regular* or S for *special*. Special customers have been members of the rental club for more than one year. They automatically receive a 50-cent discount on all rentals. The store also holds "value days" several times a year. On value days, all customers receive the 50-cent discount. Special customers do not receive an additional 50 cents off during value days, because every day is a discount for them.

The program asks for each customer's status and whether or not it is a value day. It then uses the || logical operator to test for the discount. Even before you started learning C++, you probably would have looked at this problem with the following idea in mind:

"If a customer is special or if it is a value day, deduct 50 cents from the rental."

That's basically the idea of the if decision in the following program. Even though special customers do not receive an additional discount on value days, there is one final if test for them that prints an extra message at the bottom of the screen's indicated billing.

```cpp
// Filename: VIDEO.CPP
// Program that computes video rental amounts and gives
// appropriate discounts based on the day or customer status
#include <iostream.h>
#include <iomanip.h>
void main()
{
    float tape_charge, discount, rental_amt;
    char first_name[15];
    char last_name[15];
    int num_tapes;
    char val_day, sp_stat;

    cout << "\n\n *** Video Rental Computation ***\n";
    cout << "     ----------------------\n";    // Underlines
                                                // title

    tape_charge = 2.00;    // Before-discount tape fee per tape

    // Receives input data after skipping a line
    cout << "\nWhat is customer's first name? ";
    cin >> first_name;
    cout << "What is customer's last name? ";
    cin >> last_name;

    cout << "\nHow many tapes are being rented? ";
    cin >> num_tapes;

    cout << "Is this a Value day (Y/N)? ";
    cin >> val_day;

    cout << "Is this a Special Status customer (Y/N)? ";
    cin >> sp_stat;

    // Calculates rental amount
    discount = 0.0;    // Increases discount IF the
                       // customer is eligible
```

```
    if ((val_day == 'Y') || (sp_stat == 'Y'))
      { discount = 0.5;
        rental_amt = (num_tapes * tape_charge) -
                    (discount * num_tapes); }

    cout.setf(ios::fixed);
    // Prints the bill
    cout << "\n\n** Rental Club **\n\n";
    cout << first_name << " " << last_name << " rented "
        << num_tapes << " tapes\n";
    cout << "The total was $" << setprecision(2)
        << rental_amt << "\n";
    cout << "The discount was $" << discount
        << " per tape\n";


    // Prints extra message for Special Status customers
    if (sp_stat == 'Y')
      { cout << "\nThank them for being a Special "
             << "Status customer\n";}
}
```

The output of this program appears as follows. Notice that special customers have the extra message at the bottom of the screen. This program, due to its if statements, performs differently depending on the data entered. No discount is applied for regular customers on nonvalue days.

```
*** Video Rental Computation ***
- - - - - - - - - - - - - - - - - - - - - -


What is customer's first name? Jerry
What is customer's last name? Parker

How many tapes are being rented? 3
Is this a Value day (Y/N)? Y
Is this a Special Status customer (Y/N)? Y



** Rental Club **

Jerry Parker rented 3 tapes
The total was 4.50
The discount was 0.50 per tape

Thank them for being a Special Status customer
```

165

Logical Issues

After reading Appendix B, you can understand how the logical tests work internally. The True or False results of relational tests happen at the bit level. For example, take the `if` test:

```
if (a == 6) ...
```

to determine the truth of the relation (a == 6). The computer takes a binary 6, or 00000110, and compares it, bit-by-bit, to the variable a. If a contains 7, a binary 00000111, the result of this *equal* test is False, because the right bit (called the *least-significant bit*) is different.

 If you understand binary numbers, try this quiz to test your understanding. Suppose that the integer variable named Amt contains a 9. A binary 9 is 00001001. What is the resulting bit pattern for this expression:

```
!Amt
```

C++'s Logical Efficiency

C++ attempts to be more efficient than other languages. If you combine multiple relational tests with one of the logical operators, C++ does not always interpret the full expression. This ultimately makes your programs run faster, but there are dangers. For example, if your program contains the conditional test:

```
if ((5 > 4) ¦¦ (sales < 15) && (15 != 15))...
```

C++ evaluates only the first condition, (5 > 4), and realizes that it does not have to look further. Because (5 > 4) is True and the operator is ¦¦ (OR), the result of the expression will be True, regardless of the remainder of the expression on the right side of the ¦¦. The same holds true for the following statement:

```
if ((7 < 3) && (age > 15) && (initial == 'D'))...
```

Here, C++ evaluates only the first condition, which is False. Because the operator is && (AND), the result of the expression will be False, regardless of the remainder of the expression on the right side of the &&. Most of the time, this doesn't pose a problem, but be aware that the following expression might not fulfill your expectations:

```
if ((5 > 4) ¦¦ (num = 0))...
```

166

The (num = 0) assignment never executes, because C++ has to interpret only (5 > 4) to determine whether the entire expression is True or False. Due to this danger, do not include assignment expressions in the same condition as a logical test. The following single `if` condition:

```
if ((sales > old_sales) ¦¦ (inventory_flag = 'Y'))...
```

should be broken into two statements, such as:

```
(inventory_flag) = 'Y';
if ((sales > old_sales) ¦¦ (inventory_flag))...
```

so that `inventory_flag` is always assigned the `'Y'` value, no matter how the (sales > old_sales) expression tests.

Rewrite the next `if` to ensure that `bonus` is always assigned.

```
if ((sales < 2300) && (bonus = 50))
    { cout << "Low sales."; }
```

The Precedence of Logical Operators

The math precedence order you read about in Lesson 9, "Math Operators and Precedence," did not include the logical operators. You should become familiar with the entire order of precedence, presented in Appendix D.

You might wonder why the relational and logical operators are included in the precedence table. The following partial `if` statement helps show you why:

```
if (sales < min_sal * 2 && yrs_emp > 10 * sub) ...
```

Without the complete order of operators, it is impossible to determine how such a statement would execute. Does C++ evaluate it from left to right, multiplication before &&, or what? According to the precedence order, this `if` statement executes as follows:

```
if ((sales < (min_sal * 2)) && (yrs_emp > (10 * sub))) ...
```

This still might be confusing, but it is less so. The two multiplications are performed first, followed by the relations < and >. The && is performed last because it is lowest in the precedence order of operators.

To avoid such ambiguous problems, be sure to use ample parentheses—even if the default precedence order is your intention. It is also wise to resist combining too many expressions inside a single `if` relational test.

Notice that `||` (OR) has lower precedence than `&&` (AND). Therefore, the following `if` tests are equivalent:

```
if ((first_initial == 'A') && (last_initial == 'G') ||
                          (id == 321)) ...
if (((first_initial == 'A') && (last_initial == 'G')) ||
                          (id == 321)) ...
```

The second is clearer, due to the parentheses, but the precedence table makes them identical.

 Rewrite the next partial `if` statement with parentheses to clarify the operator precedence.

```
if ((a > b && c * 2 <= yrs_emp || 10 * d == 8) ...
```

Review Questions

1. What are the three logical operators?

2. The following compound relational tests produce True or False comparisons. Determine which are True and which are False.

   (a) `! (True || False)`
   (b) `(True && False) && (False || True)`
   (c) `! (True && False)`
   (d) `True || (False && False) || False`

3. Given the statement

   ```
   int i = 12, j = 10, k = 5;
   ```

   what are the results (True or False) of the following statements? (*Hint:* Remember that C++ interprets any nonzero statement as True.)

(a) `i && j`

(b) `12 - i ¦¦ k`

(c) `j != k && i != k`

4. What is the value printed in the following program? (*Hint:* Don't be misled by the assignment operators on each side of the ¦¦.)

```cpp
// Filename: LOGO.CPP
// Logical operator test
#include <iostream.h>
void main()
{
   int f, g;

   g = 5;
   f = 8;
   if ((g = 25) ¦¦ (f = 35))
      { cout << "g is " << g << " and f got changed to " << f; }
}
```

5. Using the precedence table, determine whether the following statements produce a True or False result. After this, you should appreciate the abundant use of parentheses!

(a) `5 == 4 + 1 ¦¦ 7 * 2 != 12 - 1 && 5 == 8 / 2`

(b) `8 + 9 != 6 - 1 ¦¦ 10 % 2 != 5 + 0`

(c) `17 - 1 > 15 + 1 && 0 + 2 != 1 -- 1 ¦¦ 4 != 1`

(d) `409 * 0 != 1· * 409 + 0 ¦¦ 1 + 8 * 2 >= 17`

6. Does the following cout execute?

```cpp
if (!0)
   { cout << "C++ Programming 101 \n"; }
```

Review Exercises

1. Write a program (by using a single compound `if` statement) to determine whether the user enters an odd positive number.

2. Write a program that asks the user for two initials. Print a message telling the user if the first initial falls alphabetically before the second.

3. Write a number-guessing game. At the beginning of the program, assign a value to a variable called `number`. Give a prompt that asks for five guesses. Receive the user's five guesses with a single

cin so that you can practice with cin. Determine whether any of the guesses matches the number, and print an appropriate message if one does.

4. Write a tax-calculation routine, as follows: A family pays no tax if its income is less than $5,000. It pays a 10 percent tax if its income is $5,000 to $9,999, inclusive. It pays a 20 percent tax if its income is $10,000 to $19,999, inclusive. Otherwise, it pays a 30 percent tax.

Additional C++ Operators

To explain many of the remaining C++ operators and to continue the study of the many operators of the C++ language.

You now understand many of the C++ operators, but there are a few more to learn. The C++ language contains more operators than most other computer languages. Unless you become familiar with all the operators, you might think that C++ programs are cryptic and difficult to follow. C++'s heavy reliance on its many operators and operator precedence produces the efficiency that enables your programs to run more smoothly and quickly.

The Conditional Operator

The *conditional operator* is C++'s only *ternary* operator. It works on three values as opposed to the binary operators you have seen that operate on only two values. The conditional operator is used to replace if-else logic in some situations. It is a two-symbol operator, ?:, with the following format:

```
conditional_expression ? expression1 : expression2;
```

The *conditional_expression* is any expression in C++ that results in a True (nonzero) or False (zero) answer. If the result of *conditional_expression* is True, *expression1* executes. Otherwise, if the result of *conditional_expression* is False, *expression2* executes. Only one of the expressions following the question mark ever executes. Only a single semicolon appears at the end of *expression2*. The internal expressions, such as *expression1,* do not have a semicolon.

Figure 12.1 illustrates the conditional operator more clearly. Notice that C++ executes either *expression1* or *expression2,* but never both.

Figure 12.1.
Format of the
conditional
operator.

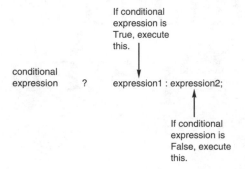

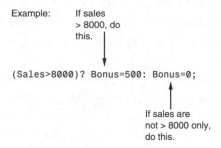

If you require simple `if-else` logic, the conditional operator usually provides a more direct and succinct method, although you should always prefer readability over compact code.

To glimpse the conditional operator at work, consider the section of code that follows:

```
if (a > b)
    { ans = 10; }
else
    { ans = 25; }
```

You can easily rewrite this kind of `if-else` code by using a single conditional operator.

```
a > b ? (ans = 10) : (ans = 25);
```

> **TIP:** Although parentheses are not required around *conditional_expression* to make it work, they usually improve readability. The following statement's readability is improved by using parentheses, as follows:
>
> ```
> (a > b) ? (ans = 10) : (ans = 25);
> ```

Rewrite the following conditional statement using parentheses to help make the three parts of the conditional clearer.

```
ActPay < 2300 ? extend_pay = 1 : extend_pay = 0;
```

Because each C++ expression has a value—in this case, the value being assigned—this statement could be even more succinct, without loss of readability, by assigning ans the answer to the left of the conditional:

```
ans = (a > b) ? (10) : (25);
```

This expression says: if a is greater than b, assign 10 to ans; otherwise, assign 25 to ans. Almost any `if-else` statement can be rewritten as a conditional, and vice versa. You should practice converting one to the other to become familiar with the conditional operator's purpose.

> **NOTE:** Any valid `if` C++ statement can be a *conditional_expression*, including all relational and logical operators and any of their possible combinations. The conditional expression is more efficient (runs faster) but it can be harder to read.

Describe what is wrong with each of these conditional operator expressions.

```
(Tolerance < 0.05) ? refine = .025; refine = .015;
```

```
(Tolerance < 0.05) ? refine = .025 : refine = .015:
```

```
if (Tolerance < 0.05) ? refine = .025 : refine = .015;
```

Just by looking at a conditional statement, you should be able to read it without thinking about it too much. Consider this conditional statement:

```
(a > b) ? (ans = 10) : (ans = 25);
```

You can read the following from left to right: "Is a greater than b? If so, assign 10 to ans; otherwise, assign 25 to ans."

Suppose that you are looking over your C++ programs, and you notice the following section of code:

```
if (production > target)
    { target *= 1.10; }
else
    { target *= .90; }
```

You should realize that such a simple `if-else` statement can be rewritten using a conditional operator, and that more efficient code results. Therefore, you can change it to the following single statement:

```
(production > target) ? (target *= 1.10) : (target *= .90);
```

The line can be further revised and shortened, like this:

```
target *= (production > target) ? (1.10) : (.90);
```

Using a conditional operator, you can write a routine to find the minimum value between two variables. This is sometimes called a *minimum routine*. The statement to do this is:

```
minimum = (var1 < var2) ? var1 : var2;
```

This statement reads like this: if var1 is less than var2, the value of var1 is assigned to minimum. If var2 is less, the value of var2 is assigned to minimum. If the variables are equal, the value of var2 is assigned to minimum, because it does not matter which is assigned.

Use logic similar to what you just saw to write a *maximum routine* below.

Taking the previous examples a step further, you also can test for the sign of a variable. The following conditional expression assigns –1 to the variable called `sign` if `testvar` is less than 0, 0 to `sign` if `testvar` is 0, and +1 to `sign` if `testvar` is 1 or more:

```
sign = (testvar < 0) ? -1 : (testvar > 0);
```

Take advantage of C++'s efficiency with the conditional operator.

It might be easy to spot why the less-than test results in a –1, but the second part of the expression can be confusing. This statement works well due to C++'s 1 and 0 (for True and False, respectively) return values from a relational test. If `testvar` is 0 or greater, `sign` is assigned the answer `(testvar > 0)`. The value of `(testvar > 0)` is 1 if True (therefore, `testvar` is greater than 0) or False if `testvar` is equal to 0. Figure 12.2 helps explain the `sign` test even further.

```
sign = (testvar<0) ?-1 : (testvar>0);
                                ↑
                        Results in either
                        a 0 or a 1,
                        depending on whether
                        it is False or True.
```

Figure 12.2. Explaining the sign conditional expression.

The preceding example explains C++'s efficient conditional operator. You might better understand if you see the statement written using typical `if-else` logic:

```
if (testvar < 0)
    { sign = -1; }
else
    { sign = (testvar > 0); }   // testvar can be only
                                // 0 or more here
```

Convert the following `if-else` to a single conditional statement.

```
if (quantity >= 24)
    { order = max + 5; }
else
    { order = max; }
```

Convert the following conditional statement to `if-else` logic.

```
n = ((a < b) ? c : d);
```

The conditional operator simply works like an `if-else` statement. Instead of spanning three or four lines of code with an `if-else`, you can pack the entire conditional test into a single conditional expression. Of course, if you understand a longer `if-else` better than a shorter conditional equivalent, use what you are comfortable with.

The Increment and Decrement Operators

C++ offers two unique operators that add 1 to variables or subtract 1 from variables. These are the *increment* and *decrement operators:* ++ and --. The increment and decrement operators offer an extremely efficient method for adding 1 to and subtracting 1 from a variable. Table 12.1 shows how these operators relate to other types of expressions you have seen. Notice that the ++ and -- can appear on either side of the modified variable. If the ++ or -- appears on the left, it is known as a *prefix* operator. If the operator appears on the right, it is a *postfix* operator.

Table 12.1. The ++ and -- operators.

Operator	Example	Description	Equivalent Statements
++	i++;	postfix	i = i + 1; i += 1;
++	++i;	prefix	i = i + 1; i += 1;
--	i--;	postfix	i = i - 1; i -= 1;
--	--i;	prefix	i = i - 1; i -= 1;

Whenever you have to add 1 to or subtract 1 from a variable, you can use these two operators. As Table 12.1 shows, if you have to increment or decrement only a single variable, these operators enable you to do so.

Increment and Decrement Efficiency

The increment and decrement operators are straightforward, efficient methods for adding 1 to a variable and subtracting 1 from a variable. You often have to do this during counting or processing loops, as discussed in Classroom 4, "Controlling Program Flow."

These two operators compile directly into their assembly language equivalents. Almost all computers include, at their lowest binary machine-language commands, increment and decrement instructions. If you use C++'s increment and decrement operators, you ensure that they compile to these low-level equivalents.

If, however, you code expressions to add or subtract 1 (as you do in other programming languages), such as the expression i = i - 1, you do not actually ensure that C++ compiles this instruction in its efficient machine-language equivalent.

If you need a program to count several hundred or thousand items, such as inventory, customers, or sales figures, use the increment operator to ensure that the counting is as efficient as possible.

Using Increment and Decrement in Expressions

It doesn't matter whether you use prefix or postfix—if you are incrementing or decrementing single variables on lines by themselves. When you combine these two operators with other operators in a single expression, however, you must be aware of their differences. Consider the following program code. Here, all variables are integers because the increment and decrement operators work only on integer variables.

```
a = 6;
b = ++a - 1;
```

What are the values of a and b after these two statements finish? The value of a is easy to determine: it is incremented in the second statement, so it is 7. However, b is either 5 or 6, depending on when the variable a increments. The following rules determine when a increments:

- If a variable is incremented or decremented with a *prefix* operator, the increment or decrement occurs *before* the variable's value is used in the remainder of the expression.

- If a variable is incremented or decremented with a *postfix* operator, the increment or decrement occurs *after* the variable's value is used in the remainder of the expression.

In the preceding code, a contains a prefix increment. Therefore, its value is first incremented to 7, then 1 is subtracted from 7, and the result, 6, is assigned to b. If a postfix increment is used, as in

```
a = 6;
b = a++ - 1;
```

a is 6. Therefore, 5 is assigned to b because a does not increment to 7 until after its value is used in the expression. The note at the end of the precedence table in Appendix D explains that prefix operators contain much higher precedence than almost any other operator. The low-priority postfix operator increments and decrements after most other operators.

> **TIP:** If the order of prefix and postfix confuses you, break your expressions into two lines of code, typing the increment or decrement before or after the expression that uses it.

By taking advantage of this tip, you can rewrite the preceding example as follows:

```
a = 6;
b = a - 1;
a++;
```

There is now no doubt as to when a is incremented: a increments after b is assigned to a-1.

> **NOTE:** Even adding parentheses cannot keep the postfix from performing after everything else. Consider the following statement:
>
> ```
> x = p + (((amt++)));
> ```
>
> There are too many unneeded parentheses, but even the redundant parentheses are not enough to increment amt before adding its value to p. Postfix increments and decrements *always* occur after their variables are used in the surrounding expression.

The increment and decrement operators are compact ways for you to add or subtract 1. Of course, you can add or subtract only variables, not numeric literals. Do not attempt to increment or decrement an expression or a numeric literal. You can apply these operators only to variables. The following expression is invalid:

```
sales = ++(rate * hours);    // Not allowed!
```

What is in x when the following code finishes?

```
n = 5;
x = n++ - 3;
```

What is in x when the following code finishes?

```
l = 10;
m = 20;
n = 15;
x = ++n - 3 + --p + l--;
```

As you should with other C++ operators, keep the precedence table in mind when you evaluate expressions that increment and decrement. Figures 12.3 and 12.4 show you some examples that illustrate these operators.

The precedence table takes on even more meaning when you see a section of code such as that shown in Figure 12.5.

*Figure 12.3.
C++ operators
incrementing by order
of precedence. ans = 0,
then i increments by 1
to its final value of 2.*

*Figure 12.4.
C++ operators
decrementing by order
of precedence. ans = 1,
then k decrements by 1
to its final value of 2.*

*Figure 12.5.
Another example of
C++ operators and
their precedence.*

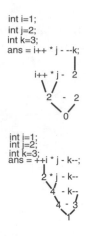

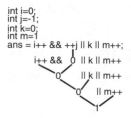

Considering the precedence table, and more important, what you know about C++'s relational efficiencies, what is the value of ans in the following section of code?

```
int i=1, j=20, k=-1, l=0, m=1, n=0, o=2, p=1;
ans = i || j-- && k++ || ++l && ++m || n-- & !o || p--;
```

At first, this exercise seems extremely complicated. Nevertheless, now that you've spent some time figuring it out, you can simply glance at it and determine the value of ans, as well as the ending value of the rest of the variables. Here is why:

Recall that when C++ performs a relation || (OR), it ignores the right side of the || if the left value is True (any nonzero value is True). Because any nonzero value is True, C++ does not evaluate the values on the right. Because the i is True, and because True anything else is still True, C++ performs this expression as shown:

```
ans = i ¦¦ j-- && k++ ¦¦ ++l && ++m ¦¦ n-- & !o ¦¦ p--;
       ¦
       1 (TRUE)
```

If the preceding example is not obvious, consider this: because i is True, C++ evaluates the entire expression as True and ignores all code after the first ¦¦. Therefore, *every other increment and decrement expression is ignored.* Because C++ ignores the other expressions, only ans is changed by this expression. The other variables, j through p, are never incremented or decremented, even though several of them contain increment and decrement operators. If you use relational operators, be aware of this problem and break all increment and decrement operators into statements by themselves, placing them on lines before the relational statements that use their values.

The `sizeof` Operator

Another operator in C++ does not look like an operator at all. It looks like a built-in function, but it is called the `sizeof` operator. In fact, if you think of `sizeof` as a built-in function, you will not be confused by it, because it works similar to built-in functions. The format of `sizeof` follows:

```
sizeof data
```

or

```
sizeof(data type)
```

The *data* can be any variable or literal. The *data type* can be any one of the data types in C++, such as `int` or `float`.

The `sizeof` operator is unary, because it operates on a single value. This operator produces a result that represents the size, in bytes, of the *data* or *data type* specified. Because most data types and variables require different amounts of internal storage on different computers, the `sizeof` operator enables programs to maintain consistency on different types of computers.

Put parentheses around the `sizeof` argument, whether that argument is *data* or *data type*. Because you *must* use parentheses around *data type* arguments and you *can* use them around *data* arguments, it doesn't hurt to always use them.

The sizeof operator is sometimes called a *compile-time operator*. At compile time, rather than at runtime, the compiler replaces each occurrence of sizeof in your program with an unsigned integer value. Because sizeof is used more in advanced C++ programming, this operator is better utilized later in this book for performing more advanced programming requirements.

If you use an array as the sizeof argument, C++ returns the number of bytes you originally reserved for that array. Data inside the array have nothing to do with its returned sizeof value—even if it's only a character array containing a short string.

sizeof returns the number of bytes of whatever you put in the parentheses. However, sizeof is not meant to return the length of a string. Therefore, given the following character array definition:

```
char ara[25] = "Programming";
```

sizeof(ara) returns a 25 because that is the size, in bytes, of the array as you defined it. To get the length of the string inside the array, you have to use the built-in strlen() function.

Suppose that you want to know the size, in bytes, of floating-point variables for your computer. You can determine this by entering the keyword float in parentheses after sizeof, as shown in the following program.

```
// Filename: SIZE1.CPP
// Prints the size of floating-point values
#include <iostream.h>
void main()
{
    cout << "The size of floating-point variables on \n";
    cout << "this computer is " << sizeof(float) << "\n";
}
```

This program might produce different results on different computers. You can use any valid data type as the sizeof argument. On most PCs, this program usually produces this output:

```
The size of floating-point variables on
this computer is 4
```

On a larger computer, such as a minicomputer or a mainframe, the program might produce this:

```
The size of floating-point variables on
this computer is 8
```

What do you think the following statement displays?

```
cout << sizeof(char);
```

If you said "It depends on the computer," you are on the right track for `sizeof` in most cases. C++, however, is designed so that a character *always* takes a single byte of storage. Therefore, the `cout` statement produces a 1 on the screen.

The Comma Operator

Another C++ operator, sometimes called a *sequence point,* works a little differently. This is the *comma operator* (,), which does not operate directly on data, but produces a left-to-right evaluation of expressions. This operator enables you to put more than one expression on a single line by separating each one with a comma.

You saw one use of a comma when you learned how to declare and initialize variables. In the following section of code, the comma separates statements. Because the comma associates from the left, the first variable, `i`, is declared and initialized before the second variable.

```
void main()
{
   int i = 10, j = 25;
   // Rest of program follows
```

> **NOTE:** The comma is *not* a sequence point when it is used inside function parentheses. Then it is said to *separate* arguments, but it is not a sequence point. Consider the `strcpy()` that follows:
>
> ```
> strcpy(ara, "George");
> ```
>
> The commas serve only to separate arguments of the `strcpy()`, and do not generate the left-to-right sequence that they do otherwise when they aren't used in functions.

183

You can put more than one expression on a line, using the comma as a sequence point. The value of the expressions becomes the value of the right side of the sequence point. For instance, the following statement:

```
Result = 4 + 5, Result = 10 + 6;    // 16 ends up in Result
```

puts a 9 in Result and then immediately puts a 16 in Result. The left-to-right order is ensured by the sequence point.

The following program also shows the left-to-right ordering of the sequence point.

```cpp
// Filename: COM.CPP
// Illustrates the sequence point
#include <iostream.h>
void main()
{
    int num, sq, cube;
    num = 5;

    // Calculates the square and cube of the number
    sq = (num * num), cube = (num * num * num);

    cout << "The square of " << num << " is " << sq <<
            " and the cube is " << cube;
}
```

This is not necessarily recommended, however, because it doesn't add anything to the program and actually decreases its readability. In this program, the square and the cube probably are better computed on two separate lines.

The comma enables some interesting statements. Consider the following section of code:

```
i = 10
j = (i = 12, i + 8);
```

After these two lines execute, what values do i and j have in them?

After the next lines execute, what values do x, y, and ans have in them?

```
ans = (y = 8, x = 12);
```

Review Questions

1. What set of statements does the conditional operator replace?

2. Why is the conditional operator called a "ternary" operator?

3. Rewrite the following conditional operator as an `if-else` statement:

   ```
   ans = (a == b) ? c + 2 : c + 3;
   ```

4. TRUE or FALSE: The following statements produce the same results:

   ```
   var++;
   ```

   and

   ```
   var = var + 1;
   ```

5. Why is using the increment and decrement operators more efficient than using the addition and subtraction operators?

6. What is a sequence point?

7. What is the output of the following program section?

   ```
   char name[20] = "Mike";
   cout << "The size of name is " << sizeof(name) << "\n";
   ```

8. What does this produce?

   ```
   cout << sizeof(int);
   ```

9. What does this produce?

   ```
   cout << sizeof(char);
   ```

Review Exercises

1. Write a program that prints the numerals from 1 to 10. Use ten different couts and only one variable called result to hold the value before each cout. Use the increment operator to add 1 to result before each cout.

2. Write a program that asks users for their ages. Using a single cout that includes a conditional operator, print on-screen the following if the input age is 21 or greater:

   You are not a minor.

   or print this otherwise:

   You are still a minor.

   This cout might be long, but it helps illustrate how the conditional operator can work in statements where if-else logic does not.

3. Use the conditional operator—and no if-else statements—to write the following tax-calculation routine: A family pays no tax if its annual salary is less than $5,000. It pays a 10 percent tax if its salary is in the range that begins at $5,000 and ends at $9,999. It pays a 20 percent tax if its salary is in the range that begins at $10,000 and ends at $19,999. Otherwise, the family pays a 30 percent tax.

The Bitwise Operators

To teach the advanced usage of bitwise operators.

You are almost through learning about every operator used in C++. This lesson introduces the *bitwise operators*. The bitwise operators operate on internal bit patterns of data instead of just "values in variables." You need to understand the material in Appendix B before you can understand bitwise operators fully.

Some people program in C++ for years and never bother to learn the bitwise operators. If you don't feel ready to tackle them just now, you can skim this lesson and return to it later.

Taking the time and patience to learn the bitwise operators might pay off, however, because there are functions your program can perform much more efficiently if you use bitwise operators. This is the last lesson that discusses operators. As soon as you have mastered the bitwise operators, you will be ready for Classroom 4, "Controlling Program Flow," which discusses control loops.

The Bitwise Operators

You have read about the logical operators &&, ¦¦, and !. The four logical operators that work on the bit level are shown in Table 13.1. The bitwise operators work at the binary level, testing internal memory bits. The bitwise operators are not just for systems programmers, although systems programmers find the bitwise operators invaluable. Application programmers also can improve portions of their programs by learning how to use these operators.

Table 13.1. The bitwise operators.

Operator	Meaning
&	Bitwise AND
¦	Bitwise OR
^	Bitwise exclusive OR
~	Bitwise 1's complement

The first two bitwise operators are easy to remember. The bitwise & (AND) operator is a single ampersand, whereas the && (logical AND) operator uses two ampersands. Also, the bitwise ¦ (OR) operator is a single vertical bar, whereas the ¦¦ (logical OR) operator uses two vertical bars.

Locate the bitwise exclusive OR symbol on your keyboard. It is sometimes called the *carat* or the *housetop* symbol. You should find it on the same key as the number 6 near the top of your keyboard. The bitwise 1's complement, called the *tilde,* usually appears on the key above the Tab key.

Each bitwise logical operator performs a bit-by-bit operation on internal data. Bitwise operators apply to only char, int, and long values. You cannot apply a bitwise operator to a float or double variable because the bit patterns for real numbers are more obscure and are not always implemented in the same way from computer to computer.

Just to keep the bitwise operators fresh in your mind, practice remembering them by drawing a line from the operator on the left to its matching description on the right.

Operator	Description
¦	Bitwise exclusive OR
&&	1's complement
^	AND
¦¦	Bitwise OR
&	OR
~	Bitwise AND

As Appendix B points out, binary numbers consist of 1s and 0s, and these 1s and 0s (called *bits*) are manipulated to produce the desired result for each bitwise operator. Before looking at some examples, you should understand Tables 13.2 through 13.5. They contain truth tables that describe the actions of the bitwise operators on the internal bit patterns.

Table 13.2. The bitwise & (AND) truth table.

First Bit	AND	Second Bit	Result
1	&	1	1
1	&	0	0
0	&	1	0
0	&	0	0

In bitwise truth tables, you can replace the 1 and the 0 with True and False, respectively, to understand the result better. For the & bitwise truth table, both bits being operated on with & must be True for the result to be True. In other words, "True AND True is equal to True."

Table 13.3. The bitwise ¦ (OR) truth table.

First Bit	OR	Second Bit	Result
1	¦	1	1
1	¦	0	1
0	¦	1	1
0	¦	0	0

The bitwise ¦ operator is sometimes called the *inclusive bitwise OR* operator. One or both sides of the ¦ operator must be 1 (True) for the result to be 1.

Table 13.4. The bitwise ^ (exclusive OR) truth table.

First Bit	OR	Second Bit	Result
1	^	1	0
1	^	0	1
0	^	1	1
0	^	0	0

The ^ bitwise operator is called the *exclusive bitwise OR* operator. One side of the ^ operator must be 1 (True) for the result to be 1, but both sides cannot be 1 at the same time for the result to be 1.

Table 13.5. The bitwise ~ (1's complement) truth table.

1's Complement	Bit	Result
~	1	0
~	0	1

The ~ bitwise operator, called the *bitwise 1's complement* operator, reverses each bit to its opposite value. For example, ~1 means 0 and ~0 means 1.

The bitwise 1's complement simply reverses each bit of whatever value you apply it to.

The following sections of this lesson show you some examples that should make things clearer. As mentioned at the beginning of this lesson, if you feel uncomfortable with these operators, you can wait a while before learning them because they are not as critical as the other C++ operators.

NOTE: The bitwise 1's complement does *not* negate a number. As Appendix B explains, most computers use 2's complement to negate numbers. The bitwise 1's complement reverses the bit pattern of numbers but does not add the additional 1, as the 2's complement requires.

You can test and change individual bits inside variables to check for patterns of data. If you apply the bitwise & operator to the numbers 9 and 14, you get the result of 8. Figure 13.1 shows why this is so. When the binary values of 9 (1001) and 14 (1110) are operated on with a bitwise &, the resulting bit pattern is 8 (1000).

```
1001    (9)
↓↓↓↓
&&&&
1110    (14)
= 1000  (8)
```

*Figure 13.1.
Performing the
bitwise & on two
numbers.*

In a C++ program, you could code this bitwise operation in the following way:

```
result = 9 & 14;    // Bitwise ANDs the values
                    // and saves the results
```

result now holds 8, which is the result of the bitwise &. The 9 or 14 (or both) could also be stored in variables with the same result.

What does result hold after this line of code finishes? *Hint:* Determine the bit patterns of 9 and 14 and perform the bitwise ¦ on each bit.

```
result = 9 ¦ 14;
```

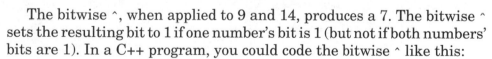

The bitwise ^, when applied to 9 and 14, produces a 7. The bitwise ^ sets the resulting bit to 1 if one number's bit is 1 (but not if both numbers' bits are 1). In a C++ program, you could code the bitwise ^ like this:

```
result = 9 ^ 14;
```

Write the result of the preceding ^ operator:

Bitwise 1's Complement

The bitwise 1's complement operator can produce some strange-looking results, depending on how your computer stores data. The bitwise ~ simply inverts each bit. ~ is a unary bitwise operator because you can apply it to only a single value at a time.

Assuming that a 9 is stored in only 4 bits, look at Figure 13.2 to see how the 1's complement converts the 9 to 6. (It is unrealistic for a 9 to be stored in only 4 bits, because most computers store integers in 2 or 4 bytes [16 to 32 bits], but this example helps show how the bitwise ^ works.)

Figure 13.2.
Performing the
bitwise 1's
complement, ~, on
the number 9.

$$\begin{array}{r} \sim \underline{1001} \quad (9) \\ = \overline{0110} \quad (6) \end{array}$$

 Table 13.6 shows how the 1's complement operator works with different lengths of data. Study the results to see how different variable types react differently to the 1's complement because they are stored in different data sizes of memory.

Table 13.6. 1's complement for different data types.

C++ Statement	Result
unsigned char uc_result = ~9;	246
signed char sc_result = ~9;	−10
unsigned int ui_result = ~9;	65526
signed int si_result = ~9;	−10
unsigned long ui_result = ~9;	4294967286
signed long si_result = ~9;	−10

 Write the results of the following bitwise operations in the space provided.

```
1 ^ 1 = _____      0 ^ 0 = _____
1 ¦ 0 = _____      0 ¦ 1 = _____
0 & 0 = _____      1 & 1 = _____
1 ^ 0 = _____         ~0 = _____
0 ¦ 0 = _____         ~1 = _____
```

192

Hint: The order of the values on each side of the bitwise operators has no bearing on the result. Therefore, `1 ^ 0` is the same as `0 ^ 1`.

What is wrong with the following statement?

```
AndIt = Test ¦ 4.564;
```

Using the Bitwise Operators

You can take advantage of the bitwise operators to perform tests on data that you could not perform as efficiently in other ways. Suppose that you want to know whether the user typed an odd or even number (assuming that the input is an integer data type). You could use the modulus operator (%) to see whether the remainder, after dividing the input value by 2, is 0 or 1. If the remainder is 0, the number is even. If the remainder is 1, the number is odd.

The bitwise operators are more efficient than other operators because bitwise operators directly compare bit patterns without using any mathematical operations. Because a number is even if its bit pattern ends in 0 and odd if its bit pattern ends in 1, you also can test for odd or even numbers by applying the bitwise & to the data and to a binary 1. This technique is more efficient than using the modulus operator. The following program tells the user whether the input value is odd or even.

```cpp
// Filename: ODDEV.CPP
// Uses a bitwise & to see whether a number is odd or even
#include <iostream.h>
void main()
{
   int input;    // Holds user's input number
   cout << "What number do you want me to test? ";
   cin >> input;

   if (input & 1)    // True if result is 1
      {              // False if result is 0
         cout << "The number " << input << " is odd\n";
      }
   else
      {
```

Lesson 13

```
            cout << "The number " << input << " is even\n";
        }
    }
}
```

Here is the program's output after the program has been run twice. The program properly checks for odd or even values with the bitwise &.

```
What number do you want me to test? 3
The number 3 is odd

What number do you want me to test? 8
The number 8 is even
```

The only difference between the bit patterns for uppercase and lowercase characters is bit number 5 (the third bit from the left, as shown in Appendix B). For lowercase letters, bit 5 is a 1. For uppercase letters, bit 5 is a 0. Figure 13.3 shows how the letters A and B differ from a and b by a single bit.

Figure 13.3. The difference between uppercase and lowercase ASCII letters.

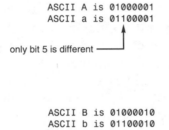

 If you are familiar with ASCII bit patterns, write the bit patterns for the letters W and w in the space below. Notice that they differ only by bit 5.

To convert an alphabetic character to uppercase, you must turn off (change to a 0) bit number 5. You can apply a bitwise & to the input character and to 223 (which is 11011111 in binary) to turn off bit 5 and convert any input character to its uppercase equivalent. If the number is already in uppercase, this bitwise & will not change it.

194

> The 223 (binary 11011111) is called a *bit mask* because it masks (just as masking tape masks areas to be painted) bit 5 so that it becomes 0 (if it isn't already).

The following program masks the bit 5 mask to convert the user's initials to uppercase if they are not already. 223 is the same as hexadecimal 0xdf.

```cpp
// Filename: UPCS1.CPP
// Converts the input characters to uppercase if
// they are not already uppercase
#include <iostream.h>

const int BITMASK = 0xdf;    // 11011111 in binary

void main()
{
   char first, middle, last;   // Will hold
                               // user's initials
   cout << "What is your first initial? ";
   cin >> first;
   cout << "What is your middle initial? ";
   cin >> middle;
   cout << "What is your last initial? ";
   cin >> last;

   // Ensures that initials are in uppercase
   first = first & BITMASK;      // Turns off bit 5
   middle = middle & BITMASK;    // if it isn't already
   last = last & BITMASK;        // turned off

   cout << "Your initials are " << first << ' '
       << middle << ' ' << last << "\n";
}
```

The following output shows what happens when two of the initials are typed with lowercase letters. The program converts them to uppercase before printing them again. Although there are other ways to convert letters to lowercase, none is as efficient as using the & bitwise operator.

```
What is your first initial? g
What is your middle initial? M
What is your last initial? p
Your initials are G M P
```

Compound Bitwise Operators

As with most of the mathematical operators, you can combine the bitwise operators with the equal sign (=) to form *compound bitwise operators*. When you want to update the value of a variable using a bitwise operator, you can shorten the expression by using the compound bitwise operators, shown in Table 13.7.

Table 13.7. The compound bitwise operators.

Operator	Result
&=	Compound bitwise AND assignment
¦=	Compound bitwise inclusive OR assignment
^=	Compound bitwise exclusive OR assignment

Write the expanded version of the three compound operators to the right of each one.

Compound	Non-Compound Equivalent
n &= a;	._____
n ¦= a;	_____
n ^= a;	_____

> **NOTE:** There is no compound 1's complement operator, such as ~=.

The preceding program that converted lowercase initials to their uppercase equivalents can be rewritten with compound bitwise & operators like this:

```
// Filename: UPCS2.CPP
// Converts the input characters to uppercase if they are
// not already uppercase by using compound operators
#include <iostream.h>
```

```
const int BITMASK = 0xdf;    // 11011111 in binary

void main()
{
    char first, middle, last;    // Will hold
                                 // user's initials
    cout << "What is your first initial? ";
    cin >> first;
    cout << "What is your middle initial? ";
    cin >> middle;
    cout << "What is your last initial? ";
    cin >> last;

    // Uses compound assignment instead of handling
    // things the way the preceding program did
    first &= BITMASK;      // Uses compound operators to
    middle &= BITMASK;     // turn off bit 5 if it isn't
    last &= BITMASK;       // already turned off

    cout << "Your initials are " << first << ' '
         << middle << ' ' << last << "\n";
}
```

Write the output of a sample run of this program.

Bitwise Shift Operators

The bitwise shift operators are shown in Table 13.8. They shift bits inside a number to the left or right. The number of bits shifted depends on the value to the right of the bitwise shift operator. The formats of the bitwise shift operators are

value << *number_of_bits*;

and

value >> *number_of_bits*;

Table 13.8. The bitwise shift operators.

Operator	Result
<<	Bitwise left shift
>>	Bitwise right shift

The *value* can be an integer, a character variable, or a literal. The *number_of_bits* determines how many bits will be shifted. Figure 13.4 shows what happens when the number 29 (binary 00011101) is left shifted 3 bits with a bitwise left shift (<<). Notice that each bit "shifts over" to the left three times, and 0s fill in from the right. If this were a bitwise right shift (>>), the 0s would fill in from the left as the rest of the bits would shift to the right three times.

Figure 13.4.
Shifting the bits in
binary 29 to the left.

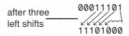

after three left shifts

00011101

11101000

C++ knows not to perform input or output when it sees the left and right bitwise shift operators. As you know, C++ also uses >> and << to perform I/O. C++ looks at the context of the operator (how it is being used) to determine the required action on the variable. The << and >> are called *overloaded operators* because they have more than one purpose.

What is the result of the following left shift? (The binary number for 40 is 00101000.) Write the bit patterns (the first 8 bits) of Result after this statement finishes.

```
Result = 40 << 2;
```

The results of bitwise shift operators are not consistent when applied to signed values. On the PC, the sign bit *propagates* with each shift. That is, for every shift position, the sign bit shifts, but the original sign is retained as well. The end result is that negative numbers fill in from the left with 1s and not with 0s when a bitwise right shift is applied to them.

The following program takes two values and shifts them 3 bits to the left and then 3 bits to the right. This program illustrates how to code the bitwise left- and right-shift operators.

```
// Filename: SHIFT1.CPP
// Demonstrates bitwise left- and right-shift operators
#include <iostream.h>
void main()
{
   int num1 = 25;    // 00011001 binary
   int num2 = 102;    // 01100110 binary
   int shift1, shift2;    // Will hold shifted numbers

   shift1 = num1 << 3;    // Bitwise left shift
   cout << "25 shifted left 3 times is " << shift1
        << "\n";
   shift2 = num2 << 3;    // Bitwise left shift
   cout << "102 shifted left 3 times is " << shift2
        << "\n";
   shift1 = num1 >> 3;    // Bitwise right shift
   cout << "25 shifted right 3 times is " << shift1
        << "\n";
   shift2 = num2 >> 3;    // Bitwise right shift
   cout << "102 shifted right 3 times is " << shift2
        << "\n";
}
```

```
25 shifted left 3 times is 200
102 shifted left 3 times is 816
25 shifted right 3 times is 3
102 shifted right 3 times is 12
```

Bitwise shifting has another useful feature. If you bitwise left shift a variable by a certain number of bit positions, the result is the same as multiplying the variable by 2^n, where n equals the number of bit positions the variable was shifted. In other words, 15 left shifted 4 times results in the same value as 15 times 2^4, or 15 times 16, which equals 240.

If you bitwise right shift a variable by a certain number of bit positions, the result is the same as dividing the variable by 2^n, where n equals the number of bit positions the variable was shifted. (Remainders get chopped off the new value.) In other words, 64 right shifted by 2 results in the same value as 64 divided by 2^2, or 64 divided by 4, which equals 16. This property is retained in signed arithmetic by the sign propagation feature mentioned earlier. For this reason, a shift right on an unsigned value often is referred to as a logical shift right, and a shift right on a signed value often is referred to as an arithmetic shift right.

If you have to multiply or divide a variable by a power of 2, you can do it much faster by simply shifting the number. In fact, this is an optimization frequently used internally by C++ compilers. The following program illustrates this:

```cpp
// Filename: SHIFT2.CPP
// Demonstrates multiplication and division
// by bitwise shifting
#include <iostream.h>
void main()
{
   signed int num1 = 15;    // Values to be shifted
   signed int num2 = -15;
   unsigned int num3 = 15;
   unsigned int num4 = 0x8000;    // Hexadecimal

   num1 = num1 << 4;    // Multiplies num1 by 16
   num2 = num2 >> 3;    // Divides num2 by 8
   num3 = num3 << 2;    // Multiplies num3 by 4
   num4 = num4 >> 1;    // Divides num4 by 2

   cout << "15 multiplied by 16 is " << num1 << "\n";
   cout << "-15 divided by 8 is (rounded) " << num2 << "\n";
   cout << "15 multiplied by 4 is " << num3 << "\n";
   cout << "0x8000 divided by 2 is 0x" << hex << num4
        << "\n";
}
```

Here is the program's output:

```
15 multiplied by 16 is 240
-15 divided by 8 is (rounded) -2
15 multiplied by 4 is 60
0x8000 divided by 2 is 0x4000
```

Compound Bitwise Shift Operators

As with most of the mathematical operators, you can combine the bitwise shift operators with the equal sign (=) to form *compound bitwise shift operators*. When you want to update the value of a variable using a bitwise shift operator, you can shorten the expression by using the compound bitwise operators, shown in Table 13.9.

Table 13.9. The compound bitwise shift operators.

Operator	Result
<<=	Compound bitwise left shift
>>=	Compound bitwise right shift

The following is the last program you saw, but its body is gone. Instead of writing out each shift operator, use the compound shift operators to perform the same shifting that the preceding program did, without using compound shift operators.

```cpp
// Filename: SHIFT2.CPP
// Demonstrates multiplication and division
// by bitwise shifting
#include <iostream.h>
void main()
{
    signed int num1 = 15;    // Values to be shifted
    signed int num2 = -15;
    unsigned int num3 = 15;
    unsigned int num4 = 0x8000;    // Hexadecimal




    cout << "15 multiplied by 16 is " << num1 << "\n";
    cout << "-15 divided by 8 is (rounded) " << num2 << "\n";
    cout << "15 multiplied by 4 is " << num3 << "\n";
    cout << "0x8000 divided by 2 is 0x" << hex << num4
    << "\n";
}
```

Review Questions

1. What are the bitwise operators? (Write each one's symbol.)

2. What is the result of each of the following bitwise True/False expressions? *Hint:* Use the operator precedence table in Appendix D.

   (a) `1 ^ 0 & 1 & 1 ¦ 0`
   (b) `1 & 1 & 1 & 1`
   (c) `1 ^ 1 ^ 1 ^ 1`
   (d) `~(1 ^ 0)`

3. TRUE or FALSE: 7 (binary 111) can be used as a bit mask to test whether the rightmost 3 bits in a variable are 1s.

4. What does the term *overloaded operator* mean?

Review Exercises

1. Write a program that converts an entered uppercase letter to a lowercase letter by applying a bit mask and one of the bitwise logical operators. If the character is already in lowercase, do not change it.

2. Write a program that asks the user for a number. Multiply that number by each power of 2, from 2^1 to 2^7, and then divide that number by each power of 2, from 2^1 to 2^7. Use shift operators, not math operators.

3. Write a program that swaps the contents of two variables without using any other variable. Use one of the bitwise operators.

C++
CLASSROOM Four

Controlling
Program Flow

Looping
with while

OBJECTIVE *To explain the concepts of loops and demonstrate the while loop.*

This lesson introduces a new feature of programming languages that will make your programs much more powerful. Computers can repeat the same set of program instructions over and over. When you write a repetitive group of statements, you are writing a *loop*. C++ offers several ways to construct a loop. This lesson introduces one such way by showing you how to use the while loop.

The repetitive capabilities of computers make them good tools for processing large amounts of information. Computers loop very fast, sometimes executing the same set of program instructions thousands of times before a single second passes. The while loops enable your programs to repeat a series of statements, over and over, as long as a certain condition is always met. Computers do not get "bored" while performing the same tasks repeatedly. This is one reason why they are so important in data processing.

After completing this lesson, you should understand the first of several methods that C++ provides for repeating sections of a program.

This lesson's discussion of loops includes one of the most important uses of looping: creating counter and total variables.

The while Loop

The while statement is one of several C++ *construct statements*. Each construct (from *construction*) is a programming language statement—or a series of statements—that controls looping. while, like other such statements, is a *looping statement* that controls the execution of a series of other statements. Looping statements cause parts of a program to execute repeatedly as long as a certain condition is being met.

The format of the while statement is

```
while (test expression)
   { block of one or more C++ statements; }
```

An example might look like this:

```
while (Count <= 10)
   { cout << "Counting is now at " << Count << "\n";
     Count++; }
```

The parentheses around *test expression* are required. As long as *test expression* is True (nonzero), the *block* of one or more C++ statements executes repeatedly until *test expression* becomes False (evaluates to zero). Braces are required before and after the body of the while loop, unless you want only one statement to execute. Each statement in the body of the while loop requires an ending semicolon.

The placeholder *test expression* usually contains relational, and possibly logical, operators. These operators provide the True-False condition checked in *test expression*. If *test expression* is False when the program reaches the while loop for the first time, the body of the while loop does not execute at all. Regardless of whether the body of the while loop executes no times, one time, or many times, the statements following the while loop's closing brace execute if *test expression* becomes False.

Because *test expression* determines when the loop finishes, the body of the while loop must change the variables used in *test expression*. Otherwise, *test expression* never changes, and the while loop repeats forever. This is known as an *infinite loop,* and you should avoid it.

Can you see why the following while loop repeats forever?

```
a = 4;
while (a <= 10)
   { Sales = a * 1.20;
     cout << "Still counting..."; }
```

The loop (the body of the while between the braces) continues forever because the a variable controls the loop, but the loop never modifies a. In other words, a is always less than or equal to 10.

TIP: If you inadvertently write an infinite loop, you must stop the program yourself. If you use a PC, this typically means pressing and holding the Ctrl key and then pressing the Break key. If you are using a UNIX-based system or a mainframe, your system administrator might have to stop your program's execution.

What is wrong with this while loop?

```
while Sales < 2500.00
   { Sales = Sales - adjustment;
     adjustment = adjustment + factor; }
```

TIP: If the body of the while loop contains only one statement, the braces surrounding it are not required. It is a good habit to enclose all while loop statements in braces, however, because if you have to add statements to the body of the while loop later, the braces are already there.

Rewrite this while loop so that it contains braces:

```
while (Sales < 2500.00)
    Sales = Sales - adjustment;
```

A regular, non-looping set of C++ statements executes only once. A loop is a set of statements that execute more than one time.

The Concept of Loops

You use the loop concept in everyday life. Whenever you have to repeat the same procedure, you are performing a loop—just as your computer does with the while statement. Suppose that you are unloading groceries. The following statements represent the looping steps (in while format) that you follow while unloading sacks of groceries:

> *while (there are still sacks of groceries)*
> *{ Get the next sack;*
> *Take groceries out of the sack;*
> *Put the cold ones in the refrigerator;*
> *Put the rest in the shelves;*
> *Put the soap and supplies in the hall pantry;*
> *Fold the sack; }*

Whether you have 3, 15, or 100 sacks of groceries to unload, you use this procedure (loop) repeatedly until every sack is put away. For an example that is more easily computerized, suppose that you want to total all the checks you wrote in the preceding month. You could perform the following loop:

> *while (there are still checks to be totaled)*
> *{ Add the amount of the next check to the total; }*

The body of this English-like while loop has only one statement, but that single statement must be performed until you have added each of the preceding month's checks. When this loop ends (when no more checks from the preceding month remain to be totaled), you have the result.

The body of a while loop can contain one or more C++ statements, including additional while loops. Your programs will be more readable if you indent the body of a while loop a few spaces to the right. The following examples illustrate this.

Because of the indented lines that make up the body of this while loop, it is easy to spot where the while begins and ends.

```
cin >> a;
cin >> b;
while (a > 5)
  { cout << "a is " << a << ", and b is " << b << "\n";
    b = 20 + a;
    a--; }
```

```
cout << "Finished.\n"
// Rest of program follows
```

Rewrite the following section of code so that its `while` loop is properly indented to make it more readable.

```
cout << "What is your first name? ";
cin >> name;
while (name[count] > 0)   // Loops until null zero reached
{count++;    // Adds 1 to the count
cout << "Still counting...";
}
cout << "Your name has " << count << " characters";
```

Some programs presented earlier in this book require user input with `cin`. If users do not enter appropriate values, these programs display an error message and ask the user to enter another value. This is an acceptable procedure.

Now that you understand the `while` loop construct, however, you should put the error message inside a loop. In this way, users see the message continually until they type proper input values, rather than once.

The following program is short, but it demonstrates a `while` loop that ensures valid keyboard input. It asks users whether or not they want to continue. You can incorporate this program into a larger one that requires user permission to continue. Put a prompt, such as the one presented here, at the bottom of a text screen. The text remains on-screen until the user tells the program to continue executing.

```
// Filename: WHIL1.CPP
// Input routine to ensure that user types a
// correct response. This routine can be part
// of a larger program.
#include <iostream.h>
void main()
{
   char ans;

   cout << "Do you want to continue (Y/N)? ";
   cin >> ans;    // Gets user's answer

   while ((ans != 'Y') && (ans != 'N'))
      { cout << "\nYou must type a Y or an N\n";      // Warns
                                                      // and asks

        cout << "Do you want to continue (Y/N)? ";  // again
        cin >> ans;
      }    // Body of while loop ends here

}
```

Notice that the two cin statements do the same thing. You must use an initial cin, outside the while loop, to provide an answer for the while loop to check. If the user types something other than Y or N, the program prints an error message, asks for another answer, then checks the new answer. This validation method is preferable to one in which the reader has only one additional chance to succeed.

The while loop tests the test expression at the top of the loop. This is why the loop might never execute. If the test is initially False, the loop does not execute even once. The output from this program is shown as follows. The program repeats indefinitely, until the relational test is True (as soon as the user types either Y or N).

```
Do you want to continue (Y/N)? k

You must type a Y or an N
Do you want to continue (Y/N)? c

You must type a Y or an N
Do you want to continue (Y/N)? s

You must type a Y or an N
Do you want to continue (Y/N)? 5
```

```
You must type a Y or an N
Do you want to continue (Y/N)? Y
```

The following program asks the user for a first name, then uses a while loop to count the number of characters in the name. This is a *string length program;* it counts characters until it reaches the null zero. Remember that the length of a string equals the number of characters in the string, not including the null zero.

```cpp
// Filename: WHIL2.CPP
// Counts the number of letters in the user's first name
#include <iostream.h>
void main()
{
    char name[15];    // Will hold user's first name
    int count = 0;    // Will hold total characters in name

    // Gets the user's first name
    cout << "What is your first name? ";
    cin >> name;

    while (name[count] > 0)   // Loops until null zero reached
        { count++; }    // Adds 1 to the count

    cout << "Your name has " << count << " characters";
}
```

The loop continues as long as the value of the next character in the name array is greater than zero. Because the last character in the array is a null zero, the test is False on the name's last character, and the statement following the body of the loop continues.

> **TIP:** If you need the length of a string that is stored inside a character array, you don't need to write your own routine to find it. C++ contains a built-in string function called strlen() that determines the length of strings.

The preceding string-length program's while loop is not as efficient as it could be. Because a while loop fails when its test expression is zero, there is no need for the greater-than test. By changing the test expression as the following program shows, you can improve the efficiency of the string length count.

```cpp
// Filename: WHIL3.CPP
// Counts the number of letters in the user's first name
#include <iostream.h>
void main()
{
   char name[15];    // Will hold user's first name
   int count = 0;    // Will hold total characters in name

   // Gets the user's first name
   cout << "What is your first name? ";
   cin >> name;

   while (name[count])    // Loops until null zero is reached
      { count++; }    // Adds 1 to the count

   cout << "Your name has " << count << " characters";
}
```

FINISH THE PROGRAM

The following section of code begins a program that prints Happy Birthday! on the screen 25 times. Finish the program so that it works.

```cpp
// Filename: HAPYWHIL.CPP
// Program that displays Happy Birthday! 25 times
#include <iostream.h>
void main()
{
   char msg[] = "Happy Birthday!\n";
   times = 0;
   while (times < 25)
```

212

The do-while Loop

Another loop, similar to the while loop, is the do-while loop. The do-while loop is like the while loop, except that the relational test occurs at the end (rather than beginning) of the loop. This ensures that the body of the loop executes at least once. The do-while tests for a *positive relational test;* as long as the test is True, the body of the loop continues to execute.

The format of the do-while is

```
do
    { block of one or more C++ statements; }
while (test expression);
```

An example might look like this:

```
do
    { cout << "Counting is now at " << Count << "\n";
      Count++; }
while (Count <= 10);
```

test expression must be enclosed in parentheses, just as it must in a while statement.

It is possible for the body of a while loop to never execute. Because the *test expression* appears at the top of the loop, if the expression is False, the program skips over the loop. Look back at the format of the do-while, though, and you will see that the body of the loop is executed once and *then* the *test expression* is evaluated. Therefore, even if the *test expression* fails, the body of the do-while loops at least once.

An earlier program in this lesson, WHIL1.CPP, shows you how to validate user input. The user enters a value, then a while loop checks to see whether the value is valid (in the example, the expected input is either a Y for Yes or an N for No). If the user does not enter a Y or an N, the while loop's body again asks the user for an answer. With a do-while loop, you can clean up the routine. Because the body of the do-while always executes at least once, you can ask for the input in the body of the loop, check it, and simply repeat the loop if the input is invalid.

 What is wrong with the following do-while?

```
do
  { cout << "Executing the do-while\n";
    a++;
  } while a < 10;
```

The following program is just like the first one you saw with the while loop (WHIL1.CPP), except that a do-while is used for the input check. Notice the placement of *test expression*. Because this expression concludes the loop, user input does not have to appear before the loop and again in the body of the loop.

```
// Filename: WHIL4.CPP
// Input routine to ensure that user types a
// correct response. This routine might be part
// of a larger program.
#include <iostream.h>
void main()
{
   char ans;

   do
    { cout << "\nYou must type a Y or an N\n";     // Warns
                                                   // and asks
      cout << "Do you want to continue (Y/N) ?";   // again
      cin >> ans; }   // Body of while loop
                      // ends here
   while ((ans != 'Y') && (ans != 'N'));
}
```

 Convert the following while loop into a do-while loop.

```
cout << "How old are you? ";
cin >> age;
while ((age <= 3) || (age >= 120))
   { cout << "You cannot be that age! Try again, please.\n";
     cout << "How old are you? ";
     cin >> age;
   }
```

if Versus the while Loop

Some beginning programmers confuse the if statement with loops. The while and do-while loops repeat a section of code multiple times, depending on the condition being tested. The if statement might or might not execute a section of code; if it does, it executes that section only once.

Use an if statement when you want to conditionally execute a section of code *once*. Use a while or do-while loop if you want to execute a section *one or more times*.

In the following if statement:

```
if (a > b)
    { cout << "Body of the if";
      b++; }
```

the body executes at most one time. If a is not greater than b, the if's body never executes. If a is greater than b, the body of the if executes once and only once. In the following while:

```
while (a > b)
    { cout << "Body of the while";
      b++; }
```

the body executes until b is finally as much as or more than a. In the following do-while:

```
do
    { cout << "Body of the do-while";
      b++; }
while (a > b);
```

the body always executes once, and maybe more times, depending on how long it takes b to equal or exceed a.

215

The `exit()` Function and the `break` Statement

C++ provides the `exit()` function as a way to leave a program early (before its natural finish). The format of `exit()` is

```
exit(status);
```

where *status* is an integer variable or a literal. If you are familiar with your operating system's return codes, *status* enables you to test the results of C++ programs. In DOS, *status* is sent to the operating system's `errorlevel` *environment variable,* where it can be tested by batch files. If you are not concerned about returning values to the operating system, just use a 1 inside the parentheses.

Often, something happens in a program that requires the program to be terminated. It might be a major problem, such as a disk drive error. Perhaps users indicate that they want to quit the program by entering a special value into `cin` that you specified. You can isolate the `exit()` function on a line by itself, or anywhere else that a C++ statement or function can appear. Typically, `exit()` is placed in the body of an `if` statement to end the program early, depending on the result of some relational test.

Always include the stdlib.h header file when you use `exit()`. This file describes to your program the operation of `exit()`. Whenever you use a function in a program, you should know its corresponding #include header file, which usually is listed in the compiler's reference manual.

Instead of exiting an entire program, however, you can use the `break` statement to exit the current loop. The format of `break` is

```
break;
```

The `break` statement can go anywhere in a C++ program that any other statement can go, but it typically appears in the body of a `while` or `do-while` loop, used to leave the loop early.

 `exit()` causes an exit from your program. `break` only causes execution of the current loop to cease.

> **NOTE:** The `break` statement exits only the most current loop. If you have a `while` loop in another `while` loop, `break` exits only the inner-most loop.

The following examples illustrate the exit() function and the break statement.

The next program shows how the exit() function works. This program looks as though it prints several messages on-screen, but it doesn't. Because exit() appears early in the code, this program quits immediately after main()'s opening brace.

```
// Filename: EXIT1.CPP
// Quits early due to exit() function
#include <iostream.h>
#include <stdlib.h>   // Required for exit()
void main()
{
   exit(0);    // Forces program to end here

   cout << "C++ programming is fun.\n";
   cout << "I like learning C++ Programming!\n";
   cout << "C++ is a powerful language that is " <<
           "not difficult to learn.";
}
```

If you were to run this program, no output would appear on your screen because exit(0) forces an early termination from the program before the first cout gets a chance to execute.

The break statement is not intended to be as strong a program exit as the exit() function. Whereas exit() ends the entire program, break quits only the loop that is currently active. In other words, break usually is placed inside a while or do-while loop to "simulate" a finished loop. The statement following the loop executes after a break occurs, but the program does not quit, as it does with exit().

The following program appears to print C++ is fun! until the user enters N to stop it. The message prints only once, however, because the break statement forces an early exit from the loop.

```
// Filename: BRK.CPP
// Demonstrates the break statement
#include <iostream.h>
void main()
{
   char user_ans;
```

```
    do
      { cout << "C++ is fun! \n";
        break;    // Causes early exit
        cout << "Do you want to see the message again (N/Y)? ";
        cin >> user_ans;
      } while (user_ans == 'Y');

    cout << "That's all for now\n";
}
```

This program always produces the following output:

```
C++ is fun!
That's all for now
```

You can tell from this program's output that the break statement does not allow the do-while loop to reach its natural conclusion, but causes it to finish early. The final cout prints because only the current loop—not the entire program—exits with the break statement.

Unlike in the preceding program, break usually appears after an if statement. This makes it a *conditional* break, which occurs only if the relational test of the if condition is True.

You can use the following program to control two other programs. This program illustrates how C++ can pass information to DOS with exit(). This is your first example of a menu program. Similar to a restaurant menu, a C++ menu program lists possible user choices. The users decide what they want the computer to do using the menu's available options.

This program returns either a 1 or a 2 to its operating system, depending on the user's selection. It is then up to the operating system to test the exit value and run the proper program.

```
// Filename: EXIT2.CPP
// Asks the user for his or her selection and returns
// that selection to the operating system with exit()
#include <iostream.h>
#include <stdlib.h>
void main()
{
    int ans;

    do
      { cout << "Do you want to:\n\n";
        cout << "\t1.  Run the word processor \n\n";
```

```
     cout << "\t2.  Run the database program \n\n";
     cout << "What is your selection? ";
     cin >> ans;
  } while ((ans != 1) && (ans != 2));   // Ensures that user
                                        // enters 1 or 2
  exit(ans);   // Returns value to operating system
}
```

Counters and Totals

Counting is important for many applications. You might need to know how many customers you have or how many people scored higher than a certain average in your class. You might want to count how many checks you wrote in the preceding month with your computerized checkbook system.

Before you develop C++ routines to count occurrences, think of how you count in your mind. If you were adding a total number of something, such as the stamps in your stamp collection or the number of wedding invitations you sent out, you probably would start at 0 and add 1 for each item being counted. When you were finished, you would have the total number (or the total count).

All you do when you count with C++ is to assign 0 to a variable and add 1 to it every time you process another data value. The increment operator (++) is especially useful for counting.

To illustrate using a counter, the following program prints Computers are fun! on-screen 10 times. You could write a program that has 10 cout statements, but that would not be efficient. It would also be too cumbersome to have 5,000 cout statements if you wanted to print that same message 5,000 times.

By adding a do-while loop and a counter that stops after a certain total is reached, you can control this printing, as the following program shows.

```
// Filename: CNT1.CPP
// Program to print a message 10 times
#include <iostream.h>
void main()
{
   int ctr = 0;   // Holds the number of times printed
```

```
do
  { cout << "Computers are fun!\n";
    ctr++;    // Adds one to the count,
              // after each cout
  } while (ctr < 10);   // Prints again if fewer
                        // than 10 times
}
```

The output of this program is shown as follows. Notice that the message prints exactly 10 times.

```
Computers are fun!
Computers are fun!
Computers are fun!
Computers are fun!
Computers are fun!
Computers are fun!
Computers are fun!
Computers are fun!
Computers are fun!
Computers are fun!
```

The heart of the counting process in this program is this increment statement:

```
ctr++;
```

You learned earlier that the increment operator adds 1 to a variable. In this program, the counter variable is incremented each time the do-while loops. Because the only operation performed on this line is the increment of ctr, the prefix increment (++ctr) produces the same results.

The preceding program not only added to the counter variable, but it also performed the loop a specific number of times. This is a common method of conditionally executing parts of a program for a fixed number of times.

The following program is a letter-guessing game. It includes a message telling users how many tries they made before guessing the correct letter. A counter counts the number of tries.

```
// Filename: GUES.CPP
// Letter-guessing game
#include <iostream.h>
void main()
{
```

```
    int tries = 0;
    char comp_ans, user_guess;

    // Saves the computer's letter
    comp_ans = 'T';    // Changes to a different
                       // letter if desired

    cout << "I am thinking of a letter...";
    do
        { cout << "What is your guess? ";
          cin >> user_guess;
          tries++;    // Adds 1 to the guess-counting variable
          if (user_guess > comp_ans)
              { cout << "Your guess was too high\n";
                cout << "\nTry again...";
              }
          if (user_guess < comp_ans)
              { cout << "Your guess was too low\n";
                cout << "\nTry again...";
              }
        } while (user_guess != comp_ans);   // Quits when a
                                            // match is found

    // The user got it right. Let him or her know.
    cout << "*** Congratulations!  You got it right! \n";
    cout << "It took you only " << tries <<
            " tries to guess.";
}
```

Here is the program's output:

```
I am thinking of a letter...What is your guess? E
Your guess was too low

Try again...What is your guess? X
Your guess was too high

Try again...What is your guess? H
Your guess was too low

Try again...What is your guess? O
Your guess was too low

Try again...What is your guess? U
Your guess was too high
```

```
Try again...What is your guess? Y
Your guess was too high

Try again...What is your guess? T
*** Congratulations!  You got it right!
It took you only 7 tries to guess.
```

Write a password-protected program. Store the password in an integer variable. The user must correctly enter the matching password in three attempts. If the user does not type the correct password in that time, the program should end. If the user types the correct password within three tries, have the program tell the user that the safe is hidden behind the picture of Mr. Duck. Passwords are used in many dial-up computer systems. The password enables a caller to try the password a fixed number of times; the program then hangs up the phone if that limit is exceeded. This helps deter people from trying hundreds of different passwords at any one sitting.

Here is the beginning of such a program. Add another `if-else` and `exit()` where needed to finish the job.

```
// Filename: PASS1.CPP
// Program to prompt for a password and
// check it against an internal one
#include <iostream.h>
#include <stdlib.h>
main()
{
   int stored_pass = 11862;
   int num_tries = 0;    // Counter for password attempts
   int user_pass;

   while (num_tries < 3)    // Loops only three times
 { cout << "What is the password (You get 3 tries...)? ";
       cin >> user_pass;
       num_tries++;    // Adds 1 to counter
```

Producing Totals

Writing a routine to add values is as easy as counting. Instead of adding 1 to the counter variable, you add a value to the total variable. For instance, if you wanted to find the total dollar amount of checks you wrote during December, you could start at nothing (0) and add the amount of every check written in December. Instead of building a count, you are building a total.

When you want C++ to add values, just initialize a total variable to zero, then add each value to the total until you have included all the values.

A counter keeps track of things by adding one to a variable counter, and a total variable keeps totals of values by adding each value to the total variable.

What value does num contain when this routing finishes?

```
num = 0;
while (num < 10)
   { num++;   }
```

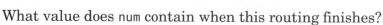

Suppose that you want to write a program that adds your grades for a class you are taking. The teacher has informed you that you earn an A if you can accumulate more than 450 points. The following program keeps asking you for values until you type −1. The −1 is a signal that you are finished entering grades and want to see the total. This program also prints a congratulatory message if you have enough points for an A.

```cpp
// Filename: GRAD.CPP
// Adds grades and determines whether you earned an A
#include <iostream.h>
#include <iomanip.h>
void main()
{
   float total_grade = 0.0;
   float grade;    // Holds individual grades

   do
   { cout << "What is your grade? (-1 to end) ";
     cin >> grade;
     if (grade >= 0.0)
      { total_grade += grade; }   // Adds to total
   } while (grade >= 0.0);   // Quits when -1 is entered
   cout.setf(ios::fixed);

   // Control begins here if no more grades
   cout << "\n\nYou made a total of " << setprecision(1) <<
           total_grade << " points\n";
   if (total_grade >= 450.00)
      { cout << "** You made an A!!"; }
}
```

Notice that the -1 response is not added to the total number of points. This program checks for the -1 before adding to total_grade. Here is the program's output:

```
What is your grade? (-1 to end) 87.6
What is your grade? (-1 to end) 92.4
What is your grade? (-1 to end) 78.7
What is your grade? (-1 to end) -1

You made a total of  258.7 points
```

 Write a program that extends the grade-calculating program. Your version should not only total the points, but also compute the average of the grades entered by the user. *Hint:* You need a counter to record the number of grades entered and a total variable to record the total. You then have enough for an average.

Review Questions

1. What is the difference between the while loop and the do-while loop?

2. What is the difference between a total variable and a counter variable?

3. What is the difference between an if and a while loop?

4. Which C++ operator is most useful for counting?

5. TRUE or FALSE: Braces are not required around the body of while and do-while loops.

6. What is wrong with the following code?

```
while (sales > 50)
    cout << "Your sales are very good this month.\n";
    cout << "You will get a bonus for your high sales\n";
```

7. What file must you include as a header file if you use exit()?

8. How many times does this cout print?

```
int a = 0;
do
    { cout << "Careful \n";
      a++; }
while (a > 5);
```

9. How can you inform DOS of the program exit status?

10. What is printed to the screen in the following section of code?

```
a = 1;
while (a < 4)
    { cout << "This is the outer loop\n";
      a++;
      while (a <= 25)
          { break;
            cout << "This prints 25 times\n"; }
    }
```

225

11. Which is considered to be the stronger terminating statement, `exit()` or `break`?

Review Exercises

1. Write a program with a `do-while` loop that prints the numerals from 10 to 20 (inclusive), with a blank line between each number.

2. Write a weather-calculator program that asks for a list of the previous 10 days' temperatures, computes the average, and prints the results. You have to compute the total as the input occurs, then divide that total by 10 to find the average. Use a `while` loop for the 10 repetitions.

3. Rewrite the program in Exercise 2 using a `do-while` loop.

4. Write a program similar to the weather calculator in Exercise 2, but generalize it so that it computes the average of any number of days' temperatures. (*Hint:* You must count the number of temperatures to compute the final average.)

The for Loop

OBJECTIVE

To explain and demonstrate the for loop.

This lesson extends the concept of a loop even further than Lesson 14, "Looping with while," did. You will learn about the for statement, which offers more control over looping than while and do-while do. Although you can use any of the loop statements—for, while, and do-while—to write almost any type of loop, sometimes one works better than another. The while and do-while loops work well when the data or user input eventually triggers a False condition. The for loop is best when you know ahead of time exactly how many iterations the loop must make.

The for loop enables you to repeat sections of your program a specific number of times. Unlike the while and do-while loops, the for loop is a *determinate loop*. This means that when you write your program, you usually can determine how many times the loop executes. Although the while and do-while loops repeat only until a condition is met, the for loop continues looping until a count (or a countdown) is reached.

The for loop is a helpful way of looping through a section of code when you want to total specified amounts, but it does not replace the while and do-while loops in every situation.

The for Statement

The for statement encloses one or more C++ statements that form the body of the loop. The statements in the loop repeat continuously for a specified number of times. As the programmer, you control the number of loop repetitions by specifying the iterations inside the for statement.

> **TIP:** If you have ever programmed in another programming language, the for statement might be familiar to you. Both BASIC and Pascal have a similar FOR statement. COBOL uses PERFORM, and FORTRAN uses do to perform the same function as the C++ for loop.

The format of the for loop is

```
for (start expression; test expression; count expression)
   { block of one or more C++ statements; }
```

For example, here is a for loop:

```
for (i = 0; i < 10; i++)
   { cout << "i is " << i << "\n"; }
```

C++ evaluates the *start expression* before the loop begins. Typically, the *start expression* is an assignment statement (such as i = 1;), but it can be any legal expression that you specify. C++ evaluates *start expression* only once, at the beginning of the loop.

> **NOTE:** Do not put a semicolon after the right parenthesis. If you do, the for loop interprets the body of the loop as zero statements long! It would continue looping—doing *nothing* each time—until the *test expression* became False.

Every time the body of the loop repeats, the *count expression* executes, usually incrementing or decrementing a variable. The *test expression* evaluates to True (nonzero) or False (zero), then determines whether the body of the loop repeats again.

> **TIP:** If only one C++ statement resides in the for loop's body, braces are not required, but they are recommended. If you add more statements, the braces are there already, reminding you that they are now needed.

You use the concept of for loops in your day-to-day life. Whenever you have to repeat a certain procedure a specified number of times, that repetition becomes a good candidate for a computerized for loop. To illustrate the concept of a for loop further, suppose that you are sitting at your kitchen table paying bills. You must do the following steps for each bill:

1. Verify the payment amount.

2. Write a check.

3. Enclose the check and bill in the payment envelope.

4. Put a stamp and a return address on the envelope.

You must perform each of these four steps exactly 10 times if you have 10 bills. After 10 times, you don't pay another bill (until the next month) because the job is finished. You are looping through a procedure that has several steps (the block of the loop). These steps are the body of the loop. It is not an endless loop because there is a fixed number of bills to pay. You run out of bills only after you pay all 10.

Notice how the sentence before these steps ended: *for each bill*. This signals an idea similar to the for loop construct.

> **NOTE:** The for loop tests the *test expression* at the top of the loop. If the *test expression* is False when the for loop begins, the body of the loop never executes.

Any loop construct can be written with a for loop, a while loop, or a do-while loop. Generally, you use the for loop when you want to count or loop a specific number of times, and you reserve the while and do-while loops for looping until a False condition is met.

To give you a glimpse of the for loop's capabilities, here are two programs—one that uses a for loop and one that does not. The first one is a counting program. Before studying its contents, look at the output. The results illustrate the for loop concept very well.

The program with a for loop follows:

```
// Filename: FOR1.CPP
// Introduces the for loop
#include <iostream.h>
void main()
{
```

```
    int ctr;
    for (ctr = 1; ctr <= 10; ctr++)    // Starts ctr at one
                                       // Increments through loop
      { cout << ctr << "\n"; }    // Body of for loop
}
```

Here is the program's output:

```
1
2
3
4
5
6
7
8
9
10
```

Here is the same program using a do-while loop:

```
// Filename: WHIFOR.CPP
// Simulating a for loop with a do-while loop
#include <iostream.h>
void main()
{
    int ctr = 1;
    do
      { cout << ctr << "\n";    // Body of do-while loop
        ctr++; }
    while (ctr <= 10);
}
```

Notice that the for loop is a cleaner way of controlling the looping process. The for loop does several things that require extra statements in a while loop. With for loops, you do not have to write extra code to initialize variables and increment or decrement them. You can see at a glance (in the expressions in the for statement) exactly how the loop executes, unlike with the do-while, which forces you to look at the *bottom* of the loop to see how the loop stops.

 See whether you can determine the output of the following program. To give you a hint, the same program using a do-while loop appears next. As soon as you understand for loops, you will see that they are easier to understand than while loops because they require less code: the three expressions inside the `for` loop do the work of several statements within `do-while`. Write the one-line output in the space provided below the `do-while` version of the program.

This program has a `for` loop:

```cpp
// Filename: FOR2.CPP
// Demonstrates totaling using a for loop
#include <iostream.h>
void main()
{
   int total, ctr;

   total = 0;    // Holds a total of 5 to 10

   for (ctr = 5; ctr <= 10; ctr++)    // ctr is 5, 6,
                                       // 7, 8, 9, 10
     { total += ctr; }    // Adds value of ctr to each iteration

   cout << "The total is " << total << "\n";
}
```

The same program without a `for` loop follows:

```cpp
// Filename: WHIFOR2.CPP
// A totaling program using a do-while loop
#include <iostream.h>
void main()
{
   int total = 0;    // Initializes total
   int num = 5;

   do
     {  total += num;    // Adds num to total
        num++;    // Increments counter
     } while (num <= 10);
   cout << "The total is " << total << "\n";;
}
```

Write the output of both programs here (the output is the same for both programs).

The body of the loop in both programs executes six times. The starting value is 0, not 1 as in the previous examples. Notice that the for loop is less complex than the do-while because the initialization, testing, and incrementing are performed in the single for statement.

Notice how the body of the for loop is indented. This is a good habit to develop, because indenting makes it easier to see the beginning and the end of the loop's body.

Isn't this easier to read:

```
for (ctr = 1; ctr <= 5; ctr++)
  { cout << "What is the next child's name? ";
    cin >> child;
    cout << "What is the child's age? ";
    cin >> age;
    if (age >= 7)
      { cout << "\n" << child << " has Mr.   "
             << "Anderson for a teacher\n"; }
  }    // Quits after five times
```

than this?

```
for (ctr = 1; ctr <= 5; ctr++)
{ cout << "What is the next child's name? ";
cin >> child;
cout << "What is the child's age? ";
cin >> age;
if (age >= 7)
{ cout << "\n" << child << " has Mr.   "
<< "Anderson for a teacher\n"; }
}    // Quits after five times
```

As the preceding section of code shows, the body of the for loop can have more than one statement. The following example requests five pairs of data values: children's first names and their ages. It prints the teacher assigned to each child, based on the child's age. This illustrates a for loop with cout functions, a cin function, and an if statement in its body. Because exactly five children are checked, the for loop ensures that the program ends after the fifth child.

```
// Filename: FOR3.CPP
// Program that uses a loop to input and print
// the teacher assigned to each child
#include <iostream.h>
void main()
{
    char child[25];   // Holds child's first name
    int age;    // Holds child's age
    int ctr;    // The for loop counter variable

    for (ctr = 1; ctr <= 5; ctr++)
      { cout << "What is the next child's name? ";
        cin >> child;
        cout << "What is the child's age? ";
        cin >> age;
        if (age <= 5)
            { cout << "\n" << child << " has Mrs. "
                   << "Jones for a teacher\n\n"; }
        if (age == 6)
            { cout << "\n" << child << " has Miss "
                   << "Smith for a teacher\n\n"; }
        if (age >= 7)
            { cout << "\n" << child << " has Mr. "
                   << "Anderson for a teacher\n\n"; }
      }    // Quits after five times
}
```

The following is this program's output. You can improve this program even more after learning about the switch statement in Lesson 17, "Controlling with switch."

```
What is the next child's name? Joe
What is the child's age? 5

Joe has Mrs. Jones for a teacher

What is the next child's name? Larry
What is the child's age? 6

Larry has Miss Smith for a teacher

What is the next child's name? Julie
What is the child's age? 9
```

```
Julie has Mr. Anderson for a teacher

What is the next child's name? Manny
What is the child's age? 6

Manny has Miss Smith for a teacher

What is the next child's name? Lori
What is the child's age? 5

Lori has Mrs. Jones for a teacher
```

The previous programs used an increment as the *count expression*. You can make the for loop increment the loop variable by any value. It does not have to increment by 1.

The following program prints the even numbers from 1 to 20, then it prints the odd numbers from 1 to 20. To do this, 2 is added to the counter variable (rather than 1 as in the previous programs) each time the loop executes.

```cpp
// Filename: EVOD.CPP
// Prints the even numbers from 1 to 20,
// then the odd numbers from 1 to 20
#include <iostream.h>
void main()
{
   int num;   // The for loop variable

   cout << "Even numbers below 21\n";   // Title
   for (num = 2; num <= 20; num += 2)
     { cout << num << " "; }   // Prints every other number

   cout << "\nOdd numbers below 20\n";   // A second title
   for (num = 1; num <= 20; num += 2)
     { cout << num << " "; }   // Prints every other number

}
```

There are two loops in this program. The body of each one consists of a single cout statement. In the first half of the program, the loop variable, num, is 2 and not 1. If it were 1, the number 1 would print first, as it does in the odd number section.

The two cout statements that print the titles are not part of either loop. If they were, the program would print a title before each number. The following shows the result of running this program:

```
Even numbers below 21
2 4 6 8 10 12 14 16 18 20
Odd numbers below 20
1 3 5 7 9 11 13 15 17 19
```

You can decrement the loop variable as well. If you do, the value is subtracted from the loop variable each time through the loop. The following example is a rewrite of the counting program. It produces the reverse effect by showing a countdown. Write the output of the program in the spaces following the code.

```cpp
// Filename: CNTD1.CPP
// Countdown to the liftoff
#include <iostream.h>
void main()
{
   int ctr;

   for (ctr = 10; ctr != 0; ctr--)
     { cout << ctr << "\n"; }   // Prints ctr as it
                                // counts down
   cout << "*** Blast off! ***\n";
}
```

Hint: When you are decrementing a loop variable, the initial value should be larger than the end value being tested. In this example, the loop variable, ctr, counts down from 10 to 1. Each time through the loop (each iteration), ctr is decremented by one.

This `for` loop test

```
for (ctr = 10; ctr != 0; ctr--)
    { cout << ctr << "\n"; }
```

illustrates a redundancy that you can eliminate, thanks to C++. The test expression `ctr != 0;` tells the `for` loop to continue looping until `ctr` is not equal to zero. However, if `ctr` becomes zero (a False value), there is no reason to add the additional `!= 0` (except for clarity). You can rewrite the `for` loop as

```
for (ctr = 10; ctr; ctr--)
```

without loss of meaning. This is more efficient and such an integral part of C++ that you should become comfortable with it. There will be little loss of clarity as soon as you adjust to it.

Another for Test

You also can make a `for` loop test for something other than a literal value. The following program combines much of what you have learned so far. It asks for student grades and computes an average. Because there might be a different number of students each semester, the program first asks the user for the number of students. Next, the program iterates until the user enters an equal number of scores. It then computes the average based on the total and the number of student grades entered.

```
// Filename: FORTST.CPP
// Computes a grade average with a for loop
#include <iostream.h>
#include <iomanip.h>
void main()
{
    float grade, avg;
    float total = 0.0;
    int num;   // Total number of grades
    int loopvar;   // Used to control the for loop
```

```
cout << "\n*** Grade Calculation ***\n\n";    // Title
cout << "How many students are there? ";
cin >> num;    // Gets total number to enter

for (loopvar = 1; loopvar <= num; loopvar++)
   { cout << "\nWhat is the next student's grade? ";
     cin >> grade;
     total += grade;  }   // Keeps a running total

avg = total / num;
cout << "\n\nThe average of this class is " <<
        setprecision(1) << avg;
}
```

Due to the for loop, the total and the average calculations do not have to be changed if the number of students changes.

Because characters and integers are so closely associated in C++, you can increment character variables in a for loop. Finish this program by making it print the letters A through Z with a simple for loop.

```
// Filename: FORALPH.CPP
// Prints the alphabet with a simple for loop
#include <iostream.h>
void main()
{
   char letter;
   cout << "Here is the alphabet:\n";
```

A `for` expression can be a blank (called a *null expression*). In the following `for` loop, all the expressions are blank:

```
for (;;)
   { cout << "Over and over..."; }
```

This `for` loop iterates forever. Although you should avoid infinite loops, your program might dictate that you make a `for` loop expression blank. If you already initialized the *start expression* earlier in the program, you are wasting computer time repeating it in the `for` loop—and C++ does not require it.

> **TIP:** Some programmers do put infinite loops in their programs using the empty `for` statement, but they make sure that there is a `break` statement (usually part of an `if`) to break out of the `for` loop eventually. You will read more about using `break` with `for` in Lesson 16, "More About Loops."

The following program omits the *start expression* and the *count expression,* leaving only the `for` loop's *test expression*. Sometimes you have to omit one or both expressions. If you use a `for` loop without two of its expressions, consider replacing it with a `while` loop or a `do-while` loop. Write the output of the program in the spaces provided to make sure that you understand the loop.

```
// Filename: FORFIV.CPP
// Uses only the test expression in
// the for loop to count by fives
#include <iostream.h>
void main()
{
   int num = 5;   // Starting value

   cout << "\nCounting by 5s: \n";   // Title
   for (; num <= 100;)   // Contains only the test expression
     { cout << num << " ";
       num += 5;   // Increments expression outside the loop
     }   // End of the loop's body
}
```

Nested for Loops

Any C++ statement can go inside the body of a for loop—even another for loop! When you put a loop in a loop, you are creating a *nested loop*. The clock in a sporting event works like a nested loop. You might think that this is stretching the analogy a bit far, but it really works. A football game counts down from 15 minutes to 0. It does this four times. The first countdown loops from 15 to 0 (for each minute). That countdown is nested in another that loops from 1 to 4 (for each of the four quarters).

If your program has to repeat a loop more than once, it is a good candidate for a nested loop. Figure 15.1 shows two outlines of nested loops. You can think of the inside loop as looping "faster" than the outside loop. In the first example, the inside for loop counts from 1 to 10 before the outside loop (the variable out) can finish its first iteration. When the outside loop finally iterates a second time, the inside loop starts over.

The second nested loop outline shows two loops in an outside loop. Both of these loops execute in their entirety before the outside loop finishes its first iteration. When the outside loop starts its second iteration, the two inside loops repeat.

Notice the order of the braces in each example of Figure 15.1. The inside loop *always* finishes; therefore, its ending brace must come before the outside loop's ending brace. Indention makes this much clearer, because you can align the braces of each loop.

```
for (out=1; out<=100; out++)
   {
     for (in=1; in<=10; in++)
        {
          // Body of inside loop
        }
   }


for (out=1; out<=100; out++)
   {
     for (in=1; in<=5; in++)
        {
          // Body of first inside loop
        }

     for (in=1; in<=10; in++)
        {
          // Body of second inside loop
        }
   }
```

inside loop — outside loop

first inner loop

second inner loop

outside loop

Figure 15.1.
Outlines of two
nested loops.

In nested loops, the inside loop or loops execute completely before the outside loop's next iteration. That is why programmers say that the inner loop always loops *fastest:* the inner loop must cycle through its every iteration before the outer loop's first iteration finishes. When the second iteration of the outer loop begins, the inner loop must start over again, looping through all its cycles, before the outer loop finishes.

The following program contains a loop in a loop—a nested loop. The inside loop counts and prints from 1 to 5. The outside loop counts from 1 to 3. The inside loop repeats, in its entirety, three times. In other words, this program prints the values 1 to 5 and does so three times.

```cpp
// Filename: NEST1.CPP
// Prints the numbers 1-5 three times
// using a nested loop
#include <iostream.h>
void main()
{
   int times, num;    // Outer and inner for loop variables

   for (times = 1; times <= 3; times++)
   {
      for (num = 1; num <= 5; num++)
         { cout << num << " "; }    // Inner loop body
      cout << "\n";
   }    // End of outer loop
}
```

The indention follows the standard of `for` loops: every statement in each loop is indented a few spaces. Because the inside loop is already indented, its body is indented another few spaces. The program's output follows:

```
1 2 3 4 5
1 2 3 4 5
1 2 3 4 5
```

The outside loop's counter variable changes each time through the loop. If one of the inside loop's control variables is the outside loop's counter variable, you see effects such as those shown in the following program.

```cpp
// Filename: NEST2.CPP
// An inside loop controlled by the outer loop's
// counter variable
```

240

```
#include <iostream.h>
void main()
{
    int outer, inner;

    for (outer = 5; outer >= 1; outer--)
      { for (inner = 1; inner <= outer; inner++)
           { cout << inner; }    // End of inner loop
      cout << "\n";
      }
}
```

The output of this program follows. The inside loop repeats five times (as outer counts down from 5 to 1) and prints from five numbers to one number.

```
12345
1234
123
12
1
```

Fill in the following table by tracing the two variables outer and inner through the preceding program. Sometimes you have to "play computer" when learning a new concept such as nested loops. By executing a line at a time and writing down each variable's contents, you create this table. The first few values are given to get you started.

The outer variable	*The* inner variable
5	1
5	2
5	3
5	4
5	5
4	1

Which variable controls the inner loop and which variable controls the outer loop in the next for loop?

```
for (ctr1 = 10; ctr1 > 5; ctr1—)
   {  for (ctr2 = 1; ctr2 < 4; ctr2++)
        { cout << ctr1 << " " << ctr2 <<   " "; }
   cout << "\n";
   }
```

Answer: _____

Write the output for this loop in the spaces provided:

TIP (for mathematicians): The for statement is identical to the mathematical summation symbol. When you need to write programs to simulate the summation symbol, the for statement is an excellent candidate. A nested for statement is good for double summations.

For example, the following summation

$$\sum_{i=1}^{30} (i / 3 * 2)$$

can be rewritten as

```
total = 0;
for (i = 1; i <= 30; i++)
   { total += (i / 3 * 2); }
```

Here is one last example to show you how nested for loops work. A factorial is a mathematical number used in probability theory and statistics. A factorial of a number is the multiplied product of every number from 1 to the number in question.

For example, the factorial of 4 is 24 because 4 * 3 * 2 * 1 = 24. The factorial of 6 is 720 because 6 * 5 * 4 * 3 * 2 * 1 = 720. The factorials of both 0 and 1 are 1 by definition.

Nested loops are good candidates for writing a factorial number-generating program. The following program asks the user for a number, then prints the factorial of that number.

```
// Filename: FACT.CPP
// Computes the factorial of numbers through
// the user's number
#include <iostream.h>
void main()
{
   int outer, num, fact, total;

   cout << "What factorial do you want to see? ";
   cin >> num;

   for (outer = 1; outer <= num; outer++)
     { total = 1;   // Initializes total for each factorial
       for (fact = 1; fact <= outer; fact++)
         { total *= fact; }   // Computes each factorial
     }

   cout << "The factorial for " << num << " is "
       << total;
}
```

The following shows the factorial of 7. You can run this program, entering different values when asked, and see various factorials. Be careful: factorials multiply quickly. (A factorial of 11 won't fit in an integer variable.)

```
What factorial do you want to see? 7
The factorial for 7 is 5040
```

Review Questions

1. What is a loop?

2. TRUE or FALSE: The body of a `for` loop contains at most one statement.

3. What is a nested loop?

4. Why might you want to leave one or more expressions out of the `for` statement's parentheses?

5. Which loop "loops" faster, the inner loop or the outer loop?

6. What is the output of the following program?

   ```
   for (ctr = 10; ctr >= 1; ctr -= 3)
      { cout << ctr << "\n"; }
   ```

7. TRUE or FALSE: A `for` loop is better to use than a `while` loop when you know in advance exactly how many iterations a loop requires.

8. What happens when the *test expression* becomes False in a `for` statement?

9. TRUE or FALSE: The following program contains a valid nested loop.

   ```
   for (i = 1; i <= 10; i++);
      { for (j = 1; j <= 5; j++)
           { cout << i << j; }
      }
   ```

10. What is the output of the following section of code?

    ```
    i = 1;
    start = 1;
    end = 5;
    step = 1;
    ```

```
for (; start >= end;)
   { cout << i << "\n";
     start += step;
     end--;}
```

Review Exercises

1. Write a program that prints the numerals 1 to 15 on-screen. Use a for loop to control the printing.

2. Write a program that prints the numerals 15 to 1 on-screen. Use a for loop to control the printing.

3. Write a program that uses a for loop to print every odd number from 1 to 100.

4. Write a program that asks the user for her or his age. Use a for loop to print Happy Birthday! for every year of the user's age.

5. Using the ASCII table numbers, write a program to print the following output, using a nested for loop. (*Hint:* The outside loop should loop from 1 to 5, and the inside loop's start variable should be 65, the value of ASCII "A.")

```
A
AB
ABC
ABCD
ABCDE
```

More About Loops

OBJECTIVE

To teach you more applications of loops and to teach you how break and continue extend the power of for loops.

Now that you have mastered the loop statements of C++, it is time to refine your knowledge of loop control. This lesson shows one application of loops, called *timing loops,* that pauses your program temporarily so that users have time to read error messages before you clear them off the screen. Timing loops are also important when writing game applications. Because of the many differences in computer speeds, it is not always possible to use timing loops, but you should learn how to program them so that you'll be able to use them when the need arises.

The break and continue statements both extend the power of for loops by giving you additional control over the way for works. There are times when you need a for loop but certain actions require an early exit from the loop. Also, there are times when you do not want to finish each iteration of a for you have set up. After this lesson, you will be able to integrate the for loop with break and continue.

Timing Loops

Computers are fast, and at times you probably would like them to be even faster. Sometimes, however, you want to slow down the computer. Often, you have to slow the execution of games because the computer's speed makes the game unplayable. Messages that appear on-screen many times clear too fast for the user to read if you don't delay them.

A nested loop is the perfect place for a *timing loop,* which simply cycles through a `for` or `while` loop many times. The larger the end value of the `for` loop, the longer the loop repeats.

A nested loop is appropriate for displaying error messages to your user. If the user requests a report, but has not entered enough data for your program to print the report, you might print a warning message on-screen for a few seconds, telling the user that you cannot yet produce the report. After displaying the message for a few seconds, you can clear the message and give the user another chance. Timing loops make the computer wait.

 Circle the number of the following application that would be appropriate for a timing loop.

1. Writing a real-time simulation of airplane take-offs.

2. Calculating your checkbook balance.

3. Beeping the computer for three seconds.

Different computers run at different speeds. There is no way to determine how many iterations a timing loop takes for one second (or minute or hour) of delay because computers run at different speeds. You therefore have to adjust your timing loop's end value to set the delay to your liking.

Timing loops are easy to write. You simply put an empty `for` loop inside the program. The following program is a rewritten version of the countdown program (CNTD1.CPP) you saw in Lesson 15, "The `for` Loop." Each number in the countdown is delayed so that the countdown does not seem to take place instantly.

```
// Filename: CNTD2.CPP
// Countdown to the lift-off with a delay
#include <iostream.h>
```

```
void main()
{
   int cd, delay;

   for (cd = 10; cd >= 0; cd--)
   { for (delay = 1; delay <= 30000; delay++);   // Delays
                                                 // program
     cout << cd << "\n";   // Prints countdown value
   }   // End of outer loop
   cout << "Blast off!!! \n";
}
```

Change the number of times the outer loop executes by increasing the initial value of the cd variable. Instead of 10, make it 20 or 30 or even 100. By changing the outer loop, you cause the inner loop, which loops 30,000 times for each of the outer loop's iterations.

The following program asks users for their ages. If a user enters an age less than 0, the program beeps (by printing \a, the alarm character), then displays an error message for a few seconds by using a nested timing loop. Because an integer does not hold a large enough value (on many computers) for a long timing loop, you must use a nested timing loop. (Depending on the speed of your computer, increase or decrease the numbers in the loop to display the message for a longer or shorter duration.)

> **NOTE:** The following program uses a rarely seen control character, \r, inside the loop. As you might recall from Lesson 6, "Characters, Strings, and Character Arrays," \r is a carriage-return character. This conversion character moves the cursor to the beginning of the current line, enabling the program to print blanks on that same line. This process overwrites the error message, so it appears as though the error disappears from the screen after a brief pause.

```
// Filename: TIM.CPP
// Displays an error message for a few seconds
#include <iostream.h>
void main()
{
   int outer, inner, age;

   cout << "What is your age? ";
```

```
    cin >> age;

    while (age <= 0)
      { cout << "*** Your age cannot be that small! ***";
        // Timing loop here
        for (outer = 1; outer <= 30000; outer++)
           { for (inner = 1; inner <= 500; inner++); }
        // Erases the message
        cout << "\r                                    \n\n";
        cout << "What is your age? ";
        cin >> age;   // Asks again
      }

    cout << "\n\nThanks, I did not think you ";
    cout << "would actually tell me your age!";
}
```

> Notice in the preceding program that the inside loop has a semicolon (;) after the for statement—with no loop body. There is no need for a loop body here because the computer is only cycling though the loop to waste some time.

Rewrite the preceding program (TIM.CPP) so that it uses a do-while loop instead of a while loop. By using a do-while, you do not have to ask the user twice for his or her age, but you have to add an if statement to the body of the do-while.

The break and for Statements

The for loop was designed to execute a specified number of times. On rare occasions, you might want the for loop to quit before the counting variable has reached its final value. As with while loops, you use the break statement to quit a for loop early.

The break statement is nested in the body of the for loop. Programmers rarely put break on a line by itself, and it almost always comes after an if test. If the break were on a line by itself, the loop would always quit early, defeating the purpose of the for loop.

How many times does each of these three loops loop?

```
for (ct = 0; ct <= 10; ct++)
  { cout << ct << "\n";
    break;}
```

```
for (ct = 1; ct <= 11; ct++)
  { cout << ct << "\n";
    break; }
```

```
for (ct = 1; ct <= 1000; ct++)
  { cout << ct << "\n";
    break; }
```

The following program shows what can happen when C++ encounters an *unconditional* break statement (one not preceded by an if statement).

```
// Filename: BRAK1.CPP
// A for loop defeated by the break statement
#include <iostream.h>
void main()
{
   int num;

   cout << "Here are the numbers from 1 to 20\n";
   for(num = 1; num <= 20; num++)
     { cout << num << "\n";
       break;  }   // This line exits the for loop immediately

   cout << "That's all, folks!";
}
```

The following shows the result of running this program. Notice that break immediately terminates the for loop. The for loop might as well not be in this program.

```
Here are the numbers from 1 to 20
1
That's all, folks!
```

251

Finish the following program so that it improves on the last one. It should ask the users if they want to see another number. If they do, make the for loop continue its next iteration. If they don't, put a break statement in the loop to terminate the for loop.

```cpp
// Filename: BRAK2.CPP
// A for loop running at the user's request
#include <iostream.h>
void main()
{
    int num;    // Loop counter variable

    char ans;
    cout << "Here are the numbers from 1 to 20\n";
    for (num = 1; num <= 20; num++)
      { cout << num << "\n";

        cout << "Do you want to see another (Y/N)? ";
        cin >> ans;
        if ((ans == 'N') || (ans == 'n'))
```

If you nest one loop inside another, the break terminates the "most active" loop (the innermost loop in which the break statement resides).

You can use the *conditional* break (an if statement followed by a break) when you are missing data. For example, when you process data files or large amounts of user data entry, you might expect 100 input numbers and receive only 95. You can use a break to terminate the for loop before it iterates the 96th time.

Suppose that a teacher wrote a grade-averaging program for her students' scores. For the program to be useful each semester, the program should ask the teacher how many grades there are to average, then loop that many times, asking for each of the students' grades. Suppose that she typed 16, but it turned out that only 14 took the test that day. A regular for loop would loop 16 times, no matter how many students there are, because it relies on the teacher's original student count.

The following grade-averaging program is sophisticated in that it asks the teacher for the total number of students, but if the teacher wants to, she can enter –99 as a student's score. The –99 is not averaged; it is used as a trigger value to break out of the for loop before its normal conclusion.

```cpp
// Filename: BRAK3.CPP
// Computes a grade average with a for loop,
// enabling an early exit with a break statement
#include <iostream.h>
#include <iomanip.h>
void main()
{
    float grade, avg;
    float total = 0.0;
    int num, count = 0;    // Total number of grades and counter
    int loopvar;    // Used to control for loop

    cout << "\n*** Grade Calculation ***\n\n";    // Title
    cout << "How many students are there? ";
    cin >> num;    // Gets total number to enter

    for (loopvar = 1; loopvar <= num; loopvar++)
       { cout << "\nWhat is the next student's " <<
                  "grade? (-99 to quit) ";
         cin >> grade;
         if (grade < 0.0)    // A negative number
                            // triggers break
           { break; }    // Leaves the loop early
         count++;
         total += grade;  }    // Keeps a running total
    cout.setf(ios::fixed);
    avg = total / count;
    cout << "\n\nThe average of this class is "<<
          setprecision(1) << avg;
}
```

Here is the program's output:

```
*** Grade Calculation ***

How many students are there? 10

What is the next student's grade? (-99 to quit) 87

What is the next student's grade? (-99 to quit) 97

What is the next student's grade? (-99 to quit) 67

What is the next student's grade? (-99 to quit) 89

What is the next student's grade? (-99 to quit) 94

What is the next student's grade? (-99 to quit) -99


The average of this class is 86.8
```

Notice that grade is tested for less than 0.0, not for −99.0. You cannot reliably use floating-point values to compare for equality (due to their bit-level representations). Because no grade is negative, *any* negative number triggers the break statement.

Write a program that totals the number of checks per month. Because the user typically writes 10 checks each month, set up the for loop to loop 10 times. However, give the user an early exit from the loop (such as entering -1.0 for an amount) in case there are fewer checks in a certain month.

The continue Statement

The break statement exits a loop early, but the continue statement forces the computer to perform another iteration of the loop. If you put a continue statement in the body of a for or a while loop, the computer ignores any statement in the loop that follows continue.

The format of continue is

```
continue;
```

You use the `continue` statement when data in the body of the loop is incorrect, out of bounds, or unexpected. Instead of acting on the incorrect data, you might want to go back to the top of the loop and try another data value. The following examples help illustrate the use of the `continue` statement.

TIP: The `continue` statement forces a new iteration of any of the three loop constructs—the `for` loop, the `while` loop, and the `do-while` loop. The loop will end when the test expression becomes false.

Figure 16.1 shows the difference between the `break` and `continue` statements.

```
for (i=0; i<=10; i++)
   {
      break; ────────────────────────────    break terminates
      cout << "Loop it \n"; // Never prints    loop immediately

for (i=0; i<=10; i++) ◄──────
   {
      cout << "Getting ready...\n";          continue causes loop to
      continue; ────────────────             perform another iteration
      cout << "Loop again \n"; // Never prints
   }
```

*Figure 16.1.
The difference
between* `break` *and*
`continue`.

How many times does each of these three loops loop?

```
for (ct = 0; ct <= 10; ct++)
   { cout << ct << "\n";
     continue;}
```

```
for (ct = 1; ct <= 11; ct++)
   { cout << ct << "\n";
     continue; }
```

```
for (ct = 1; ct <= 1000; ct++)
   { cout << ct << "\n";
     continue; }
```

Although the following program seems to print the numbers 1 through 10, each followed by "C++ Programming," it does not. The continue in the body of the for loop causes the loop to finish early. The first cout in the for loop executes, but the second does not, due to the continue.

```
// Filename: CON1.CPP
// Demonstrates the use of the continue statement
#include <iostream.h>
void main()
{
   int ctr;

   for (ctr = 1; ctr <= 10; ctr++)    // Loops 10 times
     { cout << ctr << " ";
       continue;   // Causes body to end early
       cout << "C++ Programming\n";
     }
}
```

This program produces the following output:

```
1 2 3 4 5 6 7 8 9 10
```

With some compilers, you receive a warning message when you compile this type of program. The compiler recognizes that the second cout is *unreachable* code—that is, it never executes due to the continue statement. Compile this program on your computer and check to see whether your compiler produces a warning.

Because of the warning that a stand-alone continue usually generates, most programs use a continue only after an if statement. This makes it a conditional continue statement, which is more useful. The following two programs demonstrate the conditional use of continue.

The following program asks the user for five lowercase letters, one at a time, and prints their uppercase equivalents. It uses the ASCII table (see Appendix C) to ensure that users type lowercase letters. (These are the letters whose ASCII numbers range from 97 to 122.) If the user does not type a lowercase letter, the program ignores the mistake with the continue statement.

```
// Filename: CON2.CPP
// Prints uppercase equivalents of five lowercase letters
```

```
#include <iostream.h>
void main()
{
   char letter;
   int ctr;

   for (ctr = 1; ctr <= 5; ctr++)
     { cout << "Please enter a lowercase letter ";
       cin >> letter;
       if ((letter < 97) ¦¦ (letter > 122))    // See whether
                                                // out-of-range

          { continue; }    // Go get another
       letter -= 32;    // Subtracts 32 from ASCII value
                        // to get uppercase
       cout << "The uppercase equivalent is " <<
               letter << "\n";
     }
}
```

Due to the `continue` statement, only lowercase letters are converted to uppercase.

Finish the next program so that it converts uppercase letters to lowercase.

```
// Filename: CONUP.CPP
// Prints lowercase equivalents of five uppercase
// letters
#include <iostream.h>
void main()
{
   char letter;
   int ctr;

   for (ctr = 1; ctr <= 5; ctr++)
     { cout << "Please enter an uppercase letter ";
       cin >> letter;
       if ((letter < 65) ¦¦ (letter > 90)) // See whether
                                           // out-of-range
          { continue; }    // Go get another
```

Suppose that you want to average the salaries of employees in your company who make more than $10,000 a year, but you have only their monthly gross pay figures. The following program might be useful. It prompts for each monthly employee salary, annualizes it (multiplies it by 12), and computes an average. The `continue` statement ensures that salaries less than or equal to $10,000 are ignored in the average calculation. It enables the other salaries to "fall through."

If you enter -1 as a monthly salary, the program quits and prints the result of the average.

```
// Filename: CON3.CPP
// Averages salaries more than $10,000
#include <iostream.h>
#include <iomanip.h>
void main()
{
    float month, year;    // Monthly and yearly salaries
    float avg = 0.0, total = 0.0;
    int count = 0;

    do
      { cout << "What is the next monthly salary (-1) " <<
              "to quit)? ";
        cin >> month;
        if ((year = month * 12.00) <= 10000.00)  // Do not add
          { continue; }                          // low salaries
        if (month < 0.0)
          { break; }    // Quits if user entered -1
        count++;   // Adds 1 to valid counter
        total += year;   // Adds yearly salary to total
      } while (month > 0.0);
```

```
    cout.setf(ios::fixed);
    avg = total / (float)count;    // Computes average
    cout << "\n\nThe average of high salaries " <<
            "is $" << setprecision(2) << avg;
}
```

Notice that this program uses both a `continue` and a `break` statement. The program does one of three things, depending on each user's input. It adds to the total, continues another iteration if the salary is too low, or exits the `while` loop (and the average calculation) if the user types -1.

Here is the program's output:

```
What is the next monthly salary (-1 to quit)? 500.00
What is the next monthly salary (-1 to quit)? 2000.00
What is the next monthly salary (-1 to quit)? 750.00
What is the next monthly salary (-1 to quit)? 4000.00
What is the next monthly salary (-1 to quit)? 5000.00
What is the next monthly salary (-1 to quit)? 1200.00
What is the next monthly salary (-1 to quit)? -1

The average of high salaries is $36600.00
```

Review Questions

1. For what do you use timing loops?

2. Why do timing loop ranges have to be adjusted for different types of computers?

3. Why do `continue` and `break` statements rarely appear without an `if` statement controlling them?

4. What is the output of the following section of code?

```
for (i = 1; i <= 10; i++)
   { continue;
     cout << "***** \n";
   }
```

5. What is the output of the following section of code?

```
for (i = 1; i <= 10; i++)
   { cout << "***** \n";
     break;
   }
```

6. Why do you generally have to use a nested loop to perform a long timing loop?

Review Exercises

1. Write a program that prints C++ is fun on-screen for 10 seconds. (*Hint:* You might have to try several timing loop values to get the message to print for 10 seconds.)

2. Make the program in Exercise 1 display the message C++ is fun for 10 seconds. (*Hint:* You might have to use several timing loops and also the \r character.)

3. Write a program that prints the numerals from 1 to 14 in one column. To the right of the even numbers, print each number's square. To the right of the odd numbers, print each number's cube (the number raised to its third power).

 OBJECTIVE

To explain the switch and goto statements.

This lesson focuses on the switch statement, which improves large if and else-if statements by streamlining the multiple-choice decisions your programs make. The switch statement does not replace the if statement, but it is better to use switch when your programs must select from one of many different actions.

switch and break work together. Almost every switch statement you use includes at least one break statement in the body of the switch. To conclude this lesson—and this section of the book on C++ constructs—you learn the goto statement (although C++ programmers rarely use goto).

If you have mastered the if statement, you should have little trouble with the concepts presented here. By learning the switch statement, you should be able to write menus and multiple-choice data-entry programs with ease.

The `switch` Statement

The `switch` statement is sometimes called the *multiple-choice statement*. The `switch` statement enables your program to choose from several alternatives. The format of the `switch` statement is a little longer than the format of other statements you have seen:

```
switch (expression)
   { case (expression1): { one or more C++ statements; }
     case (expression2): { one or more C++ statements; }
     case (expression3): { one or more C++ statements; }
      .    // If there are more
      .    // case statements,
      .    // they go here
     default: { one or more C++ statements; }
   }
```

A typical `switch` statement might look like this:

```
switch (day)
   { case (1): { cout <<
                "The monthly total is " << monthly << "\n"; }
     case (2): { cout <<
                "The weekly total is " << weekly << "\n"; }
     default:  { cout <<
                "The daily total is " << daily << "\n"; }
   }
```

The *expression* can be an integer expression, a character, a literal, or a variable. The *subexpressions* (*expression1, expression2,* and so on) can be any integer or character. The number of `case` expressions following the `switch` line is determined by your application. The *one or more C++ statements* is any block of C++ code.

> **TIP:** If the `switch` block is only one statement long, you do not need the braces, but they are recommended. Later, if you add additional statements to the body of the `switch`, you are more likely to enclose the statements in the braces.

How would you improve the following `switch` statement?

```
switch (a) {
   case (1) : cout << "a is 1 " << "\n";
```

```
   default  : cout << "switch is now done.\n" << "\n";
}
```

Although the `default` line is optional, most (but not all) `switch` statements include a default. The `default` line does not have to be the last line of the `switch` body.

If *expression* matches *expression1*, the statements to the right of *expression1* execute. If *expression* matches *expression2*, the statements to the right of *expression2* execute. If none of the expressions match the `switch` *expression*, the default `case` block executes. The `case` expression does not need parentheses, but parentheses sometimes make the value easier to find.

> **TIP:** Use a `break` statement after each `case` block to keep execution from "falling through" to the remaining `case` statements.

The `switch` statement has corresponding statements in many other programming languages. It is sometimes called a `CASE` statement or a `SELECT` statement. The `switch` statement provides the ability to select from one of several cases, depending on the value of the `switch` expression.

Using the `switch` statement is easier than its format might lead you to believe. Almost anywhere an `if-else-if` combination of statements can go, you usually can put a clearer `switch` statement. The `switch` statement is much easier to follow than an `if-in-an-if-in-an-if` statement, as you have had to write previously.

The `if` and `else-if` combinations of statements are not necessarily difficult to follow. When the relational test that determines the choice is complex and contains many `&&` and `||` operators, the `if` statement might be a better candidate. The `switch` statement is preferred whenever multiple-choice possibilities are based on a single literal, variable, or expression.

> **TIP:** Arrange `case` statements in the most-often to least-often executed order to improve your program's speed.

The following examples clarify the `switch` statement. They compare the `switch` statement to `if` statements to help you see the difference.

Suppose that you are writing a program to teach your child how to count. Your program will ask the child for a number. It then beeps (rings the computer's alarm bell) as many times as necessary to match that number.

The following program assumes that the child presses a number key from 1 to 5. This program uses the `if-else-if` combination to accomplish this counting-and-beeping teaching method.

```cpp
// Filename: IFBEEP.CPP
// Beeps a designated number of times
#include <iostream.h>

// Defines a beep cout to save repeating couts
// throughout the program
#define BEEP cout << "\a \n"
void main()
{
   int num;

   // Requests a number from the child (you might have to help)
   cout << "Please enter a number ";
   cin >> num;

   // Uses multiple if statements to beep
   if (num == 1)
     { BEEP; }
   else if (num == 2)
         { BEEP; BEEP; }
       else if (num == 3)
               { BEEP; BEEP; BEEP; }
             else if (num == 4)
                   { BEEP; BEEP; BEEP; BEEP; }
                 else if (num == 5)
                       { BEEP; BEEP; BEEP; BEEP; BEEP; }
}
```

No beeps are sounded if the child enters something other than 1 through 5. This program takes advantage of the #define preprocessor directive to define a shortcut to an alarm cout function. In this case, the BEEP is a little clearer to read, as long as you remember that BEEP is not a command but is replaced with the cout everywhere it appears.

One drawback to this type of if-in-an-if program is its readability. By the time you indent the body of each if and else, the program is too far to the right. There is no room for more than five or six possibilities. More important, this type of logic is difficult to follow. Because it involves a multiple-choice selection, a switch statement is much better to use, as you can see in the improved version that follows.

```cpp
// Filename: SWITBEEP.CPP
// Beeps a certain number of times using a switch
#include <iostream.h>

// Defines a beep cout to save repeating couts
// throughout the program
#define BEEP cout << "\a \n"
void main()
{
    int num;

    // Requests a number from the child (you might have to help)
    cout << "Please enter a number ";
    cin >> num;

    switch (num)
    { case (1): { BEEP;
                  break; }
      case (2): { BEEP; BEEP;
                  break; }
      case (3): { BEEP; BEEP; BEEP;
                  break; }
      case (4): { BEEP; BEEP; BEEP; BEEP;
                  break; }
      case (5): { BEEP; BEEP; BEEP; BEEP; BEEP;
                  break; }
    }
}
```

This example is much clearer than the preceding one. The value of num controls the execution, so only the case that matches num executes. The indentation helps separate each case.

If the child enters a number other than 1 through 5, no beeps are sounded because there is no case expression to match any other value and there is no default case.

Because the BEEP preprocessor directive is so short, you can put more than one on a single line. This is not a requirement, however. The block of statements following a case can also be more than one statement long.

If more than one case expression is the same, only the first expression executes. If the child does not enter a 1, 2, 3, 4, or 5, nothing happens in the preceding program. What follows is the same program modified to take advantage of the default option. The default block of statements executes if none of the previous cases match.

```cpp
// Filename: SWBEEP2.CPP
// Beeps a designated number of times using a switch
#include <iostream.h>

// Defines a beep cout to save repeating couts
// throughout the program
#define BEEP cout << "\a \n"
void main()
{
    int num;

    // Requests a number from the child (you might have to help)
    cout << "Please enter a number ";
    cin >> num;

    switch (num)  .
    { case (1): { BEEP;
                  break; }
      case (2): { BEEP; BEEP;
                  break; }
      case (3): { BEEP; BEEP; BEEP;
                  break; }
      case (4): { BEEP; BEEP; BEEP; BEEP;
                  break; }
      case (5): { BEEP; BEEP; BEEP; BEEP; BEEP;
                  break; }
      default:  { cout << "You must enter a number from " <<
                        "1 to 5\n";
```

```
                cout << "Please run this program again\n";
                break; }
        }
    }
```

The break at the end of the default case might seem redundant. After all, no other case statements execute by "falling through" from the default case. It is a good habit to put a break after the default case anyway. If you move the default higher in the switch (it doesn't have to be the last switch option), you are more inclined to move the break with it (where it is then needed).

Without the default, the switch expression *must* match one of the case values, or nothing happens. The default gives you a way to perform an action based on any value not listed in the series of case statements.

Rewrite the following if-else with a switch statement in the lines provided.

```
if (value == 10)
   { cout << "You only scored a 10." << "\n";
     cout << "Better luck next time!" << "\n"; }
else
   if (value == 20)
      { cout << "You are doing well." << "\n"; }
   else
      { cout << "Neither of your values were usable." << "\n"; }
```

What is wrong with the following switch statement?

```
switch (num)
   case (1): { break;} BEEP;
             break; }
```

```
case (2): { BEEP; BEEP;
            break; }
```

The Importance of break

To show the importance of using break statements in each case expression, here is the same beeping program as shown in the preceding section, without any break statements.

```cpp
// Filename: SWBEEP3.CPP
// Incorrectly beeps using a switch
#include <iostream.h>

// Defines a beep cout to save repeating couts
// throughout the program
#define BEEP cout << "\a \n"
void main()
{
   int num;

   // Requests a number from the child (you might have to help)
   cout << "Please enter a number ";
   cin >> num;

   switch (num)                        // Warning!
   { case (1): { BEEP; }               // Without a break, this
     case (2): { BEEP; BEEP; }         // code falls through to
     case (3): { BEEP; BEEP; BEEP; } // the rest of the beeps!
     case (4): { BEEP; BEEP; BEEP; BEEP; }
     case (5): { BEEP; BEEP; BEEP; BEEP; BEEP; }
     default:  { cout << "You must enter a number " <<
                        "from 1 to 5\n";
                 cout << "Please run this program again\n"; }
   }
}
```

If the user enters a 1, the program beeps 15 times! The break is not there to stop the execution from falling through to the other cases. Unlike with other programming languages such as Pascal, C++'s switch statement requires that you insert break statements between each case if you want only one case executed. This is not necessarily a drawback. The trade-off of having to specify break statements gives you more control in how you handle specific cases, as shown in the next example.

The next program controls the printing of end-of-day sales totals. It asks for the day of the week first. If the day is Monday through Thursday, a daily total is printed. If the day is a Friday, a weekly total and a daily total are printed. If the day happens to be the end of the month, a monthly sales total is printed as well.

In a real application, these totals would come from the disk drive rather than be assigned at the top of the program. Also, rather than individual sales figures being printed, a full daily, weekly, and monthly report of many sales totals probably would be printed. You are on your way to learning more about expanding the power of your C++ programs. For now, concentrate on the switch statement and its possibilities.

Each type of report for sales figures is handled through a hierarchy of case statements. Because the daily amount is the last case, it is the only report printed if the day of the week is Monday through Thursday. If the day of the week is Friday, the second case prints the weekly sales total and then falls through to the daily total (because Friday's daily total must be printed as well). If it is the end of the month, the first case executes, falling through to the weekly total, then to the daily sales total as well. Other languages that do not offer this "fall through" flexibility are more limiting.

```cpp
// Filename: SWISALE.CPP
// Prints daily, weekly, and monthly sales totals
#include <iostream.h>
#include <stdio.h>

void main()
{
   float daily = 2343.34;      // Later, these figures
   float weekly = 13432.65;    // come from a disk file
   float monthly = 43468.97;   // instead of being assigned
                               // as they are here
   char ans;
   int day;   // Day value to trigger correct case

   // Month is assigned 1 through 5 (for Monday through
   // Friday) or 6 if it is the end of the month. Assume
   // that a weekly and a daily total prints if it is the end of
   // the month, no matter what the day is.
```

```
cout << "Is this the end of the month? (Y/N) ";
cin >> ans;
if ((ans == 'Y') || (ans == 'y'))
  { day = 6; }    // Month value
else
  { cout << "What day number, 1 through 5 (for Mon-Fri) " <<
           "is it? ";
    cin >> day; }

switch (day)
  { case (6): { cout <<
              "The monthly total is " << monthly << "\n"; }
    case (5): { cout <<
              "The weekly total is " << weekly << "\n"; }
    default:  { cout <<
              "The daily total is " << daily << "\n"; }
  }
}
```

 What is the output of the preceding program (SWISALE.CPP) if the user indicates that the day is at the end of the month, and is a Friday?

 If you are still unsure why the switch statement is useful, consider the following few lines of code. They represent the selection logic from the preceding program if you used if and else to perform the printing. Notice how much easier switch is to understand than if-else statements.

```
if (day == 6)
   { cout << "The monthly total is " << monthly << "\n";
     cout << "The weekly total is " << weekly << "\n";
     cout << "The daily total is " << daily << "\n";
   }
else if (day == 5)
   {
     cout << "The weekly total is " << weekly << "\n";
     cout << "The daily total is " << daily << "\n";
   }
     else
       { cout << "The daily total is " << daily << "\n"; }
}
```

270

The order of the case statements is not fixed. You can rearrange the statements to make them more efficient. If only one or two cases are being selected most of the time, put those cases near the top of the switch statement.

For example, in the preceding program, most of the company's reports are daily, but the daily option is third in the case statements. By rearranging the case statements so that the daily report is at the top, you can speed up this program, because C++ does not have to scan two case expressions that it rarely executes.

Write the entire case statement from the preceding program (SWISALE.CPP) below, but change the order of the reports. Because the daily reports will be requested most often, put them first.

Character case Values

The values that you use for the case selections do not have to be integers. Because of the close association of integers and characters in C++, you can use character literals or variables for the case values. The program that follows illustrates the use of character values that trigger the case selections.

```
// Filename: SWIDEPT.CPP
// Prints message, depending on the department entered
#include <iostream.h>
void main()
{
   char choice;

   do   // Displays menu and ensures that user enters a
        // correct option
     { cout << "\nChoose your department: \n";
       cout << "S - Sales \n";
       cout << "A - Accounting \n";
       cout << "E - Engineering \n";
       cout << "P - Payroll \n";
```

271

```
        cout << "What is your choice?\n ";
        cin >> choice;
        // Converts choice to uppercase (if user
        // entered lowercase) with the ASCII table
        if ((choice >= 97) && (choice <= 122))
          { choice -= 32; }    // Subtracts enough
                               // to make uppercase
    } while ((choice != 'S') && (choice != 'A') &&
             (choice != 'E') && (choice != 'P'));

  // Put Engineering first because it occurs most often
  switch (choice)
  { case ('E') : { cout << "\n Your meeting is at 2:30";
                   break; }
    case ('S') : { cout << "\n Your meeting is at 8:30";
                   break; }
    case ('A') : { cout << "\n Your meeting is at 10:00";
                   break; }
    case ('P') : { cout << "\n Your meeting has been " <<
                          "canceled";
                   break; }
  }
}
```

To help you understand this program, the output is presented:

```
Choose your department:
S - Sales
A - Accounting
E - Engineering
P - Payroll

What is your choice? S

 Your meeting is at 8:30
```

Without the break statements, the user would also have seen the Accounting, Payroll, and the default message. The break keeps the rest of the switch options from "falling through" and executing when one of them occurs.

Finish the following program fragment so that a switch statement prints the sum, difference, product, or divided answer to this child's math program.

```cpp
#include <iostream.h>
void main()
{
    int num1, num2, answer;
    char option;
    cout << "*** Math Practice ***\n\n";
    cout << "What is the first number? ";
    cin >> num1;
    cout << "What is the second number? ";
    cin >> num2;
    cout << "Do you want to Add, Subtract, " <<
            "Multiply, or Divide?\n";
    cout << "(Enter A, S, M, or D)\n";
    cin >> option;




    cout << "The answer is " << answer << "\n";
}
```

The goto Statement

Early programming languages did not offer the flexible constructs that C++ gives you, such as for loops, while loops, and switch statements. Their only means of looping and comparing was with the goto statement. C++ still includes a goto, but the other constructs are more powerful, flexible, and easier to follow in a program.

The goto statement causes your program to jump to a different location, rather than execute the next statement in sequence. The format of the goto statement is

```
goto statement label
```

A typical goto might look like this:

```
goto CalcWages;    // Jumps to the wage calculation section
```

A *statement label* is named just as variables are (see Lesson 5, "C++ Numeric Data"). A *statement label* cannot have the same name as a C++ command, a C++ function, or another variable in the program. If you use a goto statement, there must be a *statement label* elsewhere in the program to which the goto branches. Execution then continues at the statement with the *statement label*.

A typical statement with a label might look like this:

```
CalcWages:  cout << "Calculating wages..." << "\n";
```

The *statement label* precedes a line of code. Follow all *statement labels* with a colon (:) so that C++ will recognize them as labels, not variables. The C++ programs so far in this book have not had statement labels because none of the programs needed them. A *statement label* is optional unless you have a goto statement.

> **NOTE:** As you can see, the statement label always has a colon to separate it from the rest of the line, but you should never put a colon with the label at the goto statement.

The following four lines of code each have different *statement labels*. This is not a program, but individual lines that might be included in a program. Notice that the *statement labels* are on the left.

```
pay: cout << "Place checks in the printer \n";

Again: cin >> name;

EndIt: cout << "That is all the processing.  \n";

CALC: amount = (total / .5) * 1.15;
```

The *statement labels* are not intended to replace comments, although their names reflect the code that follows. *statement labels* give goto statements a tag *to go to*. When your program finds the goto, it branches

274

to the statement labeled by the *statement label*. The program then continues to execute sequentially until the next goto changes the order again (or until the program ends).

Write a goto statement that transfers program control to a report-printing routine, then write the labeled statement that might begin the report-printing routine.

See whether you can describe what is wrong with the following statement. An example later helps clarify the problem if you cannot see it.

```
Here:    goto Here;
```

Is anything in the following pair of statements unnecessary?

```
  goto There;
There: a = 5 + 6;   // A little redundant, maybe?
```

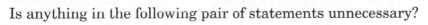

TIP: Use identifying line labels. A repetitive calculation deserves a label such as CalcIt and not x15z. Even though both are allowed, the first one is a better indication of the code's purpose.

NOTE: Use goto judiciously. It is not considered a good programming statement when it is overused. Programmers (especially beginners) have a tendency to include too many goto statements in a program. When a program branches all over the place, it becomes difficult to follow. Some people call programs with many goto statements "spaghetti code."

To eliminate goto statements and write better-structured programs, use the other looping and switch constructs discussed in the previous few lessons.

goto is not necessarily a bad statement—if it is used judiciously. Starting in Lesson 18, "Using C++ Functions," you begin to break your programs into smaller modules called *functions,* and goto becomes less and less important as you write more and more functions.

For now, become familiar with goto so that you can understand programs that use it. Some day, you might have to correct the code of someone who used goto.

The following program has a problem that is a direct result of goto, but it is still one of the best illustrations of the goto statement. The program consists of an *endless loop* (or an *infinite loop*). The first three lines (after the opening brace) execute, then the goto in the fourth line causes execution to loop back to the beginning and repeat the first three lines.

NOTE: goto continues to do this until you press Ctrl-Break or ask your system administrator to cancel the program.

```cpp
// Filename: GOTO1.CPP
// Program to show use of goto. This program ends
// only when the user presses Ctrl-Break.
#include <iostream.h>
void main()
{
   Again: cout << "This message \n";
   cout << "\t keeps repeating \n";
   cout << "\t\t over and over \n";

   goto Again;    // Repeats continuously
}
```

Here is the result of running this program:

```
This message
        keeps repeating
                over and over
```

```
This message
        keeps repeating
                over and over
This message
        keeps repeating
                over and over
This message
        keeps repeating
                over and over
This message
        keeps repeating
                over and over
This message
        keeps repeating
                over and over
This message
        keeps repeating
                over and over
This message
```

Sometimes it is easier to read your program's code when you write the statement labels on separate lines. Remember that writing maintainable programs is the goal of every good programmer. Making your programs easier to read is a prime consideration when you write them. The following program is the same repeating program just shown, except that the statement label is placed on a separate line.

```cpp
// Filename: GOTO2.CPP
// Program to show use of goto. This program ends
// only when the user presses Ctrl-Break.
#include <iostream.h>
void main()
{

Again:
   cout << "This message \n";
   cout << "\t keeps repeating \n";
   cout << "\t\t over and over \n";

   goto Again;    // Repeats continuously
}
```

The line following the statement label is the one that executes next, after control is passed to the label by goto.

Of course, these are silly examples. You probably don't want to write programs with infinite loops. If you use it at all, precede goto with an if, so that the goto transfers only upon a certain condition, or so that it stops transferring control eventually.

The following program is one of the worst-written programs ever! It is the epitome of spaghetti code! Do your best, however, to follow it and understand its output. By understanding the flow of the output, you can hone your understanding of goto. You might also appreciate the fact that the rest of this book uses goto only when needed to make the program clearer.

```cpp
// Filename: GOTO3.CPP
// This program demonstrates the overuse of goto
#include <iostream.h>
void main()
{
    goto Here;

    First:
    cout << "A \n";
    goto Final;

    There:
    cout << "B \n";
    goto First;

    Here:
    cout << "C \n";
    goto There;

    Final:;
}
```

At first glance, this program appears to print the first three letters of the alphabet, but the goto statements make them print in reverse order— C, B, A. Although this is not a well-designed program, some indentation of the lines without statement labels makes it a little more readable. This enables you to quickly separate the statement labels from the remaining code, as you can see from the following program.

```cpp
// Filename: GOTO4.CPP
// This program demonstrates the overuse of goto.
#include <iostream.h>
```

```
void main()
{
   goto Here;

First:
   cout << "A \n";
   goto Final;

There:
   cout << "B \n";
   goto First;

Here:
   cout << "C \n";
   goto There;

Final:;
}
```

This program's listing is somewhat easier to follow than the preceding one, even though both do the same thing. The remaining programs in this book with statement labels also use such indentation.

> The preceding program demonstrates the goto but has little useful-
> ness. You should realize that the program's output would be better
> produced by the following three lines:
>
> ```
> cout << "C \n";
> cout << "B \n";
> cout << "A \n";
> ```

The goto warning is worth repeating: use goto sparingly and only when its use makes your program more readable and maintainable. Usually, you can use much better commands.

Review Questions

1. Braces around a single-body switch case are not required, but they are recommended. Why?

2. `switch` often replaces which of the following statements?

   (a) `if`
   (b) `goto`
   (c) `if-else`
   (d) `while`
   (e) `do-while`

3. How does `goto` change the order in which a program normally executes?

4. What statement can substitute for an `if-else-if` construct?

5. Which statement almost always ends each `case` statement in a `switch`?

6. TRUE or FALSE: The order of your `case` statements has no bearing on the efficiency of your program.

7. Rewrite the following section of code using a `switch` statement.

```
if (num == 1)
    { cout << "Alpha"; }
else if (num == 2)
        { cout << "Beta"; }
    else if (num == 3)
            { cout << "Gamma"; }
        else
            { cout << "Other"; }
```

8. Rewrite the following program using a `do-while` loop.

```
Ask:
    cout << "What is your first name? ";
    cin >> name;
    if ((name[0] < 'A') || (name[0] > 'Z'))
        { goto Ask; }   // Keeps asking until the user
                        // enters a valid letter
```

Review Exercises

1. Write a program using the switch statement that asks users for their age, then prints a message saying You can vote! if they are 18, You can adopt! if they are 21, or Are you really that young? for any other age.

2. Write a menu-driven program for your local cable TV company. Here is how to assess charges: if you live within 20 miles of the city limits, you pay $12.00 per month; if you live 21 to 30 miles outside the city limits, you pay $23.00 per month; and if you live 31 to 50 miles outside the city limits, you pay $34.00. No one who lives more than 50 miles outside the limits receives the service. Prompt the users with a menu for their residences' distance from the city limits.

3. Write a program that calculates parking fees for a multilevel parking garage. Ask whether the driver is in a car or a truck. Charge the driver $2.00 for the first hour, $3.00 for the second, and $5.00 for more than 2 hours. If the driver is in a truck, add $1.00 to the total fee. (*Hint:* Use one switch and one if statement.)

4. Modify Exercise 3 so that the charge depends on the time of day the vehicle is parked. If the vehicle is parked before 8 a.m., charge the fees in Exercise 3. If the vehicle is parked after 8 a.m. and before 5 p.m., charge an extra fee of 50 cents. If the vehicle is parked after 5 p.m., deduct 50 cents from the computed price. You must prompt users for the starting time in a menu, as follows:

    ```
    1.   Before 8 a.m.
    2.   Before 5 p.m.
    3.   After 5 p.m.
    ```

281

C++
CLASSROOM Five

SAMS
PUBLISHING

Scope
and Functions

Using C++ Functions

OBJECTIVE

To explain the advantages of breaking your programs into groups of small routines.

Computers never get bored. They perform the same input, output, and computations that your program requires for as long as you want them to do it. You can take advantage of their repetitive nature by looking at your programs in a new way—as a series of small routines that execute whenever you need them, however many times you require.

This lesson approaches its subject somewhat differently than the previous lessons do. It concentrates on teaching you to write your own *functions,* which are *modules* of code that you execute and control from the main() function. So far, the programs in this book have consisted of a single long function called main(). As you will learn in this lesson, the main() function's primary purpose is to control the execution of other functions that follow it.

This lesson stresses the use of *structured programming,* sometimes called *modular programming.* C++ is designed so that the programmer can write programs in several modules rather than in one long block. By

breaking the program into several smaller routines (*functions*), you can isolate problems, write correct programs faster, and produce programs that are easier to maintain.

Function Basics

When you approach an application that must be programmed, it is best not to sit down at the keyboard and start typing. Rather, you should first *think* about the program and what it is supposed to do. One of the best ways to attack a program is to start with the overall goal, then divide this goal into several smaller tasks. You should never lose sight of the overall goal, but think also of how individual pieces can fit together to accomplish such a goal.

When you finally do sit down to begin coding the problem, continue to think in terms of those pieces fitting together. Don't approach a program as if it were one giant problem; rather, continue to write those small pieces individually.

When a builder builds a house, he or she does not first pick up a hammer and nails. First, the builder decides what the final house is to look like, orders the materials, gathers the workers, gets the permits, finds financing, and draws up the plans. When writing programs that are longer than the ones you have seen so far in this book, you must also plan the programs and decide what the pieces are and how they fit together before sitting down at the keyboard. Planning a program speeds the process from the idea for the program to the final debugged program.

The smaller program pieces do not mean that you must write separate programs to do everything. You can keep individual pieces of the overall program together—if you know how to write functions. Then you can use the same functions in many different programs.

C++ programs are not like BASIC or FORTRAN programs. C++ was designed to force you to think in a modular, or subroutine-like, functional style. Good C++ programmers write programs that consist of many small functions, even if their programs execute one or more of these functions only once. These functions work together to produce a program quicker and easier than if the program had to be written from scratch.

> **TIP:** Instead of coding one long program, write several smaller routines, called functions. One of those functions must be called `main()`. The `main()` function is always the first to execute. It doesn't have to be first in a program, but it usually is.

Why do you think books are divided into paragraphs, sections, and chapters? Wouldn't it be shorter to just begin at page one and keep the words going until the last word in the book, with no breaks between sections? Needless to say, partitioning a book using the "divide and conquer" approach makes it easier to read and understand. The goal of a good book is not to conserve as much space as possible, but to be as clear as possible. In the same way, the goal of your programs should be clarity. In addition to making programs more clear, writing programs in modules encapsulates your programs, putting specific individual routines in their own functions, where they impact the overall system less and make it easier for you to get your programs working faster.

Breaking Problems Down

If your program does a lot, break it into several functions. Each function should do only *one* primary task. For example, if you were writing a C++ program to retrieve a list of characters from the keyboard, alphabetize them, then print them on-screen, you could—but shouldn't—write all these instructions in one big `main()` function, as the following C++ *skeleton* (program outline) shows:

```
main()
{
   // :
   // C++ code to retrieve a list of characters
   // :
   // C++ code to alphabetize the characters
   // :
   // C++ code to print the alphabetized list on-screen
   // :
   return 0;
}
```

This skeleton is *not* a good way to write this program. Even though you can type this program in only a few lines of code, it is much better to begin

breaking every program into distinct tasks so that this process becomes a habit to you. You should not use main() to do everything. In fact, use main() to do very little except call each of the functions that does the actual work.

This program skeleton is the first time in this book that you have seen the return statement. return is optional in all the programs you have seen so far. Whether you put return at the end of main() or not, main() still finishes and returns to the operating system when the program is done. In most of the remaining programs you will see, every function includes a return. Many C++ functions don't just return control to another function or to the operating system, but they also send values back to whatever called the function (hence the return 0 in the preceding program skeleton). When you see return 0 at the end of the function, the function name does not include the void keyword, as you have seen throughout this book (void main()).

A better way to organize this program is to write a separate function for each task the program is supposed to do. This doesn't mean that each function has to be only one line long. Rather, it means that you make every function a building block that performs only one distinct task in the program.

The following program outline shows a better way to write the program just described:

```
main()
{
   getletters();   // Calls a function to retrieve the letters
   alphabetize();   // Calls a function to alphabetize
                    // letters
   printletters();   // Calls a function to print letters
                     // on-screen
   return 0;   // Returns to the operating system
}

getletters()
{
   // :
   // C++ code to get a list of characters
   // :
   return 0;   // Returns to main()
}

alphabetize()
```

288

```
{
  // :
  // C++ code to alphabetize the characters
  // :
  return 0;    // Returns to main()
}

printletters()
{
  // :
  // C++ code to print the alphabetized list on-screen
  // :
  return 0;    // Returns to main()
}
```

The program outline shows you a much better way of writing this program. It takes longer to type, but it's much more organized. The only action that the `main()` function takes is to control the other functions by calling them in a certain order. Each separate function executes its instructions, then returns to `main()`, whereupon `main()` calls the next function until no more functions remain. The `main()` function then returns control of the computer to the operating system.

Do not be too concerned about the 0 that follows the `return` statement. C++ functions return values. The functions you've seen so far have returned zero, and that return value has been ignored. Lesson 21, "Return Values and Prototypes," describes how you can use the return value for programming power.

> **TIP:** A good rule of thumb is that a function should not be more than one screen in length. If it is longer, you probably are doing too much in one function and should break it into two or more functions.

Until now you have used the function called `main()` to hold the entire program. From this point, in all but the smallest programs, `main()` simply controls other functions that do the work.

The listings seen so far in this lesson are not examples of real C++ programs; instead, they are skeletons, or outlines, of programs. From these outlines, it is easier to develop the actual program. Before going to the keyboard to write a program such as this, you should know that there are four distinct sections to the previous sample program: a primary

function-calling `main()` function, a keyboard data-entry function, an alphabetizing function, and a printing function.

Never lose sight of the original programming problem. (Using the approach just described, you never will!) Look again at the `main()` calling routine in the preceding program. Notice that you can glance at `main()` and get a feel for the overall program, without the remaining statements getting in the way. This is a good example of structured, modular programming. A large programming problem is broken into distinct, separate modules called functions, and each function performs one primary job in a few C++ statements.

Given the following program skeleton, write a better one using three more suitable functions.

```
main()
{
    // :
    // C++ code to get an employee's hours,
    // tax rate, and pay rate
    // :
    // C++ code to calculate net pay and taxes
    // :
    // C++ code to print the paycheck
    // :
    return 0;
}
```

More Function Basics

Little has been said about naming and writing functions. C++ functions generally adhere to the following rules:

1. Every function must have a name.

2. Function names are made up and assigned by the programmer following the same rules that apply to naming variables: they can contain up to 32 characters, they must begin with a letter, and they can consist of letters, numbers, and the underscore (_) character.

3. All function names have one set of parentheses immediately following them. This helps you (and C++) differentiate them from variables. The parentheses may or may not contain something. So far, all such parentheses in this book have been empty. (You learn more about functions in Lesson 20, "Passing Values.")

4. The body of each function, starting immediately after the closing parenthesis of the function name, must be enclosed by braces. This means that a block containing one or more statements makes up the body of each function.

TIP: Use meaningful function names. `Calc_balance()` is more descriptive than `xy3()`.

Although the outline shown in the preceding listing is a good example of structured code, it can be improved by using the underscore character (_) in the function names. Can you see that `get_letters()` and `print_letters()` are much easier to read than `getletters()` and `printletters()`? Some programmers prefer to use a combination of uppercase and lowercase characters instead of an underscore. They would name the `get_letters()` function `GetLetters()`. Whether you use the underscore or uppercase letters to separate parts of the function name, use descriptive names that make sense.

NOTE: Be sure to use the underscore character (_) and not the hyphen (-) when naming functions and variables. If you use a hyphen, C++ will produce an error message.

Write good function names for functions that do the following:

Description	Function Name
Calculates averages	_____
Prints a weather report	_____
Asks the user for a total	_____
Prints a name and address	_____
Converts Celsius to Fahrenheit	_____

The following listing shows you an example of a C++ function. You can already tell quite a bit about this function. You know, for instance, that it isn't a complete program because it has no `main()` function. (All programs must have a `main()` function.) You know also that the function name is `calc_it` because parentheses follow this name. These parentheses happen to have something in them (you learn more about this in Lesson 20, "Passing Values"). You know also that the body of the function is enclosed in a block of braces. Inside that block is a *smaller* block, the body of a `while` loop. Finally, you recognize that the `return` statement is the last line of the function.

```
calc_it(int n)
{
   // Function to print the square of a number
   int square;

   while (square <= 250)
     { square = n * n;
       cout << "The square of " << n <<
              " is " << square << "\n";
       n++; }    // A block in the function

   return 0;
}
```

> **TIP:** Not all functions require a `return` statement for their last line, but it is recommended that you always include one because it helps to show your intention to return to the calling function at that point. Later in this book, you will learn that the `return` is required in certain instances. For now, develop the habit of including a `return` statement. If the function has no return value, put a `0` after the `return` for now.

Calling and Returning Functions

You have been reading much about *function calling* and *returning control*. Although you might already understand these phrases from their context, you probably can learn them better through an illustration of what is meant by a function call.

A function call in C++ is like a detour on a highway. Imagine that you are traveling along the "road" of the primary function called `main()` when you run into a function-calling statement. You must temporarily leave the `main()` function and execute the function that was called. After that function finishes (its `return` statement is reached), program control reverts to `main()`. In other words, when you finish a detour, you return to the "main" route and continue the trip. Control continues as `main()` calls other functions.

> **NOTE:** Generally, the primary function that controls function calls and their order is called a *calling function*. Functions controlled by the calling function are called the *called functions*.

Given the next program, which function is the calling function and which is the called function?

```cpp
#include <iostream.h>
main()
{
    cout << "Hello! \n";
    nextMsg();
    return 0;
}

nextMsg()
{
    cout << "Goodbye! \n";
    return 0;
}
```

A complete C++ program with functions makes the calling and called function concepts clear. The following program prints several messages to the screen. Each message printed is determined by the order of the functions. Before worrying too much about what this program does, take some time to study its structure. Notice that three functions are defined in the program: `main()`, `next_fun()`, and `third_fun()`. A fourth function is used also, but it is the built-in C++ `strcpy()` function. The three defined functions appear sequentially. The body of each is enclosed in braces, and each function has a `return` statement at its end.

As you will see from the program, something new follows the `#include` directive. The first line of every function that `main()` calls is listed here, and it also appears above the actual function. C++ requires these *prototypes*. For now, just ignore them and study the overall format of multiple-function programs. Lesson 21, "Return Values and Prototypes," explains prototypes.

```cpp
// Filename: FUN1.CPP
// Illustrates function calls
```

```
#include <iostream.h>
#include <string.h>
next_fun();    // Prototypes
third_fun();

main()    // main() is always the first C++ function executed
{
   char endit[20];    // Just to hold a string
   strcpy(endit, "That is all folks!");   // A built-in function

   cout << "First function called main() \n";
   next_fun();    // Second function is called here
   third_fun();    // Last function is called here
   cout << endit << "\n";    // All control
   return 0;    // Control is returned to
                // the operating system
}    // This brace concludes main()


next_fun()    // Second function
              // Parentheses always required
{
   cout << "Inside next_fun() \n";    // No variables
                                      // are defined
                                      // in the program
   return 0;    // Control is now returned to main()
}


third_fun()    // Last function in the program
{
   cout << "Inside third_fun() \n";
   return 0;    // Always return from all functions
}
```

The output of this program follows:

```
First function called main()
Inside next_fun()
Inside third_fun()
That is all folks!
```

Figure 18.1 shows a tracing of this program's execution. Notice that main() controls which of the other functions is called, as well as the order of the calling. Control *always* returns to the calling function after the called function finishes.

Figure 18.1.
Tracing function calls.

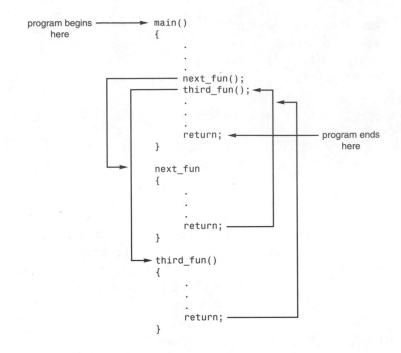

To call a function, simply type its name—including the parentheses—and follow it with a semicolon. Remember that semicolons follow all executable statements in C++, and a function call (sometimes called a *function invocation*) is an executable statement. The execution is the function's code being called. Any function can call any other function. In the preceding program, `main()` is the only function that calls other functions.

Now you can tell that the following statement is a function call:

```
print_total();
```

Because `print_total` is not a C++ command or a built-in function name, it must be a variable or a written function's name. Only function names end with parentheses, so it must be a function call or the start of a function's code. Of the last two possibilities, it must be a call to a function because it ends with a semicolon. If it didn't have a semicolon, it would have to be the start of a function definition.

When you define a function (by typing the function name and its subsequent code inside braces), you *never* follow the name with a semicolon. Notice in the preceding program that `main()`, `next_fun()`, and `third_fun()` have no semicolons when they appear in the body of the program. A semicolon follows their names only in `main()`, where the function prototypes appear and where these functions are called.

> **NOTE:** Never define a function inside another function. All function code must be listed sequentially, throughout the program. A function's closing brace *must* appear before another function's code can be listed.

Of the following three lines with the `GetAge()` function name, which is a *function prototype,* which is a *function call,* and which is a *function definition* (the first line in the function itself)?

Statement	Description
int GetAge()	_____
int GetAge();	_____
GetAge();	_____

Suppose that you are writing a program that does the following. It asks users for their departments. If they are in Accounting, they receive the accounting department's report. If they are in Engineering, they receive the engineering department's report. Finally, if they are in Marketing, they receive the marketing department's report.

The skeleton of such a program follows. The code for `main()` is shown in its entirety, but only a skeleton of the other functions are shown. The `switch` statement is a perfect function-calling statement for such multiple-choice selections.

```
// Skeleton of a departmental report program
#include <iostream.h>
main()
{
   int choice;

   do
     { cout << "Choose your department from the " <<
             "following list\n";
       cout << "\t1.  Accounting \n";
       cout << "\t2.  Engineering \n";
       cout << "\t3.  Marketing \n";
       cout << "What is your choice? ";
       cin >> choice;
     } while ((choice < 1) || (choice > 3));    // Ensures 1, 2,
                                                // or 3 is chosen
```

297

```
    switch (choice)
    { case(1): { acct_report();   // Calls accounting function
                 break; }   // Doesn't fall through
      case(2): { eng_report();   // Calls engineering function
                 break; }
      case(3): { mtg_report();   // Calls marketing function
                 break; }
    }
    return 0;   // Program returns to the operating
                // system when finished
}

acct_report()
{
    // :
    // Accounting report code goes here
    // :
    return 0;
}

eng_report()
{
    // :
    // Engineering report code goes here
    // :
    return 0;
}

mtg_report()
{
    // :
    // Marketing report code goes here
    // :
    return 0;
}
```

The bodies of switch statements normally contain function calls. You can tell that these case statements execute functions. For instance, acct_report(); (which is the first line of the first case) is not a variable name or a C++ command. It is the name of a function defined later in the program. If the user enters 1 at the menu, the function called acct_report() executes. When it finishes, control returns to the first case body, and its break statement causes the switch statement to end. The main() function returns to DOS (or to your integrated C++ environment if you are using one) when its return statement executes.

In the preceding example, the main() routine is not very modular. It displays the menu, but not in a separate function as it should. Remember that main() does very little except control the other functions, which do all the work.

Here is a rewrite of this sample program, with a fourth function to print the menu to the screen. This is truly a modular example, with each function performing a single task. Again, the last three functions are shown only as skeleton code because the goal here is simply to illustrate function calling and returning.

```cpp
// Second skeleton of a departmental report program
#include <iostream.h>
main()
{
    int choice;

    do
      { menu_print();    // Calls function to print the menu
        cin >> choice;
      } while ((choice < 1) || (choice > 3));    // Ensures 1, 2,
                                                 // or 3 is chosen
    switch (choice)
    { case(1): { acct_report();   // Calls accounting function
                 break; }    // Doesn't fall through
      case(2): { eng_report();    // Calls engineering function
                 break; }
      case(3): { mtg_report();    // Calls marketing function
                 break; }
    }
    return 0;    // Program returns to the operating system
                 // when finished
}

menu_print()
{
    cout << "Choose your department from the following list\n";
    cout << "\t1.  Accounting \n";
    cout << "\t2.  Engineering \n";
    cout << "\t3.  Marketing \n";
```

```
   cout << "What is your choice? ";
   return 0;    // Returns to main()
}

acct_report()
{
   // :
   // Accounting report code goes here
   // :
   return 0;
}

eng_report()
{
   // :
   // Engineering report code goes here
   // :
   return 0;
}

mtg_report()
{
   // :
   // Marketing report code goes here
   // :
   return 0;
}
```

The menu-printing function doesn't have to follow main(). Because it's the first function called, however, it seems best to define it there.

Readability is the key, so programs broken into separate functions result in better written code. You can write and test each function, one at a time. After you write a general outline of the program, you can list many function calls in main() and define their skeletons after main().

The body of each function should initially consist of a single return statement so that the program compiles in its skeleton format. As you complete each function, you can compile and test the program. This enables you to develop programs faster and more accurately. The separate functions enable others (who might later modify your program) to find the particular function easily and make changes without affecting the rest of the program.

300

Another useful practice, popular with many C++ programmers, is to separate functions from each other with a comment consisting of a line of asterisks (*) or hyphens (-). This makes it easy, especially in longer programs, to see where a function begins and ends. What follows is another listing of the preceding program, but with its four functions more clearly separated by this type of comment line.

```
// Third skeleton of a departmental report program
#include <iostream.h>
main()
{
   int choice;

   do
     {  menu_print();   // Calls function to print the menu
        cin >> choice;
     } while ((choice < 1) || (choice > 3));    // Ensures 1, 2,
                                                // or 3 is chosen
   switch (choice)
   { case(1): { acct_report();   // Calls accounting function
                break; }   // Doesn't fall through
     case(2): { eng_report();    // Calls engineering function
                break; }
     case(3): { mtg_report();   // Calls marketing function
                break; }
   }
   return 0;   // Program returns to the operating system
               // when finished
}


//**********************************************************
menu_print()
{
   cout << "Choose your department from the following list\n";
   cout << "\t1.  Accounting \n";
   cout << "\t2.  Engineering \n";
   cout << "\t3.  Marketing \n";
   cout << "What is your choice? ";
   return 0;   // Returns to main()
}


//**********************************************************
acct_report()
```

```
{
    // :
    // Accounting report code goes here
    // :
    return 0;
}


//**********************************************************
eng_report()
{
    // :
    // Engineering report code goes here
    // :
    return 0;
}


//**********************************************************
mtg_report()
{
    // :
    // Marketing report code goes here
    // :
    return 0;
}
```

Due to space limitations, not all program listings in this book separate the functions in this manner. You might find, however, that your listings are easier to follow if you put these separating comments between your functions.

You can execute a function more than once by simply calling it from more than one place in a program. If you put a function call in the body of a loop, the function executes repeatedly until the loop finishes.

The following program prints the message C++ is Fun! on-screen several times, forward and backward, using functions. Notice that main() does not make every function call. The second function, name_print(), calls the function named reverse_print(). Trace the execution of this program's couts.

```
// Filename: FUN2.CPP
// Prints C++ is Fun! on-screen several times
#include <iostream.h>
name_print();    // Prototypes
```

```
reverse_print();
one_per_line();

main()
{
   int ctr;    // To control loops

   for (ctr = 1; ctr <= 5; ctr++)
     { name_print(); }   // Calls function five times

   one_per_line();    // Calls program's last function once
   return 0;
}

//**********************************************************
name_print()
{
   // Prints C++ is Fun! across a line, separated by tabs
   cout << "C++ is Fun!\tC++ is Fun!\tC++ is Fun!" <<
           "\tC++ is Fun!\n";
   cout << "C++  i s  F u n! C++  i s  F u n! " <<
           "C++  i s  F u n!\n";

   reverse_print();    // Calls next function from here
   return 0;    // Returns to main()
}

//**********************************************************
reverse_print()
{
   // Prints several C++ is Fun! messages,
   // in reverse, separated by tabs
   cout << "!nuF si ++C\t!nuF si ++C\t!nuF si ++C\t\n";

   return 0;    // Returns to name_print()
}

//**********************************************************
one_per_line()
{
   // Prints C++ is Fun! down the screen
```

303

```
    cout << "C++\n \ni\ns\n \nF\nu\nn\n!\n";
    return 0;    // Returns to main()
}
```

Here is the program's output:

```
C++ is Fun!      C++ is Fun!      C++ is Fun!      C++ is Fun!
C++  i s  F u n! C++  i s  F u n! C++  i s  F u n!
!nuF si ++C       !nuF si ++C       !nuF si ++C
C++ is Fun!      C++ is Fun!      C++ is Fun!      C++ is Fun!
C++  i s  F u n! C++  i s  F u n! C++  i s  F u n!
!nuF si ++C       !nuF si ++C       !nuF si ++C
C++ is Fun!      C++ is Fun!      C++ is Fun!      C++ is Fun!
.C++  i s  F u n! C++  i s  F u n! C++  i s  F u n!
!nuF si ++C       !nuF si ++C       !nuF si ++C
C++ is Fun!      C++ is Fun!      C++ is Fun!      C++ is Fun!
C++  i s  F u n! C++  i s  F u n! C++  i s  F u n!
!nuF si ++C       !nuF si ++C       !nuF si ++C
C++ is Fun!      C++ is Fun!      C++ is Fun!      C++ is Fun!
C++  i s  F u n! C++  i s  F u n! C++  i s  F u n!
!nuF si ++C       !nuF si ++C       !nuF si ++C
C++


i

s


F
u

n

!
```

Hang on if you need more help. This lesson introduces the need for functions, but the next several lessons show you many more examples and explain additional function specifics.

Review Questions

1. TRUE or FALSE: A function should always include a `return` statement as its last command.

2. What is the name of the first function executed in a C++ program?

3. Which is better: one long function or several smaller functions? Why?

4. How do function names differ from variable names?

5. How can you use comments to help separate functions visually?

6. What is wrong with the following program section?

```
calc_it()
{
    cout << "Getting ready to calculate the square";
    cout << " of 25 \n";

    sq_25()
    {
      cout << "The square of 25 is " << (25 * 25);
      return 0;
    }

    cout << "That is a big number! \n";
    return 0;
}
```

7. Is the following a variable name, a function call, a function definition, or an expression?

```
scan_names();
```

8. TRUE or FALSE: The following line in a C++ program is a function call.

```
cout << "C++ is Fun! \n";
```

Variable Scope

 To teach why local variables offer more flexibility than global variables.

The concept of *variable scope* is most important when you write functions. Variable scope determines which functions recognize certain variables. If a function recognizes a variable, the variable is *visible* to that function. Variable scope protects variables in one function from other functions that might overwrite them. If a function doesn't need access to a variable, that function shouldn't be able to see or change the variable. In other words, the variable should not be "visible" to that particular function.

To use local variables effectively, you must be able to pass values back and forth between functions. Lesson 18, "Using C++ Functions," introduced the concept of using a different function for each task. This concept is much more useful when you learn about local and global variable scope.

Global Versus Local Variables

If you have programmed only in BASIC or COBOL, the concept of local and global variables might be new to you. In many interpreted versions of BASIC, all variables are *global,* meaning that the entire program

knows each variable and has the capability to change any of them. If you use a variable called SALES at the top of the program, even the last line in the program can use SALES. (If you don't know BASIC, don't despair—you have one less habit to break!)

Global variables can be dangerous. Parts of a program can inadvertently change a variable that shouldn't be changed. For example, suppose that you are writing a program that keeps track of a grocery store's inventory. You might keep track of sale percentages, discounts, retail prices, wholesale prices, produce prices, dairy prices, delivery prices, price changes, sale tax percentages, holiday markups, post-holiday markdowns, and so on.

The huge number of prices in such a system is confusing. When you are writing a program to keep track of every price, it is easy to mistakenly call both the dairy prices and the delivery prices d_prices. Either C++ will not enable you to do this (you can't define the same variable twice), or you will overwrite a value used for something else. Whatever happens, keeping track of all these different but similarly named prices makes this program confusing to write.

Global variables can be dangerous because code can inadvertently overwrite a variable initialized elsewhere in the program. It is better to make every variable in your programs *local*. Then, only functions that should be able to change the variables can do so.

Local variables can be seen (and changed) only from the function in which they are defined. Therefore, if a function defines a variable as local, that variable's scope is protected. The variable cannot be used, changed, or erased by any other function without special programming that you will learn about shortly.

If you use only one function, main(), the concept of local and global is academic. You know from Lesson 18, "Using C++ Functions," however, that single-function programs are not recommended. It is best to write modular, structured programs made up of many smaller functions. Therefore, you should know how to define variables as local to only those functions that use them.

Defining Variable Scope

When you first learned about variables in Lesson 5, "C++ Numeric Data," you learned that you can define variables in two places:

- before they are used inside a function
- before a function name, such as `main()`

All examples in this book have declared variables with the first method. You have yet to see an example of the second method. Because most of these programs have consisted entirely of a single `main()` function, there has been no reason to differentiate the two methods. It is only after you start using several functions in one program that these two variable definition methods become critical.

The following rules specific to local and global variables are important:

- A variable is local *if and only if* you define it after the opening brace of a block, usually at the top of a function.
- A variable is global *if and only if* you define it outside a function.

All variables you have seen so far have been local. They have all been defined immediately after the opening braces of `main()`. Therefore, they have been local to `main()`, and only `main()` can use them. Other functions have no idea that these variables even exist because they belong to `main()` only. When the function (or block) ends, all its local variables are destroyed.

> **TIP:** All local variables disappear (lose their definition) when their block ends.

In the following program, which variables are global and which are local?

```
// Filename: TRYGLLOC.CPP
#include <iostream.h>

int ageLimit = 21;
float maxDol = 100.00;

main()
{
    int age;
    float amt;

    cout << "How old are you? ";
    cin >> age;
```

```
cout << "How much do you want to pay? ";
cin >> amt;

if (age >= ageLimit)
   {
       cout << "You are old enough. \n";
   }
if (amt >= maxDol)
   {
       cout << "You have enough money. \n";
   }
   return 0;
}
```

 In the following code, what is wrong with the variable placement? (The answer is in the description following this problem).

```
doFun(i, j)
int i;
int j;
{
   // Rest of function follows
```

The two variables, i and j, are neither local nor global. This code example illustrates an outdated way of declaring variable *parameters* when they are sent to functions. If you see this style of variable definition in a program, the program is not written according to either the ANSI C or the AT&T specifications. Some Windows programs still use this method of defining variables. The next two lessons explain how to receive variables properly. If you ever see this old style of variable definition (called the *classic method of defining parameters*), move the int i, int j up into the function's parentheses to make the code more up-to-date. You probably will not see this in a C++ program, but you might see it in a C program that you want to use on a C++ compiler.

310

Differentiating Between Local and Global

Global variables are visible ("known") from their point of definition down to the end of the program. If you define a global variable, *any* line throughout the rest of the program—no matter how many functions and code lines follow it—is able to use that global variable.

The following section of code defines two local variables, i and j.

```
main()
{
   int i, j;    // Local because they're
                // defined after the brace
   // Rest of main() goes here
}
```

These variables are visible to main() and not to any other function that might follow or be called by main().

The following section of code defines two global variables, g and h.

```
#include <iostream.h>
int g, h;   // Global because they're
            // defined before a function
main()
{
   // main()'s code goes here
}
```

It doesn't matter whether your #include lines go before or after global variable declarations.

Global variables can appear before any function. In the following program, main() uses no variables. However, both of the two functions after main() can use sales and profit because these variables are global.

```
// Filename: GLO.CPP
// Program that contains two global variables
#include <iostream.h>
do_fun();
third_fun();   // Prototype discussed later
main()
{
   cout << "No variables defined in main() \n\n";
   do_fun();   // Calls the first function
   return 0;
}
```

```
float sales, profit;    // Two global variables
do_fun()
{
   sales = 20000.00;    // This variable is visible
                        // from this point down
   profit = 5000.00;    // As is this one. They are
                        // both global.

   cout << "The sales in the second function are " <<
        sales << "\n";
   cout << "The profit in the second function is " <<
        profit << "\n\n";

   third_fun();    // Calls the third function to
                   // show that globals are visible
   return 0;
}


third_fun()
{
   cout << "In the third function: \n";
   cout << "The sales in the third function are " <<
        sales << "\n";
   cout << "The profit in the third function is " <<
        profit << "\n";
   // If sales and profit were local, they would not be
   // visible to more than one function
   return 0;
}
```

Notice that the main() function can never use sales and profit because they are not visible to main()—even though they are global. Remember that global variables are visible only from their point of definition downward in the program. Statements that appear before global variable definitions cannot use those variables. Here is the result of running this program:

```
No variables defined in main()

The sales in the second function are 20000
The profit in the second function is 5000
```

```
In the third function:
The sales in the third function are 20000
The profit in the third function is 5000
```

> **TIP:** Declare all global variables at the top of your programs. Even though you can define them later (between any two functions), you can find them faster if you declare them at the top.

The following program uses both local and global variables. It should now be obvious to you that j and p are local and i and z are global.

```cpp
// Filename: GLLO.CPP
// Program with both local and global variables
// Local Variables      Global Variables
//    j, p                   i, z
#include <iostream.h>
pr_again();   // Prototype

int i = 0;   // Global variable because it's
            // defined outside main()
main()
{
   float p ;   // Local to main() only  local
   p = 9.0;   // Puts value in global variable
   cout << i << ", " << p << "\n";   // Prints global i
                                     // and local p
   pr_again();   // Calls next function
   return 0;   // Returns to DOS

 }

float z = 9.0;   // Global variable because it's
                // defined before a function
pr_again()
{
   int j = 5;   // Local to only pr_again()
   cout << j << ", " << z;   // This can't print p!
   cout << ", " << i << "\n";
   return 0;   // Returns to main()
 }
```

Even though j is defined in a function that main() calls, main() cannot use j because j is local to pr_again(). When pr_again() finishes, j is no longer defined. The variable z is global from its point of definition down. This is why main() cannot print z. Also, the function pr_again() cannot print p because p is local to main() only.

Make sure that you can recognize local and global variables before you continue. A little study here will make the rest of this lesson easy to understand.

Two variables can have the same name, as long as they are local to two different functions. They are distinct variables, even though they are named identically.

The following short program uses two variables, both named age. They have two different values, and they are considered to be two different variables. The first age is local to main(), and the second age is local to get_age().

```cpp
// Filename: LOC1.CPP
// Two different local variables with the same name
#include <iostream.h>
get_age();   // Prototype
main()
{
   int age;
   cout << "What is your age? ";
   cin >> age;

   get_age();   // Calls the second function
   cout << "main()'s age is still " << age << "\n";

   return 0;
}

get_age()
{
   int age;   // A different age. This one
              // is local to get_age().
   cout << "What is your age again? ";
   cin >> age;
   return 0;
}
```

Variables local to main() cannot be used in another function that main() calls.

314

The output of this program follows. Study the output carefully. Notice that main()'s last cout does not print the newly changed age. Rather, it prints the age known to main()—the age that is *local* to main(). Even though they are named the same, main()'s age has nothing to do with get_age()'s age. They might as well have two different variable names.

```
What is your age? 28
What is your age again? 56
main()'s age is still 28
```

You should be careful when naming variables. Having two variables with the same name is misleading. It would be easy to become confused while changing this program later. If these variables truly have to be separate, name them differently, such as old_age and new_age, or ag1 and ag2. This helps you remember that they are different.

There are a few times when overlapping local variable names does not add confusion, but be careful about overdoing it. Programmers often use the same variable name as the counter variable in a for loop. For example, the two local variables in the following program have the same name.

```
// Filename: LOC2.CPP
// Using two local variables with the same name
// as counting variables
#include <iostream.h>
do_fun();   // Prototype
main()
{
   int ctr;   // Loop counter
   for (ctr = 0; ctr <= 10; ctr++)
      { cout << "main()'s ctr is " << ctr << "\n"; }
   do_fun();   // Calls second function

   return 0;
}

do_fun()
{
```

```
    int ctr;
    for (ctr = 10; ctr >= 0; ctr--)
       { cout << "do_fun()'s ctr is " << ctr << "\n"; }
    return 0;    // Returns to main()
}
```

Although this is a nonsense program that simply prints 0 through 10 and then prints 10 through 0, it shows that using ctr for both function names is not a problem. These variables do not hold important data that must be processed; rather, they are for loop-counting variables. Calling them both ctr leads to little confusion because their use is limited to controlling for loops. Because a for loop initializes and increments variables, the one function never relies on the other function's ctr to do anything.

Be careful about creating local variables with the same name in the same function. If you define a local variable early in a function and then define another local variable with the same name inside a new block, C++ uses only the innermost variable, until its block ends.

The following example helps clarify this confusing problem. The program contains one function with three local variables. See if you can find these three variables.

```
// Filename: MULI.CPP
// Program with multiple local variables called i
#include <iostream.h>
main()
{
   int i;    // Outer i
   i = 10;

   { int i;    // New block's i
     i = 20;    // Outer i still holds a 10
     cout << i << " " << i  << "\n";    // Prints 20 20

     { int i;    // Another new block and local variable
       i = 30;    // Innermost i only
       cout << i << " " << i <<
              " " << i << "\n";    // Prints 30 30 30
     }    // Innermost i is now gone forever

   }    // Second i is gone forever (its block ended)
```

```
   cout << i << " " << i << " " <<
        i << "\n";     // Prints 10 10 10
   return 0;
}    // main() ends and so do its variables
```

All local variables are local to the block in which they are defined. This program has three blocks, each one nested within another. Because you can define local variables immediately after an opening brace of a block, there are three distinct i variables in this program.

The local i disappears completely when its block ends (when the closing brace is reached). C++ always prints the variable that it interprets as the most local—the one that resides within the innermost block.

What is the output of this short program?

```
int x = 9;
#include <iostream.h>
main()
{
   int x = 20;
   {
      int x = 35;
      cout << "x is " << x << "\n";
   }
   cout << "x is " << x << "\n";
   return 0;
}
```

Use Global Variables Sparingly

You might be asking yourself, "Why do I have to understand global and local variables?" At this point, that is an understandable question, especially if you have been programmed mostly in BASIC. Here is the bottom line: global variables can be *dangerous*. Code can inadvertently overwrite a variable that was initialized in another place in the program. It is better to have every variable in your program be *local to the function that has to access it*.

Read that last sentence again. Even though you now know how to make variables global, you should avoid doing so. Try to never use another global variable. It might seem easier to use global variables when

you write programs having more than one function. If you make every variable used by every function global, you never have to worry about whether one is visible or not to any given function. On the other hand, a function can accidentally change a global variable when that was not your intention. If you keep variables local only to functions that need them, you protect their values, and you also keep your programs fully modular.

The Need for Passing Variables

You just learned the difference between local and global variables. You saw that by making your variables local, you protect their values because the function that sees the variable is the only one that can modify it.

What do you do, however, if you have a local variable you want to use in *two or more* functions? In other words, you might need a variable to be both added from the keyboard in one function and printed in another function. If the variable is local only to the first function, how can the second one access it?

You have two solutions if more than one function has to share a variable. One, you can declare the variable globally. This is not a good idea, because you want only those two functions to have access to the variable, but all functions have access to it when it's global. The other alternative—and the better one by far—is to *pass* the local variable from one function to another. This has a big advantage: the variable is known to only those two functions. The rest of the program still has no access to it.

> You never pass a global variable to a function. There is no reason to pass global variables anyway because they are already visible to all functions.

When you pass a local variable from one function to another, you *pass an argument* from the first function to the next. You can pass more than one argument (variable) at a time, if you want several local variables to be sent from one function to another. The receiving function *receives a parameter* (variable) from the function that sends it. You shouldn't worry too much about whether you call them arguments or parameters. The important thing to remember is that you are sending local variables from one function to another.

> **NOTE:** You passed arguments to parameters when you passed data to the strcpy() function. The character literals and variables in the strcpy() parentheses are arguments. The built-in strcpy() function receives these values (called parameters on the receiving end) and copies the second argument to the first.

A little more terminology is needed before you see some examples. When a function passes an argument, it is called the *passing function*. The function that receives the argument (called a parameter when it is received) is called the *receiving function*. Figure 19.1 explains these terms.

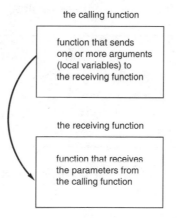

Figure 19.1. The calling and receiving functions.

To pass a local variable from one function to another, you must place the local variable in parentheses in both the calling function and the receiving function. For example, the local and global examples presented earlier did not pass local variables from main() to do_fun(). If a function name has empty parentheses, nothing is being passed to it. Given this, the following line passes two variables, total and discount, to a function called do_fun().

```
do_fun(total, discount);
```

How many variables does the following function call send to the receiving function?

```
CalcWages(hrs, rate, taxes, dependents);
```

It is sometimes said that a variable or a function is *defined*. This has nothing to do with the #define preprocessor directive, which defines literals. You define variables with statements such as the following:

```
int i, j;
int m = 9;
float x;
char ara[] = "Tulsa";
```

These statements tell the program that you need these variables to be reserved. A function is defined when the C++ compiler reads the first statement in the function that describes the name and when it reads any variables that might have been passed to that function as well. Never follow a function definition with a semicolon, but always follow the statement that calls a function with a semicolon.

NOTE: To some C++ purists, a variable is defined only when you write int i; and is initialized when you assign it a value, such as i = 7;. They say that the variable is both defined and initialized when you define the variable and assign it a value at the same time, such as int i = 7;.

The following program contains two function definitions, main() and pr_it().

```
main()   // The main() function definition
{
  int i = 5;   // Defines an integer variable
  pr_it(i);   // Calls the pr_it()
              // function and passes it i
  return 0;   // Returns to the operating system
}


pr_it(int i)   // The pr_it() function definition
{
   cout << i << "\n";   // Calls the cout operator
   return 0;   // Returns to main()
}
```

Because a passed parameter is treated like a local variable in the receiving function, the cout in pr_it() prints a 5, even though the main() function initialized this variable.

Finish the following program so that it contains a function that prints the sum of two floating-point values that `main()` passes to it.

```
#include <iostream.h>
float sum(float num1, float num2);
main()
{
   float n1, n2;
   cout << "What is the first number to add? ";
   cin >> n1;
   cout << "What is the second number to add? ";
   cin >> n2;

   sum(n1, n2);
   return 0;
}
```

The parentheses after a function name act as the "pipeline" through which the passed parameter goes from the calling function to the receiving function. In the preceding program, `main()` passes i to `pr_it()` through the parentheses.

When you pass arguments to a function, the receiving function does not know the data types of the incoming variables. Therefore, you must include each parameter's data type in front of the parameter's name. In the preceding example, the definition of `pr_it()` (the first line of the function) contains the type, `int`, of the incoming variable i. Notice that the `main()` calling function does not have to indicate the variable type. In this example, `main()` already knows the type of variable i (an integer); only `pr_it()` has to know that i is an integer.

> **TIP:** Always declare the parameter types in the receiving function. Precede each parameter in the function's parentheses with `int`, `float`, or whatever each passed variable's data type is.

Here is a program with a `main()` function that contains three local variables. `main()` passes one of these variables to the first function and two of them to the second function.

```cpp
// Filename: LOC3.CPP
// Passes three local variables to functions
#include <iostream.h>
#include <iomanip.h>
pr_init(char initial);   // Prototypes discussed later
pr_other(int age, float salary);

main()
{
   char initial;   // Three variables local to main()
   int age;
   float salary;

   // Fills these variables in main()
   cout << "What is your initial? ";
   cin >> initial;
   cout << "What is your age? ";
   cin >> age;
   cout << "What is your salary? ";
   cin >> salary;

   pr_init(initial);   // Calls pr_init() and
                       // passes it initial
   pr_other(age, salary);   // Calls pr_other() and
                            // passes it age and salary

   return 0;
}

pr_init(char initial)   // Never put a semicolon in
                        // the function definition
{
   cout << "Your initial is " << initial << "\n";
   return 0;   // Returns to main()
}
```

322

```
pr_other(int age, float salary)    // Must type both parameters
{
   cout << "You look young for " << age << "\n";
   cout << "And " << setprecision(2) << salary <<
          " is a LOT of money!";
   return 0;    // Returns to main()
}
```

Write the variables visible to main(), the variables visible to pr_init(), and the variables visible to pr_other() in the spaces provided. Because passed parameters are visible to the function to which they are passed, you can include any variables passed to pr_init() and pr_other().

A receiving function can contain its own local variables. As long as the names are not the same, these local variables do not conflict with the passed ones. In the following program, the second function receives a passed variable from main() and defines its own local variable called price_per.

```
// Filename: LOC4.CPP
// Second function has its own local variable
#include <iostream.h>
#include <iomanip.h>
compute_sale(int gallons);    // Prototypes discussed later

main()
{
   int gallons;

   cout << "Richard's Paint Service \n";
   cout << "How many gallons of paint did you buy? ";
   cin >> gallons;    // Gets gallons in main()

   compute_sale(gallons);    // Computes total in function
   return 0;
}

compute_sale(int gallons)
{
   float price_per = 12.45;    // Local to compute_sale()
```

```
    cout << "The total is " << setprecision(2) <<
          (price_per * (float)gallons) << "\n";
        // Had to typecast gallons because it was integer
    return 0;    // Returns to main()
}
```

The following sample code lines test your skill at recognizing calling functions and receiving functions. Being able to recognize the difference is half the battle of understanding them.

```
do_it()
```

This fragment must be the first line of a new function because it does not end with a semicolon.

```
do_it2(sales);
```

This line calls a function called do_it2(). The calling function passes the variable called sales to do_it2().

```
pr_it(float total)
```

This line is the first line of a function that receives a floating-point variable from another function that called it. All receiving functions must specify the type of each variable being passed.

```
pr_them(float total, int number)
```

This is the first line of a function that receives two variables. One is a floating-point variable and the other is an integer. This line cannot be calling the function pr_them because there is no semicolon at the end of the line.

Automatic Versus Static Variables

The terms *automatic* and *static* describe what happens to local variables when a function returns to the calling procedure. By default, all local variables are automatic, meaning that they are erased when their function ends. You can designate a variable as automatic by prefixing its definition with the term auto.

> **NOTE:** C++ programmers rarely use the auto keyword with local variables because they are automatic by default.

The two statements after main()'s opening brace declare automatic local variables:

```
main()
{
    int i;
    auto float x;
    // Rest of main() goes here
```

Because auto is the default, you do not have to include the term auto with x.

Write the equivalent of the following line without using auto:

```
auto double Sales;
```

The opposite of an automatic variable is a *static* variable. All global variables are static and, as mentioned, all static variables retain their values. Therefore, if a local variable is static, it too retains its value when its function ends—in case the function is called a second time. To declare a variable as static, place the static keyword in front of the variable when you define it. The following code section defines three variables, i, j, and k. The variable i is automatic, but j and k are static.

```
my_fun()    // Start of new function definition
{
    int i;
    static j = 25;    // Both j and k are static variables
    static k = 30;
```

If local variables are static, their values remain in case the function is called again.

Always assign an initial value to a static variable when you declare it, as shown in the last two lines. This initial value is placed in the static variable only the first time my_fun() executes. If you don't assign a static variable an initial value, C++ initializes it to zero.

Static variables are good to use when you write functions that keep track of a count or add to a total. If the counting or totaling variables were local and automatic, their values would disappear when the function finished—destroying the totals.

Automatic and Static Rules for Local Variables

Local automatic variables disappear when their block ends. All local variables are automatic by default. You can prefix a variable (when you define it) with the auto keyword, or you can omit it; the variable is still automatic and its value is destroyed when its local block ends.

Local static variables do not lose their values when their function ends; they remain local to that function. When the function is called after the first time, the static variable's value is still in place. You declare a static variable by placing the static keyword before the variable's definition.

In the following program, the static variable called total is initially set to 0. The 0 is assigned to total *only the first time the function executes* due to its static declaration. The idea here is to add each tripled number and print a message when the total is larger than 300.

```
// Filename: STAT.CPP
// Uses a static variable with the static declaration
#include <iostream.h>
triple_it(int ctr);

main()
{
   int ctr;   // Used in the for loop to
              // call a function 25 times
   for (ctr = 1; ctr <= 25; ctr++)
     { triple_it(ctr); }   // Pass ctr to a function
                           // called triple_it()

   return 0;
}

triple_it(int ctr)
{
```

```
    static int total = 0;    // Local and static
    int ans;    // Local and automatic
    // total is set to 0 only the first time this
    // function is called

    // Triples whatever value is passed to it and adds
    // the total

    ans = ctr * 3;    // Triples number passed
    total += ans;    // Adds triple numbers as this is called

    cout << "The number " << ctr << " multiplied by 3 is "
        << ans << "\n";

    if (total > 300)
      { cout << "The total of triple numbers is over 300 \n"; }
    return 0;
}
```

If you ever want a variable to retain its value after a function ends, you must make it static. Because local variables are automatic by default, you have to include the static keyword to override this default. Then the value of the total variable is retained each time the subroutine is called.

The preceding program's output follows. Notice that the function's cout is triggered, even though total is a local variable. Because total is static, its value is not erased when the function finishes. When main() calls the function a second time, total's previous value (at the time you left the routine) is still there.

```
The number 1 multiplied by 3 is 3
The number 2 multiplied by 3 is 6
The number 3 multiplied by 3 is 9
The number 4 multiplied by 3 is 12
The number 5 multiplied by 3 is 15
The number 6 multiplied by 3 is 18
The number 7 multiplied by 3 is 21
The number 8 multiplied by 3 is 24
The number 9 multiplied by 3 is 27
The number 10 multiplied by 3 is 30
The number 11 multiplied by 3 is 33
The number 12 multiplied by 3 is 36
The number 13 multiplied by 3 is 39
The number 14 multiplied by 3 is 42
```

```
The total of triple numbers is over 300
The number 15 multiplied by 3 is 45
The total of triple numbers is over 300
The number 16 multiplied by 3 is 48
The total of triple numbers is over 300
The number 17 multiplied by 3 is 51
The total of triple numbers is over 300
The number 18 multiplied by 3 is 54
The total of triple numbers is over 300
The number 19 multiplied by 3 is 57
The total of triple numbers is over 300
The number 20 multiplied by 3 is 60
The total of triple numbers is over 300
The number 21 multiplied by 3 is 63
The total of triple numbers is over 300
The number 22 multiplied by 3 is 66
The total of triple numbers is over 300
The number 23 multiplied by 3 is 69
The total of triple numbers is over 300
The number 24 multiplied by 3 is 72
The total of triple numbers is over 300
The number 25 multiplied by 3 is 75
The total of triple numbers is over 300
```

Local static variables do not become global. In the preceding program, main() cannot refer, use, print, or change total because it is local to the second function. static simply means that the local variable's value is still there if the program calls the function again.

What is the output of the following program? Be careful!

```cpp
#include <iostream.h>
main()
{
    int ctr;
    for (ctr = 0; ctr < 5; ctr++)
        {
            static int ctr2 = ctr;
            cout << ctr2;
        }
}
```

328

Three Issues of Parameter Passing

To have a complete understanding of programs with several functions, you have to learn about three additional concepts:

- passing arguments (variables) *by value* (also called *by copy*)

- passing arguments (variables) *by address* (also called *by reference*)

- returning values from functions

The first two concepts deal with the way local variables are passed and received. The third concept describes how receiving functions send values back to the calling functions. Lesson 20, "Passing Values," concludes this discussion by explaining these three methods for passing parameters and returning values.

Review Questions

1. TRUE or FALSE: A function should always include a return statement as its last command, even though return is not required.

2. When a local variable is passed, is it called an argument or a parameter?

3. TRUE or FALSE: A function that is passed variables from another function cannot also have its own local variables.

4. What must appear inside the receiving function's parentheses, other than the variables passed to it?

5. If a function keeps track of a total or count every time it is called, should the counting or totaling variable be automatic or static?

329

6. When would you pass a global variable to a function? (Be careful—this might be a trick question!)

7. How many arguments are there in the following statement?

```
cout << "The rain has fallen " << rainf << " inches.";
```

Review Exercises

1. Write a program that asks, in `main()`, for the age of the user's dog. Write a second function called `people()` that multiplies the dog's age by seven to compute how old the dog would be if it were human.

2. Write a function that counts the number of times it is called. Name the function `count_it()`. Do not pass it anything. In the body of `count_it()`, print the following message:

```
The number of times this function has been called is: ##
```

where ## is the number. (*Hint:* Because the variable must be local, make it static and initialize it to zero when you first define it.)

3. The following program contains several problems. Some of these problems produce errors. One problem is not an error, but a bad location for a variable declaration. (*Hint:* Find all the global variables.) See whether you can spot some of the problems, and rewrite the program so that it works better.

```
// Filename: BAD.CPP
// Program with bad uses of variable declarations
#include <iostream.h>
#define NUM 10
do_var_fun();    // Prototypes discussed later

char city[] = "Miami";
int count;

main()
{
   int abc;

   count = NUM;
```

```
    abc = 5;
    do_var_fun();

    cout << abc << " " << count << " " << pgm_var
    << " " << xyz;

    return 0;
}

int pgm_var = 7;

do_var_fun()
{
    char xyz = 'A';

    xyz = 'b';
    cout << xyz << " " << pgm_var << " " abc
    << " " << city;
    return 0;
}
```

Passing Values

 To explain how to pass variables by value and by reference.

C++ passes variables between functions using two different methods. The one you use depends on how you want the passed variables to be changed. This lesson explores these two methods. The concepts discussed here are not unique to the C++ language. Other programming languages, such as Pascal, FORTRAN, and QBasic, pass parameters using similar techniques. A computer language must have the capability to pass information between functions before it can truly be called structured.

This lesson introduces you to passing variables by value and passing variables by reference. It is especially important for you to understand these concepts because most of the remaining programs in this book rely on these methods.

NOTE: A third way that C++ can pass parameters is called *passing by address*. Passing by reference makes the more difficult passing by address obsolete.

Passing by Value (Passing by Copy)

Passing by value and *passing by copy* mean the same thing in computer terms. Some textbooks and C++ programmers state that arguments are passed *by value,* and some state that they are passed *by copy.* Both phrases describe one of the two methods by which arguments are passed to receiving functions. The other method, *by reference,* is covered later in this lesson.

When an argument (local variable) is passed by value, a copy of the variable's value is sent—and assigned—to the receiving function's parameter. If more than one variable is passed by value, a copy of each value is sent—and assigned—to the receiving function's parameters.

Figure 20.1 illustrates *passing by copy.* The value of i—not the variable—is passed to the called function, which receives it as a variable i. Two variables are called i, not one. The first is local to main(), and the second is local to pr_it(). They have the same names, but because they are local to their respective functions, there is no conflict. The variable doesn't have to be called i in both functions, and because the value of i is sent to the receiving function, it doesn't matter what the receiving function calls the variable that receives this value.

Figure 20.1.
Passing the
variable i *by*
value.

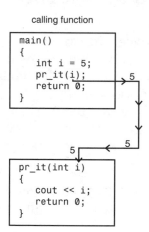

In this case, when passing and receiving variables between functions, it is wisest to retain the same names. Even though they are not the same variables, they hold the same value. In this example, the value 5 is passed from main()'s i to pr_it()'s i.

334

Because a copy of i's value (not the variable itself) is passed to the receiving function, if pr_it() changes i, it is changing only its copy of i and not main()'s i. This fact truly separates functions from variables. You now have the technique for passing a copy of a variable to a receiving function, with the receiving function unable to modify the calling function's variable.

All C++ nonarray variables you have seen so far are passed by value. You don't have to do anything special to pass variables by value, except to pass them in the calling function's argument list and receive them in the receiving function's parameter list.

> **NOTE:** The default method for passing parameters is by value, as just described, unless you pass arrays. Arrays are always passed by the other method, by reference, described in the section in this lesson called "Passing by Reference."

In the following program, is Age passed by value or by reference? How is Name passed?

```
main()
{
   char Name[] = "Julie";
   int Age = 21;

   prData(Age, Name);
   return 0;
}
prData(int Age, char Name[])
{
   cout << Age << "\n";
   cout << Name << "\n";
   return 0;
}
```

The following program asks users for their weight. It then passes that weight to a function that calculates the equivalent weight on the moon. Notice that the second function uses the passed value and calculates with it. After weight is passed to the second function, that function can treat weight as though it were a local variable.

```
// Filename: PASSV1.CPP
// Calculates the user's weight in a second function
#include <iostream.h>
moon(int weight);    // Prototypes discussed later

main()
{
    int weight;    // main()'s local weight
    cout << "How many pounds do you weigh? ";
    cin >> weight;

    moon(weight);    // Calls the moon() function and
                     // passes it the weight
    return 0;    // Returns to the operating system
}

moon(int weight)    // Declares the passed parameter
{
    // Moon weights are 1/6 Earth's weights
    weight /= 6;    // Divides the weight by six

    cout << "You weigh only " << weight <<
            " pounds on the moon!";
    return 0;    // Returns to main()
}
```

The output of this program follows:

```
How many pounds do you weigh? 120
You weigh only 20 pounds on the moon!
```

You can rename passed variables in the receiving function. They are distinct from the passing function's variable. The following is the same program as in PASSV1.CPP, except that the receiving function calls the passed variable earth_weight. A new variable, called moon_weight, is local to the called function and is used for the moon's equivalent weight.

```
// Filename: PASSV2.CPP
// Calculates the user's weight in a second function
#include <iostream.h>
moon(int earth_weight);
```

```
main()
{
   int weight;   // main()'s local weight
   cout << "How many pounds do you weigh? ";
   cin >> weight;

   moon(weight);    // Calls the moon() function and
                    // passes it the weight
   return 0;    // Returns to the operating system
}

moon(int earth_weight)    // Declares the passed parameter
{
   int moon_weight;    // Local to this function

   // Moon weights are 1/6 of Earth's weights
   moon_weight = earth_weight / 6;    // Divides weight by six

   cout << "You only weigh " << moon_weight <<
           " pounds on the moon!";
   return 0;    // Returns to main()
}
```

The resulting output is identical to that of PASSV1.CPP. Renaming the passed variable changes nothing.

The next example passes three variables—of three different types—to the called function. In the receiving function's parameter list, each of these variable types must be defined.

The next program prompts users for three values in the `main()` function. The `main()` function then passes these variables to the receiving function, which calculates and prints values related to those passed variables. When the called function modifies a variable passed to the function, notice again that this does not affect the calling function's variable. When variables are passed by value, the value—not the variable—is passed.

```
// Filename: PASSV3.CPP
// Gets grade information for a student
#include <iostream.h>
#include <iomanip.h>
check_grade(char lgrade, float average, int tests);
```

```
main()
{
   char lgrade;    // Letter grade
   int  tests;     // Number of tests not yet taken
   float average;    // Student's average based on 4.0 scale

   cout << "What letter grade do you want? ";
   cin >> lgrade;
   cout << "What is your current test average? ";
   cin >> average;
   cout << "How many tests do you have left? ";
   cin >> tests;

   check_grade(lgrade, average, tests);    // Calls function
                                           // and passes three
                                           // variables by value
   return 0;
}

check_grade(char lgrade, float average, int tests)
{
   switch (tests)
   {
     case (0): { cout << "You will get your current grade "
                      << "of " << lgrade;
                 break; }
     case (1): { cout << "You still have time to bring " <<
                        "up your average";
                 cout << "of " << setprecision(1) <<
                        average << ".  Study hard!";
                 break; }
      default:  { cout << "Relax.  You still have plenty of "
                      <<  "time.";
                 break; }
   }
   return 0;
}
```

In the preceding program, check_grade() cannot have access to main()'s local variables unless main() passes those variables to check_grade(). Because the variables are not arrays, main() passes them by value, which means that only copies of the variable's values are sent. If check_grade()

changes any of the variables (it doesn't in this program), those changes are not made in main() because copies of the variable's values, not the variables themselves, were sent.

Passing by Reference

The preceding section described passing arguments by value (or by copy). This section teaches you how to pass arguments by reference.

When you pass by reference, the same variable is worked on in both functions.

When you pass an argument (a local variable) *by reference,* the variable's address is sent—and assigned—to the receiving function's parameter. If you pass more than one variable by reference, each address is sent—and assigned—to the receiving function's parameters.

Variable Addresses

All variables in memory (RAM) are stored at memory addresses (see Figure 20.2). Refer to Appendix B for more information on the internal representation of memory.

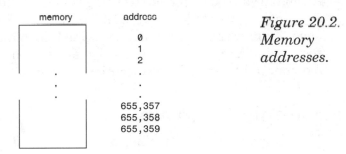

Figure 20.2. Memory addresses.

When you tell C++ to define a variable (such as int i;), you are telling C++ to find an unused place in memory and assign that place (or memory address) to i. When your program uses the variable called i, C++ goes to i's address and uses whatever is there.

If you define five variables as follows:

```
int i;
float x = 9.8;
char ara[2] = {'A', 'B'};
int j = 8, k = 3;
```

C++ might arbitrarily place them in memory at the addresses shown in Figure 20.3.

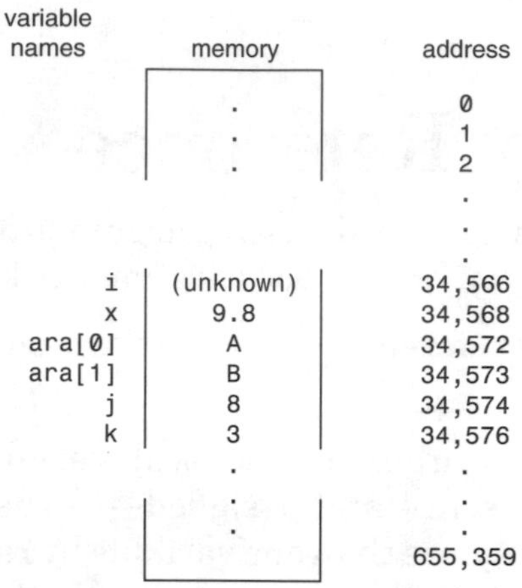

Figure 20.3.
Storing variables
in memory.

```
variable
names          memory              address

               ┌────────┐            0
               │    .   │            1
               │    .   │            2
               │    .   │            .
               │        │            .
        i      │(unknown)│         34,566
        x      │   9.8   │         34,568
    ara[0]     │    A    │         34,572
    ara[1]     │    B    │         34,573
        j      │    8    │         34,574
        k      │    3    │         34,576
               │    .   │            .
               │    .   │            .
               │    .   │            .
               └────────┘        655,359
```

You don't know what is contained in the variable called i because you haven't put anything in it yet. Before you use i, you should initialize it with a value. All variables—except character variables—usually use more than 1 byte of memory.

You do not know to what addresses C++ will store your variables. Although you could find out by using your compiler's *debugger* (a program that enables you to look at details of your program as it runs), you don't need to know the exact addresses. The important thing to know for this section is simply that all variables are stored at different locations in memory, and each of those locations has an address.

Sample Program

The address of the variable, not its value, is copied to the receiving reference function when you pass a variable by reference. In C++, *all arrays are automatically passed as if by reference.* (Actually, a copy of their starting address is passed, but you will understand this better when you learn more about arrays and pointers.) The following important rule holds true for programs that pass by reference:

> Every time you pass a variable by reference, if the receiving function changes the variable, the variable is also changed in the calling function.

Therefore, if you pass an array to a function and the function changes the array, those changes are still with the array when it returns to the calling function. Unlike passing by value, passing by reference gives you the ability to change a variable in the *called* function and to keep those changes in effect in the *calling* function. The following sample program illustrates this concept.

```
// Filename: ADD1.CPP
// Passing by reference example
#include <iostream.h>
#include <string.h>
change_it(char c[4]);    // Prototype discussed later
main()
{
   char name[4]="ABC";

   change_it(name);    // Passes by address because
                       // it is an array
   cout << name << "\n";    // Called function can
                           // change array

   return 0;
}

change_it(char c[4])    // You must tell the function
                        // that c is an array
{
   cout << c << "\n";    // Prints as it is passed
   strcpy(c, "USA");    // Changes the array, both
                        // here and in main()

   return 0;
}
```

Here is this program's output:

```
ABC
USA
```

> **NOTE:** C++ purists say that arrays are *passed by address,* but the distinction is minor for purposes of this discussion.

At this point, you should have no trouble understanding that the array is passed from main() to the function called change_it(). Even though change_it() calls the array c, it refers to the same array passed by the main() function (name).

Figure 20.4 shows how the array is passed. Although the address of the array—not its value—is passed from name to c, both arrays are the same.

Figure 20.4.
Passing an array
by reference.

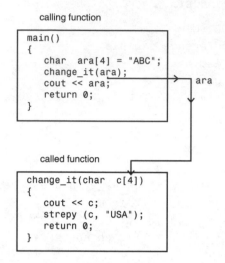

Before you read any further, a few additional comments are in order. Because the address of name is passed to the function—even though the array is called c in the receiving function—it is still the same array as name. Figure 20.5 shows how C++ accomplishes this task at the memory-address level.

Figure 20.5.
The array being
passed is the same
array in both
functions.

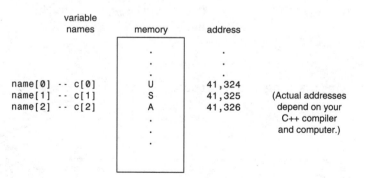

The variable array is referred to as name in main() and as c in change_it(). Because the address of name is copied to the receiving function, the variable is changed no matter what it is called in either function. Because change_it() changes the array, the array is also changed in main().

An array is being received in the following function. Obviously, the programmer is attempting to receive the array by reference, but something is amiss. Can you find what it is?

```
getAvf(int &ara[20])     // First line of function
```

The following program segment asks the user for his or her first name in main(). Write a function that reverses the name in the array so that main() can print the reversed name. To make it easy, assume that the user's name is always five characters long ("Jerry" or "Peter," for example).

```
#include <iostream.h>
void rev(char name[]);
main()
{
    char name[6];  // Room for 5-letter name
    cout << "What is your first name (5 letters, please)? ";
    cin >> name;

    rev(name);    // Calls function that reverses the name
    cout << "Your name spelled backwards is " << name << "\n";
    return 0;
}
```

You can now use a function to fill an array with user input. The following function asks users for their first name in the function called get_name(). As users type the name in the array, it is also entered in main()'s array. The main() function then passes the array to pr_name(), where it is printed. If arrays were passed by value, this program would not work. Only the array value would be passed to the called functions.

```
// Filename: ADD2.CPP
// Gets a name in an array, then prints it using
// separate functions
#include <iostream.h>
get_name(char name[25]);   // Prototypes discussed later
```

343

```
print_name(char name[25]);

main()
{
   char name[25];
   get_name(name);    // Gets the user's name
   print_name(name);   // Prints the user's name
   return 0;
}

get_name(char name[25])    // Passes the array by address
{
   cout << "What is your first name? ";
   cin >> name;
   return 0;
}

print_name(char name[25])
{
   cout << "\n\n Here you are, " << name;
   return 0;
}
```

When you pass an array, be sure to specify the array's type in the receiving function's parameter list. If the preceding program declared the passed array with

```
get_name(char name)
```

the function `get_name()` would interpret this as a single character variable, *not* as a character array. You never have to put the array size in brackets. The following statement also works as the first line of `get_name()`.

```
get_name(char name[])
```

Most C++ programmers put the array size in brackets to clarify the array size, even though the size is not needed.

 Many programmers pass character arrays to functions to erase character arrays. The following code lines contain a function called `clear_it()`. It expects two parameters—a character array and the total number of elements declared for that array. The array is passed by reference (as are all arrays), and the number of elements, `num_els`, is passed by value (as are all nonarrays). When the function finishes, the array is cleared (all its elements are reset to null zero). Subsequent functions that use the array can then have an empty array.

```
clear_it(char ara[10], int num_els)
{
   int ctr;
   for (ctr = 0; ctr < num_els; ctr++)
     { ara[ctr] = '\0'; }
   return 0;
}
```

The brackets after ara do not have to contain a number, as described in the preceding example. The 10 in this example is simply a placeholder for the brackets. Any value (or no value) would work as well.

Passing Nonarrays by Reference

You now should understand the difference between passing variables by reference and by value. Arrays can be passed by reference, and nonarrays can be passed by value. You can override the *by value* default for nonarrays. This is helpful sometimes, but it is not always recommended because the called function can damage values in the called function.

If you want a nonarray variable changed in a receiving function and you also want the changes kept in the calling function, you must override the default and pass the variable by reference. (You will understand this section better after you learn how arrays and pointers relate.) To pass a nonarray by reference, you must precede the argument in the receiving function with an ampersand (&).

The following examples demonstrate how to pass nonarray variables by reference.

The following program passes a variable by address from main() to a function. The function changes it and returns to main(). Because the variable is passed by reference, main() recognizes the new value.

```
// Filename: ADD3.CPP
// Demonstrates passing nonarrays by reference
#include <iostream.h>
do_fun(int &amt);    // Prototypes discussed later

main()
{
   int amt;

   amt = 100;    // Assigns a value in main()
   cout << "In main(), amt is " << amt << "\n";
```

```
   do_fun(amt);    // Passes amt by reference
   cout << "After return, amt is " << amt << " in main()\n";
   return 0;
}

do_fun(int &amt)    // Informs function of
                    // passing by reference
{
   amt = 85;    // Assigns new value to amt
   cout << "In do_fun(), amt is " << amt << "\n";
   return 0;
}
```

The output from this program follows:

```
In main(), amt is 100
In do_fun(), amt is 85
After return, amt is 85 in main()
```

Notice that amt changed in the called function. Because it was passed by reference, it is also changed in the calling function.

You can use a function to get the user's keyboard values. The main() function recognizes those values as long as you pass them by address. The following program calculates the cubic feet in a swimming pool. In one function, it requests the width, length, and depth. In another function, it calculates the cubic feet of water. Finally, in a third function, it prints the answer. The main() function clearly is a controlling function, passing variables between these functions by reference.

```
// Filename: POOL.CPP
// Calculates the cubic feet in a swimming pool
#include <iostream.h>
get_values(int &length, int &width, int &depth);
calc_cubic(int &length, int &width, int &depth, int &cubic);
print_cubic(int &cubic);

main()
{
   int length, width, depth, cubic;

   get_values(length, width, depth);
   calc_cubic(length, width, depth, cubic);
   print_cubic(cubic);
```

```
   return 0;
}


get_values(int &length, int &width, int &depth)
{
   cout << "What is the pool's length? ";
   cin >> length;
   cout << "What is the pool's width? ";
   cin >> width;
   cout << "What is the pool's average depth? ";
   cin >> depth;
   return 0;
}


calc_cubic(int &length, int &width, int &depth, int &cubic)
{
   cubic = (length) * (width) * (depth);
   return 0;
}


print_cubic(int &cubic)
{
   cout << "\nThe pool has " << cubic << " cubic feet\n";
   return 0;
}
```

The output follows:

```
What is the pool's length? 16
What is the pool's width? 32
What is the pool's average depth? 6
The pool has 3072 cubic feet
```

All variables in a function must be preceded with an ampersand if they are to be passed by reference.

Rewrite the following function so that it receives its nonarray arguments by reference.

```
do_fun(int i, float j)
{
   i += 25;
   j *= 4.0;
   return 0;
}
```

You now have a complete understanding of the various methods for passing data to functions. Because you will be using local variables as much as possible, you must know how to pass local variables between functions but also keep the variables away from functions that don't need them.

You can pass data in two ways: by value and by reference. When you pass data by value, which is the default method for nonarrays, only a copy of the variable's contents is passed. If the called function modifies its parameters, those variables are not modified in the calling function. When you pass data by reference, as is done with arrays and nonarray variables preceded by an ampersand, the receiving function can change the data in both functions.

Whenever you pass values, you must ensure that they match in number and type. If you don't match them, you could have problems. For example, suppose that you pass an array and a floating-point variable, but in the receiving function, you receive a floating-point variable followed by an array. The data doesn't reach the receiving function properly because the parameter data types do not match the variables being passed. Lesson 21, "Return Values and Prototypes," shows you how to protect against such disasters by prototyping all your functions.

Review Questions

1. What is another name for *passing by value?*

2. What kind of variables are automatically passed by reference?

3. What kind of variables are automatically passed by value?

4. TRUE or FALSE: If a variable is passed by value, it is also passed by copy.

5. If a variable is passed to a function by value and the function changes the variable, is it changed in the calling function?

6. If a variable is passed to a function by reference and the function changes the variable, is it changed in the calling function?

7. What is wrong with the following function?

```
do_fun(x, y, z)
{
    cout << "The variables are " << x << y << z;
    return 0;
}
```

8. Suppose that you pass a nonarray variable and an array to a function at the same time. What is the default?

    (a) Both are passed by reference.

    (b) Both are passed by value.

    (c) One is passed by reference and the other is passed by value.

Review Exercises

1. Write a `main()` function and a second function that `main()` calls. Ask users for their annual income in `main()`. Pass the income to the second function and print a congratulatory message if the user makes more than $50,000 or an encouragement message if the user makes less.

2. Write a three-function program consisting of the following functions:

```
main()
fun1()
fun2()
```

   Declare a 10-element character array in `main()`, fill it with the letters A through J in `fun1()`, then print that array backward in `fun2()`.

3. Write a program whose `main()` function passes a number to a function called `print_aster()`. The `print_aster()` function prints that many asterisks on a line, across the screen. If `print_aster()` is passed a number greater than 80, display an error because most screens cannot print more than 80 characters on one line. When execution is finished, return control to `main()` and then return to the operating system.

4. Write a function that is passed two integer values by reference. The function should declare a third local variable. Use the third variable as an intermediate variable and swap the values of both passed integers. For example, suppose that the calling function passes your function old_pay and new_pay, as in

```
swap_it(old_pay, new_pay);
```

The swap_it() function reverses the two values, so when control returns to the calling function, the values of old_pay and new_pay are swapped.

Return Values and Prototypes

To explain how to return values from functions and prototype all your functions to help eliminate possible errors.

So far, you have passed variables to functions in only one direction—a calling function passed data to a receiving function. You have yet to see how data is passed back *from* the receiving function to the calling function. When you pass variables by reference, the data is changed in both functions. This is different from specifically passing back data. This lesson focuses on writing function return values that improve your programming power.

After you learn to pass and return values, you need to *prototype* your own functions, as well as C++'s built-in functions such as strcpy(). By prototyping all functions, you ensure the accuracy of passed and returned values.

Function Return Values

All functions discussed in this book so far have acted like *subroutines* or *subfunctions*. A C++ subroutine is a function that is called from another function but that does not return any values. The difference between subroutines and functions is not as critical in C++ as it is in other languages. All functions, whether they are subroutines or functions that return values, are defined in the same way. You can pass variables to each of them, as you have seen throughout Classroom 5, "Scope and Functions."

In the last few lessons, you have seen a `return` statement at the end of each function. Those lessons explained that not all functions need `return`. Whenever you want to return values from a function, however, you must put `return` at the end of the function. The `return` is the mechanism whereby C++ sends a value back to the calling function.

 Functions that return values offer a new approach to programming. In addition to passing data in one direction, from a calling to a receiving function, you can pass data back from a receiving function to its calling function. When you want to return a value from a function to its calling function, put the return value after the `return` statement. To clarify the return value even more, many programmers put parentheses around the return value, as shown in the following syntax:

```
return (return value);
```

> **TIP:** Do not return global variables. There is no need to do so because their values are already known throughout the code.

The calling function must have a use for the return value. For example, suppose that you wrote a function that calculated the average of any three integer variables passed to it. If you return the average, the calling function has to receive that return value. The following sample program illustrates this principle.

```cpp
// Filename: AVGRET.CPP
// Calculates the average of three input values
#include <iostream.h>
int calc_av(int num1, int num2, int num3);   //Prototype

main()
{
```

```
    int num1, num2, num3;
    int avg;    // Holds the return value

    cout << "Please type three numbers (such as 23 54 85) ";
    cin >> num1 >> num2 >> num3;

    // Calls the function, passes the numbers,
    // and accepts the return value amount
    avg = calc_av(num1, num2, num3);        passes num1, num2, num3 to calc_av

    cout << "\n\nThe average is " << avg;    // Prints the
                                             // return value
    return 0;
}


int calc_av(int num1, int num2, int num3)
{
    int local_avg;    // Holds the average for these numbers
    local_avg = (num1 + num2 + num3) / 3;

    return (local_avg);      This variable gets returned for calc_av
}
```

Here is a sample output from this program:

```
Please type three numbers (such as 23 54 85) 30 40 50
```

```
The average is 40
```

Study this program carefully. It is similar to many you have seen, but a few additional points must be considered now that the function returns a value. It might help to walk through this program a few lines at a time.

Figure 21.1 shows you how main() passes calc_av() three values, then gets calc_av()'s return value.

The first part of main() is similar to other programs you have seen. It declares its local variables—three for user input and one for the calculated average. cout and cin are familiar to you. The function call to calc_av() is also familiar. It passes three variables (num1, num2, and num3) by value to calc_av(). If it passed them by reference, an ampersand (&) would have to precede each argument, as discussed in Lesson 20, "Passing Values."

Figure 21.1.
Passing three
values and
returning one.

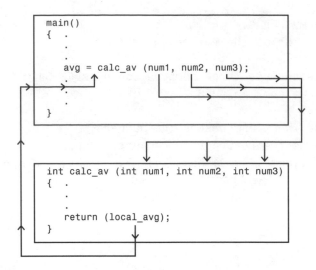

 Of the following three `return` statements, only the first and third return values. A `return` statement can return at most one value.

```
return (a);
return;
return Age;    // The parentheses are not required
```

Put the function's return type before its name. If you don't specify a return type, `int` is the default.

The receiving function, `calc_av()`, seems similar to others you've seen. The only difference is that the first line, the function's definition line, has one addition—the `int` before its name. This is the *type* of the return value. You must always precede a function name with its return data type. If you do not specify a type, C++ assumes a type of `int`. Therefore, if this example had no return type, it would work just as well because an `int` return type would be assumed.

Because the variable being returned from `calc_av()` is an integer, the `int` return type was placed before `calc_av()`'s name.

You also can see that the return statement of `calc_av()` includes the return value, `local_avg`. This is the variable being sent back to the calling function, `main()`. You can return only a single variable to a calling function.

Even though a function can receive more than one parameter, it can return only a single value to the calling function. If a receiving function is modifying more than one value from the calling function, you must pass the parameters by reference. You cannot return multiple values using a `return` statement.

After the `calc_av()` receiving function returns the value, `main()` must do something with that returned value. So far, you have seen function calls on lines by themselves. Notice in `main()` that the function call appears on the right side of the following assignment statement:

```
avg = calc_av(num1, num2, num3);
```

When the `calc_av()` function returns its value—the average of the three numbers—that value replaces the function call. If the average computed in `calc_av()` is 40, the C++ compiler interprets the following statement in place of the function call:

```
avg = 40;
```

You typed a function call to the right of the equal sign, but the program replaces a function call with its return value when the `return` takes place. In other words, a function that returns a value becomes that value. You must put such a function anywhere you put any variable or literal (usually to the right of an equal sign, in an expression, or in `cout`). The following is an *incorrect* way of calling `calc_av()`:

```
calc_av(num1, num2, num3);
```

If you did this, C++ would have nowhere to put the return value.

A function call that calls another function becomes the called function's return value. Therefore, in the preceding function call, `calc_av(num1, num2, num3);` becomes whatever value `calc_av()` returns. Suppose that `calc_av()`'s return value is 45.6. Unless you assign that value to a variable, you are letting 46.6 sit on the line by itself, in effect having this "statement":

```
45.6;
```

Function calls that return values usually don't appear on lines by themselves. Because the function call is replaced by the return value, you should do something with that return value (such as assign it to a variable or use it in an expression). Return values can be ignored, but doing so usually defeats the purpose of creating them.

Assuming that all of the following function calls return values, which of the four example lines handle the return value in some way?

```
x = MyNum(i, j);
```

```
cout << TestIt(n, o, p);
```

```
GetValues(v1, v2);

num = addIt(d, e) + addIt(f, g);
```

A few examples help further clarify return values. The following program passes a number to a function called doub(). The function doubles the number and returns the result.

```cpp
// Filename: DOUB.CPP
// Doubles the user's number
#include <iostream.h>
int doub (int num);
main()
{
    int number;    // Holds user's input
    int d_number;    // Holds double the user's input
    cout << "What number do you want doubled? ";
    cin >> number;

    d_number = doub(number);    // Assigns return value
    cout << number << " doubled is " << d_number;
    return 0;
}

int doub(int num)
{
    int d_num;
    d_num = num * 2;    // Doubles the number
    return (d_num);    // Returns the result
}
```

The program produces output such as this:

```
What number do you want doubled? 5
5 doubled is 10
```

doub() cannot directly use main()'s number variable because number is local to main(). Therefore, main() must pass number to doub(). Because main() needs the result of the doub() function, doub() sends the doubled result back to main(), where main() then prints the returned value.

You can use function return values *anywhere* that literals, variables, and expressions are used. The following program is similar to the preceding one. The difference is in main().

356

The function call is performed not on a line by itself, but from a cout. This is a nested function call. You call the built-in function cout using the return value from one of the program's functions named doub(). Because the call to doub() is replaced by its return value, the cout has enough information to proceed as soon as doub() returns. This gives main() less overhead because it no longer needs a variable called d_number, although you must judge whether this program is easier to maintain. Sometimes it is wise to include function calls in other expressions. At other times, it is clearer to call the function and assign its return value to a variable before using it.

```cpp
// Filename: DOUB2.CPP
// Doubles the user's number
#include <iostream.h>
int doub(int num);    // Prototype

main()
{
   int number;    // Holds user's input
   cout << "What number do you want doubled? ";
   cin >> number;

   // The third cout parameter is
   // replaced with a return value
   cout << number << " doubled is " << doub(number);

   return 0;
}

int doub(int num)
{
   int d_num;
   d_num = num * 2;    // Doubles the number
   return (d_num);    // Returns the result
}
```

Write the called function for the following program that computes and returns the square of the number passed to it. (The square of a number is the number multiplied by itself.)

```
#include <iostream.h>
int doub(int num);    // Prototype
main()
{
    int number;    // Holds user's input
    cout << "What number do you want squared? ";
    cin >> number;
    // The third cout parameter is
    // replaced with a return value
    cout << number << " squared is " << sq(number);
    return 0;
}
```

The following program asks the user for a number. That number is then passed to a function called sum(), which adds the numbers from 1 to that number. In other words, if the user types a 6, the function returns the result of the following calculation:

```
1 + 2 + 3 + 4 + 5 + 6
```

This is known as the *sum of the digits* calculation. It is sometimes used for depreciation in accounting.

```
// Filename: SUMD.CPP
// Computes the sum of the digits
#include <iostream.h>
int sum(int num);    // Prototype

main()
{
    int num, sumd;
```

```cpp
   cout << "Please type a number: ";
   cin >> num;

   sumd = sum(num);
   cout << "The sum of the digits is " << sumd;
   return 0;
}

int sum(int num)
{
   int ctr;    // Local loop counter
   int sumd = 0;    // Local to this function
   if (num <= 0)    // Checks whether parameter is too small
     { sumd = num; }    // Returns parameter if too small
   else
     { for (ctr = 1; ctr <= num; ctr++)
          { sumd += ctr; }
     }
   return(sumd);
}
```

What is the result of the preceding program, assuming that the user types a 5?

The following program contains a function that returns values. The function, `maximum()`, returns the larger of two numbers entered by the user.

```cpp
// Filename: MAX.CPP
// Finds maximum of two values in a function
#include <iostream.h>

int maximum(int num1, int num2);    // Prototypes
main()
{
   int num1, num2;    // User's two numbers
   int max;

   cout << "Please type two numbers (such as 46 75) ";
   cin >> num1 >> num2;
```

```
   max = maximum(num1, num2);   // Assigns the return
                                // value of each
                                // function to variables
   cout << "The maximum number is " << max << "\n";
   return 0;
}

int maximum(int num1, int num2)
{
   int max;    // Local to this function only
   max = (num1 > num2) ? (num1) : (num2);
   return (max);
}
```

Here is a sample output from this program:

```
Please type two numbers (such as 46 75) 72 55
The maximum number is 72
```

If the user types the same number twice, maximum returns that number. The maximum() function can be passed any two integer values. In an example as simple as this one, the user certainly already knows which number is higher. The point of this example is to show how to code return values. You might want to use similar functions in a more useful application, such as finding the highest paid employee from a payroll disk file.

Write a minimum() function that finds the minimum of two values.

Function Prototypes

The word *prototype* is sometimes defined as a model. In C++, a function prototype models the actual function. Before completing your study of functions, parameters, and return values, you must understand how to prototype each function in your program.

C++ requires you to prototype all functions in your program. When prototyping, you inform C++ of the function's parameter types and its return value, if any.

To prototype a function, copy the function's definition line to the top of your program (immediately before or after the #include <iostream.h> line). Place a semicolon at the end of the function definition line, and you have the prototype. The definition line (the function's first line) contains the return type, the function name, and the type of each argument, so the function prototype serves as a model of the function that follows.

If a function does not return a value, or if that function has no arguments passed to it, you should still prototype it. Place the keyword void in place of the return type or the parameters. main() is the only function that you do not have to prototype, because it is *self-prototyping*. This means that main() is not called by another function. The first time main() appears in your program (assuming that you follow the standard approach and make main() your program's first function), it is executed.

If a function returns nothing, void must be its return type. Put void in the argument parentheses of function prototypes with no arguments. All functions must match their prototypes.

C++ assumes functions return int unless you use a different data return type or use the void keyword.

All main() functions in the last few lessons return a 0. Why? You now know enough to answer that question. Because main() is self-prototyping, and because the void keyword never appears before main() in these programs, C++ assumes an int return type. All C++ functions prototyped as returning int or those without any return data type prototype assume int. If you don't want to put return 0; at the end of main()'s functions, you must insert void before main(), as in:

```
void main()    // main() self-prototypes to return nothing
```

The first several lessons in this book did not return a value in main() because return 0; is difficult to explain until you understand passing and returning values. You can look at a statement and tell if it's a prototype or a function definition (the function's first line) by whether or not it has a semicolon at the end. All prototypes end with a semicolon.

Prototype for Safety

Prototyping protects you from programming mistakes. Suppose that you write a function that expects two arguments—an integer followed by a floating-point value. Here is the first line of such a function:

```
my_fun(int num, float amount)
```

What if you passed incorrect data types to my_fun()? If you were to call this function by passing two literals to it, a floating-point followed by an integer, as in

```
my_fun(23.43, 5);   // Calls the my_fun() function
```

the function would not receive correct parameters. It is expecting an integer followed by a floating-point, but you did the opposite and sent it a floating-point followed by an integer.

In regular C programs, mismatched arguments such as these generate no error message, even though the data is not passed correctly. C++ requires prototypes so that you cannot send the wrong data types to a function (or expect the wrong data type to be returned). Prototyping the preceding function results in this:

```
void my_fun(int num, float amount);   // Prototype
```

In doing so, you tell the compiler to check this function for accuracy. You tell the compiler to expect nothing after the return statement, not even 0 (due to the void keyword), and to expect an integer followed by a floating-point in the parentheses.

If you break any of the prototype's rules, the compiler informs you of the problem so that you can correct it.

 Here is the first line of a function. Write its prototype below it.

```
float CalcPay(float rate, int hrs, float taxes)
```

 Here is a prototype and its corresponding function. The prototype is incomplete. What is wrong with it?

```
float GetAvg(int i, int j, float x, float y);   // Prototype

GetAvg(int i, int j, float x, float y)  // 1st line of function
```

Prototype All Functions

You should prototype every function in your program. As just described, the prototype defines (for the rest of the program) which functions follow, their return types, and their parameter types. You should also prototype C++'s built-in functions, such as strcpy(), if you use them.

Think about how you prototype strcpy(). Why should you need to prototype strcpy() when your compiler supplies the definition? Prototyping functions that you write is easy, because the prototype is basically the first line in the function. Prototyping functions that you do not write might seem difficult, but it isn't—you've already done it with every program in this book!

The designers of C++ realized that all functions have to be prototyped. They also realized that you cannot prototype built-in functions, so they did it for you and placed the prototypes in header files on your disk. You have been including the strcpy() prototype in each program that used it in this book with the following statement:

```
#include <string.h>
```

Inside the string.h file is a prototype of many of C++'s string manipulation functions. By having prototypes of these functions, you ensure that they cannot be passed bad values. If someone attempts to pass incorrect values, C++ catches the problem.

The cout and cin operators have their own header file, called iostream.h, that you also have seen included in this book's programs. iostream.h does not actually include prototypes for cout and cin because they are operators and not functions, but iostream.h does include some needed definitions to make cout and cin work.

Remember, too, that iomanip.h must be included if you use a setw or setprecision modifier in cout. Whenever you use a new built-in C++ function or a manipulating operator, check your compiler's manual to find the name of the prototype file to include.

Prototyping is the primary reason that you should always include the matching header file when you use C++'s built-in functions. The strcpy() function you have seen in previous lessons requires the following line:

```
#include <string.h>
```

This is the header file for the strcpy() function. Without it, the program does not work.

> **NOTE:** Throughout this book, when you learn a new built-in function, the lesson gives the full name of the prototype.

Prototype all functions in all programs except `main()`. (Even `main()` can be prototyped, however, if it returns nothing (not even 0).) The following program includes two prototypes—one for `main()` that shows you how to prototype `main()`, and one for the built-in `cout` and `cin` object definitions.

```cpp
// Filename: PRO1.CPP
// Calculates sales tax on a sale
#include <iostream.h>   // Prototypes built-in functions
void main(void);

void main(void)
{

  float total_sale;
  float tax_rate = .07;    // Assumes seven percent tax rate

  cout << "What is the sale amount? ";
  cin >> total_sale;

  total_sale += (tax_rate * total_sale);
  cout << "The total sale is " << total_sale;
  return;    // No 0 required!
}
```

Notice that `main()`'s return statement needed only a semicolon after it. As long as you prototype `main()` with a `void` return type, the last line in `main()` can be `return;` instead of `return 0;`.

> **NOTE:** Check to ensure that your C++ compiler is not set to compile with the ANSI C option turned on. Many C++ compilers give you this option. ANSI C always returns a value from `main()`. Even if your `return` statement does not return a specific value, ANSI C returns one for you. If the compiler is set up for ANSI C, you cannot specify `void main()`. If you are writing C++ programs, you have no need for the ANSI C option anyway.

The following program asks the user for a number in main() and passes that number to ascii(). The ascii() function returns the ASCII character that matches the user's number. This example illustrates a character return type. Functions can return any data type.

```cpp
// Filename: ASC.CPP
// Prints the ASCII character of the user's number
// Prototypes follow
#include <iostream.h>
char ascii(int num);

void main()
{
    int num;
    char asc_char;

    cout << "Enter an ASCII number? ";
    cin >> num;

    asc_char = ascii(num);
    cout << "The ASCII character for " << num
         << " is " << asc_char;
    return;
}

char ascii(int num)
{
    char asc_char;
    asc_char = char(num);   // Typecasts to a character
    return (asc_char);
}
```

The output from this program follows:

```
Enter an ASCII number? 67
The ASCII character for 67 is C
```

 Write a function that returns the ASCII number when passed the user's entered character.

Review Questions

1. What statement returns a value from one function to another?

2. What is the maximum number of return values a function can return?

3. What are header files for?

4. What is the default function return type?

5. TRUE or FALSE: A function that returns a value can be passed only a single parameter.

6. How do prototypes protect the programmer from bugs?

7. Why don't you need to return global variables?

8. What is the return type, given the following function prototype?

   ```
   float my_fun(char a, int b, float c);
   ```

   How many parameters are passed to `my_fun()`? What are their types?

Review Exercises

1. Write a program that contains two functions. The first function returns the square of the integer passed to it, and the second function returns the cube. Prototype `main()` so that you do not have to return a value.

2. Write a function that returns the double-precision area of a circle, given that a double-precision radius is passed to it. The formula for calculating the area of a circle is

```
area = 3.14159 * (radius * radius)
```

3. Write a function that returns the value of a polynomial, given this formula:

```
9x4 + 15x2 + x1
```

Assume that x is passed from `main()` and is supplied by the user.

4. Suppose that you have to calculate net pay for a company. You find yourself multiplying the hours worked by the hourly pay, then deducting taxes to compute the net pay. Write a program that includes a function that does this for you. It requires three arguments: the hours worked, the hourly pay, and the tax rate (as a floating-point decimal, such as .30 for 30 percent). The function should return the net pay. Test the `main()` calling function by sending three different payroll values to the function, and print the three return values.

Default Arguments and Function Overloading

To explain how to utilize default arguments and overload functions so that you can write clearer code.

C++ has two capabilities that regular C does not have. *Default argument lists* and *overloaded functions* speed your function writing and make your code clearer. All functions that receive arguments do not have to be sent values. When you specify default argument lists, you write functions that assume certain argument values even if you do not pass them any arguments. Overloaded functions enable you to write more than one function with the same function name. As long as their argument lists differ, the functions are differentiated by C++. Default argument lists and overloaded functions are not available in regular C. C++ extends the power of your programs by providing these time-saving procedures.

Default Argument Lists

Suppose that you are writing a program that must display a message on-screen for a short period of time. For instance, you might pass a function an error message that is stored in a character array, and the function displays the error message for a certain period of time.

The prototype for such a function can be this:

```
void pr_msg(char note[]);
```

Therefore, to request that pr_msg() display the line Turn printer on, you call it this way:

```
pr_msg("Turn printer on");   // Passes a message to be printed
```

This command displays the message Turn printer on for five seconds or so. To request that pr_msg() display the line Press any key to continue..., you call it this way:

```
pr_msg("Press a key to continue...");   // Passes a message
```

As you write more of the program, you begin to realize that you are displaying one message—for instance, the Turn printer on message—more often than any other message. It seems as if the pr_msg() function is receiving that message more often than any other. This could be the case if you are writing a program that prints many reports to the printer. You want to use pr_msg() for other delayed messages, but the printer is the most used.

Instead of calling the function over and over, typing the same message each time, you can set up the prototype for pr_msg() so that it defaults to the Turn printer on message in this way:

```
void pr_msg(char note[]="Turn printer on");   // Prototype
```

List default argument values in the prototype.

After prototyping pr_msg() with the default argument list, C++ assumes that you want to pass Turn printer on to the function unless you override the default by passing something else to it. For example, in main(), you call pr_msg() like this:

```
pr_msg();   // C++ assumes that you mean "Turn printer on"
```

This makes your programming job easier. Because you would usually want pr_msg() to display Turn printer on, the default argument list takes care of the message and you don't have to pass the message when you call the function. However, for those few times when you want to pass something else, simply pass a different message. For example, to make pr_msg() display Incorrect value on-screen, you type:

```
pr_msg("Incorrect value");    // Passes a new message
```

> **TIP:** Whenever you call a function several times and find yourself passing the same parameters to that function most of the time, consider using a default argument list.

This is *not* a prototype for a function with a default argument:

```
double CalcWages(float rate);    // Not a default list
```

This is the same function's prototype with a default argument:

```
double CalcWages(float rate=7.85); // A default prototype list
```

Write a default argument list that passes an integer value of 17 to a function named DoIt() if you do not pass it an argument.

Multiple Default Arguments

You can specify more than one default argument in the prototype list. Here is a prototype for a function with three default arguments:

```
float funct1(int i = 10, float x = 7.5, char c = 'A');
```

You can call this function in several ways. Here are some examples:

`funct1();`	All default values are assumed.
`funct1(25);`	25 is sent to the integer argument, and the default values are assumed for the rest.
`funct1(25, 31.25);`	25 is sent to the integer argument, 31.25 to the floating-point argument, and the default value of 'A' is assumed for the character argument.

> **NOTE:** If only some of a function's arguments are default arguments, those default arguments must appear on the far *right* of the argument list. No default arguments can appear to the left of those not specified as default. This is an *invalid* default argument prototype:
>
> ```
> float func2(int i=10, float x, char c, long n=10.232);
> ```
>
> This is invalid because a default argument appears on the left of a nondefault argument. To fix this, you must move the two default arguments to the far right (the end) of the argument list. Therefore, if you rearrange the prototype (and the resulting function calls) as follows, C++ enables you to accomplish the same objective that you attempted with the preceding line:
>
> ```
> float func2(float x, char c, int i=10, long n=10.232);
> ```

What is wrong with this function prototype?

```
float GetValues(int i, float x, double j = 24355.2, int k);
```

The following is a complete program that illustrates the message-printing function described earlier in this lesson. The main() function simply calls the delayed message-printing function three times, each time passing a different set of argument lists to it.

```
// Filename: DEFP1.CPP
// Illustrates default argument list
#include <iostream.h>

void pr_msg(char note[]="Turn printer on");    // Prototype

void main()
{
   pr_msg();   // Prints default message
   pr_msg("A new message");   // Prints another message
   pr_msg();   // Prints default message again
   return;
}

void pr_msg(char note[])    // Only prototype contains defaults
{
```

```
      long int delay;
      cout << note << "\n";
      for (delay = 0; delay < 500000; delay++)
         { ;   /* Do nothing while waiting */ }
      return;
   }
```

This program produces the following output:

```
Turn printer on
A new message
Turn printer on
```

The delay loop causes each line to display for a couple of seconds or more, depending on the speed of your computer, until all three lines print.

The following program illustrates the use of defaulting several arguments. main() calls the function de_fun() five times, sending de_fun() five sets of arguments. The de_fun() function prints five different things, depending on main()'s argument list.

```
// Filename: DEFP2.CPP
// Demonstrates default argument list with several parameters
#include <iostream.h>
#include <iomanip.h>

void de_fun(int i = 5, long j = 40034, float x = 10.25,
            char ch = 'Z', double d = 4.3234);   // Prototype

void main()
{
   de_fun();   // All defaults used
   de_fun(2);   // First default overridden
   de_fun(2, 75037);   // First and second default overridden
   de_fun(2, 75037, 35.88);   // First, second, and third
   de_fun(2, 75037, 35.88, 'G');   // First, second, third,
                                   // and fourth
   de_fun(2, 75037, 35.88, 'G', .0023);   // No defaulting
   return;
}

void de_fun(int i, long j, float x, char ch, double d)
{
   cout << setprecision(4) << "i: " << i << "    "
        << "j: " << j;
```

373

```
cout << "   x: " << x << "   " << "ch: " << ch;
cout << "   d: " << d << "\n";
return;
}
```

Here is this program's output:

```
i: 5    j: 40034    x: 10.25    ch: Z    d: 4.3234
i: 2    j: 40034    x: 10.25    ch: Z    d: 4.3234
i: 2    j: 75037    x: 10.25    ch: Z    d: 4.3234
i: 2    j: 75037    x: 35.88    ch: Z    d: 4.3234
i: 2    j: 75037    x: 35.88    ch: G    d: 4.3234
i: 2    j: 75037    x: 35.88    ch: G    d: 0.0023
```

Notice that each call to de_fun() produces a different output because main() sends a different set of parameters each time main() calls de_fun().

What does the following program display?

```
// Filename: DEFTRY.CPP
// "Try This" default argument list with several parameters
#include <iostream.h>
#include <iomanip.h>

void tryFun(char ch[10] = "Jim", int i = 15);   // Prototype

main()
{
   tryFun();   // All defaults used
   tryFun("Nancy");   // First default used
   tryFun("Nancy", 20);   // All defaults used
   return 0;
}

void tryFun(char ch[], int i)
{
   cout << ch << "\n";
   cout << i << "\n";
   return;
}
```

Overloaded Functions

Unlike regular C, C++ enables you to have more than one function with the same name. In other words, you can have three functions called abs() in the same program. Functions with the same name are called *overloaded functions*. C++ requires that each overloaded function differ in its argument list. Overloaded functions enable you to have similar functions that work on different types of data.

For example, suppose that you wrote a function that returned the absolute value of whatever number you passed to it. The absolute value of a number is its positive equivalent. For instance, the absolute value of 10.25 is 10.25, and the absolute value of −10.25 is 10.25.

Absolute values are used in distance, temperature, and weight calculations. The difference in the weights of two children is always positive. If Joe weighs 65 pounds and Mary weighs 55 pounds, their difference is a positive 10 pounds. You can subtract the 65 from 55 (−10) or 55 from 65 (+10) and the weight difference is always the absolute value of the result.

Suppose that you had to write an absolute-value function for integers and an absolute-value function for floating-point numbers. Without function overloading, you need these two functions:

```
int iabs(int i)    // Returns absolute value of an integer
{
   if (i < 0)
   { return (i * -1); }    // Makes positive
   else
   { return (i); }    // Already positive
}


float fabs(float x)    // Returns absolute value of a float
{
   if (x < 0.0)
   { return (x * -1.0); }    // Makes positive
   else
   { return (x); }    // Already positive
}
```

Without overloading, if you have a floating-point variable for which you need the absolute value, you pass it to the fabs() function, as in

```
ans = fabs(weight);
```

If you need the absolute value of an integer variable, you pass it to the `iabs()` function, as in

```
ians = iabs(age);
```

Because the code for these two functions differs only in the parameter lists, they are perfect candidates for overloaded functions. Call both functions `abs()`, prototype both of them, and code each of them separately in your program. After overloading the two functions (each of which works on two different types of parameters with the same name), you pass your floating-point or integer value to `abs()`. The C++ compiler determines which function you want to call.

> **NOTE:** If two or more functions differ only in their return types, C++ cannot overload them. Two or more functions that differ only in their return types must have different names and cannot be overloaded.

This process simplifies your programming considerably. Instead of having to remember several different function names, you have to remember only one function name. C++ passes the arguments to the proper function.

Here is a complete absolute-value program using overloaded functions. Notice that both functions are prototyped. The two prototypes signal C++ that it must perform overloading to determine the correct function names to call.

```cpp
// Filename: OVF1.CPP
// Overloads two absolute-value functions
#include <iostream.h>   // Prototypes cout and cin
#include <iomanip.h>    // Prototypes setprecision(2)

int abs(int i);       // abs() is overloaded twice,
float abs(float x);   // as shown by these prototypes

void main()
{
   int ians;   // To hold return values
   float fans;
   int i = -15;    // To pass to the two overloaded functions
   float x = -64.53;
```

```
    ians = abs(i);    // C++ calls the integer abs()
    cout << "Integer absolute value of -15 is " << ians << "\n";

    fans = abs(x);    // C++ calls the floating-point abs()
    cout << "Float absolute value of -64.53 is " <<
            setprecision(2) << fans << "\n";

    // Notice that you no longer have to keep track of two
    // different names. C++ calls the appropriate
    // function that matches the parameters.
    return;
}

int abs(int i)    // Integer absolute-value function
{
    if (i < 0)
    { return (i * -1); }    // Makes positive
    else
    { return (i); }    // Already positive
}

float abs(float x)    // Floating-point absolute-value function
{
    if (x < 0.0)
    { return (x * -1.0); }    // Makes positive
    else
    { return (x); }    // Already positive
}
```

Here is the program's output:

```
Integer absolute value of -15 is 15
Float absolute value of -64.53 is 64.53
```

As you write more and more C++ programs, you will find many uses for overloaded functions. The following demonstration program shows how you can build your own output functions to suit your needs. main() calls three functions named output(). Each time it's called, main() passes a different value to the function.

When main() passes a string to output(), output() prints the string, formatted to a width of 30 characters (using the setw() manipulator described in Lesson 8, "I/O with cout and cin"). When main() passes an integer to output(), output() prints the integer with a width of five. When

main() passes a floating-point value to output(), output() prints the value to two decimal places and generalizes the output of different types of data. You do not have to format your own data, because output() properly formats the data. You have to remember only one function name that outputs all three types of data.

```cpp
// Filename: OVF2.CPP
// Outputs three different types of
// data with same function name
#include <iostream.h>
#include <iomanip.h>
void output(char []);    // Prototypes for overloaded functions
void output(int i);
void output(float x);

void main()
{
   char name[] = "C++ Programming 101 makes C++ easy!";
   int ivalue = 2543;
   float fvalue = 39.4321;

   output(name);    // C++ chooses the appropriate function
   output(ivalue);
   output(fvalue);

return;
}

void output(char name[])
{
   cout << setw(30) << name << "\n";
   // The width truncates string if it is longer than 30
   return;
}

void output(int ivalue)
{
   cout << setw(5) << ivalue << "\n";
   // Just printed integer within a width of five spaces
   return;
}
```

```
void output(float fvalue)
{
   cout << setprecision(2) << fvalue << "\n";
   // Limits the floating-point value to two decimal places
   return;
}
```

Here is the program's output:

```
C++ Programming 101 makes C++ easy!
 2543
39.43
```

Each of the three lines, containing three different types of data, was printed with the same function call.

Name-Mangling

C++ uses *name-mangling* to accomplish overloaded functions. Understanding name-mangling helps you to become an advanced C++ programmer.

When C++ realizes that you are overloading two or more functions with the same name, each function differing only in its parameter list, C++ changes the name of the function and adds letters that match the parameters to the end of the function name. Different C++ compilers mangle function names differently.

To understand what the compiler does, consider the absolute-value function described earlier. C++ might change the integer absolute-value function to absi() and the floating-point absolute-value function to abst(). When you call the function with this function call:

```
ians = abs(age);
```

C++ determines that you want the absi() function called. As far as you know, C++ is not mangling the names; you never see the name differences in your program's source code. However, the compiler performs the name-mangling so that it can keep track of different functions that have the same name.

If you do not want C++ to mangle a function name, you can wrap the following code around the function:

```
extern "C" {
   fun1(int i);    // Prototype
};
```

You can list more than one function inside the `extern "C"` declaration. Then C++ does not mangle the function names when it compiles the program. This becomes important when you begin using multiple source files, mixing C and C++ code.

Write a declaration that keeps `prFun1()`, `prFun2()`, and `prFun3()` from being mangled.

Review Questions

1. Where in a program do you specify the defaults for default argument lists?

2. What is the term for C++ functions that have the same name?

3. Does name-mangling help support default argument lists or overloaded functions?

4. TRUE or FALSE: You can specify only a single default argument.

5. Fix the following prototype for a default argument list.

   ```
   void my_fun(int i = 7, float x, char ch = 'A');
   ```

6. TRUE or FALSE: The following prototypes specify overloaded functions:

   ```
   int   sq_rt(int n);
   float sq_rt(int n);
   ```

Review Exercises

1. Write a program that contains two functions. The first function returns the square of the integer passed to it, and the second function returns the square of the float passed to it.

2. Write a program that computes net pay based on the values the user types. Ask the user for the hours worked, the rate per hour, and the tax rate. Because most employees work 40 hours per week and earn $5.00 per hour, use these values as default values in the function that computes the net pay. If the user presses Enter in response to your questions, use the default values.

C++
CLASSROOM Six

Supplied
Functions

Input and Output Functions

OBJECTIVE **To show you additional ways to input and output data besides using the cin and cout operators.**

Unlike many programming languages, C++ does not contain any input or output commands. C++ is a very *portable* language; a C++ program that compiles and runs on one computer also can compile and run on another type of computer. Most incompatibilities between computers reside in their input/output mechanics. Different devices require different methods of performing I/O (input/output).

By putting all I/O capabilities in common functions supplied with each computer's compiler instead of in C++ statements, the designers of C++ ensured that programs are not tied to specific hardware for input and output. A compiler must be modified for every computer for which it is written. This ensures that the compiler works with the specific computer and its devices. Compiler writers write I/O functions for each machine.

When your C++ program writes a character to the screen, it works the same whether you have a color PC screen or a UNIX X/Windows terminal.

Stream and Character I/O

C++ views all input and output as streams of characters. Whether your program receives input from the keyboard, a disk file, a modem, or a mouse, C++ views only a stream of characters. C++ does not have to know what type of device is supplying the input; the operating system handles the device specifics. The designers of C++ want your programs to operate on characters of data without regard to the physical method taking place.

This stream I/O means that you can use the same functions to receive input from the keyboard as from the modem. You can use the same functions to write to a disk file, printer, or the screen. Of course, you need some way of routing that stream input or output to the proper device, but each program's I/O functions work in a similar manner. Figure 23.1 illustrates this concept.

Figure 23.1.
All I/O
consists of
streams of
characters.

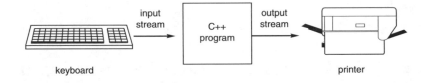

The stream is like a pipe that sends characters through it from one device to another.

The Newline Special Character: \n

Portability is the key to the success of C++. Few companies have the resources to rewrite every program they use when they change computer equipment. They need a programming language that works on many platforms (hardware combinations). C++ achieves true portability better than almost any other programming language.

It is because of portability that C++ uses the generic newline character, \n, rather than the specific carriage return and line feed sequences that other languages use. This also is why C++ uses the \t for tab, as well as for the other control characters used in I/O functions.

If C++ used ASCII code to represent these special characters, your programs would not be portable. If you wrote a C++ program on one computer and used a carriage return value such as 12, 12 might not be the carriage return value on another type of computer.

By using the newline and other control characters available in C++, you ensure that your program is compatible with any computer on which it is compiled. The specific compilers substitute their computer's actual codes for the control codes in your programs.

Standard Devices

Table 23.1 shows a list of standard I/O devices. C++ always assumes that input comes from `stdin`, meaning the *standard input device*. This usually is the keyboard, although you can reroute this default. C++ assumes that all output goes to `stdout`, or the *standard output device*. There is nothing magical about the words `stdin` and `stdout`, but many people learn their meanings for the first time in C++.

Table 23.1. Standard devices in C++.

Description	*C++ Name*	*C++ Object*	*MS-DOS Name*
Screen	stdout	cout	CON:
Keyboard	stdin	cin	CON:
Printer	stdprn		PRN: or LPT1:
Serial Port	stdaux		AUX: or COM1:
Error Messages	stderr	cerr	CON:
Disk Files			Filename

Take a moment to study Table 23.1. It might seem confusing that three devices are named CON:. MS-DOS differentiates between the screen device called CON: (which stands for *console*) and the keyboard device called CON: from the context of the data stream. If you send an output stream (a stream of characters) to CON:, MS-DOS automatically routes it to the screen. If you request input from CON:, MS-DOS retrieves the input from the keyboard. (These defaults hold true as long as you do not redirect these devices, as you will see in the following section.) MS-DOS sends all error messages to the screen (CON:) as well.

> If you were writing an error message, you would send it to the `cerr` object, like this:
>
> ```
> cerr << "Turn the printer on.";
> ```

> **NOTE:** If you want to route I/O to a second printer or serial port, see how to do so in Lesson 32, "Sequential Files."

Redirecting Devices from MS-DOS

`cout` goes to the screen because `stdout` is routed to the screen by default on most computers. `cin` inputs from the keyboard because most computers consider the keyboard to be the standard input device, `stdin`. After compiling your program, C++ does not send data to the screen or retrieve it from the keyboard. Instead, the program sends output to `stdout` and receives input from `stdin`. The operating system routes the data to the appropriate device.

MS-DOS enables you to reroute I/O from its default location to other devices through the use of the *output redirection symbol* (>) and the *input redirection symbol* (<). It is not the goal of this book to delve deeply into operating-system redirection. To learn more about the handling of I/O, read a good book on MS-DOS, such as *The Best Book of DOS 5* (Sams, 1991).

The output redirection symbol informs the operating system that you want standard output to go to a device other than the default (the screen). The input redirection symbol routes input away from the keyboard to another input device. The following example illustrates how this is done in MS-DOS.

Suppose that you write a program that uses only `cin` and `cout` for input and output. Instead of receiving input from the keyboard, you want the program to get the input from a file called MYDATA. Because `cin` receives input from `stdin`, you must redirect `stdin`. After compiling the program in a file called MYPGM.EXE, you can redirect its input away from the keyboard with the following DOS command:

```
C:>MYPGM < MYDATA
```

NOTE: You can include a full pathname before either the program name or the filename.

How would you execute from DOS a program called COMPUTE that gets its input from SALES.DAT?

You also can route a program's output to the printer by typing

```
C:>MYPGM > PRN:
```

There is a danger in redirecting all output such as this, however. All output, including screen prompts for keyboard input, goes to MYDATA. This probably is not acceptable to you in most cases; you still want prompts and some messages to go to the screen. In the next section, you learn how to separate I/O and send some output to one device, such as the screen, and the rest to another device, such as a file or a printer.

If the program requires much input, and that input is stored in a file called ANSWERS, you can override the keyboard default device that cin uses by typing

```
C:>MYPGM < ANSWERS
```

You can redirect both the input and the output. Write the line needed to get the input from the file ANSWERS and place the output to the DOS name for the printer.

TIP: You can route the output to a serial printer or a second parallel printer port by substituting COM1: or LPT2: for PRN:.

What is wrong with this redirection of the output of the program named PAYROLL to the printer?

```
C:>PAYROLL < PRN:
```

Lesson 23

Printing Formatted Output to the Printer

It's easy to send program output to the printer by using the `ofstream` function. The format of `ofstream` is

```
ofstream device(device_name);
```

The following examples show how you can combine `cout` and `ofstream` to write to both the screen and the printer.

> **NOTE:** `ofstream` uses the fstream.h header file.

The following program asks the user for his or her first and last name. It then prints the name, last name first, to the printer.

```
// Filename: FPR1.CPP
// Prints a name on the printer

#include <fstream.h>

void main()
{
   char first[20];
   char last[20];

   cout << "What is your first name? ";
   cin >> first;
   cout << "What is your last name? ";
   cin >> last;

   // Sends names to the printer
   ofstream prn("PRN");
   prn << "In a phone book, your name looks like this: \n";
   prn << last << ", " << first << "\n";
   return;
}
```

The line with `ofstream prn("PRN");` connects the DOS name for the printer, PRN, to the `ofstream` (another name for *output file stream* because DOS makes all devices look like disk files to your program). In effect, this program creates a new output object called `prn` that works with

390

your printer just as cout works with your screen. There is no need for iostream.h, because ofstream.h includes all the necessary information contained in iostream.h, as well as some for writing to devices other than your screen.

If you connect a printer to your second parallel port, you can direct output to it with this line:

```
ofstream prn("LPT2");
```

Finish this program that prints the stored name and address to the printer.

```
#include <fstream.h>

void main()
{
    char name[] = "Judy Venice";
    char address[] = "1432 E. Oak"
    char city[] = "Miami";
    char state[] = "FL"
    char zip[] = 31923;
```

Character I/O Functions

Because all I/O is actually character I/O, C++ provides many functions you can use to perform character input and output. The cout and cin functions are called *formatted I/O functions* because they give you formatting control over your input and output. The cout and cin functions are not character I/O functions.

391

There's nothing wrong with using cout for formatted output, but cin has many problems, as you have seen. You will now see how to write your own character input routines to replace cin, as well as use character output functions to prepare you for the discussion of disk files in Classroom 8, "Structures, Files, and OOP."

The get() and put() Functions

The most fundamental character I/O functions are get() and put(). The put() function writes a single character to the standard output device (the screen if you don't redirect it from your operating system). The get() function inputs a single character from the standard input device (the keyboard by default).

The format of get() is

```
device.get(char_var);
```

The get() *device* can be any standard input device. If you receive character input from the keyboard, you use cin as the device. If you initialize your modem and want to receive characters from it, use ofstream to open the modem device and read from the device.

The format of put() is

```
device.put(char_val);
```

char_val can be a character variable, expression, or constant. You output character data with put(). The device can be any standard output device. To write a character to your printer, open PRN with ofstream.

The following program asks the user for his or her initials a character at a time. Notice that the program uses both cout and put(). The cout is still useful for formatted output such as messages to the user. Writing individual characters is best achieved with put().

The program must call two get() functions for each character typed. When you answer a get() prompt by typing a character and pressing Enter, C++ interprets the input as a stream of two characters. get() first receives the letter you typed, then it receives \n (the newline, supplied to C++ when you press Enter). The following examples fix this double-get() problem.

```
// Filename: CH1.CPP
// Introduces get() and put()
```

```
#include <fstream.h>

void main()
{
    char  in_char;    // Holds incoming initial
    char first, last;    // Holds converted first and last initial

    cout << "What is your first name initial? ";
    cin.get(in_char);    // Waits for first initial
    first = in_char;
    cin.get(in_char);    // Ignores newline
    cout << "What is your last name initial? ";
    cin.get(in_char);    // Waits for last initial
    last = in_char;
    cin.get(in_char);    // Ignores newline
    cout << "\nHere they are: \n";
    cout.put(first);
    cout.put(last);
return;
}
```

Here is the program's output:

```
What is your first name initial? G
What is your last name initial? P

Here they are:
GP
```

You can add carriage returns to space the output better. To print the two initials on two separate lines, use put() to add a newline character to cout. Finish the following program so that it does just that.

```
#include <fstream.h>
void main()
{
    char in_char;    // Holds incoming initial
    char first, last;  // Holds converted first
                       // and last initial

    cout << "What is your first name initial? ";
    cin.get(in char);    // Waits for first initial
```

```
first = in_char;
cin.get(in_char);   // Ignores newline
cout << "What is your last name initial? ";
cin.get(in_char);   // Waits for last initial
last = in_char;
cin.get(in_char);   // Ignores newline
cout << "\nHere they are: \n";
```

THINK...

It might have been clearer to define the newline character as a constant. At the top of the program you would see:

```
const char NEWLINE = '\n'
```

`put()` then would read:

```
cout.put(NEWLINE);
```

Some programmers prefer to define their character formatting constants and refer to them by name. It's up to you to decide whether you want to use this method or continue using the \n character constant in `put()`.

The `get()` function is a *buffered* input function. As you type characters, the data does not go to your program immediately; instead, it goes to a buffer. The buffer is a section of memory (having nothing to do with your PC's type-ahead buffers) managed by C++.

Figure 23.2 shows how this buffered function works. When your program approaches a `get()`, the program waits as you type the input. The program doesn't view the characters, because they're going to the buffer of memory. There is practically no limit to the size of the buffer; it fills with input until you press Enter. Pressing Enter signals the computer to release the buffer to your program.

Most PCs accept either buffered or nonbuffered input. The `getch()` function discussed later in this lesson is nonbuffered. With `get()`, all input is buffered. Buffered text affects the timing of your program's input. Your program receives no characters from `get()` until you press Enter. Therefore, if you ask a question such as

```
Do you want to see the report again (Y/N)?
```

and use `get()` for input, the user can press Y, but the program does not receive the input until the user also presses Enter. The Y and Enter are then sent, one character at a time, to the program, which processes the input. If you want immediate response to what a user types (similar to what the `INKEY$` in BASIC allows), you must use `getch()`.

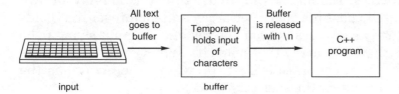

Figure 23.2. `get()` *input goes to a buffer. The buffer is released when you press Enter.*

By using buffered input, the user can type a string of characters in response to a loop with `get()`, receive characters, and correct the input by pressing Backspace before pressing Enter. If the input were nonbuffered, the Backspace would be another character of data.

One of the programs presented earlier, CH1.CPP, had to discard the newline character. It did so by assigning the input character (from `get()`) to an extra variable. Obviously, `get()` returns a value (the character typed). In this case it's acceptable to ignore the return value by not using the character returned by `get()`. You know that the user has to press Enter (to end the input), so it's acceptable to discard Enter with an unused `get()` function call.

When inputting strings such as names and sentences, `cin` enables you to enter only one word at a time. The following string asks for the user's full name with these two lines:

```
cout << "What are your first and last names? ";

cin >> names;    // Receives name in character array names
```

The names array receives only the first name; cin ignores all data to the right of the first space.

Using get(), you can build your own input function that doesn't have a single-word limitation. When you want to receive a string of characters from the user, such as the user's first and last name, you can call the get_in_str() function shown in the next program.

The main() function defines an array and prompts the user for a name. After the prompt, the program calls the get_in_str() function and builds the input array one character at a time using get(). The function keeps looping, using the while loop, until the user presses Enter (signaled by the newline character, \n, to C++) or until the user types the maximum number of characters. You might want to use this function in your own programs. Be sure to pass it a character array and an integer that holds the maximum array size (because you don't want the input string to be longer than the character array that holds it). When control returns to main() (or whatever function called get_in_str()), the array has the user's full input, including the spaces.

```
// Filename: IN.CPP
// Program that builds an input string array using get()

#include <fstream.h>
void get_in_str(char str[], int len);

const int MAX = 25;    // Size of character array to be typed

void main()
{
   char input_str[MAX];    // Keyboard input fills this
   cout << "What is your full name? ";
   get_in_str(input_str, MAX);    // String from keyboard
   cout << "After return, your name is " << input_str << "\n";
   return;
}


//*************************************************************
// The following function requires that a string and the
// maximum length of the string be passed to it. It accepts
// input from the keyboard and sends keyboard input in the
// string. On return, the calling routine has access to the
// string.
//*************************************************************
```

```
void get_in_str(char str[ ], int len)
{
   int i = 0;    // Index
   char input_char;   // Character typed

   cin.get(input_char);   // Gets next character in string
   while (i < (len - 1) && (input_char != '\n'))
     {
       str[i] = input_char;   // Builds string
       i++;                    // one character at a time
       cin.get(input_char);   // Receives next character
                               // in string
     }
   str[i] = '\0';   // Makes the char array a string
   return;
}
```

> **NOTE:** The loop checks for len - 1 to save room for the null-terminating zero at the end of the input string.

Write a program that uses the get_in_str() function to ask for the user's full name and address. When you have the data, print it to the printer.

The getch() and putch() Functions

The getch() and putch() functions are somewhat different from the character I/O functions discussed earlier. Their format is similar to get() and put(): they read from the keyboard, write to the screen, and cannot be redirected, even from the operating system. The formats of getch() and putch() are

```
int_var = getch();
```

and

```
putch(int_var);
```

getch() and putch() are not AT&T C++ standard functions, but they usually are available with most C++ compilers. getch() and putch() are

397

nonbuffered functions. The putch() character output function is a mirror-image function of getch(): it is a nonbuffered output function. Because almost every output device made (except for the screen and the modem) is inherently buffered, putch() effectively does the same thing as put().

Another way that getch() differs from the other character input functions is that getch() does not echo (display) the input characters on-screen as it receives them. When you type characters in response to get(), you see the characters as you type them (as they are sent to the buffer). If you want to see characters received by getch(), you must follow getch() with putch(). It is handy to echo the characters on-screen so that users can verify that they typed correctly.

Some programmers like to make users press Enter after answering a prompt or selecting from a menu. They feel that the extra time given with buffered input gives users more time to decide whether they want to give a particular answer. The user can press Backspace and correct the input before pressing Enter.

> **NOTE:** getch() and putch() use the conio.h header file.

Other programmers like to grab the user's response to a single-character answer, such as a menu response, and act on it immediately. They feel that pressing Enter is an added and unneeded burden for the user, so they use getch(). The choice is yours. You should understand both buffered and nonbuffered input so that you can use both.

> **TIP:** You also can use getche() where you would use getch(). getche() is a nonbuffered input identical to getch(), except that it echoes the input characters to the screen as the user types them. Using getche() rather than getch() keeps you from having to call putch() to echo the user's input to the screen.

The following program shows the getch() and putch() functions. The program asks the user to enter five letters. These five letters are added (by way of a for loop) to the character array named letters. As you run this program, notice that the characters are not echoed to the screen as you type them. Because getch() is unbuffered, the program actually receives each character, adds it to the array, and loops again as you type them. (If this were buffered input, the program would not loop through the five iterations until you pressed Enter.)

A second loop prints the five letters using `putch()`. A third loop prints the five letters to the printer using `put()`.

```
// Filename: GCH1.CPP
// Uses getch() and putch() for input and output

#include <fstream.h>
#include <conio.h>

void main()
{
   int ctr;   // for loop counter
   char letters[5];   // Holds five input characters. No
                      // room is needed for the null zero
                      // because this array will never be
                      // treated as a string.
   cout << "Please type five letters...  \n";
   for (ctr = 0; ctr < 5; ctr++)
     {
       letters[ctr] = getch();   // Adds input to array
     }
   for (ctr = 0; ctr < 5; ctr++)   // Prints them to screen
   {
      putch(letters[ ctr ]);
   }
   ofstream prn("PRN");
   for (ctr = 0; ctr < 5; ctr++)   // Prints them to printer
   {
      prn.put(letters[ ctr ]);
   }
return;
}
```

When you run this program, do not press Enter after the five letters. The `getch()` function does not use Enter. The loop ends automatically after the fifth letter because of the unbuffered input and the `for` loop.

A Better Way to Input Strings

The string-input function shown earlier in this lesson was a nice exercise for you to follow, but C++ offers you an additional way to get strings from the keyboard without your having to resort to writing functions. The get() function is nice to use when you need to input a string that might contain spaces, such as an address or a full name. Earlier you saw get() used to get single characters, but it also works well for strings.

When reading character strings using get(), use the following format:

```
cin.get(char [], num);
```

num is the maximum length of the string the user is going to enter (the user can enter strings shorter than *num*). The *char []* can be any character array (or a pointer to a character array, as you will learn about in later lessons).

The following program illustrates getting strings with get(). It asks the user for his or her full name and prints the results.

```
// Filename: GETS.CPP
// Gets a string from the keyboard into a character array
#include <iostream.h>
void main()
{
   char str[81];    // Reserves space for up to 80 characters
                    // with null

   cout << "What is your full name? ";
   cin.get(str, 80);

   cout << "Thank you, " << str << ", for answering me.\n";
   return;
}
```

Finish the following program that asks for the user's name and address. Print the name and address to the printer.

```
#include <iostream.h>
#include <fstream.h>
void main()
{
   char name[30];
```

```
    char addr[30];
    char city[10];
    char st[3];
    char zip[6];

    cout << "What is your full name? ";
    cin.get(name, 30);
```

Review Questions

1. Why are there no input or output commands in C++?

2. TRUE or FALSE: If you use the character I/O functions to send output to stdout, it always goes to the screen.

3. What is the difference between getch() and get()?

4. What function sends formatted output to devices other than the screen?

5. What are the MS-DOS redirection symbols?

6. What nonstandard function most similar to getch() echoes the input character to the screen as the user types it?

7. TRUE or FALSE: When you use get(), the program receives your input as you type it.

8. Which keypress releases the buffered input to the program?

9. TRUE or FALSE: Using devices and functions described in this lesson, it is possible to write one program that sends some output to the screen, some to the printer, and some to the modem.

10. How can you get a string with spaces from the keyboard?

Review Exercises

1. Write a program that asks the user for five letters and prints them to the screen in reverse order, and then to the printer.

2. Write a miniature typewriter program using get() and put(). In a loop, get characters until the user presses Enter while getting a line of user input. Print the line of user input to the printer. Because get() is buffered, nothing goes to the printer until the user presses Enter at the end of each line of text. (Use the string-building input function shown in IN.CPP.)

3. Rewrite the program in Exercise 2 using cin.get() to get the string.

4. Add a putch() inside the first loop of CH1.CPP (this lesson's first get() sample program) so that the characters are echoed to the screen as the user types them.

5. A *palindrome* is a word or a phrase spelled the same forward and backward. Two sample palindromes are

   Madam, I'm Adam

   Golf? No sir, prefer prison flog!

   Write a C++ program that asks the user for a phrase. Build the input, one character at a time, using a character input function such as get(). When you have the full string (store it in a character array), determine whether the phrase is a palindrome. You have to filter special (nonalphabetic) characters, storing only alphabetic characters to a second character array. You also must convert the characters to uppercase as you store them. The first palindrome would become

   MADAMIMADAM

   Using one or more for or while loops, you now can test the phrase to determine whether it is a palindrome. Print the result of the test on the printer. Sample output should look like this:

   "Madam, I'm Adam" is a palindrome.

C++ Built-In Functions

To explain some of the many built-in functions that come with your C++ compiler that speed program development.

You do not have to write everything from scratch. C++ provides many built-in functions in addition to the cout, getch(), and strcpy() functions you have seen so far. These built-in functions increase your productivity and save you programming time. You don't have to write as much code because the built-in functions perform many useful tasks for you.

There are functions that perform character conversion, character and string testing, string manipulation, mathematical operations, and random-number generation. This lesson teaches you about the more common functions and how to use them.

Character Functions

This section explores many of the character functions available in AT&T C++. Generally, you pass character arguments to the functions, and the

functions return values that you can store or print. By using these functions, you off-load much of your work to C++ and allow it to perform the more tedious manipulations of character and string data.

Character Testing Functions

Several functions test for certain characteristics of your character data. You can determine whether your character data is alphabetic, digital, uppercase, lowercase, and much more. You must pass a character variable or a literal argument to the function (by placing the argument in the function parentheses) when you call it. These functions return a True or False result, so that you can test their return values inside an `if` statement or a `while` loop.

> **NOTE:** All character functions presented in this section are prototyped in the ctype.h header file. Be sure to include ctype.h at the beginning of any programs that use these functions.

Alphabetic and Digital Testing

The following functions test for alphabetic conditions:

- `isalpha(c)`: Returns True (nonzero) if c is an uppercase or lowercase letter. Returns False (zero) if c is not a letter.

- `islower(c)`: Returns True (nonzero) if c is a lowercase letter. Returns False (zero) if c is not a lowercase letter.

- `isupper(c)`: Returns True (nonzero) if c is an uppercase letter. Returns False (zero) if c is not an uppercase letter.

 What is this program's output?

```
// Filename: AD1.CPP
#include <iostream.h>
#include <ctype.h>
void main()
{
   if (isalpha('2'))
      { cout << "Yes"; }
   else
      ( cout << "No"; }
}
```

What is this program's output?

```
// Filename: AD2.CPP
#include <iostream.h>
#include <ctype.h>
void main()
{
   char ch = 'a';
   if (islower(ch))
      { cout << "Yes"; }
   else
      { cout << "No"; }
}
```

What is this program's output?

```
// Filename: AD3.CPP
#include <iostream.h>
#include <ctype.h>
void main()
{
   char ch = 'a';
   if (isupper(ch))
      { cout << "Yes"; }
   else
      { cout << "No"; }
}
```

What is wrong with the following program?

```
#include <ctype.h>
#include <iostream.h>
void main()
{
   char initial;
   cout << "What is your first initial? ";
   cin >> initial;
   if (isalpha(initial))
      { cout << "Nice job, " << initial << "!\n"; }
```

```
   else
      { cout << "That is not an initial!\n"; }
}
```

Remember that any nonzero value is True in C++, and zero is always False. If you use the return values of these functions in a relational test, the True return value is not always 1 (it can be any nonzero value), but it is always considered True for the test.

The following functions test for digits:

- isdigit(*c*): Returns True (nonzero) if *c* is a digit 0 through 9. Returns False (zero) if *c* is not a digit.

NOTE: Although some character functions test for digits, the arguments still are character data and cannot be used in mathematical calculations, unless you calculate using the ASCII values of characters.

What is this program's output?

```
// Filename: AD4.CPP
#include <iostream.h>
#include <ctype.h>
void main()
{
   char ch = 'a';
   if (isdigit(ch))
      { cout << "Yes"; }
   else
      { cout << "No"; }
}
```

- isxdigit(*c*): Returns True (nonzero) if *c* is any of the hexadecimal digits 0 through 9 or A, B, C, D, E, F, a, b, c, d, e, or f. Returns False (zero) if *c* is anything else. (See Appendix B for more information on the hexadecimal numbering system.)

What is this program's output?

```
// Filename: AD5.CPP
#include <iostream.h>
#include <ctype.h>
void main()
{
   char ch = 'x';
   if (isxdigit(ch))
      { cout << "Yes"; }
   else
      { cout << "No"; }
}
```

The following function tests for numeric or alphabetical arguments:

isalnum(c): Returns True (nonzero) if c is a digit 0 through 9 or an alphabetic character (either uppercase or lowercase). Returns False (zero) if c is not a digit or a letter.

What is this program's output?

```
// Filename: AD6.CPP
#include <iostream.h>
#include <ctype.h>
void main()
{
   char ch = '!';
   if (isalnum(ch))
      { cout << "Yes"; }
   else
      { cout << "No"; }
}
```

NOTE: You can pass to these functions only a character value or an integer value holding the ASCII value of a character. You cannot pass an entire character array to character functions. If you want to test the elements of a character array, you must pass the array one element at a time.

Lesson 24

Special Character-Testing Functions

A few character functions become useful when you have to read from a disk file, a modem, or another operating system device from which you route input. These functions are not used as much as the character functions you saw in the preceding section, but they are useful for testing specific characters for readability. The character-testing functions do not change characters.

The remaining character-testing functions follow:

- `iscntrl(c)`: Returns True (nonzero) if c is a *control character* (any character from the ASCII table numbered 0 through 31). Returns False (zero) if c is not a control character.

- `isgraph(c)`: Returns True (nonzero) if c is any printable character (a noncontrol character) except a space. Returns False (zero) if c is a space or anything other than a printable character.

- `isprint(c)`: Returns True (nonzero) if c is a printable character (a noncontrol character) from ASCII 32 to ASCII 127, including a space. Returns False (zero) if c is not a printable character.

- `ispunct(c)`: Returns True (nonzero) if c is any punctuation character (any printable character other than a space, a letter, or a digit). Returns False (zero) if c is not a punctuation character.

- `isspace(c)`: Returns True (nonzero) if c is a space, newline (\n), carriage return (\r), tab (\t), or vertical tab (\v) character. Returns False (zero) if c is anything else.

Some people program in C++ for years and never need any of these functions. Programmers often use them to *parse,* or interpret, lines of input. Specialized applications such as language translators need special character testing functions such as these. Other times, a programmer produces a file that contains many control characters, and the programmer needs to strip out any data that is not a text or numeric character.

Character Conversion Functions

The two remaining character functions are handy. Rather than testing characters, these functions change characters to their lowercase or uppercase equivalents.

- `tolower(c)`: Converts c to lowercase. Nothing changes if you pass `tolower()` a lowercase letter or a nonalphabetic character.

408

- `toupper(c)`: Converts *c* to uppercase. Nothing changes if you pass `toupper()` an uppercase letter or a nonalphabetic character.

These functions return their changed character values.

These functions are useful for user input. Suppose that you ask users a yes-or-no question, such as the following:

```
Do you want to print the checks (Y/N)?
```

Before `toupper()` and `tolower()` were developed, you had to check for both a Y and a y to print the checks. Instead of testing for both conditions, you can convert the character to uppercase, and test for a Y.

Here is a program that prints an appropriate message if the user is a girl or a boy. The program tests for G and B after converting the user's input to uppercase. No check for lowercase has to be done.

```cpp
// Filename: GB.CPP
// Determines whether the user typed a G or a B.
#include <iostream.h>
#include <conio.h>
#include <ctype.h>
void main()
{
    char ans;    // Holds user's response
    cout << "Are you a girl or a boy (G/B)? ";
    ans = getch();    // Gets answer
    getch();    // Discards newline

    cout << ans << "\n";
    ans = toupper(ans);    // Converts answer to uppercase
    switch (ans)
    {   case ('G'): { cout << "You look pretty today!\n";
                      break; }
        case ('B'): { cout << "You look handsome today!\n";
                      break; }
        default :   { cout << "Your answer makes no sense!\n";
                      break; }
    }
    return;
}
```

Here is the output from this program:

```
Are you a girl or a boy (G/B)? B
You look handsome today!
```

Would the output be the same if the user had typed a b (in lowercase)?

String Functions

Some of the most powerful built-in C++ functions are the string functions. They perform much of the tedious work for which you have been writing code so far, such as inputting strings from the keyboard and comparing strings.

As with the character functions, there is no need to "reinvent the wheel" by writing code when built-in functions do the same task. Use these functions as much as possible.

Now that you have a good grasp of the foundations of C++, you can master the string functions. They enable you to concentrate on your program's primary purpose rather than spend time coding your own string functions.

Useful String Functions

You can use a handful of useful string functions for string testing and conversion. In earlier lessons you saw the strcpy() string function, which copies a string of characters to a character array.

> **NOTE:** All string functions in this section are prototyped in the string.h header file. Be sure to include string.h at the beginning of any program that uses the string functions.

The string functions work on string literals or on character arrays that contain strings.

The following are string functions that test or manipulate strings:

- strcat(*s1*, *s2*): Concatenates (merges) the *s2* string to the end of the *s1* character array. The *s1* array must have enough reserved elements to hold both strings.

If st1 were a character array that you had reserved 25 characters for, and it currently holds the string "First," it would hold "First National" if you performed the following strcat() function call:

```
strcat(st1, " National");
```

- `strcmp(`*s1*`, `*s2*`)`: Compares the *s1* string with the *s2* string on an alphabetical, element-by-element basis. If *s1* alphabetizes before *s2*, `strcmp()` returns a negative value. If *s1* and *s2* are the same strings, `strcmp()` returns 0. If *s1* alphabetizes after *s2*, `strcmp()` returns a positive value.

The following code tests to see whether two strings (strings stored in character arrays) hold the same value:

```
if (!strcmp(s1, s2))
   { cout << "They are the same\n"; }
```

This is one time when the NOT operator (`!`), is clear. Because `strcmp()` returns 0, or False, if the strings compare, you must test for NOT False to perform the comparison and print if they truly do compare.

- `strlen(`*s1*`)`: Returns the length of *s1*. Remember that the length of a string is the number of characters, not including the null zero. The number of characters defined for the character array has nothing to do with the length of the string.

The following code stores the length of the string in `n`:

```
n = strlen("A string");    // Stores 8 in n
```

TIP: Before using `strcat()` to concatenate strings, use `strlen()` to ensure that the target string (the string being concatenated to) is large enough to hold both strings.

What is wrong with the following program?

```
#include <string.h>
#include <iostream.h>
void main()
{
   char full[10] = "\0";   // Will hold both names
   char first[10];
   char last[10];
```

411

```
cout << "What is your first name? ";
cin >> first;
cout << "What is your last name? ";
cin >> last;
strcat(full, first);
strcat(full, last);
cout << "Your full name is " << full << "\n";
return;
}
```

Converting Strings to Numbers

Sometimes you have to convert numbers stored in character strings to a numeric data type. AT&T C++ provides three functions that enable you to do this:

- atoi(s): Converts s to an integer. The name stands for *alphabetic to integer*.

- atol(s): Converts s to a long integer. The name stands for *alphabetic to long integer*.

- atof(s): Converts s to a floating-point number. The name stands for *alphabetic to floating-point*.

> **NOTE:** These three ato() functions are prototyped in the stdlib.h header file. Be sure to include stdlib.h at the beginning of any program that uses the ato() functions.

The string must contain a valid number. Here is a string that can be converted to an integer:

`"1232"`

The string must hold a string of digits short enough to fit in the target numeric data type. The following string could not be converted to an integer with the atoi() function:

`"-1232495.654"`

It could, however, be converted to a floating-point number with the atof() function.

C++ cannot perform any mathematical calculation with such strings, even if the strings contain digits that represent numbers. Therefore, you must convert any string to its numeric equivalent before performing arithmetic with it.

> **NOTE:** If you pass a string to an `ato()` function and the string does not contain a valid representation of a number, the `ato()` function returns 0.

The following code fragment gets a number from the user as a string and converts that string to a floating-point number:

```
float fv;    // Will hold the converted number
char cnum[20];   // Will hold the user's number
cout << "How much was your check? ";
cin >> cnum;   // Gets the number into the character
                // array
fv = atof(cnum);   // Converts the string to a
                    // floating-point
```

The conversion functions will become more useful to you after you learn about disk files and pointers in later lessons.

Numeric Functions

The following sections present many of the built-in C++ numeric functions. As with the string functions, these functions convert and calculate numbers. They save you time because you don't have to write functions that do the same thing. Many of these are trigonometric and advanced mathematical functions. You might use some of these numeric functions only rarely, but they are there if you need them.

These sections conclude the discussion of C++'s standard built-in functions. After mastering the concepts in this lesson, you will be ready to learn more about arrays and pointers. As you develop more skills in C++, you might find yourself relying on these numeric, string, and character functions when you write more powerful programs.

Useful Mathematical Functions

Several built-in numeric functions return results based on numeric variables and literals passed to them. Even if you write only a few science and engineering programs, some of these functions are useful.

> **NOTE:** All mathematical and trigonometric functions are prototyped in the math.h header file. Be sure to include math.h at the beginning of any program that uses the numeric functions.

These numeric functions return double-precision values. Here are the functions and their descriptions:

- ceil(*x*): The ceil(), or *ceiling,* function rounds numbers up to the nearest integer.

> The following statement
>
> ```
> cout << ceil(11.2);
> ```
>
> prints 12 to the screen.

- fabs(*x*): Returns the absolute value of *x*. The absolute value of a number is its positive equivalent.

> The following statement
>
> ```
> cout << fabs(-412);
> ```
>
> prints 412 to the screen.

> **TIP:** Absolute value is used for distances (which are always positive), accuracy measurements, age differences, and other calculations that require a positive result.

- floor(*x*): The floor() function rounds numbers down to the nearest integer.

What do you think this prints?

```
cout << floor(11.2);
```

- fmod(x, y): The fmod() function returns the floating-point remainder of (x/y) with the same sign as x, and y cannot be zero. Because the modulus operator (%) works only with integers, this function is used to find the remainder of floating-point number divisions.

- pow(x, y): Returns x raised to the y power, or x^y. If x is less than or equal to zero, y must be an integer. If x equals zero, y cannot be negative.

- sqrt(x): Returns the square root of x. x must be greater than or equal to zero.

The following program uses the fabs() function to compute the difference between two ages.

```
// Filename: ABS.CPP
// Computes the difference between two ages
#include <iostream.h>
#include <math.h>
void main()
{
    float age1, age2, diff;
    cout << "\nWhat is the first child's age? ";
    cin >> age1;
    cout << "What is the second child's age? ";
    cin >> age2;

    // Calculates the positive difference
    diff = age1 - age2;
    diff = fabs(diff);   // Determines the absolute value

    cout << "\nThey are " << diff << " years apart.";
    return;
}
```

The output from this program follows. Due to fabs(), the order of the ages doesn't matter. Without absolute value, this program would produce a negative age difference if the first age were less than the second. Because the ages are relatively small numbers, floating-point variables are used in this example. C++ automatically converts floating-point arguments to double precision when passing them to fabs().

415

```
What is the first child's age? 10
What is the second child's age? 12

They are 2 years apart.
```

Trigonometric Functions

The following functions are available for trigonometric applications:

- `cos(x)`: Returns the cosine of the angle *x*, expressed in radians.

- `sin(x)`: Returns the sine of the angle *x*, expressed in radians.

- `tan(x)`: Returns the tangent of the angle *x*, expressed in radians.

These probably are the least-used functions. This is not to belittle the work of scientific and mathematical programmers who need them, however. Certainly they are grateful that C++ supplies these functions! Otherwise, programmers would have to write their own functions to perform these three basic trigonometric calculations.

Most C++ compilers supply additional trigonometric functions, including hyperbolic equivalents of these three functions.

If you are confused, you probably are in good company. Trigonometric functions are not used in everyday applications. If you don't have a need for them, leave them alone and you'll be just fine.

> **TIP:** If you have to pass an angle that is expressed in degrees to these functions, convert the angle's degrees to radians by multiplying the degrees by /180.0. (equals approximately 3.14159.)

Logarithmic Functions

Three highly mathematical functions are sometimes used in business and mathematics:

- `exp(x)`: Returns *e*, the base of the natural logarithm, raised to a power specified by *x* (e^x). *e* is the mathematical expression for the approximate value of 2.718282.

- `log(x)`: Returns the natural logarithm of the argument *x*, mathematically written as `ln(x)`. *x* must be positive.

- `log10(x)`: Returns the base-10 logarithm of argument *x*, mathematically written as `log10(x)`. *x* must be positive.

Random-Number Processing

Random events happen every day. You wake up and it is sunny or rainy. You have a good day or a bad day. You receive a phone call from an old friend or you don't. Your stock portfolio goes up or down in value.

Random events are especially important in games. Part of the fun in games is your luck with rolling dice or drawing cards, combined with your playing skills.

Simulating random events is an important task for computers. Computers, however, are finite machines. Given the same input, they always produce the same output. This fact can make for some boring games!

The designers of C++ knew about this computer setback and found a way to overcome it. They wrote a random-number generating function called rand(). You can use rand() to compute a dice roll or draw a card, for example.

To call the rand() function and assign the returned random number to test, use the following syntax:

```
test = rand();
```

The rand() function returns an integer from 0 to 32767. Never use an argument in the rand() parentheses.

Every time you call rand() in the same program, you receive a different number. If you run the same program over and over, however, rand() returns the same set of random numbers. One way to receive a different set of random numbers is to call the srand() function. The format of srand() follows:

```
srand(seed);
```

seed is an integer variable or literal. If you don't call srand(), C++ assumes a seed value of 1.

> **NOTE:** The rand() and srand() functions are prototyped in the stdlib.h header file. Be sure to include stdlib.h at the beginning of any program that uses rand() or srand().

The seed value reseeds, or resets, the random-number generator, so the next random number is based on the new seed value. If you call srand() with a different seed value at the top of a program, rand() returns a different random number each time you run the program.

If you need a random number between two values, such as between 1 and 6 (for a dice roll), use the modulus operator to supply it. The following statement produces a value between 1 and 6:

```
dice = (rand() % 6) + 1;
```

The following program computes a random number between 1 and 100 and asks the user to guess it. Finish the program to give the user "Too high" or "Too low" hints. Print the total number of correct guesses when the user finally guesses the number.

```
#include <stdlib.h>
#include <iostream.h>
void main()
{
   int rnum, guess;

   rnum = (rand() % 100) + 1;    // Between 1 and 100

   cout << "I am thinking of a number...\n";
   do
   {   cout << "What is your guess? ";
```

Review Questions

1. How do the character testing functions differ from the character conversion functions?

2. What are the string handling functions?

3. What is the difference between `floor()` and `ceil()`?

4. What does the following nested function return?

   ```
   isalpha(islower('s'));
   ```

5. If the character array `str1` contains the string `Peter` and the character array `str2` contains `Parker`, what does `str2` contain after the following line of code executes?

   ```
   strcat(str1, str2);
   ```

6. What is the output of the following `cout`?

   ```
   cout << floor(8.5) << " " << ceil(8.5);
   ```

7. TRUE or FALSE: The `isxdigit()` and `isgraph()` functions could return the same value, depending on the character passed to them.

8. TRUE or FALSE: The following statements print the same results.

   ```
   cout << pow(64.0, (1.0/2.0)) ;
   cout << sqrt(64.0);
   ```

9. How would you produce a random number from 100 to 200?

Review Exercises

1. Write a program that asks users for their ages. If a user types anything other than two digits, display an error message.

2. Write a program that stores a password in a character array called `pass`. Ask users for the password. Use `strcmp()` to inform users whether they typed the proper password.

3. Write a program that rounds up and rounds down the numbers −10.5, −5.75, and 2.75.

419

4. Ask users for their names. Print every name in *reverse* case—that is, print the first letter of each name in lowercase and the rest of the name in uppercase.

5. Write a program that asks users for five movie titles. Print the longest title.

6. Write a program that computes the square root, cube root, and fourth root of the numbers from 10 to 25, inclusive.

7. Ask users for the titles of their favorite songs. Discard all the special characters in each title. Print the words in the title, one per line. For example, if they enter `My True Love Is Mine, Oh, Mine!`, you should output the following:

```
My
True
Love
Is
Mine
Oh
Mine
```

8. Ask users for the first names of ten children. Using `strcmp()` on each name, write a program to print the name that comes first in the alphabet.

C++

CLASSROOM Seven

Arrays and Pointers

Array Processing

OBJECTIVE ***To introduce the programming of array techniques in C++.***

This lesson discusses different types of arrays. You are familiar with character arrays, which are the only method for storing character strings in the C++ language. A character array isn't the only kind of array you can use, however. There is an array for every data type in C++. By learning how to process arrays, you greatly improve the power and efficiency of your programs.

The sample programs in the next few lessons are the most advanced that you have seen in this book. Arrays are not difficult to use, but their power makes them well-suited to more advanced programming.

Think of an array as a list of items. With a character array, you store strings of characters, or lists of characters, in sequential storage locations. You also can have an array of integers or floating-point values.

Array Basics

Although you have seen arrays used as character strings, you will benefit from a review of arrays in general. An array is a list of more than one variable having the same name. Not *all* lists of variables are arrays. The following list of four variables, for example, does not qualify as an array.

```
sales      bonus92     firstInitial     ctr
```

This is a list of variables (four of them), but it isn't an array because each variable has a different name. You might wonder how more than one variable can have the same name; this seems to violate the rules for variables. If two variables have the same name, how can C++ determine which one you are referring to when you use that name?

Array variables (array elements) are differentiated by a *subscript*, which is a number inside brackets. Suppose that you want to store a person's name in a character array called `name`. You can do this with

```
char name[] = "Heath Barkley";
```

or

```
char name[14] = "Heath Barkley";
```

Because C++ reserves an extra element for the null zero at the end of every string, you don't have to specify the 14 as long as you initialize the array with a value. The variable `name` is an array because brackets follow its name. The array has a single name, `name`, and it contains 14 elements. The array is stored in memory, as shown in Figure 25.1. Each element is a character.

Figure 25.1.
Storing the name
character array
in memory.

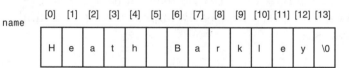

NOTE: All array subscripts begin with 0.

You can manipulate individual elements in the array by referencing their subscripts. For instance, the following cout prints Heath's initials:

```
cout << name[0] << " " << name[6];
```

You can define an array as any data type in C++. You can have integer arrays, long integer arrays, double floating-point arrays, short integer arrays, and so on. C++ recognizes that the brackets [ ] following the array name signify that you are defining an array, not a single nonarray variable.

What does the following print?

```
cout << name[1] << " " << name[2];
```

The following line defines an array called ages, consisting of five integers:

```
int ages[5];
```

The first element in the ages array is ages[0]. The second element is ages[1], and the last one is ages[4]. This declaration of ages does not assign values to the elements, so you don't know what is in ages and your program does not automatically zero ages for you.

Here are some more array definitions:

```
int weights[25], sizes[100];   // Declares two integer arrays
float salaries[8];   // Declares a floating-point array
double temps[50];   // Declares a double floating-point
                    // array
char letters[15];   // Declares an array of characters
```

When you define an array, you instruct C++ to reserve a specific number of memory locations for that array. C++ protects those elements, ensuring that the memory space will not be used by other variables. In the preceding lines of code, if you assign a value to letters[2], you don't overwrite any data in weights, sizes, salaries, or temps. Also, if you assign a value to sizes[94], you don't overwrite data stored in weights, salaries, temps, or letters.

How would you define a floating-point array called amounts that will hold 20 values?

You might wonder why there is not an extra array element for the null zero. Think for a moment about when you need a null zero at the end of an array. You need the null zero only when you store character strings in a character array because every string in C ends with a null zero. Neither

floating-point arrays nor integer arrays require the extra element for the null zero because they do not hold strings.

The following line attempts to print the first element from an array named ara. What is wrong with the line?

```
cout << ara[1] << "\n";
```

Each element in an array occupies the same amount of storage as a nonarray variable of the same data type. In other words, each element in a character array occupies one byte. Each element in an integer array occupies two or more bytes of memory—depending on the computer's internal architecture. The same is true for every other data type.

Your program can reference elements by using formulas for subscripts. As long as the subscript can evaluate to an integer, you can use a literal, a variable, or an expression for the subscript. All of the following are references to individual array elements:

```
ara[4]
sales[ctr + 1]
bonus[month]
salary[month[i] * 2]
```

All array elements are stored in a contiguous, back-to-back fashion. This is important to remember, especially as you write more advanced programs. You can always count on an array's first element preceding the second. The second element is always placed immediately before the third, and so on. Memory is not "padded," meaning that C++ guarantees that there is no extra space between array elements. This is true for character arrays, integer arrays, floating-point arrays, and every other type of array. If a floating-point value occupies four bytes of memory on your computer, the next element in a floating-point array always begins exactly four bytes after the preceding element.

The Size of Arrays

The sizeof() function returns the number of bytes needed to hold its argument. If you request the size of an array, sizeof() returns the number of bytes *reserved* for the entire array.

For example, suppose that you declare an integer array of 100 elements called scores. If you were to find the size of the array, as in the following:

```
n = sizeof(scores);
```

n holds either 200 or 400 bytes, depending on the integer size of your computer. The `sizeof()` function always returns the reserved amount of storage, no matter what data are in the array. Therefore, a character array's contents—even if it holds a very short string—do not affect the size of the array that was originally reserved in memory. If you request the size of an individual array element, however, as in the following:

```
n = sizeof(scores[6]);
```

n holds either 2 or 4 bytes, depending on the integer size of your computer.

Given the following array definition:

```
char values[200];
```

what does `sizeof(values)` produce? What does `sizeof(values[0])` produce? What does `sizeof(values[200])` produce?

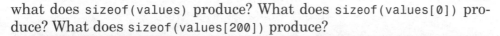

The size of a character array has nothing to do with the length of the string stored in the array. `sizeof(ara)` always returns the number of bytes (characters) it takes to store the entire array named ara in memory. If you declared a character array with 50 elements, but put a string of only 25 characters in that array (with `strcpy()`), the `sizeof()` that array would still be 50, even though the string length (produced with `strlen()`) would be 25.

Array Boundaries

You must never go out-of-bounds with any array. For example, suppose that you want to keep track of the exemptions and salary codes of five employees. You can reserve two arrays to hold such data, like this:

```
int  exemptions[5];   // Holds up to five employee exemptions
char sal_codes[5];    // Holds up to five employee codes
```

Figure 25.2 shows how C++ reserves memory for these arrays. The figure assumes a two-byte integer size, although this might differ on some computers. Notice that C++ reserves five elements for `exemptions` from the array declaration. C++ starts reserving memory for `sal_codes` after it reserves all five elements for `exemptions`. If you declare several more variables—either locally or globally—after these two lines, C++ always protects these five reserved elements for `exemptions` and `sal_codes`.

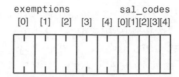

Figure 25.2.
Locating two
arrays in memory.

Because C++ does its part to protect data in the array, so must you. If you reserve five elements for `exemptions`, you have five integer array elements, referred to as `exemptions[0]`, `exemptions[1]`, `exemptions[2]`, `exemptions[3]`, and `exemptions[4]`. C++ does not protect more than five elements for `exemptions`! Suppose that you put a value in an `exemptions` element that you did not reserve:

```
exemptions[6] = 4;    // Assigns a value to an
                      // out-of-range element
```

C++ enables you to do this, but the results are damaging! C++ overwrites other data (in this case, `sal_codes[2]` and `sal_codes[3]` because they are reserved in the location of the seventh element of `exemptions`). Figure 25.3 shows the damaging results of assigning a value to an out-of-range element.

Figure 25.3.
The arrays in
memory after
overwriting part
of `sal_codes`.

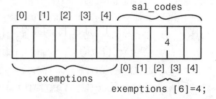

TIP: Some C++ compilers enable you to set an option to check for array boundary violations.

NOTE: Unlike most programming languages, AT&T C++ enables you to assign values to out-of-range (nonreserved) subscripts. You must be careful not to do this; otherwise, you start overwriting your other data or code.

Although you can define an array of any data type, you cannot declare an array of strings. A *string* is not a C++ variable data type. You learn how to hold multiple strings in an array-like structure in Lesson 29, "Pointers and Arrays."

What is wrong with the following program? The problem is not obvious. Keep an eye on array boundaries.

```cpp
#include <iostream.h>
#include <string.h>
main()
{
   char Company[] = "Widgets";
   cout << "The first company is " << Company << endl;

   strcpy(Company, "Micro Amalgamated, Inc.");
   cout << "The next is " << Company << endl;
   return 0;
}
```

Initializing Arrays

You must assign values to array elements before using them. Here are the two ways to initialize elements in an array:

- initialize the elements at declaration time
- initialize the elements in the program

> **NOTE:** C++ automatically initializes global arrays to null zeros. Therefore, global character array elements are null, and all numeric array elements contain zero. You should limit your use of global arrays. If you use global arrays, explicitly initialize them to zero, even though C++ does this for you, to clarify your intentions.

Sometimes you know all of an array's values at the beginning of a program, such as the number of days in each month of the current year. Other times, you do not know the values of the array, such as when you want the user to enter values in a list.

Initializing Elements at Declaration Time

You already know how to initialize character arrays that hold strings when you define the arrays: you simply assign them a string. For example, the following declaration reserves six elements in a character array called city:

```
char city[6];    // Reserves space for city
```

If you also want to initialize city with a value, you can do it like this:

```
char city[6] = "Tulsa";    // Reserves space and
                           // initializes city
```

The 6 is optional because C++ counts the elements needed to hold Tulsa, plus an extra element for the null zero at the end of the quoted string.

You also can reserve a character array and initialize it—a single character at a time—by placing braces around the character data. The following line of code declares an array called initials and initializes it with eight characters:

```
char initials[8] = {'Q', 'K', 'P', 'G', 'V', 'M', 'U', 'S'};
```

The array initials is not a string! Its data does not end in a null zero. There is nothing wrong with defining an array of characters such as this one, but you must remember that you cannot treat the array as if it were a string. Do not use string functions with it or attempt to print the array with cout.

By using brackets, you can initialize any type of array. For example, if you want to initialize an integer array that holds your five children's ages, you can do it with the following declaration:

```
int child_ages[5] = {2, 5, 6, 8, 12};    // Declares and
                                         // initializes array
```

In another example, if you want to keep track of the previous three years' total sales, you can declare an array and initialize it at the same time with the following:

```
double sales[] = {454323.43, 122355.32, 343324.96};
```

As with character arrays, you do not have to state the array size explicitly when you declare and initialize an array of any type. C++ determines, in this case, to reserve three double floating-point array elements for sales. Figure 25.4 shows the representation of child_ages and sales in memory.

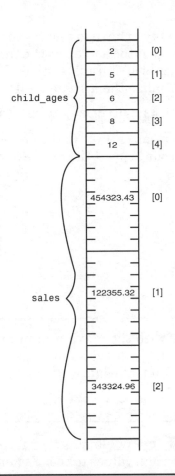

*Figure 25.4.
In-memory
representation of
two different types
of arrays.*

NOTE: You cannot initialize an array using the assignment operator and braces *after* you declare it. You can initialize arrays in this manner only when you declare them. If you want to fill an array with data after you declare the array, you must do so element-by-element or by using functions, as described in the next section.

Although C++ does not automatically initialize the array elements, if you initialize some but not all of the elements when you declare the array, C++ finishes the job for you by assigning the remainder to zero.

TIP: To initialize every element of a large array to zero at the same time, declare the entire array and initialize only its first value to zero. C++ fills the rest of the array to zero.

431

For instance, suppose that you have to reserve array storage for profit figures of the three previous months as well as the three months to follow. You must reserve six elements of storage, but you know values for only the first three. You can initialize the array as follows:

```
double profit[6] = {67654.43, 46472.34, 63451.93};
```

Because you explicitly initialize three of the elements, C++ initializes the rest to zero. If you use cout to print the entire array, one element per line, you receive:

```
67654.43
46472.34
63451.93
00000.00
00000.00
00000.00
```

Always declare an array with the maximum number of subscripts, unless you initialize the array at the same time you declare it. The following array declaration is illegal:

```
int count[];    // Bad array declaration!
```

C++ does not know how many elements to reserve for count, so it reserves none. If you then assign values to count's nonreserved elements, you can (and probably will) overwrite other data.

The only time you can leave the brackets empty is when you also assign values to the array, such as the following:

```
int count[] = {15, 9, 22, -8, 12};    // Good definition
```

C++ can determine, from the list of values, how many elements to reserve. In this case, C++ reserves five elements for count.

Suppose that you want to track the stock market averages for the previous 90 days. Instead of storing them in 90 different variables, it is much easier to store them in an array. You can declare the array like this:

```
float stock[90];
```

The remainder of the program can assign values to the averages.

Suppose that you just finished taking classes at a local university and you want to average your six class scores. The following program initializes one array for the school name and another for the six classes. The body of the program averages the six scores.

```cpp
// Filename: ARA1.CPP
// Averages six test scores
#include <iostream.h>
#include <iomanip.h>
void main()
{
   char s_name[] = "Tri Star University";
   float scores[6] = {88.7, 90.4, 76.0, 97.0, 100.0, 86.7};
   float average = 0.0;
   int ctr;

   // Computes total of scores
   for (ctr = 0; ctr < 6; ctr++)
      { average += scores[ctr]; }

   // Computes the average
   average /= float(6);

   cout << "At " << s_name << ", your class average is "
        << setprecision(2) << average << "\n";
   return;
}
```

The output follows:

```
At Tri Star University, your class average is 89.8.
```

Notice that using arrays makes processing lists of information much easier. Instead of averaging six differently named variables, you can use a for loop to step through each array element. If you had to average 1,000 numbers, you still can do so with a simple for loop. If the 1,000 variables were not in an array, but were individually named, you would have to write a considerable amount of code just to add them.

Expand on the preceding program. Make it print the six scores before computing the average. Notice that you must print array elements individually; you cannot print an entire array in a single cout. (You

433

can print an entire character array with cout, but only if it holds a
null-terminated string of characters.)

```cpp
// Filename: ARA2.CPP
// Prints and averages six test scores
#include <iostream.h>
#include <iomanip.h>
void pr_scores(float scores[]);    // Prototype

void main()
{
   char s_name[] = "Tri Star University";
   float scores[6] = {88.7, 90.4, 76.0, 97.0, 100.0, 86.7};
   float average = 0.0;
   int ctr;

   // Calls function to print scores
   pr_scores(scores);

   // Computes total of scores




   cout << "At " << s_name << ", your class average is "
       << setprecision(2) << average;
   return;
}

void pr_scores(float scores[6])
{
   // Prints the six scores
   int ctr;

   cout << "Here are your scores:\n";    // Title
   for (ctr = 0; ctr < 6; ctr++)
     cout << setprecision(2) << scores[ctr] << "\n";
   return;
}
```

> **NOTE:** To pass an array to a function, you must specify its name only. In the receiving function's parameter list, you must state the array type and include its brackets, which tell the function that it is an array. (You do not have to explicitly state the array size in the receiving parameter list, as shown in the prototype.)

To improve the maintainability of your programs, define all array sizes with the `const` instruction. What if you took four classes next semester but still wanted to use the same program? You could modify it by changing all the 6s to 4s, but if you had defined the array size with a constant, you would have to change only one line to change the program's subscript limits. Using a separate sheet of paper or one of the blank pages provided at the end of this book, rewrite the preceding program so that it uses constants for the class size.

For such a simple example, using a constant for the maximum subscript might not seem like a big advantage. If you were writing a larger program that processed several arrays, however, changing the constant at the top of the program would be much easier than searching the program for each occurrence of that array reference.

Using constants for array sizes has the added advantage of protecting you from going outside of the subscript bounds. You do not have to remember the subscript while looping through arrays; you can use the constant instead.

The following program asks the user for three numbers and then attempts to initialize an integer array with the three values. Something is wrong with the initialization method. What is it? (The next section explains how to fix bugs such as this.)

```
#include <iostream.h>
void main()
{
    int num1, num2, num3;
    int iara[3];
    cout << "What is the first number? ";
    cin >> num1;
    cout << "What is the second number? ";
    cin >> num2;
    cout << "What is the third number? ";
    cin >> num3;
```

```
      iara = {num1, num2, num3};    // Attempts to initialize
                                    // the array
   cout << "Thanks for your help!\n";
}
```

Initializing Elements in the Program

Rarely do you know the contents of arrays when you declare them. You usually fill an array with user input or a disk file's data. The for loop is a perfect tool for looping through arrays when you fill them with values.

> **NOTE:** An array name cannot appear on the left side of an assignment statement.

You cannot assign one array to another. Suppose that you want to copy an array called total_sales to a second array called saved_sales. You cannot do so with the following assignment statement:

```
saved_sales = total_sales;    // Invalid!
```

Instead, you have to copy the arrays one element at a time, using a loop, such as the following section of code does:

```
for (ctr = 0; ctr < ARRAY_SIZE; ctr++)
   { saved_sales[ctr] = total_sales[ctr]; }
```

The following examples illustrate methods for initializing arrays in a program. After learning about disk processing later in this book, you will learn to read array values from a disk file.

The following program uses the assignment operator to assign 10 temperatures to an array.

```
// Filename: ARA3.CPP
// Fills an array with 10 temperature values
#include <iostream.h>
#include <iomanip.h>
const int NUM_TEMPS = 10;
void main()
{
```

```cpp
float temps[NUM_TEMPS];
int ctr;

temps[0] = 78.6;    // Subscripts always begin at 0
temps[1] = 82.1;
temps[2] = 79.5;
temps[3] = 75.0;
temps[4] = 75.4;
temps[5] = 71.8;
temps[6] = 73.3;
temps[7] = 69.5;
temps[8] = 74.1;
temps[9] = 75.7;

// Prints the temps
cout << "Daily temperatures for the last " <<
        NUM_TEMPS << " days:\n";
for (ctr = 0; ctr < NUM_TEMPS; ctr++)
   { cout << setprecision(1) << temps[ctr] << "\n"; }

return;
}
```

The following program uses a `for` loop and `cin` to assign eight integers entered individually by the user. The program then prints a total of the numbers.

```cpp
// Filename: TOT.CPP
// Totals eight input values from the user
#include <iostream.h>
const int NUM = 8;
void main()
{
   int nums[NUM];
   int total = 0;   // Holds total of user's eight numbers
   int ctr;

   for (ctr = 0; ctr < NUM; ctr++)
     { cout << "Please enter the next number...";
       cin >> nums[ctr];
       total += nums[ctr]; }

   cout << "The total of the numbers is " << total << "\n";
   return;
}
```

437

Out-of-Order Arrays

You don't have to access an array in the same order you initialized it. Lesson 26, "Working with Arrays," shows you how to change the order of an array. You also can use the subscript to select items from an array of values.

The following program requests sales data for the preceding 12 months. Users can then type a month they want to see. That month's sales figure is then printed, without figures from other months getting in the way. This is how you begin to build a search program to find requested data: you store the data in an array (or in a disk file that can be read into an array, as you learn later in Lesson 32, "Sequential Files"), then wait for a user's request to see specific pieces of the data.

```
// Filename: SAL.CPP
// Stores twelve months of sales and
// prints selected ones
#include <iostream.h>
#include <ctype.h>
#include <conio.h>
#include <iomanip.h>
const int NUM = 12;
void main()
{
   float sales[NUM];
   int ctr, ans;
   int req_month;    // Holds user's request

   // Fills the array
   cout << "Please enter the twelve monthly sales values\n";
   for (ctr = 0; ctr < NUM; ctr++)
     { cout << "What are sales for month number "
           << ctr + 1 << "? \n";
       cin >> sales[ctr]; }

   // Waits for a requested month
   for (ctr = 0; ctr < 25; ctr++)
     { cout << "\n"; }    // Clears the screen

   cout << "*** Sales Printing Program ***\n";
   cout << "Prints any sales from the last " << NUM
       << " months\n\n";
```

```
     do
       { cout << "\nFor what month (1-" << NUM << ") do you want "
              << "to see a sales value? ";
         cin >> req_month;
         // Adjusts for zero-based subscript
         cout << "\nMonth " << req_month <<
                 "'s sales are " << setprecision(2) <<
                 sales[req_month - 1];
         cout << "\nDo you want to see another (Y/N)? ";
         ans = getch();
         ans = toupper(ans);
       } while (ans == 'Y');
     return;
}
```

Notice the helpful screen-clearing routine that prints 25 newline characters. This routine scrolls the screen until it is blank. (Most compilers come with a better built-in screen-clearing function, but the AT&T C++ standard does not offer one because the compiler is too closely linked with specific hardware.)

The following is the second screen from this program. After the 12 sales values are entered in the array, any or all can be requested, one at a time, simply by supplying the month's number (the number of the subscript).

```
*** Sales Printing Program ***
Prints any sales from the last 12 months


For what month (1-12) do you want to see a sales value? 2

Month 2's sales are 433.22
Do you want to see another (Y/N)?
For what month (1-12) do you want to see a sales value? 5

Month 5's sales are 123.45
Do you want to see another (Y/N)?
```

Review Questions

1. TRUE or FALSE: A single array can hold several values of different data types.

2. How do C++ programs tell one array element from another if all elements have identical names?

3. Why must you initialize an array before using it?

4. Given the following definition of an array, called `weights`, what is the value of `weights[5]`?

```
int weights[10] = {5, 2, 4};
```

5. If you pass an integer array to a function and change it, does the array change in the calling function also? (*Hint:* Remember how character arrays are passed to functions.)

6. How does C++ initialize global array elements?

Review Exercises

1. Write a program to store the ages of six of your friends in a single array. Store each of the six ages using the assignment operator. Print the ages on-screen.

2. Modify the program in Exercise 1 to print the ages in reverse order.

3. Write a simple data program to track a radio station's ratings (1, 2, 3, 4, or 5) for the previous 18 months. Use `cin` to initialize the array with the ratings. Print the ratings on-screen with an appropriate title.

4. Write a program to store the numbers from 1 to 100 in an array of 100 integer elements. (*Hint:* The subscripts should begin at 0 and end at 99.)

5. Write a program that a small business owner can use to track customers. Assign each customer a number (starting at 0). Whenever a customer purchases something, record the sale in the element that matches the customer's number (that is, the next unused array element). When the store owner signals the end of the day, print a report consisting of each customer number with its matching sales, a total sales figure, and an average sales figure per customer.

440

Working with Arrays

OBJECTIVE ***To teach some of the array processing techniques possible in C++.***

This lesson shows you ways to access and manipulate arrays. C++ provides many ways to access arrays. If you have programmed in other computer languages, you will find that some of C++'s array indexing techniques are unique. Arrays in the C++ language are closely linked with *pointers*. Lesson 28, "Introduction to Pointers," describes the many ways pointers and arrays interact. Because pointers are so powerful, and because learning about arrays provides a good foundation for learning about pointers, this lesson attempts to describe in detail how to reference arrays.

This lesson discusses the different types of array processing. You will learn how to search an array for one or more values, find the highest and lowest values in an array, and sort an array into numerical or alphabetical order.

Searching Arrays

Arrays are one of the primary means by which data is stored in C++ programs. Many types of programs lend themselves to processing lists (arrays) of data, such as an employee payroll program, scientific research of several chemicals, or customer account processing. As mentioned in Lesson 25, "Array Processing," array data usually is read from a disk file. Later lessons describe disk file processing. For now, you should understand how to manipulate arrays so that you can see data exactly the way you want to see it.

Lesson 25 showed how to print arrays in the same order that you entered the data. This is sometimes done, but it is not always the most appropriate method of looking at data.

For instance, suppose that a high school used C++ programs for its grade reports. Suppose also that the school wanted to see a list of the top 10 grade-point averages (GPAs). You could not print the first 10 GPAs in the list of student averages because the top 10 GPAs might not (and probably will not) appear as the first 10 array elements. Because the GPAs would not be in any sequence, the program would have to sort the array into numeric order, from high GPAs to low, or else search the array for the 10 highest GPAs.

You need a method for putting arrays in a specific order. This is called *sorting* an array. When you sort an array, you put that array in a specific order, such as in alphabetical or numerical order. A dictionary is in sorted order, and so is a phone book.

When you reverse the order of a sort, it is called a *descending sort*. For instance, if you wanted to look at a list of all employees in descending salary order, the highest-paid employees would be printed first.

 The following 10 numbers are sorted in *ascending* order:

2 5 10 23 54 102 454 677 678 1029

The following 10 numbers are sorted in *descending* order:

1029 678 677 454 102 54 23 10 5 2

Before you learn to sort, it would be helpful to learn how to search an array for a value. This is a preliminary step in learning to sort. What if one of those students received a grade change? The computer must be able to access that specific student's grade to change it (without affecting the others). As the next section shows, programs can search for specific array elements.

> **NOTE:** C++ provides a method for sorting and searching lists of strings, but you cannot understand how to do this until you learn about pointers, starting in Lesson 28, "Introduction to Pointers." The sorting and searching examples and algorithms presented in this lesson demonstrate sorting and searching arrays of numbers. The same concepts will apply (and actually will be much more usable for "real-world" applications) when you learn how to store lists of names in C++.

What is the difference between *sorting* an array and *searching* an array for a value?

Searching for Values

You do not have to know any new commands to search an array for a value. The `if` and `for` loop statements are all you need. To search an array for a specific value, look at each element in that array, comparing it with the `if` statement to see whether they match. If they do not, you keep searching down the array. If you run out of array elements before finding the value, it is not in the array.

You can perform several different kinds of searches. You might have to find the highest or the lowest value in a list of numbers. This is informative when you have a lot of data and want to know the extremes of the data (such as the highest and lowest sales region in your division). You also can search an array to see whether it contains a matching value. For example, you can see whether an item is already in an inventory by searching a part number array for a match.

To find the highest number in an array, compare each element with the first one. If you find a higher value, it becomes the basis for the rest of the array. Continue until you reach the end of the array, and you will have the highest value, as the following program shows.

```
// Filename: HIGH.CPP
// Finds the highest value in the array
#include <iostream.h>
const int SIZE = 15;
void main()
```

```
{
    // Puts some numbers in the array
    int ara[SIZE] = {5,2,7,8,36,4,2,86,11,43,22,12,45,6,85};
    int high_val, ctr;

    high_val = ara[0];    // Initializes with first
                          // array element
    for (ctr = 1; ctr < SIZE; ctr++)
       {                        // Stores current value if it
                                // is higher than the highest
         if (ara[ctr] > high_val)
           { high_val = ara[ctr]; }
       }

    cout << "The highest number in the list is "
         << high_val << "\n";
    return;
}
```

The output of the program is the following:

```
The highest number in the list is 86
```

You have to save the element if and only if it is higher than the one you are comparing. Finding the smallest number in an array is just as easy, except that you compare to see whether each succeeding array element is less than the lowest value found so far.

Finish the following program so that it finds both the highest and the lowest value in the array. The code fragment that you see uses the rand() function from Lesson 24, "C++ Built-In Functions," to fill the array with random values from 0 to 99. The program prints the entire array before starting the search for the highest and the lowest.

```
// Finds the highest and the lowest value in the array
#include <iostream.h>
#include <stdlib.h>
const int SIZE = 15;
void main()
{
    int ara[SIZE];
    int high_val, low_val, ctr;
```

```
    // Fills array with random numbers from 0 to 99
    for (ctr = 0; ctr < SIZE; ctr++)
      { ara[ctr] = rand() % 100; }

    // Prints the array to the screen
    cout << "Here are the " << SIZE << " random numbers:\n";
    for (ctr = 0; ctr < SIZE; ctr++)
      {   cout << ara[ctr] << "\n"; }

    cout << "\n\n";   // Prints a blank line
    high_val = ara[0];   // Initializes first element to
                         // both high and low

    low_val = ara[0];




    cout << "The highest number in the list is " <<
            high_val << "\n";
    cout << "The lowest number in the list is " <<
            low_val << "\n";
    return;
}
```

Describe what the following program does.

```
// Filename: ARASRCH.CPP
#include <iostream.h>
void main()
{
   int mult, ctr, found = 0;
   int iara[] = {20, 40, 100, 80, 10, 60, 50, 90, 30, 70};
   cout << "Enter a number from 10 to 100 ";
   cin >> mult;
```

```
    for (ctr = 0; ctr < 10; ctr++)
    {   if (iara[ctr] == mult)
            { found = 1; break; }
    }

    if (found)
        { cout << "The number is at position " << ctr << endl; }
    else
        { cout << "I could not find the number." << endl; }
    return;
}
```

Sorting Arrays

There are many times when you must sort one or more arrays. Suppose that you were to take a list of numbers, write each number on a separate piece of paper, and throw all the pieces of paper into the air. The steps you would take trying to put the pieces of paper back in order—shuffling and changing the order—are similar to what your computer goes through to sort numbers or character data.

Because sorting arrays requires exchanging values of elements back and forth, it helps if you first learn the technique for swapping variables. Suppose that you had two variables named score1 and score2. What if you wanted to reverse their values (putting score2 into the score1 variable, and vice versa)? You could not do this:

```
score1 = score2;    // Does not swap the two values
score2 = score1;
```

Why doesn't this work? In the first line, the value of score1 is replaced with score2's value. When the first line finishes, both score1 and score2 contain the same value. Therefore, the second line cannot work as you want it to.

To swap two variables, you have to use a third variable to hold the intermediate result. (This is the only function of this third variable.) For instance, to swap score1 and score2, use a third variable (called hold_score in this code), as in:

```
hold_score = score1;    // These three lines properly
score1 = score2;        // swap score1 and score2
score2 = hold_score;
```

This exchanges the values in the two variables.

There are several different ways to sort arrays. These methods include the *bubble sort,* the *quicksort,* and the *shell sort.* The basic goal of each method is to compare each array element to another array element and swap them if the first value is less than the other.

Although the theory behind these sorts is beyond the scope of this book, the bubble sort is one of the easiest to understand. Values in the array are compared to each other, a pair at a time, and swapped if they are not in back-to-back order. The lowest value eventually "floats" to the top of the array, like a bubble in a glass of soda.

Figure 26.1 shows a list of numbers before, during, and after a bubble sort. The bubble sort steps through the array, comparing pairs of numbers, to see whether they have to be swapped. Several passes might have to be made through the array before it is finally sorted (no more passes are needed). Other types of sorts improve on the bubble sort. The bubble sort procedure is easy to program, but it is slower compared to many of the other methods.

Start	Pass 1	Pass 2	Pass 3	Pass 4
3	1	1	1	1
2	3	2	2	2
5	5	5	3	3
1	2	3	5	4
4	4	4	4	5

Figure 26.1. Sorting a list of numbers using the bubble sort.

The following function shows the bubble sort in action. The function receives an integer array and the maximum number of elements in the array. It then rearranges the array, using the bubble sort. When the function ends, the array is sorted.

```
void sortArray(int ara[], int max)
{
   // Sorts the array
   int temp;    // Temporary variable to swap with
   int ctr1, ctr2;    // Need two loop counters to
                      // swap pairs of numbers
   for (ctr1 = 0; ctr1 < (max - 1); ctr1++)
      { for (ctr2=(ctr1+1); ctr2<max; ctr2++)   // Tests pairs
          { if (ara[ctr1] > ara[ctr2])   // Swaps if this pair
             { temp = ara[ctr1];         // is not in order
```

447

```
                    ara[ctr1] = ara[ctr2];
                    ara[ctr2] = temp;    // "Floats" the lowest
                                         // to the highest
            }
        }
    }
   return;
}
```

Write a program that uses this bubble sort function. Assign an array 25 random numbers, sort the array, then print it in sorted (ascending) order.

A descending sort is as easy to write as an ascending sort. With the ascending sort (from low to high values), you compare pairs of values, testing to see whether the first is greater than the second. With a descending sort, you test to see whether the first is less than the second.

You have to change only one line in the bubble sort function—the `if` statement—to make it sort in descending order. Write the `if` statement so that it sorts in descending order.

TIP: You can save the sort functions in two separate files named sortAscend.h and sortDescend.h. When you must sort two different arrays, `#include` these files inside your own programs. Even better, compile each of these routines separately and link the one you need to your program. (You must check your compiler's manual to learn how to do this.)

NOTE: You can sort character arrays just as easily as you sort numeric arrays. C++ uses the ASCII character set for its sorting comparisons. If you look at the ASCII table in Appendix C, you will see that numbers sort before letters and that uppercase letters sort before lowercase letters.

Advanced Referencing of Arrays

The array notation you have seen so far is common in computer programming languages. Most languages use subscripts inside brackets (or parentheses) to refer to individual array elements. For instance, you know that the following array references describe the first and fifth elements of the array called `sales` (remember that the starting subscript is always 0):

```
sales[0]
sales[4]
```

C++ provides another approach to referencing arrays. Even though the title of this section includes the word *advanced,* this array-referencing method is not difficult. It is very different, however, especially if you are familiar with another programming language's approach.

There is nothing wrong with referring to array elements in the manner you have seen so far. The second approach, however, is unique to C and C++ and will be helpful when you learn about pointers in upcoming lessons. Actually, C++ programmers who have programmed for several years rarely use the subscript notation you have seen.

In C++, an array's name is not just a label for you to use in programs. To C++, the array name is the actual address where the first element begins in memory. Suppose that you define an array called `amounts` with the following statement:

```
int amounts[6] = {4, 1, 3, 7, 9, 2};
```

Figure 26.2 shows how this array is stored in memory. The figure shows the array beginning at address 405,332. (The actual addresses of variables are determined by the computer when you load and run your compiled program.) Notice that the name of the array, `amounts`, is located somewhere in memory and contains the address of `amounts[0]`, or 405,332.

You can refer to an array by its regular subscript notation, or by modifying the address of the array. Both of the following refer to the fourth element of `amounts`:

```
amounts[3] and (amounts + 3)[0]
```

Because C++ considers the array name to be an address in memory that contains the location of the first array element, nothing keeps you from using a different address as the starting address and referencing from there. Taking this one step further, each of the following also refers to the third element of `amounts`:

```
(amounts + 0)[3] and (amounts + 2)[1] and (amounts - 2)[5]
(1 + amounts)[2] and (3 + amounts)[0] and (amounts + 1)[2]
```

You can print any of these array elements with cout.

Figure 26.2.
The array name amounts *holds the* address of amounts[0].

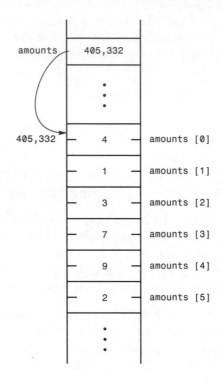

 THINK...

The hierarchy table in Appendix D shows that array subscripts have precedence over addition and subtraction. Therefore, you must enclose array names in parentheses if you want to modify the name, as shown in these examples. The following are not equivalent:

```
(2 + amounts)[1] and 2 + amounts[1];
```

The first example refers to amounts[3] (which is 7). The second example takes the value of amounts[1] (which is 1 in this sample array) and adds 2 to it (resulting in a value of 3).

This second method of array referencing might seem like more trouble than it is worth, but learning to reference arrays in this fashion will make your transition to pointers much easier. An array name is actually a pointer itself, because the array contains the address of the first array element (it "points" to the start of the array).

When you print strings inside character arrays, referencing the arrays by their modified addresses is more useful than with integer arrays. Suppose that you stored three strings in a single character array. You could initialize this array with the following statement:

```
char names[] = {'T','e','d','\0','E','v','a','\0'};
```

Figure 26.3 shows how this array might look in memory. The array name, names, contains the address of the first element, names[0] (the let-ter T).

	[0]	[1]	[2]	[3]	[4]	[5]	[6]	[7]
names	T	e	d	\0	E	v	a	\0

Figure 26.3. Storing more than one string in a single character array.

You have yet to see a character array that holds more than one string, but C++ allows it. The problem with such an array is how you reference, and especially how you print, the second and third strings. If you were to print this array using cout:

```
cout << names;
```

C++ would print the following:

```
Ted
```

Because cout requires a starting address, you can print both strings with the following couts:

```
cout << names;    // Prints Ted
cout << (names + 4);    // Prints Eva
cout << (names + 8);    // Prints Sam
```

What do the following couts print?

```
cout << (names + 1);
cout << (names + 6);
```

To help you review character arrays, the following refer to individual array elements (single characters):

```
names[2] and (names + 1)[1]
```

The following refer to addresses only, and as such, you can print the full strings with cout:

`names` and `(names + 4)`

The following program stores the numbers from 100 to 600 in an array, then prints elements using the new method of array subscripting.

```cpp
// Filename: REF1.CPP
// Prints elements of an integer array in different ways
#include <iostream.h>
void main()
{
   int num[6] = {100, 200, 300, 400, 500, 600};

   cout << "num[0] is \t" << num[0] << "\n";
   cout << "(num + 0)[0] is \t" << (num + 0)[0] << "\n";
   cout << "(num - 2)[2] is \t" << (num - 2)[2] << "\n\n";

   cout << "num[1] is \t" << num[1] << "\n";
   cout << "(num + 1)[0] is \t" << (num + 1)[0] << "\n\n";

   cout << "num[5] is \t" << num[5] << "\n";
   cout << "(num + 5)[0] is \t" << (num + 5)[0] << "\n";
   cout << "(num + 2)[3] is \t" << (num + 2)[3] << "\n\n";

   cout << "(3 + num)[1] is \t" << (3 + num)[1] << "\n";
   cout << "3 + num[1] is \t" << 3 + num[1] << "\n";
   return;
}
```

Here is this program's output:

```
num[0] is        100
(num + 0)[0] is   100
(num - 2)[2] is   100

num[1] is        200
(num + 1)[0] is   200

num[5] is        600
(num + 5)[0] is   600
(num + 2)[3] is   600

(3 + num)[1] is   500
3 + num[1] is     203
```

The following program prints strings and characters from a character array. All the `cout`s print properly.

```
// Filename: REF2.CPP
// Prints elements and strings from an array
#include <iostream.h>
void main()
{
   char names[] = {'T','e','d','\0','E','v','a','\0','S',
                   'a','m','\0'};

   // Must use extra percent (%) to print %s and %c
   cout << "names " << names << "\n";
   cout << "names + 0 " << names + 0 << "\n";
   cout << "names + 1 " << names + 1 << "\n";
   cout << "names + 2 " << names + 2 << "\n";
   cout << "names + 3 " << names + 3 << "\n";
   cout << "names + 5 " << names + 5 << "\n";
   cout << "names + 8 " << names + 8 << "\n\n";

   cout << "(names + 0)[0] " << (names + 0)[0] << "\n";
   cout << "(names + 0)[1] " << (names + 0)[1] << "\n";
   cout << "(names + 0)[2] " << (names + 0)[2] << "\n";
   cout << "(names + 0)[3] " << (names + 0)[3] << "\n";
   cout << "(names + 0)[4] " << (names + 0)[4] << "\n";
   cout << "(names + 0)[5] " << (names + 0)[5] << "\n\n";

   cout << "(names + 2)[0] " << (names + 2)[0] << "\n";
   cout << "(names + 2)[1] " << (names + 2)[1] << "\n";
   cout << "(names + 1)[4] " << (names + 1)[4] << "\n\n";

   return;
}
```

Here is the first part of this program's output. Write the remaining six lines of output after the ones shown here.

```
names Ted
names + 0 Ted
names + 1 ed
names + 2 d
names + 3
names + 5 va
names + 8 Sam

(names + 0)[0] T
(names + 0)[1] e
(names + 0)[2] d
```

Review Questions

1. Where did the bubble sort get its name?

2. Are the following values sorted in ascending or descending order?

   33   55   78   78   90   102   435   859   976   4092

3. How does C++ interpret the name of an array?

4. Consider the following array definition:

   ```
   char teams[] = {'E','a','g','l','e','s','\0','R',
                   'a','m','s','\0'};
   ```

   What is printed with each of these statements? (Answer "invalid" if the cout is illegal.)

   (a) `cout << teams;`
   (b) `cout << teams + 7;`
   (c) `cout << (teams + 3);`
   (d) `cout << teams[0];`
   (e) `cout << (teams + 0)[0];`
   (f) `cout << (teams + 5);`

Review Exercises

1. Write a program to store six of your friends' ages in a single array. Assign the ages in random order. Print the ages, from low to high, on-screen.

2. Modify the program in Exercise 1 to print the ages in descending order.

3. Using the new approach of subscripting arrays, rewrite the programs in Exercises 1 and 2. Always put a 0 in the subscript brackets, modifying the address instead (use `(ages + 3)[0]` rather than `ages[3]`).

Multi-Dimensional Arrays

OBJECTIVE

To explain how to access and manipulate C++ arrays of more than one dimension.

This lesson teaches you how to store tables of data in your C++ program. Some data fits in lists, such as the data discussed in the preceding two lessons, and other data is better suited for tables of information. This lesson takes arrays one step further. The previous lessons introduced single-dimensional arrays—arrays that have only one subscript and represent lists of values.

This lesson introduces arrays of more than one dimension, called *multidimensional arrays*. Multidimensional arrays, sometimes called *tables* or *matrices,* have at least two dimensions (rows and columns). Often they have more than two. If you understand single-dimensional arrays, you should have no trouble understanding arrays that have more than one dimension.

Multidimensional Array Basics

A multidimensional array has more than one subscript. Whereas a single-dimensional array is a list of values, a multidimensional array simulates a table of values, or multiple tables of values. The most commonly used table is a two-dimensional table (an array with two subscripts).

C++ does not store multidimensional arrays in the same way as other programming languages. In C++, a multidimensional array is nothing more than an *array of arrays*. Most of the time, however, you can treat a C++ multidimensional array as you would multidimensional arrays in other programming languages.

Suppose that a football team wanted to track its players' total yardage. The team has eight games scheduled, and there are six rushing players on the team. Table 27.1 shows the team's yardage record.

Table 27.1. A football team's yardage record.

Player Name	Game 1	Game 2	Game 3	Game 4	Game 5	Game 6	Game 7	Game 8
Downing	1	0	2	1	0	0	0	0
Edwards	0	3	6	4	6	4	5	3
Franks	2	2	3	2	1	0	2	3
Grady	1	3	2	0	1	5	2	1
Howard	3	1	1	1	2	0	1	0
Williams	2	3	1	0	1	2	1	2

Do you see that the football table is a two-dimensional table? It has rows (the first dimension) and columns (the second dimension). Therefore, this is a two-dimensional table with six rows and eight columns. (Generally, the number of rows is specified first.)

Each row has a player's name, and each column has a game number, but these are not part of the actual data. The data consists of only 48 values (six rows by eight columns). The data in a two-dimensional table always is the same type of data; in this case, every value is an integer. If it were a table of salaries, every element would be a floating-point or a double floating-point number.

How many elements would a 10-by-15 multidimensional table have?

The number of dimensions, in this case two, corresponds to the dimensions in the physical world. The single-dimensional array is a line, or list of values. Two dimensions represent both length and width. You write on a piece of paper in two dimensions; two dimensions represent a flat surface. Three dimensions represent width, length, and depth. You have seen 3-D movies. Not only do the images have width and height, but they also seem to have depth. Figure 27.1 shows what a three-dimensional array looks like if it has a depth of four, six rows, and three columns. Notice that a three-dimensional table resembles a cube.

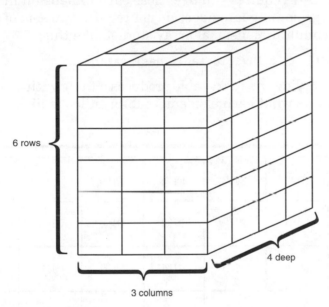

Figure 27.1.
A representation of a three-dimensional table (a cube).

6 rows

4 deep

3 columns

It is difficult to visualize more than three dimensions. However, you can think of each dimension after three as another occurrence. In other words, a list of one player's season yardage record can be stored in an array. The team's yardage record is two-dimensional (as shown in Table 27.1). The league, made of up several teams' yardage records, would represent a three-dimensional table. Each team (the depth of the table) has rows and columns of yardage data. Each additional league becomes an additional dimension (another set of data).

C++ enables you to store several dimensions, although "real-world" data rarely requires more than two or three.

Reserving Multidimensional Arrays

When you define storage for a multidimensional array, you must inform C++ that the array has more than one dimension by putting more than one subscript in brackets after the array name. You must include a separate number in brackets for each dimension in the table. For example, to reserve the team data from Table 27.1, you use the following multidimensional array declaration:

```
int teams[8][6];    // Reserves a two-dimensional table
```

Notice that C++ requires you to enclose each dimension in brackets. Most other programming languages do not require two sets of brackets. Do not reserve multidimensional array storage like this:

```
int teams[8,6];    // Invalid table declaration
```

Properly reserving the teams table produces a table with 48 elements. Figure 27.2 shows what each element's subscript looks like.

Figure 27.2. Subscripts for the football team table.

columns					
[0] [0]	[0] [1]	[0] [2]	[0] [3]	[0] [4]	[0] [5]
[1] [0]	[1] [1]	[1] [2]	[1] [3]	[1] [4]	[1] [5]
[2] [0]	[2] [1]	[2] [2]	[2] [3]	[2] [4]	[2] [5]
[3] [0]	[3] [1]	[3] [2]	[3] [3]	[3] [4]	[3] [5]
[4] [0]	[4] [1]	[4] [2]	[4] [3]	[4] [4]	[4] [5]
[5] [0]	[5] [1]	[5] [2]	[5] [3]	[5] [4]	[5] [5]
[6] [0]	[6] [1]	[6] [2]	[6] [3]	[6] [4]	[6] [5]
[7] [0]	[7] [1]	[7] [2]	[7] [3]	[7] [4]	[7] [5]

rows

458

If you had to track three teams, each with 15 players and 10 games, the three-dimensional table would be created as follows:

```
int teams[3][15][10]; // Reserves a three-dimensional
                      // table
```

When creating a two-dimensional table, always put the maximum number of rows first and the maximum number of columns second. C++ always uses 0 as the starting subscript of each dimension. The last element, the lower-right element of the `teams` table, is `teams[7][5]`.

A programmer wants to print the first and last values of a four-dimensional table named `MyData` that she defined with this statement:

```
double MyData[2][10][3][60];   // Defines the table
```

After filling the table with values, she writes the following cout statements, but they do not produce the first or the last values in the table as she wants to do. What is she doing wrong?

```
cout << MyData[1][1][1][1] << "\n"; // Prints the first value
cout << MyData[2][10][3][60] << "\n";  // Prints the last value
```

How would you define an array named `utilities` that holds five years' worth of monthly utility bill payments from your four utility companies?

Mapping Arrays to Memory

C++ approaches multidimensional arrays a little differently than most programming languages do. When you use subscripts, you do not have to understand the internal representation of multidimensional arrays. However, most C++ programmers think that a deeper understanding of these arrays is important, especially when programming advanced applications.

Remember, a two-dimensional array is actually an *array of arrays*. You program multidimensional arrays as though they were tables with

rows and columns. A two-dimensional array is actually a single-dimensional array, but each of its elements is not an integer, floating-point, or character, but another array.

Knowing that a multidimensional array is an array of other arrays is critical when passing and receiving such arrays. C++ passes all arrays, including multidimensional arrays, by address. Suppose that you were using an integer array called scores, reserved as a 5-by-6 table. You could pass scores to a function called print_it(), as follows:

```
print_it(scores);   // Passes table to a function
```

The function print_it() must identify the type of parameter being passed to it. The print_it() function also must recognize that the parameter is an array. If scores were single-dimensional, you could receive it as

```
print_it(int scores[])   // Works only if scores
                         // is single-dimensional
```

or

```
print_it(int scores[10])   // Assuming that scores
                           // has 10 elements
```

If scores were a multidimensional table, you would have to designate each pair of brackets and put the maximum number of subscripts in its brackets, as in

```
print_it(int scores[5][6])   // Informs print_it() of
                             // the array's dimensions
```

or

```
print_it(int scores[][6])   // Informs print_it() of
                            // the array's dimensions
```

Notice that you do not have to explicitly state the maximum subscript on the first dimension when receiving multidimensional arrays, but you must designate the second. If scores were a three-dimensional table, dimensioned as 10-by-5-by-6, you would receive it with print_it() as

```
print_it(int scores[][5][6])   // Only first dimension
                               // is optional
```

or

```
print_it(int scores[10][5][6])   // Inform print_it() of
                                 // array's dimensions
```

Write a statement that passes a four-dimensional table named `Bills`, defined with this statement:

```
double Bills[3][5][2][7];
```

to a function named `PayThem()`.

Write the first line of `Bills` that receives the `Bills` table.

Initializing Multidimensional Arrays

C++ enables you to initialize a multidimensional array when you define it. As with single-dimensional arrays, you initialize multidimensional arrays with braces that designate dimensions. Because a multidimensional array is an array of arrays, you can nest braces when you initialize them.

The following three array definitions fill the three arrays `ara1`, `ara2`, and `ara3`, as shown in Figure 27.3:

```
int ara1[5] = {8, 5, 3, 25, 41};    // Single-dimensional array
int ara2[2][4] = {{4, 3, 2, 1},{1, 2, 3, 4}};
int ara3[3][4] = {{1, 2, 3, 4},{5, 6, 7, 8},{9, 10, 11, 12}};
```

Notice that the multidimensional arrays are stored in row order. In `ara3`, the first row receives the first four elements of the definition (1, 2, 3, and 4).

Fill in the boxes of Figure 27.4 to show how the following statement initializes a table.

```
int Table[4][2] = {2, 1, 5, 4, 6, 7, 4, 2};    // Fill up Table
```

To make a multidimensional array initialization look more like the array's subscripts, some programmers like to show how arrays are filled. Because C++ programs are free-form, you can initialize `ara2` and `ara3` as

```
int ara2[2][4] = {{4, 3, 2, 1},    // Does exactly the same
                  {1, 2, 3, 4}};   // thing as before
```

and

```
int ara3[3][4] = {{1, 2, 3, 4},
                   {5, 6, 7, 8},
                   {9,10, 11, 12};    // Visually more
                                      // obvious
```

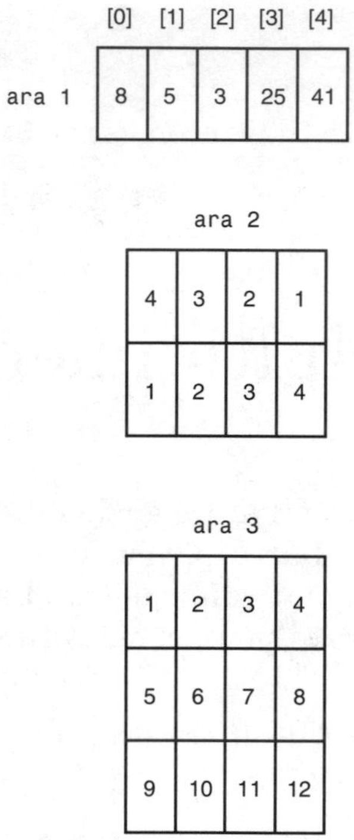

Figure 27.3.
After initializing
a table.

	[0]	[1]	[2]	[3]	[4]
ara 1	8	5	3	25	41

ara 2

4	3	2	1
1	2	3	4

ara 3

1	2	3	4
5	6	7	8
9	10	11	12

Figure 27.4.
Fill in the values
for the Table
elements.

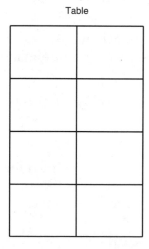
Table

You can initialize a multidimensional array as if it were single-dimensional in C++. You must keep track of the row order if you do this. For instance, the following two definitions also reserve storage for and initialize ara2 and ara3:

```
int ara2[2][4] = {4, 3, 2, 1, 1, 2, 3, 4};
int ara3[3][4] = {1, 2, 3, 4, 5, 6, 7, 8, 9, 10, 11, 12, 13};
```

There is no difference between initializing ara2 and ara3 with or without the nested braces. The nested braces seem to show the dimensions and how C++ fills them a little better, but the choice of using nested braces is yours.

Rewrite the following array definition to show its two dimensions in the list of values that initialize it. (Break the list of values into a row-and-column appearance using more braces.)

```
char Initials[3][3] = {9,8,7,6,5,4,3,2,1};
```

> **TIP:** Multidimensional arrays (unless they are global) are not initialized to specific values unless you assign them values at declaration time or in the program. As with single-dimensional arrays, if you initialize one or more of the elements, but not all of them, C++ fills the rest with zeros. If you want to fill an entire multidimensional array with zeros, you can do so with the following:
>
> ```
> float sales[3][4][7][2] = {0};    // Fills all sales
>                                   // with zeros
> ```

Tables and for Loops

As the following examples show, nested for loops are useful when you want to loop through every element of a multidimensional table.

For instance, this section of code

```
for (row = 0; row < 2; row++)
   { for (col = 0; col < 3; col++)
```

```
        { cout << row << " " << col "\n"; }
    }
```

produces the following output:

```
0    0
0    1
0    2
1    0
1    1
1    2
```

These numbers are the subscripts, in row order, for a two-row by three-column table dimensioned with

```
int table[2][3];
```

Notice that there are as many for loops as there are subscripts in the array (two). The outside loop represents the first subscript (the rows), and the inside loop represents the second subscript (the columns). The nested for loop steps through each element of the table.

You can use cin, gets(), get, and other input functions to fill a table, and you also can assign values to the elements when declaring the table. More often, the data comes from data files on the disk. Regardless of what method is used to store the values in multidimensional arrays, nested for loops are excellent control statements to step through the subscripts.

Suppose that you used the following statement to reserve enough memory elements for a television station's ratings (A through D) for one week:

```
char ratings[7][48];
```

These statements reserve enough elements to hold seven days (the rows) of ratings for each 30-minute time slot (48 of them in a day). Every element in a table is always the same type. In this case, each element is a character variable. Some are initialized with the following assignment statements:

```
shows[3][12] = 'B';    // Stores B in 4th row, 13th column
shows[1][5] = 'A' ;    // Stores C in 2nd row, 6th column
shows[6][20] = getch();   // Stores the letter that the
                          // user types
```

The following complete program defines, initializes, and prints the values from a two-dimensional table. Suppose that a video store sells two grades of video tapes, High Grade and Regular. Each grade of tape comes in one of four lengths: 2-hour, 4-hour, 6-hour, or 8-hour. The tape inventory is well-suited for a two-dimensional table. The store determined that the tapes should have the following retail prices:

	2-Hour	4-Hour	6-Hour	8-Hour
High Grade	2.39	2.85	3.29	3.99
Regular	1.75	2.19	2.69	2.95

The store wants to store the price of each tape in a table for easy access. Typically, you use a nested for loop to print rows and columns.

To add the titles, simply print a row of titles before the first row of values, then print a new column title before each column. The following program stores the tape table, initializes it, and prints the output to the screen.

```
// Filename: TAPE.CPP
// Initializes and prints tape prices
// in a table format with titles
#include <iostream.h>
#include <iomanip.h>
void main()
{
    float tapes[2][4];    // Table of tape prices
    int row, col;

    tapes[0][0] = 2.39;    // Row 1, column 1
    tapes[0][1] = 2.85;    // Row 1, column 2
    tapes[0][2] = 3.29;    // Row 1, column 3
    tapes[0][3] = 3.99;    // Row 1, column 4
    tapes[1][0] = 1.75;    // Row 2, column 1
    tapes[1][1] = 2.19;    // Row 2, column 2
    tapes[1][2] = 2.69;    // Row 2, column 3
    tapes[1][3] = 2.95;    // Row 2, column 4

    // Prints the column titles
    cout << "\t\t2-Hour\t\t4-Hour\t\t6-Hour\t\t8-Hour\n";

    // Prints the prices
    for (row = 0; row < 2; row++)
```

```
    { if (row == 0)
     { cout << "High Grade\t"; }
      else
        { cout << "Regular\t\t"; }
      for (col=0; col<4; col++)    // Prints the current row
          { cout << setprecision(2) << "$" << tapes[row][col]
                 << "\t\t";
          }
  }

  return;
}
```

Here is the program's output:

```
             2-Hour     4-Hour     6-Hour     8-Hour
High Grade   $2.39      $2.85      $3.29      $3.99
Regular      $1.75      $2.19      $2.69      $2.95
```

Review Questions

1. What statement reserves a two-dimensional table of integers called scores with five rows and six columns?

2. What statement reserves a three-dimensional table of four character arrays called initials with 10 rows and 20 columns?

3. In the following statement, which subscript (first or second) represents rows and which represents columns?

   int weights[5][10];

4. How many elements are reserved with the following statement?

   int ara[5][6];

5. The following table of integers is called ara:

4	1	3	5	9
10	2	12	1	6
25	42	2	91	8

What values do the following elements contain?

(a) `ara[2][2]`

(b) `ara[0][1]`

(c) `ara[2][3]`

(d) `ara[2][4]`

6. What control statement is best for stepping through multidimensional arrays?

7. Notice the following section of a program:

```
int grades[3][5] = {80,90,96,73,65,67,90,68,92,84,70,
                    55,95,78,100};
```

What are the values of the following?

(a) `grades[2][3]`

(b) `grades[2][4]`

(c) `grades[0][1]`

Review Exercises

1. Write a program that stores and prints the numbers from 1 to 21 in a 3-by-7 table. (*Hint:* Remember that C++ begins subscripts at 0.)

2. Write a program that reserves storage for three years' worth of sales data for five salespeople. Use assignment statements to fill the table with data, then print it, one value per line.

3. Instead of using assignment statements, use the `cin` function to fill the salespeople data from Exercise 2.

4. Write a program that tracks the grades for five classes, each having 10 students. Input the data using the `cin` function. Print the table in its native row-and-column format.

5. Rewrite the TAPE.CPP program presented in this lesson so that it prints a title at the top of the table that says "Tape Inventory," and add a third row to the table for a new Medium grade of tape.

Introduction to Pointers

OBJECTIVE

To teach how pointers are stored in memory and how they ease programming tasks.

C++ reveals its true power through pointer variables. Pointer variables (or *pointers,* as they generally are called) are variables that contain addresses of other variables. All variables you have seen so far have held data values. You understand that variables hold various data types—character, integer, floating-point, and so on. Pointer variables contain the location of regular data variables; in effect they point to the data because they hold the address of the data.

When first learning C++, students of the language tend to shy away from pointers, thinking that pointers are difficult to learn. Pointers do not have to be difficult. In fact, after you work with them for a while, you will find that they are easier to use than arrays (and much more flexible).

Pointers offer a highly efficient means of accessing and changing data. Because pointers contain the actual address of your data, your compiler has less work to do when finding that data in memory. Pointers do not have to link data to specific variable names. A pointer can point to an unnamed data value. With pointers, you gain a different "view" of your data.

Introduction to Pointer Variables

Pointers are variables. They follow all the normal naming rules of regular, nonpointer variables. As with regular variables, you must declare pointer variables before using them. There is a type of pointer for every data type in C++. There are integer pointers, character pointers, floating-point pointers, and so on. You can declare pointers globally or locally, depending on where you declare them.

The only difference between pointer variables and regular variables is the data they hold. Pointers do not contain data in the usual sense of the word; pointers contain addresses of data. If you need a quick review of addresses and memory, see Appendix B.

There are two pointer operators in C++:

   & The *address of* operator
   * The *dereferencing* operator

Don't let these operators throw you; you might have seen them before! The & is the bitwise AND operator (from Lesson 13, "The Bitwise Operators") and the *, of course, means multiplication. These are called *overloaded* operators. They perform more than one function, depending on how you use them in your programs. C++ does not confuse * with multiplication when you use it as a dereferencing operator with pointers.

Whenever you see the & used with pointers, think of the words "address of." The & operator always produces the memory address of whatever it precedes. The * operator, when used with pointers, either declares a pointer or dereferences the pointer's value. The next section explains each of these operators.

Declaring Pointers

Because you must declare all pointers before using them, the best way to begin learning about pointers is to understand how to declare and define them. Actually, declaring pointers is almost as easy as declaring regular variables. After all, pointers are variables.

If you must declare a variable that holds your age, you could do so with the following variable declaration:

```
int age = 30;    // Declares a variable to hold my age
```

Declaring age like this does several things. It enables C++ to identify a variable called age and to reserve storage for that variable. Using this format also enables C++ to recognize that you store only integers in age, not floating-point or double floating-point data. The declaration also requests that C++ store the value of 30 in age after it reserves storage for age.

Where did C++ store age in memory? As the programmer, you should not really care where C++ stores age. You do not have to know the variable's address because you never refer to age by its address. If you want to calculate with or print age, you call it by its name, age.

> **TIP:** Make your pointer variable names meaningful. The name `file_ptr` makes more sense than `x13` for a file-pointing variable, although either name is permissible.

Suppose that you want to declare a pointer variable. This pointer variable will not hold your age, but it will *point* to age, the variable that holds your age. (Why you would want to do this is explained in this and the next few lessons.) p_age might be a good name for the pointer variable. Figure 28.1 illustrates what you want to do. The figure assumes that C++ stored age at the address 350,606. Your C++ compiler arbitrarily determines the address of age, however, so it could be anything.

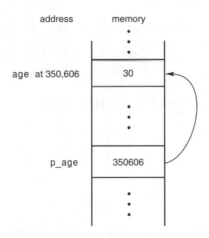

Figure 28.1. p_age contains the address of age; p_age points to the age variable.

The name p_age by itself has nothing to do with pointers, except that it is the name you made up for the pointer to age. Because you can name variables anything (as long as the name follows the legal naming rules of variables), p_age could have been named house, x43344, space_trek, or

471

whatever else you wanted to call it. This fact reinforces the idea that a pointer is simply a variable you reserve in your program. Create meaningful variable names, even for pointer variables. p_age is a good name for a variable that points to age (as would be ptr_age and ptr_to_age).

To declare the p_age pointer variable, do the following:

```
int * p_age;    // Declares an integer pointer
```

Similar to the declaration for age, this declaration reserves a variable called p_age. The p_age variable is not a normal integer variable, however. Because of the dereferencing operator, *, C++ recognizes it as a pointer variable. Some C++ programmers prefer to declare such a variable without a space after the *, as follows:

```
int *p_age;    // Declares an integer pointer
```

Either method is acceptable, but you must remember that the * is *not* part of the name. When you later use p_age, you will not prefix the name with the * unless you are dereferencing it at the time (as later examples show).

 Whenever the dereferencing operator, *, appears in a variable definition, the variable being declared is *always* a pointer variable. Consider the declaration for p_age if the asterisk were not there: C++ would recognize it as a declaration of a regular integer variable. The * is important because it tells C++ to interpret p_age as a pointer variable, not as a normal, data variable.

 Define a character pointer variable named cPtr.

Assigning Values to Pointers

p_age is an integer pointer. The type of a pointer is very important. p_age can point only to integer values, never to floating-point, double floating-point, or even character variables. If you had to point to a floating-point variable, you would do so with a pointer declared as

```
float *point;    // Declares a floating-point pointer
```

As with any automatic variable, C++ does not initialize pointers when you declare them. If you declared p_age as an integer pointer, and you wanted p_age to point to age, you would have to explicitly assign p_age to the address of age. The following statement does so:

```
p_age = &age;    // Assigns the address of age to p_age
```

What value is now in p_age? You do not know exactly, but you know it is the address of age, whatever that is. Rather than assigning the address of age to p_age with an assignment operator, you can declare and initialize pointers at the same time. These lines declare and initialize both age and p_age:

```
int age = 30;      // Declares a regular integer
                   // variable, putting 30 in it
int *p_age = &age;   // Declares an integer pointer,
                     // initializing it with the address
                     // of p_age
```

These two lines produce the variables described in Figure 28.1.

If you wanted to print the value of age, you could do so with the following cout:

```
cout << age;     // Prints the value of age
```

You also can print the value of age like this:

```
cout << *p_age;    // Dereferences p_age
```

The dereference operator produces a value that tells the pointer where to point. Without the *, the last cout would print an address (the address of age). With the *, the cout prints the value at that address.

You can assign a different value to age with the following statement:

```
age = 41;    // Assigns a new value to age
```

You also can assign a value to age like this:

```
*p_age - 41;
```

This declaration assigns 41 to the value p_age points to.

> **TIP:** The * appears before a pointer variable in only two places: when you declare a pointer variable and when you dereference a pointer variable (to find the data it points to).

Declaring and using pointers might seem troublesome at this point. Why assign *p_num a value when it is easier (and clearer) to assign a value directly to num? If you are asking yourself that question, you probably understand everything you should from this lesson so far. The rest of this lesson helps eliminate your confusion.

Pointers and Parameters

You might recall from Lesson 20, "Passing Values," that you can override C++'s normal default of passing by copy (or by value). To pass by address, receive the variable preceded by an & in the receiving function. The following function receives `tries` by address:

```
pr_it(int &tries);     // Receives integer tries in pr_it() by
                       // address (pr_it normally would receive
                       // tries by copy)
```

Now that you understand the & and * operators, you can understand the passing by address of nonarray parameters to functions. (Arrays default to passing by address without requiring that you use &.)

 How would you pass by address an integer variable named `Age` to a function named `PrAge()`?

Just to review pointer initialization, the following section of code declares three regular variables of three different data types, and three corresponding pointer variables:

```
char initial = 'Q';    // Declares three regular variables
int num = 40;          // of three different types
float sales = 2321.59;

char *p_initial = &initial;    // Declares three pointers
int * ptr_num = &num;          // Pointer names and spacing
float * sales_add = &sales;    // after * are not critical
```

The next few lines of code are equivalent to the preceding code:

```
char initial;   // Declares three regular variables
int num;        // of three different types
float sales;

char *p_initial;   // Declares three pointers but does
int * ptr_num;     // not initialize them
float * sales_add;

initial = 'Q';   // Initializes the regular variables
num = 40;        // with values
sales = 2321.59;
```

```
p_initial = &initial;    // Initializes the pointers with
ptr_num = &num;          // the addresses of their
sales_add = &sales;      // corresponding variables
```

Do not put the * operator before the pointer variable names when assigning them values. You prefix a pointer variable with the * only if you are dereferencing it.

> **NOTE:** In the preceding code, the pointer variables could have been assigned the addresses of the regular variables before the regular variables were assigned values. There would be no difference in the operation. The pointers are assigned the addresses of the regular variables no matter what the data in the regular variables is.

Pointer variable types dictate the type of data the pointer variable points to. For example, an integer pointer cannot point to a long integer variable.

What is wrong with the following variable definitions?

```
double dv = 2324.565;     // Defines a variable
char * dvPtr = &dv;       // Makes dvPtr point to dv
```

Review of Pointer Storage

The following program is one you should study closely. It shows more about pointers and the pointer operators, & and *, than several pages of text could do.

```
// Filename: POINT.CPP
// Demonstrates the use of pointer declarations
// and operators
#include <iostream.h>

void main()
{
    int num = 123;    // A regular integer variable
    int *p_num;    // Declares an integer pointer
```

```
      cout << "num is " << num << "\n";    // Prints value of num
      cout << "The address of num is " << &num << "\n";  // Prints
                                              // num's location
      p_num = &num;   // Puts address of num in p_num,
                      // in effect making p_num point
                      // to num
                      // No * in front of p_num
      cout << "*p_num is " << *p_num << "\n";   // Prints value of
                                              // num
      cout << "p_num is " << p_num << "\n";   // Prints location
                                              // of num


      return;
}
```

Here is the output from this program:

```
num is 123
The address of num is 0x8fbd0ffe
*p_num is 123
p_num is 0x8fbd0ffe
```

If you run this program, you probably will get different results for the value of p_num because your compiler will place num at a different location, depending on your memory setup. The value of p_num prints in hexadecimal because it is an address of memory. The actual address does not matter, however. Because the pointer p_num always contains the address of num, and because you can dereference p_num to get num's value, the actual address is not critical.

There is no way you can predict the address where C++ will store a variable. By using a pointer variable, however, you can indirectly reference the variable as if you knew the address, because the address will be stored in the pointer variable. You will see uses for pointers in this and the next two lessons.

The following program includes a function that swaps the values of any two integers passed to it. You might recall that a function can return only a single value. Therefore, before now, you could not write a function that changed two different values and returned both values to the calling function.

To swap two variables (reversing their values for sorting, as you saw in Lesson 26, "Working With Arrays"), you need the ability to pass both variables by address. This way, when the function reverses the variables, the calling function's variables are swapped also.

Be sure to receive arguments with the prefix & in functions that receive by address, as follows.

```
// Filename: SWAP.CPP
// Program that includes a function that swaps
// any two integers passed to it
#include <iostream.h>
void swap_them(int &num1, int &num2);

void main()
{
    int i = 10, j = 20;
    cout << "\n\nBefore swap, i is " << i <<
            " and j is " << j << "\n\n";
    swap_them(i, j);
    cout << "\n\nAfter swap, i is " << i <<
            " and j is " << j << "\n\n";
    return;
}
void swap_them(int &num1, int &num2)
{
   int temp;    // Variable that holds
                // in-between swapped value
   temp = num1;    // The calling function's variables
   num1 = num2;    // (not copies of them) are
   num2 = temp;    // changed in this function
   return;
}
```

Arrays of Pointers

If you have to reserve many pointers for many different values, you might want to declare an array of pointers. You know that you can reserve an array of characters, integers, long integers, and floating-point values, as well as an array of every other data type available. You also can reserve an array of pointers, with each pointer being a pointer to a specific data type.

The following reserves an array of 10 integer pointer variables:

```
int *iptr[10];    // Reserves an array of 10 integer pointers
```

Figure 28.2 shows how C++ views this array. After being assigned a value, each element holds an address that points to other values in memory. Each value pointed to must be an integer. You can assign an element from `iptr` an address just as you would for nonarray pointer variables. You can make `iptr[4]` point to the address of an integer variable named `age` by assigning it like this:

```
iptr[4] = &age;    // Makes iptr[4] point to address of age
```

Figure 28.2. An array of 10 integer pointers.

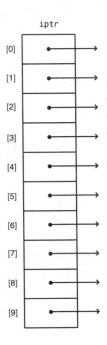

The following reserves an array of 20 character pointer variables:

```
char *cpoint[20];    // Array of 20 character pointers
```

Again, the asterisk is not part of the array name. The asterisk informs C++ that this is an array of character pointers and not simply an array of characters.

Some beginning C++ students become confused when they see such a declaration. Pointers are one thing, but reserving storage for arrays of pointers tends to confuse novices. However, reserving storage for arrays of pointers is easy to understand. Remove the asterisk from the preceding declaration

```
char cpoint[20];
```

and what do you have? You have just reserved a simple array of 20 characters. Adding the asterisk tells C++ to go one step further: rather than an array of character variables, you want an array of character pointing variables. Rather than having each element be a character variable, you have each element hold an address that points to characters.

Reserving arrays of pointers will be much more meaningful after you learn about structures in the next few lessons. As with regular, nonpointing variables, an array makes processing several pointer variables much easier. You can use a subscript to reference each variable (element) without having to use a different variable name for each value.

Write a definition that reserves storage for an array of 50 `double` pointer variables named `payAmts`.

What is wrong with the following array definition? The programmer is attempting to define storage for an array of 100 integer pointers named `iPtrs`.

```
int iPtrs[100];
```

Review Questions

1. What type of variable is reserved in each of the following?

    (a) `int *a;`

    (b) `char * cp;`

    (c) `float * dp;`

2. What words should come to mind when you see the & operator?

3. What is the dereferencing operator?

4. How would you assign the address of the floating-point variable `salary` to a pointer called `pt_sal`?

5. TRUE or FALSE: You must define a pointer with an initial value when declaring it.

6. In both of the following sections of code:

    ```
    int i;
    int * pti;
    i = 56;
    pti = &i;
    ```

and

```
int i;
int * pti;
pti = &i;    // These two lines are reversed
i = 56;      // from the preceding code lines
```

is the value of pti the same after the fourth line of each section?

7. In the following section of code:

```
float pay;
float *ptr_pay;
pay = 2313.54;
ptr_pay = &pay;
```

what is the value of each of the following (answer "invalid" if it cannot be determined)?

(a) pay

(b) *ptr_pay

(c) *pay

(d) &pay

8. What does the following declare?

```
double *ara[4][6];
```

(a) An array of double floating-point values

(b) An array of double floating-point pointer variables

(c) An invalid declaration statement

> **NOTE:** Because this is a theory-oriented lesson, review exercises are saved until you master Lesson 29, "Pointers and Arrays."

Lesson

Pointers and Arrays

29

OBJECTIVE

To compare and contrast arrays and pointer variables, to show how pointers often substitute for arrays in C++ programs, and to show how to store arrays of strings using pointer variables.

Arrays and pointers are closely related in the C++ programming language. You can address arrays as if they were pointers and address pointers as if they were arrays. Being able to store and access pointers and arrays gives you the ability to store strings of data in array elements. Without pointers, you could not store strings of data in arrays because there is no fundamental string data type in C++ (no string variables, only string literals).

This lesson introduces concepts that you will use for much of your future programming in C++. Pointer manipulation is important to the C++ programming language.

Array Names as Pointers

An array name is just a pointer, nothing more. To prove this, suppose that you have the following array declaration:

```
int ara[5] = {10, 20, 30, 40, 50};
```

If you printed ara[0], you would see 10. Because you now fully understand arrays, this is the value you would expect. But what if you were to print *ara? Would *ara print anything? If so, what? If you thought an error message would print because ara is not a pointer but an array, you would be wrong. An array name is a pointer. If you printed *ara you would see 10.

Recall how arrays are stored in memory. Figure 29.1 shows how ara would be mapped in memory. The array name, ara, is nothing more than a pointer pointing to the first element of the array. Therefore, if you dereference that pointer, you dereference the value stored in the first element of the array, which is 10. Dereferencing ara is exactly the same thing as referencing to ara[0], because they both produce the same value.

Figure 29.1. Storing the array called ara *in memory.*

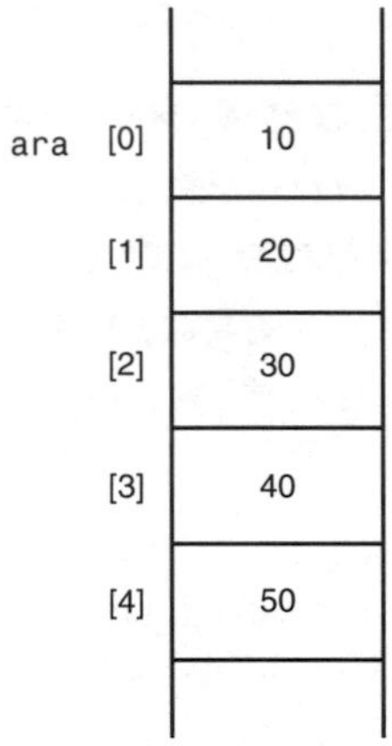

ara	[0]	10
	[1]	20
	[2]	30
	[3]	40
	[4]	50

You now see that you can reference an array with subscripts or with pointer dereferencing. Can you use pointer notation to print the third element of ara? Yes, and you already have the tools to do so. The following cout prints ara[2] (the third element of ara) without using a subscript:

```
cout << *(ara + 2) ;    // Prints ara[2]
```

The expression *(ara + 2) is not vague at all if you remember that an array name is just a pointer that always points to the array's first element. *(ara + 2) takes the address stored in ara, adds 2 to the address, and dereferences that location. The following holds true:

482

```
ara + 0 points to ara[0]
ara + 1 points to ara[1]
ara + 2 points to ara[2]
ara + 3 points to ara[3]
ara + 4 points to ara[4]
```

Therefore, to print, store, or calculate with an array element, you can use either the subscript notation or the pointer notation. Because an array name contains the address of the array's first element, you must dereference the pointer to get the element's value.

Consider the following character array:

```
char Name[] = "C++ Programming 101";
```

What output do the following cout statements produce?

cout *Statement*	*Output*
cout << Name[0];	_____
cout << *Name;	_____
cout << *(Name + 3);	_____
cout << *(Name + 0);	_____

Internal Locations

C++ knows the internal data size requirements of characters, integers, floating-points, and the other data types on your computer. Therefore, because ara is an integer array, and because each element in an integer array consumes 2 to 4 bytes of storage, depending on the computer, C++ adds 2 or 4 bytes to the address if you reference arrays as just shown.

If you write *(ara + 3) to refer to ara[3], C++ adds 6 or 12 bytes to the address of ara to get the third element. C++ does not add an actual 3. You do not have to worry about this, because C++ handles these internals. When you write *(ara + 3), you are actually requesting that C++ add the size (in bytes) of three integers to the address of ara. If ara were a floating-point array, C++ would add three floating-point addresses to ara.

Pointer arithmetic (adding to a pointer) enables you to point to any value within a list whose first value is pointed to by the pointer variable. Just as an array name is really a pointer to the beginning element, ara[0], *ara, and *(ara + 0) all refer to the same location. So do ara[5] and *(ara + 5). Sometimes, advanced C++ programming is easier when you use pointer notation (such as *(ara + 5)) instead of array notation (such as

483

ara[5]) to refer to an individual element in a list. At first, pointer notation might seem new to you and more difficult than using array notation, but try to become comfortable with pointer notation as you advance in your C++ programming knowledge.

> **TIP:** Pointer notation is more efficient and allows for faster processing than array notation.

Pointer Advantages

Although arrays are actually pointers in disguise, they are special types of pointers. An array name is a *pointer constant,* not a pointer variable. You cannot change the value of an array name, because you cannot change constants. This explains why you cannot assign an array new values during a program's execution. For instance, even if cname is a character array, the following is not valid in C++:

```
cname = "Christine Chambers";   // Invalid array assignment
```

> The array name cname cannot be changed because it is a constant. You would not attempt the following
>
> ```
> 5 = 4 + 8 * 21;   // Invalid assignment
> ```
>
> because you cannot change the constant 5 to any other value. C++ knows that you cannot assign anything to 5, and C++ prints an error message if you attempt to change 5. C++ also knows that an array name is a constant and that you cannot change an array to another value. (You can assign values to an array only at declaration time, one element at a time during execution, or by using functions such as strcpy().)

This brings you to the most important reason to learn pointers: pointers (except arrays referenced as pointers) are variables. You can change a pointer variable, and being able to do so makes processing virtually any data, including arrays, much more powerful and flexible.

By changing pointers, you make them point to different values in memory. The following program demonstrates how to change pointers. The program first defines two floating-point values. A floating-point pointer points to the first variable, v1, and is used in cout. The pointer is then changed so that it points to the second floating-point variable, v2.

```cpp
// Filename: PTRCH.CPP
// Changes the value of a pointer variable
#include <iostream.h>
#include <iomanip.h>
void main()
{
   float v1 = 676.54;   // Defines two
   float v2 = 900.18;   // floating-point variables
   float * p_v;   // Defines a floating-point pointer

   p_v = &v1;   // Makes pointer point to v1
   cout << "The first value is " << setprecision(2) <<
           *p_v << "\n";   // Prints 676.54

   p_v = &v2;   // Changes the pointer so
                // that it points to v2
   cout << "The second value is " << setprecision(2) <<
           *p_v << "\n";   // Prints 900.18
   return;
}
```

Because they can change the address values in pointers but not addresses pointed to by arrays, most C++ programmers use pointers rather than arrays. Because arrays are easy to declare, C++ programmers sometimes declare arrays and then use pointers to reference those arrays. If the array data changes, the pointer helps to change it.

You can use pointer notation and reference pointers as arrays with array notation. The following program declares an integer array and an integer pointer that points to the start of the array. The array and pointer values are printed using subscript notation. Afterwards, the program uses array notation to print the array and pointer values.

Study this program carefully. It shows the inner workings of arrays and pointer notation.

```cpp
// Filename: ARPTR.CPP
// References arrays like pointers and pointers like arrays
#include <iostream.h>
void main()
{
```

```
   int ctr;
   int iara[5] = {10, 20, 30, 40, 50};
   int *iptr;

   iptr = iara;    // Makes iptr point to array's first
                   // element. This would work also:
                   // iptr = &iara[0];

   cout << "Using array subscripts:\n";
   cout << "iara\tiptr\n";
   for (ctr = 0; ctr < 5; ctr++)
      { cout << iara[ctr] << "\t" << iptr[ctr] << "\n";   }

   cout << "\nUsing pointer notation:\n";
   cout << "iara\tiptr\n";
   for (ctr = 0; ctr < 5; ctr++)
      { cout << *(iara+ctr) << "\t" << *(iptr+ctr) << "\n"; }

   return;
}
```

Here is the program's output:

```
Using array subscripts:
iara    iptr
10      10
20      20
30      30
40      40
50      50

Using pointer notation:
iara    iptr
10      10
20      20
30      30
40      40
50      50
```

What is the output of the following program?

```
// Filename: TTPTR.CPP
// Program that references arrays like pointers and
// pointers like arrays
#include <iostream.h>
```

```
void main()
{
   int ctr;
   char cara[3] = {'A', 'B', 'C'};
   char *cptr;

   cptr = cara;    // Makes iptr point to array's first
                   // element. This would work also:
                   // cptr = &iara[0];

   cout << cara[1] << "\n";
   cout << *cara << "\n";
   cout << *(cara + 2) << "\n";
   cout << *(cara + 1) << "\n";
   cout << *(cara + 10 - 9) << "\n";
 return;
}
```

Using Character Pointers

The ability to change pointers is best seen when working with character strings in memory. You can store strings in character arrays, or point to them with character pointers. Consider the following two string definitions:

```
char cara[] = "C++ is fun";    // An array holding a string

char *cptr = "C++ Programming";   // A pointer to the string
```

Figure 29.2 shows how C++ stores these two strings in memory. C++ stores both in basically the same way. You are familiar with the array definition. When assigning a string to a character pointer, C++ finds enough free memory to hold the string and assigns the address of the first character to the pointer. The preceding two string definition statements do almost exactly the same thing. The only difference between them is that the two pointers can easily be interchanged (the array name and the character pointers).

487

Figure 29.2. Storing two strings, one in an array and one pointed to by a pointer variable.

cara
[0] [1] [2] [3] [4] [5] [6] [7] [8] [9][10]

| c | + | + | | i | s | | f | u | n | \0 |

• • •

cptr

| c | + | + | | p | r | o | g | r | a | m | m | i | n | g | \0 |

Because cout prints strings starting at the array or pointer name until the null zero is reached, you can print each of these strings with the following cout statements:

```
cout << "String 1: " << cara << "\n";
```

```
cout << "String 2: " << cptr << "\n";
```

Notice that you print strings in arrays and strings that pointers point to in the same way. You might wonder what advantage one method of storing strings has over the other. The seemingly minor difference between these stored strings makes a big difference when you change them.

Suppose that you want to store the string Hello in the two strings. You cannot assign the string to the array like this:

```
cara = "Hello";   // Invalid
```

Because you cannot change the array name, you cannot assign it a new value. The only way to change the contents of the array is by assigning the array characters from the string an element at a time, or by using a built-in function such as strcpy(). You can, however, make the character array point to the new string like this:

```
cptr = "Hello";   // Changes the pointer so that
                  // it points to the new string
```

TIP: If you want to store user input in a string pointed to by a pointer, first you must reserve enough storage for that input string. The easiest way to do this is to reserve a character array, then assign a character pointer to the beginning element of that array, like this:

```
char input[81];   // Holds a string as long as
                  // 80 characters
char *iptr = input;   // Also could have done this:
                      // char *iptr = &input[0];
```

Now you can input a string by using the pointer:

```
gets(iptr);   // Makes sure that iptr points to
              // the string typed by the user
```

> You can use pointer manipulation, arithmetic, and modification on the input string.

Suppose that you want to store your sister's full name and print it. Rather than using arrays, you can use a character pointer. The following program does just that.

```cpp
// Filename: CP1.CPP
// Stores a name in a character pointer
#include <iostream.h>
void main()
{
   char *c = "Bettye Lou Horn";

   cout << "My sister's name is " << c << "\n";
   return;
}
```

This prints the following:

```
My sister's name is Bettye Lou Horn
```

Suppose that you must change a string pointed to by a character pointer. If your sister changed her last name to Henderson, your program could show both strings in the following manner:

```cpp
// Filename: CP2.CPP
// Illustrates changing a character string
#include <iostream.h>
void main()
{
   char *c = "Bettye Lou Horn";

   cout << "My sister's maiden name was " << c << "\n";

   c = "Bettye Lou Henderson";   // Assigns new string to c

   cout << "My sister's married name is " << c << "\n";
   return;
}
```

The output is as follows:

```
My sister's maiden name was Bettye Lou Horn
My sister's married name is Bettye Lou Henderson
```

489

When you define and initialize a character pointer so that it points to a string:

```
char * MyName = "Astronaut Steve Austin";
```

you can, at any time, make it point to another string just by using an equal sign:

```
MyName = "R. Lim Baugh";
```

If MyName were a character array, you could never assign it directly because an array name cannot be changed. The preceding statement instructs the character pointer MyName to point to the string.

> **NOTE:** When you define and initialize a string as just shown, you then can copy any string into it as long as the new string never exceeds the length of the first one. If you ever have to put longer strings into it, you will have to use a character array until you master the very advanced technique of dynamic memory allocation later in your C++ career.

Pointer Arithmetic

You saw an example of pointer arithmetic when you accessed array elements with pointer notation. By now you should be comfortable with the fact that both of these array or pointer references are identical:

```
ara[sub] and *(ara + sub)
```

You can increment or decrement a pointer. If you increment a pointer, the address inside the pointer variable increments. The pointer does not always increment by 1, however.

Suppose that f_ptr is a floating-point pointer indexing the first element of an array of floating-point numbers. You could initialize f_ptr as follows:

```
float fara[] = {100.5, 201.45, 321.54, 389.76, 691.34};
f_ptr = fara;
```

Figure 29.3 shows what these variables look like in memory. Each floating-point value in this example takes 4 bytes of memory.

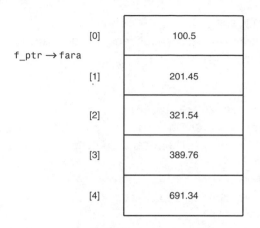

Figure 29.3. A floating-point array and a pointer.

If you print the value of *f_ptr, you see 100.5. Suppose that you increment f_ptr by 1 with the following statement:

```
f_ptr++;
```

C++ does not add 1 to the address in f_ptr, even though it seems as though 1 should be added. In this case, because floating-point values take 4 bytes each on this machine, C++ adds 4 to f_ptr. How does C++ know how many bytes to add to f_ptr? C++ knows from the pointer's declaration how many bytes of memory pointers take. This is why you have to declare the pointer with the correct data type.

After incrementing f_ptr, if you were to print *f_ptr, you would see 201.45, the second element in the array. If C++ added only 1 to the address in f_ptr, f_ptr would point only to the second byte, 100.5. This would output garbage to the screen.

NOTE: When you increment a pointer, C++ adds one full data type size (in bytes) to the pointer, not 1 byte. When you decrement a pointer, C++ subtracts one full data type size (in bytes) from the pointer.

The following program defines an array with five values. An integer pointer is then initialized to point to the first element in the array. The rest of the program prints the dereferenced value of the pointer, then increments the pointer so that it points to the next integer in the array.

Just to show you what is going on, the size of integer values is printed at the bottom of the program. Because (in this case) integers take 2 bytes, C++ increments the pointer by 2 so that it points to the next integer. (The integers are 2 bytes apart from each other.)

491

```
// Filename: PTI.CPP
// Increments a pointer through an integer array
#include <iostream.h>
void main()
{
    int iara[] = {10,20,30,40,50};
    int *ip = iara;    // The pointer points to
                       // the start of the array

    cout << *ip << "\n";
    ip++;   // Two are actually added
    cout << *ip << "\n";
    ip++;      // Two are actually added
    cout << *ip << "\n";
    ip++;      // Two are actually added
    cout << *ip << "\n";
    ip++;      // Two are actually added
    cout << *ip << "\n\n";
    cout << "The integer size is " << sizeof(int);
    cout << " bytes on this machine \n\n";
    return;
}
```

Here is the program's output:

```
10
20
30
40
50


The integer size is 2 bytes on this machine
```

The next program shows the many ways you can add to, subtract from, and reference arrays and pointers. The program defines a floating-point array and a floating-point pointer. The body of the program prints the values from the array using array and pointer notation.

```
// Filename: ARPT.CPP
// Comprehensive reference of arrays and pointers
#include <iostream.h>
void main()
{
    float ara[] = {100.0, 200.0, 300.0, 400.0, 500.0};
    float *fptr;    // Floating-point pointer
```

```
    // Makes pointer point to array's first value
    fptr = &ara[0];    // Also could have been this:
                       // fptr = ara;

    cout << *fptr << "\n";    // Prints 100.0
    fptr++;    // Points to next floating-point value
    cout << *fptr << "\n";    // Prints 200.0
    fptr++;    // Points to next floating-point value
    cout << *fptr << "\n";    // Prints 300.0
    fptr++;    // Points to next floating-point value
    cout << *fptr << "\n";    // Prints 400.0
    fptr++;    // Points to next floating-point value
    cout << *fptr << "\n";    // Prints 500.0

    fptr = ara;    // Points to first element again
    cout << *(fptr + 2) << "\n";    // Prints 300.00 but
                                    // does not change fptr

    // References both array and pointer using subscripts
    cout << (fptr + 0)[0] << " " << (ara + 0)[0] << "\n";
                                    // 100.0   100.0
    cout << (fptr + 1)[0] << " " << (ara + 1)[0] << "\n";
                                    // 200.0   200.0
    cout << (fptr + 4)[0] << " " << (ara + 4)[0] << "\n";
                                    // 500.0   500.0
    return;
}
```

The following is the program's output:

```
100.0
200.0
300.0
400.0
500.0
300.0
100.0   100.0
200.0   200.0
500.0   500.0
```

Arrays of Strings

Now you are ready for one of the most useful applications of character pointers: storing arrays of strings. Actually, you cannot store an array of strings, but you can store an array of character pointers, and each character pointer can point to a string in memory.

By defining an array of character pointers, you define a *ragged-edge array*. A ragged-edge array is similar to a two-dimensional table, except that each row contains a different number of characters (instead of being the same length).

The word *ragged-edge* derives from the use of word processors. A word processor typically can print text fully justified or with a ragged-right margin. The columns of a newspaper are fully justified, because both the left and the right columns align evenly. Letters you write by hand and type on typewriters (remember typewriters?) generally have ragged-right margins. It is difficult to type so that each line ends in exactly the same right column.

All two-dimensional tables you have seen so far have been fully justified. For example, if you declared a character table with five rows and 20 columns, each row would contain the same number of characters. You could define the table with the following statement:

```
char names[5][20] = { {"George"},
                      {"Michelle"},
                      {"John"},
                      {"Kim"},
                      {"Barbara"} };
```

This table is shown in Figure 29.4. Notice that much of the table is wasted space. Each row takes 20 characters, even though the data in each row takes far fewer characters. The unfilled elements contain null zeros because C++ nullifies all elements you do not initialize in arrays. This type of table uses too much memory.

To fix the memory-wasting problem of fully justified tables, you should declare a single-dimensional array of character pointers. Each pointer points to a string in memory, and the strings do not have to be the same length.

Here is the definition for such an array:

```
char *names[5] = { {"George"},
                   {"Michelle"},
```

```
   {"John"},
   {"Kim"},
   {"Barbara"} };
```

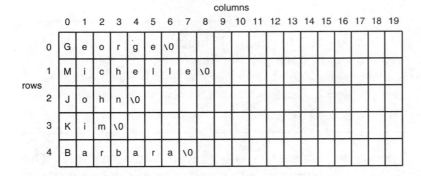

Figure 29.4. A fully justified table.

This array is single-dimensional. The definition should not confuse you, even though it is something you have not seen. The asterisk before names makes this an array of pointers. The data type of the pointers is character. The strings are not being assigned to the array elements, but they are being pointed to by the array elements. Figure 29.5 shows this array of pointers. The strings are stored elsewhere in memory. Their actual locations are not critical because each pointer points to the starting character. The strings waste no data. Each string takes only as much memory as is needed by the string and its terminating zero. This gives the data its ragged-right appearance.

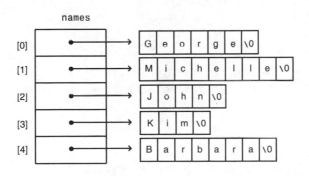

Figure 29.5. The array that points to each of the five strings.

To print the first string, you would use this cout:

```
cout << *names;    // Prints George
```

To print the second string, you would use this cout:

```
cout << *(names + 1);    // Prints Michelle
```

495

Whenever you dereference any pointer element with the * dereferencing operator, you access one of the strings in the array. You can use a dereferenced element anyplace you use a string constant or character array (with strcpy(), strcmp(), and so on).

> **TIP:** Working with pointers to strings is much more efficient than working directly with the strings. For instance, sorting a list of strings takes a lot of time if they are stored as a fully justified table. Sorting strings pointed to by a pointer array is much faster. You swap only pointers during the sort, not entire strings.

Here is a full program that uses the pointer array with five names. The for loop controls the cout function, printing each name in the string data. Now you can see why learning about pointer notation for arrays pays off!

```cpp
// Filename: PTST1.CPP
// Prints strings pointed to by an array
#include <iostream.h>
void main()
{
    char *name[5] = { {"George"},      // Defines a ragged-edge
                      {"Michelle"},    // array of pointers to
                      {"John"},        // strings
                      {"Kim"},
                      {"Barbara"} };
    int ctr;

    for (ctr = 0; ctr < 5; ctr++)
       { cout << "String #" << (ctr + 1) <<
                " is " << *(name + ctr) << "\n"; }

    return;
}
```

The following is the output from this program:

```
String #1 is George
String #2 is Michelle
String #3 is John
String #4 is Kim
String #5 is Barbara
```

The following program stores the days of the week in an array. What happens when the user types a 4 at the prompt?

```cpp
// Filename: PTST2.CPP
// Prints the day of the week based on an input value
#include <iostream.h>
void main()
{
    char *days[] = {"Sunday",    // The seven separate sets
                    "Monday",    // of braces are optional
                    "Tuesday",
                    "Wednesday",
                    "Thursday",
                    "Friday",
                    "Saturday"};
    int day_num;

    do
      { cout << "What is a day number (from 1 to 7)? ";
        cin >> day_num;
      } while ((day_num < 1) || (day_num > 7));    // Ensures an
                                                   // accurate number


    day_num--;    // Adjusts for subscript
    cout << "The day is " << *(days + day_num) << "\n";
    return;
}
```

Review Questions

1. What is the difference between an array name and a pointer?

2. If you performed the following statement (assume that `ipointer` points to integers that take 4 bytes of memory):

   ```cpp
   ipointer += 2;
   ```

   how many bytes are added to `ipointer`?

497

3. Which of the following are equivalent, assuming that `iary` is an integer array and that `iptr` is an integer pointer pointing to the start of the array?

   (a) `iary` and `iptr`

   (b) `iary[1]` and `iptr + 1`

   (c) `iary[3]` and `*(iptr + 3)`

   (d) `*iary` and `iary[0]`

   (e) `iary[4]` and `*iptr + 4`

4. Why is it more efficient to sort a ragged-edge character array than a fully justified string array?

5. Given the following array and pointer definition:

   ```
   int ara[] = {1, 2, 3, 4, 5, 6, 7, 8, 9, 10};
   int *ip1, *ip2;
   ```

   which of the following is allowed?

   (a) `ip1 = ara;`

   (b) `ip2 = ip1 = &ara[3];`

   (c) `ara = 15;`

   (d) `*(ip2 + 2) = 15;`   `// Assuming that ip2 and`
                                      `// ara are equal`

Review Exercises

1. Write a program to store your family members' names in an array of character pointers. Print the names.

2. Write a program that asks the user for 15 daily stock market averages and stores those in a floating-point array. Using only pointer notation, print the array forward and backward. Again, using only pointer notation, print the highest and lowest stock market quotes in the list.

3. Modify the bubble sort shown in Lesson 26, "Working with Arrays," so that it sorts using pointer notation. Add this bubble sort to the program in Exercise 2 to print the stock market averages in ascending order.

4. Write a program that requests 10 song titles from the user. Store the titles in an array of character pointers (a ragged-edge array). Print the original titles, the alphabetized titles, and the titles in reverse alphabetical order (from Z to A).

C++

CLASSROOM Eight

Structures, Files, and OOP

Structures

 To teach the aggregate `struct` data type so that you can treat several variables of different types as a single entity.

Using structures, you have the ability to group data and work with the grouped data as a whole. Business data processing uses the concept of structures in almost every program. Being able to manipulate several variables as a single group makes your programs easier to manage.

This lesson explains how to define structures, initialize structures, and work with structures using the dot operator.

Introduction to Structures

A *structure* is a collection of one or more variable types grouped together. You can refer to a structure as a single variable, and you also can initialize, read, and change the parts of a structure (the individual variables that make it up). As you know, each element in an array must be the same data type, and you must refer to the entire array by its name. Each element (called a *member*) in a structure can be a different data type.

You can use a structure any time you would naturally collect a set of values into a single group. For example, suppose that you owned a

hardware store and needed to keep track of your inventory. You might want to track the following pieces of information about each inventory part:

Item description
Part number
Quantity
Cost
Retail price

Each of these five items would be a *member* of the inventory structure. The structure would be a collection of the members.

> **TIP:** If you have programmed in other computer languages, or if you have ever used a database program, C++ structures are analogous to file records, and members are analogous to fields in those records.

After deciding on the members, you must decide what data type each member is. The description and part number are character arrays, the quantity is an integer, and the cost and retail price are floating-point values. This information is represented as follows:

Member Name	Data Type
Item Description	Character array of 15 characters
Part number	Character array of 6 characters
Quantity	Integer
Cost	Floating-point
Retail price	Floating-point

Here is how you could define this structure:

```
struct Inventory {
   char  Descript[15];
   char  PartNo[6];
   int   Quantity;
   float Cost;
   float Retail;
};   // All structures end with a semicolon
```

Figure 30.1 shows the parts of this `struct` definition.

```
                              Structure tag
struct    Inventory {
    char      Descript[15];
    char      PartNo[6];
    int       Quantity;              Members
    float     Cost;                  of the
    float     Retail;               structure
};
              Ends the
              structure
              declaration
```

Figure 30.1.
The components
of a struct
declaration.

Each structure you define can have an associated structure name called a *structure tag*. Structure tags are not required in most cases, but it is generally best to define one for each structure in your program. The structure tag is not a variable name. Unlike array names, which reference the array as variables, a structure tag is simply a label for the structure's format.

You name structure tags yourself, using the same naming rules as for variables. The inventory structure has a structure tag named Inventory. This tag informs C++ that the tag called Inventory looks like two character arrays, followed by an integer, followed by two floating-point values.

A structure tag is actually a newly defined data type that you, the programmer, define. When you want to store an integer, you do not have to define for C++ what an integer is. C++ already recognizes an integer. When you want to store an inventory's data, however, C++ is not capable of recognizing what format your inventory data takes. You have to tell C++ (using the example described here) that you need a new data type. That data type will be your structure tag, called Inventory in this example, and it looks like the structure described earlier (two character arrays, an integer, and two floating-points).

Given the following structure declaration:

```
struct Car {
    float Price;
    int   NumTires;
    int   MPG;
    char  Name[20];
    long  YrBuilt;
};
```

1. What is the structure tag?

2. How many members are there?

> **NOTE:** No memory is reserved for structure tags. A structure tag is your own data type. C++ does not reserve memory for the integer data type until you declare an integer variable. C++ does not reserve memory for a structure until you declare a structure variable.

Figure 30.2 shows the Inventory structure, graphically representing the data types in the structure. Notice that there are five members and that many of the members are different data types. The entire structure is called Inventory because that is the structure tag.

Figure 30.2. The layout of the Inventory *structure.*

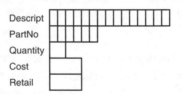

Suppose that you were asked to write a program for a hotel's room reservation system. The hotel had been using a card-file inventory system to track the following items:

> Room number
> Price
> Color code (1, 2, 3)
> Square feet

This would be a perfect use for a structure containing four members. Before defining the structure, you must determine the data types of each member. After asking questions about the range of data (you must know the largest room number, and the highest possible price that would appear on the order to ensure that your data types can hold data that large), you decide to use the following data types:

Member	*Data Type*
RoomNum	int
Price	float
ColorCd	unsigned short int
SquareFt	long int

Write an appropriate `struct` that matches this data. Use `Hotel` as the structure tag.

Suppose that the same company also wanted you to write a program to keep track of their monthly and annual employee salaries and to print a report at the end of the year that showed each month's individual salary and the total salary at the end of the year.

What would the salary structure look like? Be careful! This type of data probably does not need a structure. Because all the monthly salaries must be the same data type, a floating-point or a double floating-point array holds the monthly salaries nicely without the complexity of a structure.

Structures are useful for keeping track of data that must be grouped, such as inventory data, a customer's name and address data, or an employee data file.

Defining Structures

This section helps you better understand the format of the `struct` statement. As you saw earlier, to define a structure, you must use the `struct` statement. The `struct` statement defines a new data type, with more than one member, for your program. The format of the `struct` statement is this:

```
struct [structure tag]
   {
      member definition;
      member definition;
        :
      member definition;
   } [one or more structure variables];
```

As mentioned earlier, *structure tag* is optional (hence the brackets in the format). Each *member definition* is a normal variable definition, such as `int i;` or `float sales[20];` or any other valid variable definition, including variable pointers if the structure requires a pointer as a member. At the end of the structure's definition, before the final semicolon, you can specify one or more structure variables.

The previous `struct` declarations in this lesson had no structure variables; they declared only the structure's look and feel. By defining a structure without structure variables, you inform the compiler that you want it to recognize that structure, named by its structure tag, when the time comes for you to define structure variables.

If you specify a structure variable, you request that C++ reserve space for that variable. This enables C++ to recognize that the variable is not an integer, character, or any other internal data type. C++ also recognizes that the variable must be a type that looks like the structure. It might seem strange that the members do not reserve storage, but they don't. The structure variables do. This is made clear in the examples that follow.

Here is how you declare the hotel structure with three structure variables:

```
struct Hotel  {
    int RoomNum;
    float Price;
    unsigned short int ColorCd;
    long int SquareFt;
} SouthHotel, WestHotel, NorthHotel;
```

 Before going any further, you should be able to answer the following questions about this structure:

1. What is the structure tag?

2. How many members are there?

3. What are the member data types?

4. What are the member names?

5. How many structure variables are there?

6. What are their names?

The structure tag is called Hotel. There are four members: an integer, a floating-point, an unsigned short integer, and a long integer. The member names are RoomNum, Price, ColorCd, and SquareFt. There are three structure variables: SouthHotel, WestHotel, and NorthHotel.

If the parent company owned 100 hotels, it would have to declare 100 structure variables. Obviously, you would not want to list that many structure variables at the end of a structure definition. To help define structures for a large number of occurrences, you must define an *array of structures*. Lesson 31, "Arrays of Structures," shows you how to do so. For now, concentrate on becoming familiar with structure definitions.

Here is a structure definition of the inventory application described earlier in this lesson:

```
struct Inventory {
    char  Descript[15];
    char  PartNo[6];
    int   Quantity;
    float Cost;
    float Retail;
} Item1, Item2, Item3, Item4;
```

Four inventory structure variables are defined. Each structure variable—Item1, Item2, Item3, and Item4—looks like the structure.

Suppose that a company wanted to track its customers and personnel. The following two structure definitions would create five structure variables for each structure. This example, having five employees and five customers, is very limited, but it shows how structures can be defined.

```
struct employees
{
    char empName[25];    // Employee's full name
    char address[30];    // Employee's address
    char city[10];
    char state[2];
    long int zip;
    double salary;    // Annual salary
} emp1, emp2, emp3, emp4, emp5;
```

```
struct customers
{
    char custName[25];    // Customer's full name
    char address[30];     // Customer's address
    char city[10];
    char state[2];
    long int zip;
    double balance;       // Balance owed to company
} cust1, cust2, cust3, cust4, cust5;
```

Each structure has similar data. Later in this lesson you learn how to consolidate similar member definitions by creating nested structures.

> **TIP:** Put comments to the right of members in order to document the purpose of the members.

Suppose that the same company also needed to track its vendors' (the companies from which they purchase their inventory and supplies) names and addresses. About the only difference is that you need to add an extra member named venCode (an integer) and a totPurchase (a double floating-point) member to hold the total amount bought from that vendor. Write the structure that defines the vendor and three vendor structure variables.

Initializing Structure Data

There are two ways to initialize members of a structure. You can initialize members when you declare a structure, or you can initialize a structure in the body of the program. Most programs lend themselves to the latter method, because you do not always know structure data when you write your program.

Here is an example of a structure declared and initialized at the same time:

```
struct cdCollection
   {
     char title[25];
     char artist[20];
     int numSongs;
     float price;
     char datePurch[9];
   } cd1 = {"Red Moon Men", "Sam and the Sneeds",
           12, 11.95, "08/13/93"};
```

When first learning about structures, you might be tempted to initialize members inside the structure individually, such as

```
char artist[20] = "Sam and the Sneeds";   // Invalid
```

You cannot initialize individual members, because they are not variables. You can assign only values to variables. The only structure variable in this structure is cd1. The braces must enclose the data you initialize in the structure variables, just as they enclose data when you initialize arrays.

This method of initializing structure variables becomes tedious when there are several structure variables (as there usually are). Putting the data in several variables, each set of data enclosed in braces, becomes messy and takes up too much space in your code.

More important, you usually cannot even know the contents of the structure variables. Generally, the user enters data to be stored in structures, or you read them from a disk file.

A better approach to initializing structures is to use the *dot operator* (.). The dot operator is one way to initialize individual members of a structure variable in the body of your program. With the dot operator, you can treat each structure member almost as if it were a regular nonstructure variable.

The format of the dot operator is

structureVariableName.memberName

A structure variable name must always precede the dot operator, and a member name must always appear after the dot operator. Using the dot operator is easy, as the following examples show.

Here is a simple program using the CD collection structure and the dot operator to initialize the structure. Notice that the program treats members as if they were regular variables when they are combined with the dot operator.

```cpp
// Filename: ST1.CPP
// Structure initialization with the CD collection
#include <iostream.h>
#include <string.h>
void main()
{
  struct cdCollection
  {
    char title[25];
    char artist[20];
    int numSongs;
    float price;
    char datePurch[9];
  } cd1;

  // Initializes members here
  strcpy(cd1.title, "Red Moon Men");
  strcpy(cd1.artist, "Sam and the Sneeds");
  cd1.numSongs = 12;
  cd1.price = 11.95;
  strcpy(cd1.datePurch, "02/13/92");

  // Prints the data to the screen
  cout << "Here is the CD information:\n\n";
  cout << "Title: " << cd1.title << "\n";
  cout << "Artist: " << cd1.artist << "\n";
  cout << "Songs: " << cd1.numSongs << "\n";
  cout << "Price: " << cd1.price << "\n";
  cout << "Date purchased: " << cd1.datePurch << "\n";

  return;
}
```

Here is the program's output:

```
Here is the CD information:

Title: Red Moon Men
Artist: Sam and the Sneeds
```

```
Songs: 12
Price: 11.95
Date purchased: 02/13/92
```

By using the dot operator, you can receive structure data from the keyboard with any of the data-input functions you know, such as cin, gets(), and get.

The following program asks the user for student information. To keep the example reasonably short, only two students are defined in the program.

```cpp
// Filename: ST2.CPP
// Structure input with student data
#include <iostream.h>
#include <string.h>
#include <iomanip.h>
#include <stdio.h>
void main()
{
   struct students
   {
     char name[25];
     int age;
     float average;
   } student1, student2;

   // Gets data for two students
   cout << "What is first student's name? ";
   gets(student1.name);
   cout << "What is the first student's age? ";
   cin >> student1.age;
   cout << "What is the first student's average? ";
   cin >> student1.average;

   fflush(stdin);   // Clears input buffer for next input

   cout << "\nWhat is second student's name? ";
   gets(student2.name);
   cout << "What is the second student's age? ";
   cin >> student2.age;
   cout << "What is the second student's average? ";
   cin >> student2.average;
```

```
// Prints the data
cout << "\n\nHere is the student information you " <<
        "entered:\n\n";
cout << "Student #1:\n";
cout << "Name:     " << student1.name << "\n";
cout << "Age:      " << student1.age << "\n";
cout << "Average: " << setprecision(2) << student1.average
                    << "\n";

cout << "\nStudent #2:\n";
cout << "Name:     " << student2.name << "\n";
cout << "Age:      " << student2.age << "\n";
cout << "Average: " << student2.average << "\n";

return;
}
```

Here is the program's output:

```
What is first student's name? Larry
What is the first student's age? 14
What is the first student's average? 87.67

What is second student's name? Judy
What is the second student's age? 15
What is the second student's average? 95.38



Here is the student information you entered:

Student #1:
Name:    Larry
Age:     14
Average: 87.67

Student #2:
Name:    Judy
Age:     15
Average: 95.38
```

Structure variables are passed by copy, not by address as with arrays. Therefore, if you fill a structure in a function, you must return it to the calling function in order for the calling function to recognize the structure, or use global structure variables, which generally is not recommended.

514

> **TIP:** A good solution to the local/global structure problem is this: define your structures globally without any structure variables. Define all your structure variables locally to the functions that need them. As long as your structure definition is global, you can declare local structure variables from that structure. All subsequent examples in this book use this method.

The structure tag plays an important role in the local/global problem. Always use the structure tag to define local structure variables. In the following program fragment, the student structure is first declared globally with no structure variables. In each function, as shown here in `main()`, you can then define local structure variables by referring to the structure tag. The structure tag keeps you from having to redefine the structure members every time you define a new structure variable.

```
// Structure input with student data passed to functions
struct students fill_structs(struct students student_var);


struct students   {   // A global structure
    char name[25];
    int age;
    float average;
};   // No memory reserved


void main()
{
    students student1, student2;   // Defines two
                                   // local variables
    // Rest of program follows
```

Because structure data is nothing more than regular variables grouped together, feel free to calculate using structure members. As long as you use the dot operator, you can treat structure members just as you would other variables.

The following program asks for a customer's balance and uses a discount rate, included in the customer's structure, to calculate a new balance. To keep the program short, the structure's data is initialized at variable declaration time.

This program does not actually require structures because only one customer is used. Individual variables could have been used, but they don't illustrate the concept of calculating with structures.

515

```
// Filename: CUST.CPP
// Updates a customer balance in a structure
#include <iostream.h>
#include <iomanip.h>

struct customerRec
   {
      char custName[25];
      double balance;
      float disRate;
   } ;

void main()
{
   struct customerRec customer = {"Steve Thompson",
                                       431.23, .25};

   cout << "Before the update, " << customer.custName;
   cout << " has a balance of $" << setprecision(2) <<
           customer.balance << "\n";

   // Updates the balance
   customer.balance *= (1.0-customer.disRate);

   cout << "After the update, " << customer.custName;
   cout << " has a balance of $" << customer.balance << "\n";
   return;
}
```

You can copy the members of one structure variable to the members of another as long as both structures have the same format. Being able to copy one structure variable to another will seem more meaningful when you read Lesson 31, "Arrays of Structures."

Nested Structures

C++ gives you the ability to nest one structure definition in another. This saves time when you are writing programs that use similar structures. You have to define the common members only once in their own structure and then use that structure as a member in another structure.

The following two structure definitions illustrate this point:

```
struct employees
{
   char empName[25];    // Employee's full name
   char address[30];    // Employee's address
   char city[10];
   char state[2];
   long int zip;
   double salary;    // Annual salary
};

struct customers
{
   char custName[25];    // Customer's full name
   char address[30];    // Customer's address
   char city[10];
   char state[2];
   long int zip;
   double balance;    // Balance owed to company
};
```

These structures hold different data. One structure is for employee data and the other holds customer data. Even though the data should be kept separate (you don't want to send a customer a paycheck!), the structure definitions have a lot of overlap and can be consolidated by creating a third structure.

Suppose that you created the following structure:

```
struct addressInfo
{
   char address[30];    // Common address information
   char city[10];
   char state[2];
   long int zip;
};
```

This structure could then be used as a member in the other structures, like this:

```
struct employees
{
   char empName[25];    // Employee's full name
   struct addressInfo eAddress;    // Employee's address
   double salary;    // Annual salary
};
```

```
struct customers
{
    char custName[25];    // Customer's full name
    struct addressInfo cAddress;    // Customer's address
    double balance;    // Balance owed to company
};
```

It is important to realize that there is a total of three structures, and that they have the tags addressInfo, employees, and customers. How many members does the employees structure have? If you answered three, you are correct. There are three members in both employees and customers. The employees structure has the structure of a character array, followed by the addressInfo structure, followed by the double floating-point member, salary.

When you define a structure, that structure becomes a new data type in the program and can be used anywhere a data type (such as int, float, and so on) can appear.

You can assign members values using the dot operator. To assign the customer balance a number, type something like this:

```
customer.balance = 5643.24;
```

The nested structure might seem to pose a problem. How can you assign a value to one of the nested members? By using the dot operator, you must nest the dot operator just as you nest the structure definitions. You would assign a value to the customer's ZIP code like this:

```
customer.cAddress.zip = 34312;
```

To assign a value to the employee's ZIP code, you would do this:

```
employee.eAddress.zip = 59823;
```

How would you assign a value to the customer's city member? (*Hint:* You must use a built-in function to assign data to the character array.)

Review Questions

1. How do structures differ from arrays?
2. What are the individual elements of a structure called?

3. What are the two ways to initialize members of a structure?
4. Do you pass structures by copy or by address?
5. TRUE or FALSE: The following structure definition reserves storage in memory:

```
struct crec
   { char name[25];
   int age;
   float sales[5];
   long int num;
};
```

6. Should you declare a structure globally or locally?
7. Should you declare a structure variable globally or locally?
8. How many members does the following structure declaration contain?

```
struct item {
   int quantity;
   partRec item Disc;
   float price;
   char dataPurch[*];
};
```

Review Exercises

1. Write a structure in a program that tracks a video store's tape inventory. Be sure that the structure includes the tape title, the length of the tape (in minutes), the initial purchase price of the tape, the rental price of the tape, and the date of the movie's release.
2. Write a program using the structure you declared in Exercise 1. Define three structure variables and initialize them when you declare the variables with data. Print the data to the screen.
3. Write a teacher's program to keep track of 10 students' names, ages, letter grades, and IQs. Use 10 different structure variable names and retrieve the data for the students in a `for` loop from the keyboard. Print the data on the printer when the teacher finishes entering the information for all the students.

Arrays of Structures

To teach you ways you can store many occurrences of structure variables in arrays.

This lesson builds on the preceding one by showing you how to create many structures for your data. After creating an array of structures, you can store many occurrences of your data values. So far, all arrays you have seen have been arrays of built-in data types such as int and char. You also can store arrays of your own data types by holding an array of structures.

Arrays of structures are good for storing a complete employee file, inventory file, or any other set of data that fits in the structure format. Whereas arrays provide a handy way to store several values that are the same type, arrays of structures store several values of different types together, grouped as structures.

Many C++ programmers use arrays of structures as a prelude to storing their data in a disk file. You can input and calculate your disk data in arrays of structures, then store those structures in memory. Arrays of structures also provide a means of holding data you read from the disk.

Declaring Arrays of Structures

It is easy to declare an array of structures. You only need to specify the number of reserved structures inside array brackets when you declare the structure variable. Consider the following structure definition:

```
struct stores  {
    int employees;
    int registers;
    double sales;
} store1, store2, store3, store4;
```

This structure should not be difficult for you to understand because no new commands are used in the structure declaration. This structure declaration creates four structure variables. Figure 31.1 shows how C++ stores these four structures in memory. Each of the structure variables has three members—two integers followed by a double floating-point value.

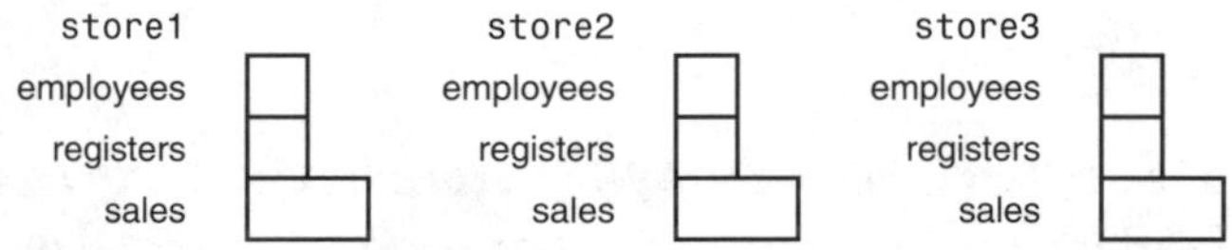

Figure 31.1.
The structure
of store1,
store2,
store3, *and*
store4.

If the fourth store increased its employee count by three, you could update the store's employee number with the following assignment statement:

```
store4.employees += 3;    // Adds three to this store's
                          // employee count
```

Suppose that the fifth store just opened and you want to initialize its members with data. If the stores are a chain and the new store is similar to one of the others, you can begin initializing the store's data by assigning each of its members the same data as another store's, like this:

```
store5 = store2;    // Defines initial values for
                    // the members of store5
```

Such structure declarations are fine for a small number of structures, but if the stores were a national chain, five structure variables would not be enough. Suppose that there were 1,000 stores. You would not want to create 1,000 different store variables and work with each one individually. It would be much easier to create an array of store structures.

Consider the following structure declaration:

```
struct Company  {
    int employees;
    int registers;
    double sales;
} store[1000];
```

In one quick declaration, this code creates 1,000 store structures, each one containing three members. Figure 31.2 shows how the first four of these structure variables would appear in memory. Notice the name of each individual structure variable: store[0], store[1], store[2], and store[3].

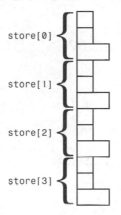

Figure 31.2.
An array of
Company
structures.

Be sure that your computer does not run out of memory when you create a large number of structures. Arrays of structures quickly consume valuable memory. You might have to create fewer structures, storing more data in disk files and less data in memory.

You also can define the array of structures after the declaration of the structure. As long as a structure has a tag, you can define variables later in the program. For instance, here is how you would define the array of store structure variables locally in main(), using the global Company tag:

```
struct Company  {
    int employees;
    int registers;
    double sales;
```

```
};    // No structure variables defined yet
#include <iostream.h>
main()
{
   struct Company store[1000];   // Defines the array
   // Rest of program follows
```

> **NOTE:** You do not have to repeat the `struct` keyword when you define the `store` array of structure variables. In C, the `struct` would be required, but C++ lets you use `struct` if you want to without requiring it.

Referencing the Array Structures

The element `store[2]` is an array element. This array element, unlike the other arrays you have seen, is a structure variable. Therefore, it contains three members, each of which you can reference with the dot operator.

The dot operator works the same way for structure array elements as it does for regular structure variables. If the number of employees for the fifth store (`store[4]`) increased by three, you could update the structure variable like this:

```
store[4].employees += 3;    // Adds three to this store's
                            // employee count
```

You also can assign complete structures to one another by using array notation. To assign all the members of the 20th store to the 45th store, you would do this:

```
store[44] = store[19];    // Copies all members from the
                          // 20th store to the 45th
```

 The rules of arrays are still in force here. Each element of the array called `store` is of the same data type. The data type of `store` is the structure `stores`. As with any array, each element must be the same data type; you cannot mix data types in the same array. This array's data type happens to be a structure you created containing three members. The data type for `store[316]` is the same for `store[981]` and `store[74]`.

Write the line of code that adds the fifth structure's sales to the third structure's sales.

The name of the array, store, is a pointer constant to the starting element of the array, store[0]. Therefore, you can use pointer notation to reference the stores. To assign store[60] the same value as store[23], you can reference the two elements like this:

```
*(store +  60) = *(store + 23);
```

You also can mix array and pointer notation, such as

```
store[60] = *(store + 23);
```

and receive the same results.

You can increase the sales of store[8] by 40 percent using pointer or subscript notation as well, as in

```
store[8].sales = (*(store + 8)).sales * 1.40;
```

The extra pair of parentheses is required because the dot operator has precedence over the dereferencing symbol in C++'s hierarchy of operators (see Appendix D). Of course, in this case, the code is not helped by the pointer notation. The following is a much clearer way to increase the sales by 40 percent:

```
store[8].sales *= 1.40;
```

Building a Structure Array

The following programs build an inventory data-entry system for a mail-order firm using an array of structures. There is very little new you have to know when working with arrays of structures. To become comfortable with the arrays of structure notation, concentrate on the notation used when accessing arrays of structures and their members.

Suppose that you work for a mail-order company that sells disk drives. You are given the task of writing a tracking program for the 125 different drives you sell. You must keep track of the following information:

Storage capacity
Access time in milliseconds
Vendor code (A, B, C, or D)
Cost
Price

Because there are 125 different disk drives in the inventory, the data fits nicely into an array of structures. Each array element is a structure containing the five members described in the list.

The following structure definition defines the inventory:

```
struct inventory  {
    long int storage;
    int accessTime;
    char vendorCode;
    double cost;
    double price;
} drive[125];    // Defines 125 occurrences of the structure
```

When you are working with a large array of structures, your first concern should be how the data inputs into the array elements. The best method of data entry depends on the application.

For example, if you are converting from an older computerized inventory system, you must write a conversion program that reads the inventory file in its native format and saves it to a new file in the format required by your C++ programs. This is no easy task. It demands that you have extensive knowledge of the system from which you are converting.

If you are writing a computerized inventory system for the first time, your job is a little easier because you do not have to convert the old files. You still must realize that someone has to type the data into the computer. You have to write a data-entry program that receives each inventory item from the keyboard and saves it to a disk file. You should give the user a chance to edit inventory data to correct any data that he or she originally typed incorrectly.

One of the reasons disk files are introduced in the last half of this book is that disk-file formats and structures share a common bond. When you store data in a structure, or more often, in an array of structures, you can easily write that data to a disk file using straightforward disk I/O commands.

The following program takes the array of disk drive structures shown earlier and adds a data-entry function so that the user can enter data into the array of structures. The program is menu driven. The user has a choice, when starting the program, to add data, print data on-screen, or exit the program. Because you have yet to learn about disk I/O commands, the data in the array of structures goes away when the program ends. As mentioned earlier, saving those structures to disk is an easy task after you learn C++'s disk I/O commands. For now, concentrate on the manipulation of the structures.

This program is longer than many you have seen in this book, but if you have followed the discussions of structures and the dot operator, you should have little trouble following the code.

```cpp
// Filename: DSINV.CPP
// Data-entry program for a disk drive company
#include <iostream.h>
#include <stdlib.h>
#include <iomanip.h>
#include <stdio.h>

struct inventory   // Global structure definition
{
   long int storage;
   int accessTime;
   char vendorCode;
   float cost;
   float price;
};   // No structure variables defined globally

void dispMenu(void);
struct inventory enterData();
void seeData(inventory disk[125], int numItems);

void main()
{
   inventory disk[125];   // Local array of structures
   int ans;
   int numItems = 0;   // Total number of items
                       // in the inventory

   do
     {
        do
         { dispMenu();   // Displays menu of user choices
           cin >> ans;   // Gets user's request
         } while ((ans < 1) || (ans > 3));
```

```
        switch (ans)
     { case (1): { disk[numItems] = enterData();  // Enters
                                                  // disk data
                numItems++;   // Increments number of items
                break; }
       case (2): { seeData(disk, numItems);   // Displays
                                              // disk data
              break; }
       default : { break; }
     }
     } while (ans != 3);   // Quits program
                           // when user is done
     return;
}


void dispMenu(void)
{

   cout << "\n\n*** Disk Drive Inventory System ***\n\n";
   cout << "Do you want to:\n\n";
   cout << "\t1.  Enter new item in inventory\n\n";
   cout << "\t2.  See inventory data\n\n";
   cout << "\t3.  Exit the program\n\n";
   cout << "What is your choice? ";
   return;
}


inventory enterData()
{
   inventory diskItem;   // Local variable to fill
                         // with input

   cout << "\n\nWhat is the next drive's storage in bytes? ";
   cin >> diskItem.storage;
   cout << "What is the drive's access time in ms? ";
   cin >> diskItem.accessTime;
   cout << "What is the drive's vendor code (A, B, C, or D)? ";
   fflush(stdin);   // Discards input buffer
                    // before accepting character
   diskItem.vendorCode = getchar();
   getchar();   // Discards carriage return
   cout << "What is the drive's cost? ";
```

```
   cin >> diskItem.cost;
   cout << "What is the drive's price? ";
   cin >> diskItem.price;

   return (diskItem);
}

void seeData(inventory disk[125], int numItems)
{
   int ctr;
   cout << "\n\nHere is the inventory listing:\n\n";
   for (ctr = 0; ctr < numItems; ctr++)
      {
      cout << "Storage: " << disk[ctr].storage << "\t";
      cout << "Access time: " << disk[ctr].accessTime << "\n";
      cout << "Vendor code: " << disk[ctr].vendorCode << "\t";
      cout << setprecision(2);
      cout << "Cost: $" << disk[ctr].cost << "\t";
      cout << "Price: $" << disk[ctr].price << "\n";
      }
   return;
}
```

You can add many features and error-checking functions, but this program is the foundation of a more comprehensive inventory system. You can easily adapt it to a different type of inventory, a videotape collection, a coin collection, or any other tracking system by changing the structure definition and the member names throughout the program.

Add the lines necessary to the preceding program's seeData() function to print an error message if the user attempts to see an inventory listing (via the program's menu option 2) before he or she has entered any data (with option 1). *Hint:* If NumItems is zero, you probably don't want to print the listing.

Arrays as Members

Members of structures can be arrays. Array members pose no new problems, but you have to be careful when you access individual array elements. Keeping track of arrays of structures that contain array members might seem to require a great deal of work on your part, but there is nothing to it.

Consider the following structure definition. This statement declares an array of 100 structures, each structure holding payroll information for a company. Two of the members, name and department, are arrays.

```
struct payroll {
    char name[25];    // Employee name array
    int dependents;
    char department[10];   // Department name array
    float salary;
} employee[100];    // An array of 100 employees
```

Figure 31.3 shows what these structures look like. The first and third members are arrays. name is an array of 25 characters, and department is an array of 10 characters.

Figure 31.3. The payroll data.

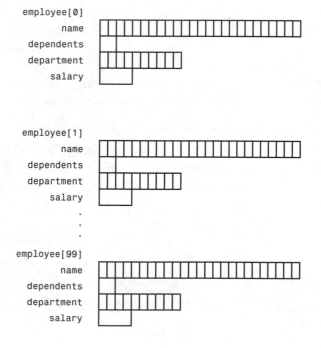

Suppose that you must save the 25th employee's initial in a character variable. Assuming that `initial` is already declared as a character variable, the following statement assigns the employee's initial to `initial`:

```
initial = employee[24].name[0];
```

The double subscripts might look confusing, but the dot operator requires a structure variable on its left (`employee[24]`) and a member on its right (`name`'s first array element). Being able to refer to member arrays makes the processing of character data in structures simple.

Suppose that an employee got married and wanted her name changed in the payroll file. (She happens to be the 45th employee in the array of structures.) Given the payroll structure just described, write the statement that would assign a new name to her structure.

TIP: When you refer to a structure variable using the dot operator, you can use regular commands and functions to process the data in the structure members.

What is wrong with the following assignment statement (given the payroll structure just shown)?

```
employee.salary[43] = 212.32;  // Assigns 43rd employee a salary
```

A bookstore might want to catalog its inventory of books. The following program creates an array of 100 structures. Each structure contains several types of variables, including arrays. This program is the data-entry portion of a larger inventory system. Study the references to the members to see how member arrays are used.

```
// Filename: BOOK.CPP
// Bookstore data-entry program
#include <iostream.h>
#include <stdio.h>
#include <ctype.h>

struct inventory
  { char title[25];    // Book's title
    char pubDate[19];   // Publication date
```

```
      char author[20];    // Author's name
      int num;    // Number in stock
      int onOrder;    // Number on order
      float retail;    // Retail price
   };

void main()
{
   inventory book[100];
   int total = 0;    // Total books in inventory
   int ans;

   do    // This program enters data into the structures
      { cout << "Book #" << (total + 1) << ":\n", (total + 1);
      cout << "What is the title? ";
      gets(book[total].title);
      cout << "What is the publication date? ";
      gets(book[total].pubDate);
      cout << "Who is the author? ";
      gets(book[total].author);
      cout << "How many books of this title are there? ";
      cin >> book[total].num;
      cout << "How many are on order? ";
      cin >> book[total].onOrder;
      cout << "What is the retail price? ";
      cin >> book[total].retail;
      fflush(stdin);
      cout << "\nAre there more books? (Y/N) ";
      ans = getchar();
      fflush(stdin);    // Discards carriage return
      ans = toupper(ans);    // Converts to uppercase
      if (ans == 'Y')
        { total++;
          continue; }
      } while (ans == 'Y');
   return;
}
```

You need much more to make this a usable inventory program. Expand on this book data-entry program (BOOK.CPP) by adding a print routine that displays the book titles. Also, change the program to put the data-entry routine into its own separate function.

Seeing the Steps

Here is a comprehensive walk-through of the steps you might go through to write a C++ program. You should begin to understand the C++ language enough to start writing some advanced programs.

Assume that you have been hired by a local bookstore to write a magazine inventory system. You have to track the following:

Magazine title (at most, 25 characters)
Publisher (at most, 25 characters)
Month (1, 2, 3,...12)
Year of publication
Number of copies in stock
Number of copies on order
Price of magazine (dollars and cents)

Suppose that there is a projected maximum of 200 magazine titles that the store will ever carry. This means that you need 200 occurrences of the structure, not 200 magazines total. Here is a good structure definition for such an inventory:

```
struct magInfo  {
   char title[25];
   char pub[25];
   int month;
   int year;
   int stockCopies;
   int orderCopies;
   float price;
} mags[200];    // Defines 200 occurrences
```

Because this program consists of more than one function, declare the structure globally and the structure variables locally in the functions that need them.

This program needs three basic functions: a main() controlling function, a data-entry function, and a data printing function. You can add much more, but this is a good start for an inventory system. To keep the length of this program reasonable, assume that the user wants to enter several magazines, then print them. (To make the program more "usable," you should add a menu so that the user can control when she or he adds and prints the information. You also should add more error-checking and editing capabilities.)

Here is the complete data-entry and printing program with prototypes. The arrays of structures are passed between the functions from main().

```cpp
// Filename: MAG.CPP
// Magazine inventory program for adding and displaying
// a bookstore's magazines
#include <iostream.h>
#include <ctype.h>
#include <stdio.h>

struct magInfo
   { char title[25];
     char pub[25];
     int month;
     int year;
     int stockCopies;
     int orderCopies;
     float price;
   };

magInfo fillMags(magInfo mag);
void printMags(magInfo mags[], int magCtr);

void main()
{
   magInfo mags[200];
   int magCtr = 0;    // Number of magazine titles
   char ans;

   do
   {   // Assumes that at least
       // one magazine is filled
      mags[magCtr] = fillMags(mags[magCtr]);
      cout << "Do you want to enter another magazine? ";
      fflush(stdin);
      ans = getchar();
      fflush(stdin);    // Discards carriage return
      if (toupper(ans) == 'Y')
        { magCtr++; }
        } while (toupper(ans) == 'Y');
      printMags(mags, magCtr);
      return;    // Returns to operating system
}

void printMags(magInfo mags[], int magCtr)
{
```

```
   int i;
   for (i = 0; i <= magCtr; i++)
     { cout << "\n\nMagazine " << (i+1) << ":\n";// Adjusts for
                                                 // subscript
       cout << "\nTitle: " << mags[i].title << "\n";
       cout << "\tPublisher: " << mags[i].pub << "\n";
       cout << "\tPub.  Month: " << mags[i].month << "\n";
       cout << "\tPub.  Year: " << mags[i].year << "\n";
       cout << "\tIn-stock: " << mags[i].stockCopies << "\n";
       cout << "\tOn order: " << mags[i].orderCopies << "\n";
       cout << "\tPrice: " << mags[i].price << "\n";
     }
   return;
}


magInfo fillMags(magInfo mag)
{
   puts("\n\nWhat is the title? ");
   gets(mag.title);
   puts("Who is the publisher? ");
   gets(mag.pub);
   puts("What is the month (1, 2, ..., 12)? ");
   cin >> mag.month;
   puts("What is the year? ");
   cin >> mag.year;
   puts("How many copies in stock? ");
   cin >> mag.stockCopies;
   puts("How many copies on order? ");
   cin >> mag.orderCopies;
   puts("How much is the magazine? ");
   cin >> mag.price;
   return (mag);
}
```

Where would the following line go in the preceding program if you
wanted to pause after each magazine is displayed to the screen?

```
cout << "\nPress Enter to see next magazine...\n";
getch();    // Doesn't save the Enter key
```

Review Questions

1. TRUE or FALSE: Each element in an array of structures must be of the same type.

2. What is the advantage of creating an array of structures rather than using individual variable names for each structure variable?

3. Given the following structure declaration:

```
struct item  {
   char partNo[8];
   char descr[20];
   float price;
   int inStock;
} inventory[100];
```

   (a) How would you assign a price of 12.33 to the 33rd item's in-stock quantity?

   (b) How would you assign the first character of the 12th item's part number the value of X?

   (c) How would you assign the 97th inventory item the same values as the 63rd?

4. Consider the following structure declaration:

```
struct item  {
   char desc[20];
   int num;
   float cost;
} inventory[25];
```

   (a) What is wrong with the following statement?

```
item[1].cost = 92.32;
```

   (b) What is wrong with the following statement?

```
strcpy(inventory.desc, "Widgets");
```

   (c) What is wrong with the following statement?

```
inventory.cost[10] = 32.12;
```

Review Exercises

1. Write a program that stores an array of friends' names, phone numbers, and addresses and prints them two ways: with the friend's name, address, and phone number, or with only the friend's name and phone number.

2. Add a search function to the book program (BOOK.CPP) so that the user can enter a book title. Display all of that book's related information (or an error message saying that the book does not exist). Use C++'s built-in strcmp() function to do the title-matching. strcmp() returns a nonzero value if its two string arguments do not match, and it returns a zero if they do.

Sequential Files

OBJECTIVE *To teach you how to read and write to C++ disk files.*

Most "real-world" computer applications need to store data long after the computer is turned off. So far, every program in this book has processed data that resided inside the program listing or came from the keyboard. You assigned constants and variables to other variables and created new data values from expressions. The programs also received input with `cin`, `gets()`, and the character input functions.

The data created by the user and assigned to variables with assignment statements is sufficient for some applications. With the large volume of data most real-world applications must process, however, you need a better way of storing that data. For all but the smallest computer programs, disk files offer the solution. This lesson focuses on disk- and file-processing concepts and teaches you the first of two methods of disk access—*sequential file access.*

If you have programmed computerized data files in another programming language, you might be surprised at how C++ borrows from other programming languages, especially BASIC, when working with disk files. If you are new to disk-file processing, disk files are simple to create and read.

Why Use a Disk?

The typical computer system has much less memory storage than hard disk storage. Your disk drive holds much more data than can fit in your computer's RAM. Also, data on the disk lasts longer than that in your computer's memory. When you turn your computer off, the disk memory is not erased, whereas RAM is.

Most disks that come with today's computer systems hold much more data than RAM memory can hold. The capacity of your disk makes it a perfect place to store your data as well as your programs.

What if the Social Security Office in Washington, D.C. asked you to write a C++ program to compute, average, filter, sort, and print the name and address of each person in their files? Would you want your program to include millions of assignment statements? You would not want the program to hold that much data, and it could not do so because only relatively small amounts of data fit in a program before you run out of RAM.

By storing data on your disk, you are much less limited because you have more storage. Your disk can hold as much data as you have disk capacity. Also, if your program requirements grow, you usually can increase your disk space, whereas you cannot always add more RAM to your computer.

NOTE: Regular C++ programs cannot access the special extended or expanded memory that some computers have. (This is memory that exists above the usual 640K of computer RAM that comes with most PCs.) Although some compilers offer functions that take advantage of the extra memory, many do not. Therefore, disk files are critical for processing large amounts of data.

When working with disk files, C++ does not have to access much RAM because C++ reads data from your disk drive and processes the data only parts at a time. Not all your disk data has to reside in RAM for C++ to process it. C++ reads some data, processes it, and then reads some more. If C++ requires disk data a second time, it rereads that place on the disk.

Types of Disk File Access

Your programs can access files in two ways—through sequential access or random access. Your application determines the method you should choose. The access mode of a file determines how you read, write, change, and delete data from the file. Most C++ data files can be accessed in both ways, sequentially and randomly, as long as your programs are written properly and the data lends itself to both types of file access.

A sequential file has to be accessed in the same order as the file was written. This is analogous to cassette tapes: you play music in the same order it was recorded. (You can quickly fast-forward or rewind through songs you do not want to hear, but the order of the songs dictates what you do to play the song you want.) It is difficult, and sometimes impossible, to insert data in the middle of a sequential file. How easy is it to insert a new song in the middle of two other songs on a tape? The only way to truly add or delete records from the middle of a sequential file is to create a completely new file that combines both old and new records.

It might seem that sequential files are limiting, but it turns out that many applications lend themselves to sequential file processing.

Unlike with sequential files, you can access random-access files in any order you want. Think of data in a random-access file as being similar to songs on a compact disc or a record: you can go directly to any song you want without having to play or fast-forward through the other songs. If you want to play the first song, the sixth song, then the fourth song, you can do so. The order of play has nothing to do with the order in which the songs were recorded. Random file access sometimes takes more programming but rewards your effort with a more flexible file-access method. Lesson 33, "Random-Access Files," discusses how to program for random-access files.

Suppose that a company keeps its sales history in disk files for several years. The company rarely needs to change the data, but it keeps the data to make end-of-the-year predictions for sales forecasts. Which programming method do you think the company should use: sequential files, which are easier to program, or random-access files? *Hint:* Even though you have not yet read Lesson 33, "Random-Access Files," you probably can tell that they require more programming effort but are necessary when a company needs to change disk file data often.

Sequential File Concepts

You can perform three operations on sequential disk files. You can:

- create disk files
- add to disk files
- read from disk files

Your application determines what you must do. If you are creating a disk file for the first time, you must create the file and write the initial data to it. Suppose that you wanted to create a customer data file. You would create a new file and write your current customers to that file. The customer data might originally be in arrays, arrays of structures, pointed to with pointers, or placed in regular variables by the user.

Over time, as your customer base grew, you could add new customers to the file (*append* to the file). When you add to the end of a file, you append to that file. As customers entered your store, you would read their information from the customer data file.

 As mentioned earlier, a sequential file is analogous to music on a cassette tape. You can either create a new tape (record songs), add to the end of a tape, or read the tape (play the songs). You cannot easily change or add music in the middle of the tape because of its sequential nature.

Customer disk processing is not always a good use for sequential files, however. Suppose that a customer moves and wants you to change his or her address in your files. Sequential-access files do not lend themselves to changing data stored in them. It is also difficult to remove information from sequential files. Random files, described in the next lesson, provide a much easier approach to changing and removing data.

> The primary approach to changing or removing data from a sequential-access file is to create a new one from the old one with the updated data. Because of the updating ease provided with random-access files, this lesson concentrates on creating, reading, and adding to sequential files.

Opening and Closing Files

Before you can create, write to, or read from a disk file, you must open the file. This is analogous to opening a file cabinet before working with a file stored in the cabinet. When you are done with a cabinet's file, you close the file drawer. You also must close a disk file when you finish with it.

When you open a disk file, you only have to inform C++ of the filename and what you want to do (write to, add to, or read from). C++ and your operating system work together to make sure that the disk is ready, and they create an entry in your file directory for the filename (if you are creating a file). When you close a file, C++ writes any remaining data to the file, releases the file from the program, and updates the file directory to reflect the file's new size.

To open a file, you must call the `open()` function. To close a file, call the `close()` function. Here is the format of these two function calls:

```
filePtr.open(fileName, access);
```

and

```
filePtr.close();
```

filePtr is a special type of pointer that points only to files, not to data variables. When you open the file, you will use *filePtr* for the rest of the program to access the file.

Your operating system handles the exact location of your data in the disk file. You don't want to worry about the exact track and sector number of your data on the disk. Therefore, you let *filePtr* point to the data you are reading and writing. Your program only has to manage *filePtr*, whereas C++ and your operating system take care of locating the actual physical data.

fileName is a string (or a character pointer that points to a string) containing a valid filename for your computer. *fileName* can contain a complete disk and directory pathname. You can specify the filename in uppercase or lowercase letters.

access must be one of the values in Table 32.1.

Table 32.1. Possible access modes.

Mode	Description
app	Opens the file for appending (adding to it)
ate	Seeks to end of file on opening it
in	Opens the file for reading
out	Opens the file for writing
binary	Opens the file in binary mode
trunc	Discards contents if file exists
nocreate	If file doesn't exist, open fails
noreplace	If file exists, open fails unless appending or seeking to end of file on opening

The default access mode for file access is *text mode*. A text file is an ASCII file, compatible with most other programming languages and applications. Text files do not always contain text, in the word-processing sense of the word. Any data you have to store can go in a text file. Programs that read ASCII files can read data you create as C++ text files.

If you specify binary access, C++ creates or reads the file in a binary format. Binary data files are "squeezed"—that is, they take less space than text files. The disadvantage of using binary files is that other programs cannot always read the data files. Only C++ programs written to access binary files can read and write to them. The advantage of binary files is that you save disk space because your data files are more compact. Other than the access mode in the open() function, you use no additional commands to access binary files with your C++ programs.

> **NOTE:** The binary format is a system-specific file format. In other words, not all computers can read a binary file created on another computer.

If you open a file for writing, C++ creates the file. If a file by that name already exists, C++ overwrites the old file with no warning. You must be careful when opening files to not overwrite existing data that you want to save.

If an error occurs during the opening of a file, C++ does not create a valid file pointer. Instead, C++ creates a file pointer equal to zero. For example, if you open a file for output, but use an invalid disk name, C++ cannot open the file and therefore makes the file pointer equal to zero. Always check the file pointer when writing disk file programs to ensure that the file opened properly.

> **TIP:** Beginning programmers like to open all files at the beginning of their programs and close them at the end. This is not always the best method. Open files immediately before you access them and close them as soon as you are done with them. This protects the files, keeping them open only as long as needed. A closed file is more likely to be protected in the unfortunate (but possible) event of a power failure or computer breakdown.

Suppose that you want to create a file for storing your house payment records for the preceding year. Here are the first few lines in the program that creates a file called HOUSE.DAT on your disk:

```
#include <fstream.h>

main()
{
    ofstream filePtr;   // Declares a file pointer for writing
    filePtr.open("house.dat", ios::out);   // Creates the file
```

The remainder of this program writes data to the file. The program never has to refer to the filename again. The program uses the *filePtr* variable to refer to the file. Programs in the next few sections illustrate how. There is nothing special about *filePtr*, other than its name (although the name is meaningful in this case). You can name file pointer variables XYZ or a908973 if you like, but these names are not meaningful.

You must include the fstream.h header file because it contains the definition for the ofstream and ifstream declarations. You don't have to worry about the physical specifics. The *filePtr* "points" to data in the file as you write it. Put the declarations in your programs where you declare other variables and arrays.

> **TIP:** Because files are not part of your program, you might find it useful to declare file pointers globally. Unlike data in variables, there is rarely a reason to keep file pointers local.

Before finishing with the program, you should close the file. The following `close()` function closes the house file:

```
filePtr.close();   // Closes the house payment file
```

Write an `open()` function that opens a file named `house.dat` and that resides on drive D in a directory named `mydata`.

If you want to, you can store a filename in a character array or point to it with a character pointer. Each of the following sections of code is equivalent:

```
char fn[] = "house.dat";   // Filename in character array
filePtr.open(fn, ios::out);   // Creates the file

char *myfile = "house.dat";   // Filename pointed to
filePtr.open(myfile, ios::out);   // Creates the file

// Enables the user to enter the filename
cout << "What is the name of the household file? ";
gets(filename);   // Filename must be a character pointer
filePtr.open(filename, ios::out);   // Creates the file
```

No matter how you specify the filename when opening the file, close the file with the file pointer. This `close()` function closes the open file, no matter which method you used to open the file:

```
filePtr.close();   // Closes the house payment file
```

You should check the return value from `open()` to ensure that the file opened properly. Here is code after `open()` that checks for an error:

```
#include <fstream.h>

main()
{
   ofstream filePtr;   // Declares a file pointer

   filePtr.open("house.dat", ios::out);   // Creates the file
   if (!filePtr)
   { cout << "Error opening file.\n"; }
   else
   {
      // Rest of output commands go here
}
```

You can open and write to several files in the same program. Suppose that you wanted to read data from a payroll file and create a backup payroll data file. You would have to open the current payroll file using the in reading mode and the backup file in the output out mode.

For each open file in your program, you must declare a different file pointer. The file pointers that your input and output statements use determine on which file they operate. If you have to open many files, you can declare an array of file pointers.

Here is a way you can open the two payroll files:

```
#include <fstream.h>

ifstream   fileIn;    // Input file
ofstream   fileOut;   // Output file

main()
{
    fileIn.open("payroll.dat", ios::in);    // Existing file
    fileOut.open("payroll.BAK", ios::out);   // New file
```

Writing to a File

Any input or output function that requires a device performs input and output with files. You have seen most of these already. The most common file I/O functions are

```
get() and put()
gets() and puts()
```

You also can use *filePtr* as you do with cout or cin.

The following function call reads three integers from a file pointed to by *filePtr*:

```
filePtr >> num1 >> num2 >> num3;    // Reads three variables
```

There is always more than one way to write data to a disk file. Most of the time, more than one function will work. For example, if you write many names to a file, both puts() and *filePtr* << work. You also can write the names using put(). You should use whichever function you are most comfortable with. If you want a newline character (\n) at the end of each line in your file, *filePtr* << and puts() probably would be easier than put(), but all three will do the job.

> **TIP:** Each line in a file is called a record. By putting a newline character at the end of file records, you make the input of those records easier.

The following program creates a file called NAMES.DAT, which writes five names to a disk file using *filePtr* <<.

```
// Filename: WR1.CPP
// Writes five names to a disk file
#include <fstream.h>

ofstream fp;

void main()
{
    fp.open("NAMES.DAT", ios::out);   // Creates a new file

    fp << "Daniel Marino\n";
    fp << "Donny Shula\n";
    fp << "Lawrence Csonka\n";
    fp << "Marc Duper\n";
    fp << "Joe Robbie\n";
    fp.close();   // Releases the file
    return;
}
```

To keep this program simple, error checking was not done on the open() function. The next few programs check for errors.

NAMES.DAT is a text data file. If you want to, you can read this file into your word processor (use your word processor's command for reading ASCII files) or use the MS-DOS TYPE command (or your operating system's equivalent command) to display this file on-screen. If you were to display NAMES.TXT, you would see:

```
Daniel Marino
Donny Shula
Lawrence Csonka
Marc Duper
Joe Robbie
```

The following file writes the numbers from 1 to 100 to a file called NUMS.1.

```
// Filename: WR2.CPP
// Writes 1 to 100 to a disk file

#include <fstream.h>

ofstream  fp;

void main()
{
   int ctr;

   fp.open("NUMS.1", ios::out);    // Creates a new file
   if (!fp)    // Checks for error
     {  cout << "Error opening file.\n"; }
   else
     {
        for (ctr = 1; ctr < 101; ctr++)
           {  fp << ctr << " "; }
     }
   fp.close();
   return;
}
```

The numbers are not written one per line, but with a space between each of them. The format of the *filePtr* << determines the format of the output data. When writing data to disk files, keep in mind that you have to read the data later. You have to use "mirror-image" input functions to read data you output to files.

Writing to a Printer

Functions such as open() and others were not designed to write only to files. They were designed to write to any device, including files, the screen, and the printer. If you must write data to a printer, you can treat the printer as if it were a file. The following program opens a file pointer using the MS-DOS name for a printer located at LPT1 (the MS-DOS name for the first parallel printer port):

```
// Filename: PRNT.CPP
// Prints to the printer device

#include <fstream.h>
```

```
ofstream prnt;    // Points to the printer

void main()
{
   prnt.open("LPT1", ios::out);
   prnt << "Printer line 1\n";   // First line printed
   prnt << "Printer line 2\n";   // Second line printed
   prnt << "Printer line 3\n";   // Third line printed
   prnt.close();
return;
}
```

Make sure that your printer is on and has paper before you run this program. When you run the program, you see this printed on the paper:

```
Printer line 1
Printer line 2
Printer line 3
```

Adding to a File

You can easily add data to an existing file, or create new files, by opening the file in append access mode. Data files on the disk rarely are static; they grow almost daily (hopefully!) due to increased business. Being able to add to data already on the disk is very useful.

Files you open for append access (using ios::app) do not have to exist. If the file exists, C++ appends data to the end of the file when you write the data. If the file does not exist, C++ creates the file (as is done when you open a file for write access).

The following program adds three more names to the NAMES.DAT file created in an earlier program (WR1.CPP).

```
// Filename: AP1.CPP
// Adds three names to a disk file
#include <fstream.h>
ofstream  fp;
void main()
{
   fp.open("NAMES.DAT", ios::app);   // Adds to file
   fp << "Johnny Smith\n";
   fp << "Laura Hull\n";
```

```
    fp << "Mark Brown\n";
    fp.close();    // Releases the file
    return;
}
```

Write the contents of NAMES.DAT after this program finishes. Remember that the three names are appended to the end of the previous five names that were written.

> **NOTE:** If the file does not exist, C++ creates it and stores the three names to the file.

Basically, you have to change only the open() function's access mode to turn a file-creation program into a file-appending program.

Reading from a File

As soon as the data is in a file, you must be able to read that data. You must open the file in a read-access mode. There are several ways to read data. You can read character data one character at a time or one string at a time. The choice depends on the data's format.

Files you open for read access (using ios::in) must exist already, or C++ gives you an error message. You cannot read a file that does not exist. open() returns zero if the file does not exist when you open it for read access.

Another event happens when you read files. Eventually, you read all the data. Subsequent reading produces errors because there is no more data to read. C++ provides a solution to the end-of-file occurrence. If you

attempt to read from a file that you have completely read the data from, C++ returns the value of zero. To find the end-of-file condition, be sure to check for zero when reading information from files.

The following program asks the user for a filename and prints the contents of the file to the screen. If the file does not exist, the program displays an error message.

```cpp
// Filename: RE1.CPP
// Reads and displays a file

#include <fstream.h>
#include <stdlib.h>

ifstream fp;

void main()
{
   char filename[12];   // Holds user's filename
   char inChar;    // Inputs character

   cout << "What is the name of the file you want to see? ";
   cin >> filename;
   fp.open(filename, ios::in);
   if (!fp)
   {
     cout << "\n\n*** That file does not exist ***\n";
     exit(0);   // Exits program
   }
   while (fp.get(inChar))
     {  cout << inChar;  }
   fp.close();
   return;
}
```

Here is the output when the NAMES.DAT file is requested:

```
What is the name of the file you want to see? NAMES.DAT
Daniel Marino
Donny Shula
Lawrence Csonka
Marc Duper
Joe Robbie
Johnny Smith
```

552

Laura Hull

Mark Brown

Because newline characters are in the file at the end of each name, the names appear on-screen, one per line. If you attempt to read a file that does not exist, the program displays the following message:

```
*** That file does not exist ***
```

This program is supposed to read one file and copy it to another, one character at a time. You might want to use such a program to back up important data in case the original file is damaged.

The program must open two files, the first for reading and the second for writing. The file pointer determines which of the two files is being accessed. Finish the program so that it copies the file correctly.

```cpp
// Filename: FCOPY.CPP
// Makes a copy of a file
#include <fstream.h>
#include <stdlib.h>

ifstream inFp;
ofstream outFp;

void main()
{
   char inFilename[12];   // Holds original filename
   char outFilename[12];   // Holds backup filename
   char inChar;   // Inputs character

   cout << "What is the name of the file you want to"
        << " back up? ";
   cin >> inFilename;
   cout << "What is the name of the file ";
   cout << "you want to copy " << inFilename << " to? ";
   cin >> outFilename;
   inFp.open(inFilename, ios::in);
   if (!inFp)
   {
     cout << "\n\n*** " << inFilename
          << " does not exist ***\n";
     exit(0);   // Exits program
   }
```

```
outFp.open(outFilename, ios::out);
   if (!outFp)
   {
      cout << "\n\n*** Error opening "
           << inFilename << " ***\n";
      exit(0);   // Exits program
   }
   cout << "\nCopying...\n";   // Waiting message




   cout << "\nThe file is copied.\n";
   inFp.close();
   outFp.close();
   return;
}
```

Review Questions

1. What are the three ways to access sequential files?

2. What advantage do disk files have over holding data in memory?

3. How do sequential files differ from random-access files?

4. What happens if you open a file for read access and the file does not exist?

5. What happens if you open a file for write access and the file already exists?

6. What happens if you open a file for append access and the file does not exist?

7. How does C++ inform you that you have reached the end-of-file condition?

Review Exercises

1. Write a program that creates a file containing the following data:

   Your name
   Your address
   Your phone number
   Your age

2. Write a second program that reads and prints the data file you created in Exercise 1.

3. Write a program that takes the data created in Exercise 1 and writes it to the screen, one word per line.

4. Write a program for PCs that backs up two important files—the AUTOEXEC.BAT and the CONFIG.SYS. Call the backup files AUTOEXEC.SAV and CONFIG.SAV.

5. Write a program that reads a file and creates a new file with the same data, but reverse the case on the second file. In other words, everywhere uppercase letters appear in the first file, write lowercase letters to the new file, and everywhere lowercase letters appear in the first file, write uppercase letters to the new file.

Random-Access Files

To teach you how to read and write random-access files that give you the ability to "move around" in the file, reading and writing nonsequentially.

Random file access enables you to read or write any data in your disk file without having to read or write every piece of data that precedes it. You can quickly search for, add, retrieve, change, and delete information in a random-access file. Although you need to learn a few new functions to access files randomly, the extra effort pays off in flexibility, power, and speed of disk access.

This lesson ends the basics of C++ programming. When you began reading this book, you might have been a beginning programmer. After this lesson, you will know all the fundamentals needed to write C++ programs that do what you want.

Random File Records

Random files exemplify the power of data processing with C++. Sequential file processing can be slow unless you read the entire file into arrays and process them in memory. As explained in Lesson 32, "Sequential Files," you have much more disk space than RAM, and most disk files do not even fit in your RAM at one time. Therefore, you need a way to quickly read individual pieces of data from a file in any order and process them one at a time.

Generally, you read and write file *records*. A record to a file is analogous to a C++ structure. A record is a collection of one or more data values (called *fields*) that you read and write to disk. Generally, you store data in structures and write the structures to disk, where they are called records. When you read a record from disk, you generally read that record into a structure variable and process it with your program.

Unlike with most programming languages, not all disk data for C++ programs must be stored in record format. Typically, you write a stream of characters to a disk file and access that data either sequentially or randomly by reading it into variables and structures.

The process of randomly accessing data in a file is simple. Think about the data files of a large credit card organization. When you make a purchase, the store calls the credit card company to receive authorization. Millions of names are in the credit card company's files. There is no quick way that the company can read every record sequentially from the disk that comes before yours. Sequential files do not lend themselves to quick access. It is not feasible, in many situations, to look up individual records in a data file with sequential access.

Credit card companies must use random file access so that their computers can go directly to your record, just as you go directly to a song on a compact disk or a record album. The functions that you use are different from the sequential functions, but the power that results from learning the added functions is worth the effort.

When your program reads and writes files randomly, it treats the file like a big array. You know that with arrays you can add, print, or remove values in any order. You do not have to start with the first array element, sequentially looking at the next one, until you get the element you need. You can view your random-access file in the same way, accessing the data in any order.

Most random file records are *fixed-length* records. Each record (usually a row in the file) takes the same amount of disk space. Most of the sequential files you read and wrote in the previous lessons were variable-length records. When you are reading or writing sequentially, there is no need for fixed-length records because you input each value one character, word, string, or number at a time, and look for the data you want. With fixed-length records, your computer can better calculate where on the disk the desired record is located.

Although you waste some disk space with fixed-length records (because of the spaces that pad some of the fields), the advantages of random file access compensate for the "wasted" disk space (when the data does not actually fill the structure size).

> **TIP:** With random-access files, you can read or write records in any order. Therefore, even if you want to perform sequential reading or writing of the file, you can use random-access processing and "randomly" read or write the file in sequential record number order.

A record in C++ is nothing more than a structure variable. Because all variables of the same structure are the same size, when you read and write structure variables, you are reading and writing fixed-length data values. Working with fixed-length (all the same size) data values gives you the capability to move around in the file, reading and writing any structure in the file. If structure variables (derived from the same structure definition) were variable-length, you would never know how far to "move" in the file when you wanted to skip ahead five records.

Opening Random-Access Files

As with sequential files, you must open random-access files before reading or writing to them. You can use any of the read access modes (such as ios::in) mentioned in Lesson 32, "Sequential Files," if you are only going to read a file randomly. However, to modify data in a file, you must open the file in one of the update modes listed in Table 33.1.

Table 33.1. Random-access update modes.

Mode	Description
app	Opens file for appending (adding to it)
ate	Seeks to end of file on opening it
in	Opens file for reading
out	Opens file for writing
binary	Opens file in binary mode
trunc	Discards contents if file exists
nocreate	If file doesn't exist, open fails
noreplace	If file exists, open fails unless you are appending or seeking to end of file on opening

There is really no difference between sequential files and random files in C++. The difference between the files is not physical, but lies in the method that you use to access them and update them.

Suppose that you want to write a program to create a file of your friends' names. The following open() function call suffices, assuming that fp is declared as a file pointer:

```
fp.open("NAMES.DAT", ios::out);
if (!fp)
   { cout << "\n*** Cannot open file ***\n";
     exit(1);}   // Exits the program if an error occurs
```

No update open() access mode is needed if you are only creating the file. The !fp check ensures that the file opened properly. If an error occurred (such as an open disk drive door), open() would return a null pointer (equal to zero), so !fp means if *not true*. If it is not true that the file opened properly, issue an error message.

However, what if you wanted to create the file, write names to it, and give the user a chance to change any of the names before closing the file? You then would have to open the file like this:

```
fp.open("NAMES.DAT", ios::in ¦ ios::out);
if (!fp)
   { cout << "\n*** Cannot open file ***\n";
     exit(1); }   // Exits the program if an error occurs
```

560

This code enables you to create the file, then change data you wrote to the file. The ¦ symbol is called a *bitwise OR operator*. The bitwise OR operator is used for very advanced programming applications. Despite its advanced use, all you have to do to use the bitwise OR operator in the open() function is put it between two or more of the modes you want C++ to use for open().

Write the open() (along with an error check) that opens a file for append mode (meaning that you want to add to it). Make sure that the file exists. If it doesn't, print an error message and exit the program. *Hint:* You must use two of the modes from Table 33.1.

As with sequential files, the only difference between using a binary open() access mode and a text mode is that the file you create is more compact and saves disk space. You cannot, however, read that file from other programs as an ASCII text file. The preceding open() function can be rewritten to create and allow updating of a binary file. All other file-related commands and functions work for binary files just as they do for text files.

```
fp.open("NAMES.DAT", ios::in ¦ ios::out ¦ ios::binary);
if (!fp)
    { cout << "\n*** Cannot open file ***\n";
      exit(1); }   // Exits the program if an error occurs
```

The seekg() Function

As you read and write disk files, C++ keeps track of a file pointer. When you first open the file for reading or writing, the file pointer points to the very first byte in the file. When you open the file for appending, the file pointer points to the end of the file (so that you can write to the end of it). You do not always want to begin reading or writing at the location of the file pointer. (If you did, you probably would be using a sequential mode.)

C++ provides the seekg() function, which enables you to move the file pointer to a specific point in a random-access data file. The format of seekg() is

```
filePtr.seekg(longNum, origin);
```

filePtr is the pointer to the file that you want to access, initialized with an open() statement. *longNum* is the number of bytes you want to skip in the file. C++ does not read this many bytes, but it literally skips the data by the number of bytes specified in *longNum*. Skipping the bytes on the disk is much faster than reading them. If *longNum* is negative, C++ skips backwards in the file (which allows for rereading of data several times). Because data files can be large, you must declare *longNum* as a long integer to hold a large number of bytes.

origin is a value that tells C++ where to begin the skipping of bytes specified by *longNum*. *origin* can be any of the three values shown in Table 33.2.

Table 33.2. Possible origin values.

C++ Name	Description
ios::beg	Beginning of file
ios::cur	Current file position
ios::end	End of file

The names ios::beg, ios::cur, and ios::end are defined in fstream.h.

No matter how far into a file you have read, the following seekg() function positions the file pointer at the beginning of a file:

```
fp.seekg(0L, ios::beg);  // Positions file pointer at beginning
```

The constant 0L passes a long integer 0 to the seekg() function. Without the L, C++ passes a regular integer. This does not match the prototype for seekg() that is located in fstream.h. Lesson 5, "C++ Numeric Data," explained the use of data type suffixes on numeric constants, but the suffixes have not been used until now.

This seekg() function literally reads "Move the file pointer 0 bytes from the beginning of the file."

The following program reads a file named MYFILE.TXT twice, once to send the file to the screen and once to send the file to the printer. Three file pointers are used, one for each device (the file, the screen, and the printer).

```
// Filename: TWIC.CPP
// Writes a file to the printer, rereads it,
// and sends it to the screen

#include <fstream.h>
#include <stdlib.h>
#include <stdio.h>

ifstream inFile;   // Inputs file pointer
ofstream scrn;     // Screen pointer
ofstream prnt;     // Printer pointer

void main()
{
   char inChar;

   inFile.open("MYFILE.TXT", ios::in);
   if (!inFile)
   {
      cout << "\n*** Error opening MYFILE.TXT ***\n";
      exit(0);
   }
   scrn.open("CON", ios::out);   // Opens screen device
   while (inFile.get(inChar))
   { scrn << inChar; }    // Outputs characters to the screen
   scrn.close();   // Closes screen because it
                   // is no longer needed
   inFile.seekg(0L, ios::beg);   // Repositions file pointer
   prnt.open("LPT1", ios::out);   // Opens printer device
   while (inFile.get(inChar))
     { prnt << inChar; }   // Outputs characters to the printer
   prnt.close();   // Always close all open files
   inFile.close();
   return;
}
```

The important aspect of this program is that the file is opened only once, although it is read twice. The seekg() function backs up the file pointer to the beginning of the file before rereading it.

You could also close and then reopen a file to position the file pointer at the beginning, but using seekg() is more efficient.

 You could have used regular I/O functions to write to the screen, rather than opening the screen as a separate device. This program simply shows that the screen can be treated as another file (a special file, however) that you can perform output to.

The following `seekg()` function positions the file pointer at the 30th byte in the file. (The next byte read is the 31st byte.)

```
filePtr.seekg(30L, ios::beg);   // Positions file pointer
                                // at the 30th byte
```

This `seekg()` function literally reads "Move the file pointer 30 bytes from the beginning of the file."

If you write structures to a file, you can quickly seek any structure in the file using the `sizeof()` function. Suppose that you want the 123rd occurrence of the structure tagged with `inventory`. You would search using the following `seekg()` function:

```
filePtr.seekg((123L * sizeof(struct inventory)), ios::beg);
```

 Write the `seekg()` function that would move the file pointer to the second structure (whose structure tag is `Data`) in a file.

The following program writes the letters of the alphabet to a file called ALPH.TXT. The `seekg()` function is then used to read and display the ninth and 17th letters (I and Q).

```cpp
// Filename: ALPH.CPP
// Stores the alphabet in a file, then reads
// two letters from it

#include <fstream.h>
#include <stdlib.h>
#include <stdio.h>

fstream fp;

void main()
{
    char ch;    // Holds A through Z

    // Opens in update mode so that you can
    // read file after writing to it
    fp.open("alph.txt", ios::in | ios::out);
```

```
    if (!fp)
    {
      cout << "\n*** Error opening file ***\n";
      exit(0);
    }
    for (ch = 'A'; ch <= 'Z'; ch++)
    { fp << ch;  }    // Writes letters
    fp.seekg(8L, ios::beg);  // Skips eight letters, points to I
    fp >> ch;
    cout << "The first character is " << ch << "\n";
    fp.seekg(16L, ios::beg);   // Skips 16 letters, points to Q
    fp >> ch;
    cout << "The second character is " << ch << "\n";
    fp.close();
    return;
}
```

To point to the end of a data file, you can use the seekg() function to position the file pointer at the last byte. Subsequent seekg()s should then use a negative *longNum* value to skip backwards in the file. The following seekg() function makes the file pointer point to the end of the file:

```
filePtr.seekg(0L, ios::beg);    // Positions file
                                // pointer at the end
```

This seekg() function literally reads "Move the file pointer 0 bytes from the end of the file." The file pointer now points to the end-of-file marker, but you can seekg() backwards to find other data in the file.

The following program is supposed to read the ALPH.TXT file (created in the preceding program, ALPH.CPP) backwards, printing each character as it skips back in the file. Finish the body of the code (with an appropriate seekg() function) so that it does this.

Be sure that your seekg() in this program seeks two bytes backwards from the *current position,* not from the beginning or the end as the previous programs in this lesson have. The for loop toward the end of the program needs to perform a "skip-two-bytes-back, read-one-byte-forward" method to skip through the file backwards.

```
// Reads and prints a file backwards
#include <fstream.h>
#include <stdlib.h>
#include <stdio.h>
```

```
ifstream fp;

void main()
{
   int ctr;    // Steps through the 26 letters in the file
   char inChar;

   fp.open("ALPH.TXT", ios::in);
   if (!fp)
   {
     cout << "\n*** Error opening file ***\n";
     exit(0);
   }
   fp.seekg(-1L, ios::end);   // Points to last byte
                              // in the file
   for (ctr = 0; ctr < 26; ctr++)
   {
      fp >> inChar;


      cout << inChar;
   }
   fp.close();
   return;
}
```

The following program attempts to perform the same action as ALPH.CPP, with one addition. When the letters I and Q are found, the letter x is written over the I and the Q. Something is wrong, however, in two lines. See whether you can fix the program. To see what the program does when it contains the two bugs, run the program as is and look at the data file it creates (by loading the ALPH.TXT data file into your program editor).

```
// Filename: CHANGBUG.CPP
// Stores the alphabet in a file, reads two letters from it,
// and changes those letters to x

#include <fstream.h>
#include <stdlib.h>
#include <stdio.h>
```

```
fstream fp;

void main()
{
   char ch;    // Holds A through Z

   // Opens in update mode so that you can
   // read file after writing to it
   fp.open("alph.txt", ios::in | ios::out);
   if (!fp)
   {
     cout << "\n*** Error opening file ***\n";
     exit(0);
   }
   for (ch = 'A'; ch <= 'Z'; ch++)
      { fp << ch; }    // Writes letters
   fp.seekg(8L, ios::beg);  // Skips eight letters, points to I
   fp >> ch;
   // Changes the Q to an x
   fp.seekg(-2L, ios::cur);
   fp << 'x';
   cout << "The first character is " << ch << "\n";
   fp.seekg(16L, ios::beg);   // Skips 16 letters, points to Q
   fp >> ch;
   cout << "The second character is " << ch << "\n";
   // Changes the Q to an x
   fp.seekg(-2L, ios::cur);
   fp << 'x';
   fp.close();
   return;
}
```

The preceding program (as soon as it works correctly) forms the basis of a more complete data file management program. After you master the seekg() functions and become more familiar with disk data files, you will begin to write programs that store more advanced data structures and access them.

Other Helpful I/O Functions

Several more disk I/O functions that you might find useful are available. They are mentioned here for completeness. As you perform more powerful disk I/O, you might find a use for many of these functions.

- read(*array, count*): Reads the data specified by *count* into the array or pointer specified by *array*. read() is called a *buffered I/O function*. read() enables you to read much data with a single function call. This function is prototyped in fstream.h.

- write(*array, count*): Writes *count array* bytes to the specified file. write() is a buffered I/O function that enables you to write much data in a single function call. *Note:* The write() function is a perfect complement to the read() function. Try not to mix your I/O routines. If you write to a file using write(), read from it using read(). This function is prototyped in fstream.h.

- remove(*filename*): Erases the file named by *filename*. remove() returns a 0 if the file was erased successfully or –1 if an error occurred. This function is prototyped in stdio.h

Many of these functions (and other built-in I/O functions that you will learn in your C++ programming career) are helpful functions that you could duplicate using what you already know.

The following program requests a filename from the user and erases the file from the disk using the remove() function.

```
// Filename: ERAS.CPP
// Erases the file specified by the user

#include <stdio.h>
#include <iostream.h>

void main()
{
   char filename[12];

   cout << "What is the filename you want me to erase? ";
   cin >> filename;
   if (remove(filename) == -1)
   {  cout << "\n*** I could not remove the file ***\n"; }
   else
   {  cout << "\nThe file " << filename
           << " is now removed\n";}
   return;
}
```

The following function is part of a larger program that receives inventory data in an array of structures from the user. This function is passed the array name and the number of elements (structure variables) in the array. The `write()` function then writes the complete array of structures to the disk file pointed to by `fp`.

```
void writeStr(inventory items[ ], int invCnt)
{
   fp.write(items, invCnt * sizeof(inventory);
   return;
}
```

`write()` (and its mirror-image, `read()`) is extremely powerful. If the inventory array had 1,000 elements, this one-line function would still write the entire array to the disk file! You could use the `read()` function to read the entire array of structures from the disk in a single function call.

Review Questions

1. What is the difference between records and structures?

2. TRUE or FALSE: You have to create a random-access file before reading from it randomly.

3. Where is the file pointer pointing when you first open a disk file for append mode?

4. What happens to the file pointer as you read from a file?

5. What are the two buffered file I/O functions?

6. What is wrong with this program?

   ```
   #include <fstream.h>
   ifstream  fp;
   void main()
   {
      char inChar;
      fp.open(ios::in ¦ ios::binary);
      if (fp.get(inChar))
      { cout << inChar;  }   // Writes to the screen
      fp.close();
      return;
   }
   ```

569

Review Exercises

1. Write a program that asks the user for a list of five names, then writes the names to a file. Display its contents on-screen using the seekg() and get() functions.

2. Rewrite the program in Exercise 1 so that it displays every other character in the file of names.

3. Write a program that reads characters from a file. If the input character is a lowercase letter, change it to uppercase. If the input character is an uppercase letter, change it to lowercase. Do not change other characters in the file.

4. Write a program that displays the number of nonalphabetic characters in a file.

5. Write a grade-keeping program for a teacher. Allow the teacher to enter up to 10 students' grades. Each student has three grades for the semester. Store the students' names and their three grades in an array of structures and store the data on the disk. Make the program menu-driven. Include options of adding more students, viewing the file's data, or printing the grades to the printer with a calculated class average.

Introduction to OOP

To explain the concepts that separate object-oriented programming techniques from those that are non-object-oriented.

This lesson introduces the future of programming—object-oriented programming with C++. Many people believe that object-oriented programming, or *OOP,* will become the dominant programming technique of the 1990s. Several OOP programming languages are available today, but the one known and used most is C++.

This lesson presents an overview of some of the easier OOP techniques. Although veteran C++ programmers sometimes debate the issue, the majority (including this author) feel that a mastery of non-OOP C++ is a prerequisite to understanding object-oriented programming.

OOP Overview

When you program using objects, your data immediately becomes active instead of passive. Throughout this book, you have seen and written

programs that operated on data. The data just sat in variables and disk files until code in the program did something with the data (printed it, changed it, or whatever).

In OOP, data begins to take on responsibility for itself. It can initialize itself, print itself, and perform calculations on itself. This removes the burden of the programming task from the rest of the program. Instead of having to worry about the details of the data, you, the programmer, can concentrate on the important job at hand—the application you are writing.

An *object* is nothing more than a variable. Even integer variables and character variables are C++ objects. Generally, however, C++ program-mers reserve the term *object* for structure variables (as well as for *class* variables, which this lesson addresses in a later section). Because data becomes active, it takes on behaviors (the actions it is capable of) as well as properties (the data itself, such as the structure members).

It is in this way that objects begin to mirror real-world objects. If you write a program to track airplane flights, your data more closely simu-lates an airplane. It has properties (engine size, flight speed, maximum distance, and so on) and behaviors (it takes off, lands, radios to the control tower, and so on). Because the real-world objects you are programming are more closely simulated, a layer of abstraction is taken away from your programming chores. It is easier for you to model the real-world objects your program is simulating.

If your structure data "knows" how to initialize itself, if your structure data "knows" how to calculate itself, and if your structure data "knows" how to print itself, you would only have to write the code that triggers these actions and add a framework (the code around the objects) that deals with the user's I/O and puts the right objects in the right places. The petty details of programming would be lifted from your shoulders. Even most of a program's error checking would be done by the data itself so that your own program (main() and the rest of the code) would be cleaner and you would finish the program faster.

OOP also gives your data protection that goes far beyond that of local variables. Through *data hiding,* your variables are protected from acci-dentally being overwritten by the rest of the program. Only code that you specifically write for the data can access that data. The rest of the program must go through special functions called *member functions* to change or even look at your data.

One primary advantage of OOP is its maintainability. OOP programs are much easier to change when the application's needs change. Because all the code is *encapsulated* with the data (belongs to the data), you can easily "zero in" on the code that works with data and modify it without messing up anything else in the program. The data's code, through the data-hiding process just described, is the only code that can access the data. If the data format changes, such as the data type for one of the variables in a structure, you need to change only the variable's code, and the rest of the program implements the change seamlessly.

Another advantage of OOP is its *extensibility*. Extensibility means that you can extend the capabilities of a C++ program easily. In Lesson 22, "Default Arguments and Function Overloading," you learned about C++'s capability to overload functions. Overloading functions is C++'s first step in overloading operators as well. By overloading operators, you can make C++'s built-in operators work on data you define, such as adding together two structures. Objects also can be inherited so that you don't always have to "reinvent the wheel" by rewriting similar code. You only have to inherit code from a similar object.

Some concepts, such as operator overloading and inheritance, go far beyond the scope of this book. Therefore, if you are still confused as to what these techniques are all about, be assured that a full understanding of OOP does not come without some patience and work.

Data with Functions

After the earlier lessons in this book, you should have no trouble understanding the following:

```
struct Inventory {
   char name[15];
   int quantity;
   float price;
};
```

This code simply declares a structure tagged with the name Inventory. You can define variables that take on the format of the Inventory structure like this:

```
struct Inventory part1, part2, part3;
```

The struct keyword is optional. There are now three occurrences of Inventory variables. In OOP terminology, you would say that you have defined three objects named part1, part2, and part3.

As mentioned earlier in this lesson, OOP data can take on active roles in the program, including initializing themselves and printing themselves. If you have programmed before, the following concept might seem strange to you, but it is the foundation of C++ OOP.

To make your data active, you can *add functions to your structure definitions*. These functions, called *member functions* (and sometimes called *methods*) operate on the rest of the structure data. Here is an example of very short functions inside the Inventory structure:

```
struct Inventory {
   char name[15];
   int quantity;
   float price;
   void init(char n[], int q, float p)    // Member function
               { strcpy(name, n);
                 quantity = q;
                 price = p; }
   void prInv() { cout << "\nName: " << name << "\n";
                  cout << "Quantity: " << quantity << "\n";
                  cout << "Price: " << price << "\n"; }
};
```

Now the data is active! It contains not only data, but also member functions.

> **NOTE:** In reality, the C++ compiler does not really put the member functions inside the structure variables (the objects). Nevertheless, you can program as though the data and functions are closely tied, with the structure variables actually containing code.

By placing the member function code inside the structure itself, you help ensure that C++ will inline those functions. Although C++ does not guarantee that an inline will take place, short member functions defined directly inside the structure almost always are placed inline by the C++ compiler, thereby improving the function's efficiency.

 The member functions inside the structure perform the actions on your data. Because data items inside structures are called *members,* C++ programmers call the functions inside structures *member functions.*

In order to keep the object's description cleaner, most C++ program-mers prefer to prototype their member functions and place the code below the structure declaration. Here is how you do so:

```
struct Inventory {
   char name[15];
   int quantity;
   float price;
   void init(char n[], int q, float p);   // Prototype
   void prInv();
};

void Inventory::init(char n[], int q, float p)   // Member
                                                 // function
{ strcpy(name, n);
  quantity = q;
  price = p; }


void Inventory::prInv()
{ cout << "\nName: " << name << "\n";
  cout << "Quantity: " << quantity << "\n";
  cout << "Price: " << price << "\n"; }
```

The member functions `init()` and `prInv()` can go anywhere later in the program, even after `main()`. Sometimes they are not even in the same source file as the structure declaration. The only requirement for placing them outside the structure is that you must precede their name with the structure tag name, followed by the *scope resolution operator,* `::`. The scope resolution operator tells C++ that the functions are members of the structure tagged with the `Inventory` structure.

NOTE: If there were several different structures in the program, each of them could have their own version of the `init()` and `prInv()` member functions. Because each of their member functions' code would be scoped with `::`, C++ would know how to match the proper member functions to the proper structure.

Rewrite the following structure definition with the member functions appearing after the structure declaration.

```
struct sData {
   int i;
   void pr() {cout << "\n"; cout << "i is " << i << "\n";}
```

```
    int doub() { return 2 * i;}
    void in(int I) { i = I; };
};
```

You can define three of the `Inventory` structure variables (three objects) just as you would before you learned about member functions. Here is the statement that does so:

```
Inventory part1, part2, part3;
```

Executing the Member Functions

As you have seen throughout the last few lessons of this book, you can access a data member in a structure variable by using the dot operator, such as this:

```
part1.quantity = 14;    // Assigns 14 to the quantity
                        // of first part
```

You also execute member functions with the dot operator. The following line calls the member function `init()` for part3:

```
part3.init("Widget", 43, 12.95);   // Initializes first part
```

In effect, the object, part3, is doing the work. `main()` does not have to have any printing code cluttering up its code. All the printing of the part3 object is included in the object's description.

In C++ terminology, the preceding statement *sends a message* to the object. The message tells part3 to initialize itself with the three values in the member function's parentheses. Because the code is localized in the structure, you can easily find it and modify it instead of searching throughout the primary program, looking for something related to printing an Inventory object.

Data Hiding with Classes

The Inventory objects are not yet hidden from the rest of the program. Therefore, nothing stops you from doing this:

```
part3.quantity = -56;    // Assigns a bad quantity!
```

There can be no negative quantity of an inventory item. Nevertheless, the structure is just too available to main() and other functions in which part3 is visible. To achieve the true data hiding mentioned earlier, you must learn how to program with classes.

The designers of C++ added *classes* to better protect data members. A class is nothing more than a structure, with one and only one exception: a class is all *private* and a structure is *public*. By being public, a structure makes its members available to any part of the program that has access to the structure variables.

If you declare your objects with a class statement instead of a struct statement, no code in the rest of the program can change or even look at the data members. Here is the previous Inventory structure rewritten as a class:

```
class Inventory {
   char name[15];
   int quantity;
   float price;
   void init(char n[], int q, float p);    // Prototype
   void prInv();
};
```

The code in the member functions can follow a class, just as they can a struct, as long as you precede the member function name with the class name followed by the scope resolution operator. This class definition is exactly the same as the corresponding struct, except that all of its

members, both data and functions, are private. Therefore, no code in the rest of the program has any access to the data members or the member functions. The following is not allowed:

```
main()
{
    class part1, part2, part3;   // Okay
    part1.quantity = 31;   // * Not valid *
    // Rest of program follows
```

main() can define three class variables, but it cannot access the private members in the class variables. main() cannot assign quantity or any other data member a value, even though part1 is visible to main(). All of part1 is private, even the member functions of part1. main() is not allowed to initialize any of the class variables. The following is not allowed in main():

```
part1.init("Gizmo", 53, 9.29);   // Not allowed in main()
```

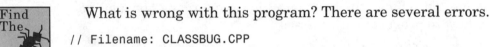

What is wrong with this program? There are several errors.

```
// Filename: CLASSBUG.CPP
#include <iostream.h>
class Date {
    int day;
    int month;
    int year;
    void prDate();
    void setDay(int d);
    void setMonth(int m);
    void setYear(int y);
};

void prDate()
{
    cout << "Date: " << day << "/" << month << "/"
        << year << "\n";
}

void setDay(int d)
{
    day = d;
}

void setMonth(int m)
```

```
{
   month = m;
}

void setyear(int y)
{
   year = y;
}

main()
{
   Date today;
   today.setDay(20);
   today.setMonth(6);
   today.setyear(1993);
   today.prDate();
}
```

Redefining Access

Structures are too accessible and classes are not accessible enough! There must be a way for the rest of the program to get to class data, or it would be useless. Therefore, C++ includes *access specifiers* that enable you to specify exactly which members of a class are private and which are public to the rest of the program. Appropriately enough, the access specifiers are named private and public.

> **NOTE:** You will learn more about a third access specifier, protected, when you tackle inheritance later in your OOP career.

Any class member function or data that follows a public access specifier is available to the rest of the program. All member functions and data that follow the private access specifier are hidden from (unavailable to) the rest of the program. In the following Date class, the three data members are private and the rest of the class is public:

```
class Date {
private:   // Not available to rest of program
   int day;
   int month;
   int year;
public:   // Available to rest of program
   void prDate();
   void setDay(int d);
   void setMonth(int m);
   void setYear(int y);
};
```

Because all `class` members are private by default (unlike structures, which are public by default), the `private` access specifier in the `Date` class is not necessary.

Now a wall is put between the `class` and the rest of the program. The rest of the program can change the private members, but only through controlled access via the `setDay()`, `setMonth()`, and `setYear()` member functions. The rest of the program also can see the private members, but only though the controlled access function named `prDate()`.

One big advantage of controlling the access to data is that the rest of the program does not care how the day, month, and year are stored. Because `main()` can print the values only by calling the `prDate()` member function of an object, `main()` neither knows nor cares how the `Date` class actually stores the date. Therefore, if the programmer decides to store the date in a different format, such as a compacted form in a `long int`, the rest of the program does not have to be changed. Only the access functions that set and print the data need to be changed.

Your OOP Future

OOP with C++ is not difficult. You can learn to program using OOP and program just as well and probably much better than if you had stayed with non-OOP C++. Object-oriented programming is just another way of approaching parts of programming problems. Even after you master OOP, not all of your code will look like an OOP program; a large

580

percentage of your code will look exactly like non-OOP programs look. Not all programming problems lend themselves to OOP, and not all C++ programs require OOP (as you have seen throughout this book).

If you are not ready to tackle the layers of OOP, rest assured that it will be a while before C++ with OOP is as popular a programming paradigm as non-OOP C and C++ are. Nevertheless, ready yourself for a future in OOP. If you still are uncomfortable with non-OOP C++, take the time to master it before moving to OOP. The foundation you acquire will pay off when you decide to tackle objects.

Where Do You Go From Here?

First of all, take a deserved rest! You have learned the fundamentals of C++, and you now know something about object-oriented programming with C++. Now you must write as many programs in C++ as you can to hone your skills until C++ programming becomes second nature.

To help guide you through some advanced C++ concepts, such as dynamic memory allocation and linked list programming, you should check out *Mastering Borland C++* or *Microsoft C/C++ 7 Developer's Guide*, both from Sams Publishing, which take a C++ programmer through more ad-vanced concepts than this book does. Although these books are not for C++ beginners, you are ready for them. You can begin to incorporate some more-advanced concepts into your programming repertoire.

As soon as you are comfortable with non-OOP C++, you might want to read *Moving from C to C++ (Sams Publishing, 1992)*. This book walks you through OOP concepts from the beginning, taking it easy in the early chapters so that you are prepared to tackle the heavy-duty OOP techniques toward the end. *Moving from C to C++* progresses though objects, classes, data hiding, inheritance (creating a `class` from an existing one), and many more OOP concepts. Although *Moving from C to C++* assumes that you know non-OOP C or C++, it does not assume that you know anything about objects. It takes you by the hand until you know the ins and outs of OOP.

Review Questions

1. What are objects?

2. Why do OOP objects have both properties *and* behaviors?

3. What are member functions?

4. What is the scope resolution operator? Why is it needed when you put member function code outside of a class?

5. TRUE or FALSE: When you put member function code directly inside a class, you are requesting that the function be inlined.

6. What is the OOP equivalent (almost) of a struct?

7. What is the only difference between a struct and a class?

8. What access specifiers were mentioned in this lesson?

9. Do you need the public access specifier when defining classes? Why or why not?

10. What is meant by "passing a message to an object"?

Review Exercises

1. Add to this lesson's Date class so that simple error checking is performed. Make sure that a day can never be more than 31, a month can never be more than 12, and a year can never be less than 1990.

2. Write a Time class program that tracks the current hour, minute, and second. Create an object called clock that is an instance (variable) of the Time class. Write a member function that initializes the time and one that prints it. Do not worry about recording accurate time. To initialize this "clock," call a single initialization function.

C++ Keywords

These are the 48 C++ standard keywords:

asm*	double	new*	switch
auto	else	operator*	template
break	enum	private*	this*
case	extern	protected*	throw*
catch*	float	public*	try*
char	for	register	typedef
class*	friend*	return	union
const	goto	short	unsigned
continue	if	signed	virtual*
default	inline*	sizeof	void
delete*	int	static	volatile
do	long	struct	while

*These keywords are specific to C++. All others exist in both C and C++.

> **NOTE:** The catch, throw, and try keywords are reserved for a future version of C++.

Memory and Numbering Systems

If you did not understand the discussion on hexadecimal numbers in Lesson 5, "C++ Numeric Data," this appendix provides a brief introduction to hexadecimal numbers. You do not have to understand the concepts in this appendix to become well-versed in C++. Some people program in C++ for years without ever learning about binary and hexadecimal numbering systems.

Many believe, however, that the more you know about what goes on "under the hood," the better you will be at programming, even if you never use hexadecimal numbers or the bitwise operators at all. The material presented here is not difficult, but many programmers choose not to take the time to study it.

Because this appendix is brief, you will not master these concepts just from reading it. Nevertheless, you will get a glimpse of the inner workings of your computer at the bit level. This appendix first teaches you about binary numbers and then moves on to hexadecimal numbers.

Computer Memory

Each memory location inside your computer holds a single character called a *byte*. If your computer contains 640K of memory, it can hold a total of approximately 640,000 bytes of memory. The *K* stands for 1,024, so 640K equals exactly 655,360 bytes, or characters, of memory. As soon as you fill your computer's memory with 640K of programs and data, there is no room for additional characters unless you overwrite something.

Each memory location in your computer has a unique *address*. A memory address is simply a sequential number, starting at 0, that labels each memory location. The second memory location is address 1, the third is address 2, and so on.

NOTE: Not all of your memory is available to C++ programs because the operating system uses some of it.

Eight Bits Make a Byte

The computer does not store characters in the same way that humans think of characters. For example, if you type a letter W on your keyboard while working in your C++ editor, you see the W on-screen, and you also know that the W is stored in a memory location at some unique address. Your computer does not actually store the letter W; it stores electrical impulses that stand for the letter W.

Electricity, which runs through the components of your computer and makes it understand and execute your programs, can exist in only two states—on or off. As with a light bulb, electricity is either flowing (it is on) or it is not flowing (it is off). Even though you can dim some lights, the electricity is still either on or off.

Your computer is nothing more than millions of on-and-off switches. You might have heard about the integrated circuits, transistors, and even vacuum tubes that computers have contained over the years. These electrical components are nothing more than switches that rapidly turn electrical impulses on and off.

This two-state on-and-off mode of electricity is called a *binary* state of electricity. Computers use a 1 to represent an on state (a switch in the computer that is on) and a 0 to represent an off state (a switch that is off). These numbers, 1 and 0, are called *binary digits,* often shortened to *bits.* A bit is either a 1 or a 0, representing an on or an off state of electricity. Different combinations of bits represent different characters.

A PC can represent 256 different characters. The 256 ASCII characters are listed in Appendix C.

In the ASCII table, a different combination of bits (1s and 0s strung together) represents each of the 256 ASCII characters. The ASCII table is a standard table used by almost every PC in the world. ASCII stands for American Standard Code for Information Interchange.

It turns out that if you take every different combination of eight 0s strung together, to eight 1s strung together (that is, from 00000000, 00000001, 00000010, and so on until you get to 11111110, and finally, 11111111), you have a total of 256 combinations. (256 is 2 to the 8th power.) Each memory location in your computer holds 8 bits each. These bits can be any combination of eight 1s and 0s. This brings us to the following fundamental rule of computers:

> Because it takes a combination of eight 1s and 0s to represent a character, and because each byte of computer memory can hold exactly one character, 8 bits equals 1 byte.

To bring this into better perspective, consider that the bit pattern needed for the uppercase letter A is 01000001. No other character in the ASCII table "looks" like this to the computer because each of the 256 characters is assigned a unique bit pattern.

Suppose that you press the A key on your keyboard. Your keyboard does *not* send a letter A to the computer; rather, it looks in its ASCII table for the on-and-off states of electricity that represent the letter A. Your computer simply stores this bit pattern for A in a memory location. Even though you can think of the memory location as holding an A, it really holds the byte 01000001.

If you were to print that A, your computer would not send an A to the printer; it would send the 01000001 bit pattern for an A to the printer. The printer receives that bit pattern, looks up the correct letter in the ASCII table, and prints an A.

There are times when your computer treats two bytes as a single value. Even though memory locations typically are 8 bits wide, many CPUs access memory 2 bytes at a time. If this is the case, the two bytes are called a *word* of memory. On other computers (commonly mainframes), the word size might be 4 bytes (32 bits) or even 8 bytes (64 bits).

Binary Numbers

Because a computer works best with 1s and 0s, its internal numbering method is limited to a *base-2* (binary) numbering system. People work in a *base-10* (or *decimal*) numbering system in "the real world." There are always as many different digits as the base in a numbering system. For example, in the base-10 system, there are 10 digits, 0 through 9. As soon as you count to 9 and run out of digits, you must combine some that you already used. The number 10 is a representation of ten values, but it combines the digits 1 and 0.

The same is true of base-2. There are only two digits, 0 and 1. As soon as you run out of digits, after the second one, you have to reuse digits. The first seven binary numbers are 0, 1, 10, 11, 100, 101, and 110.

It is okay if you do not understand how these numbers were derived; you will see how in a moment. For the time being, you should realize that no more than two digits, 0 and 1, can be used to represent any base-2 number, just as no more than 10 digits, 0 through 9, can be used to represent any base-10 number in the regular "real-world" numbering system.

You should know that a base-10 number, such as 3412, does not really mean anything by itself. You must assume what base it is. You get very used to working with base-10 numbers because you use them every day. However, the number 3412 actually represents a quantity based on powers of 10. For example, Figure B.1 shows what the number 3412 actually represents. Notice that each digit in the number represents a certain number of a power of 10.

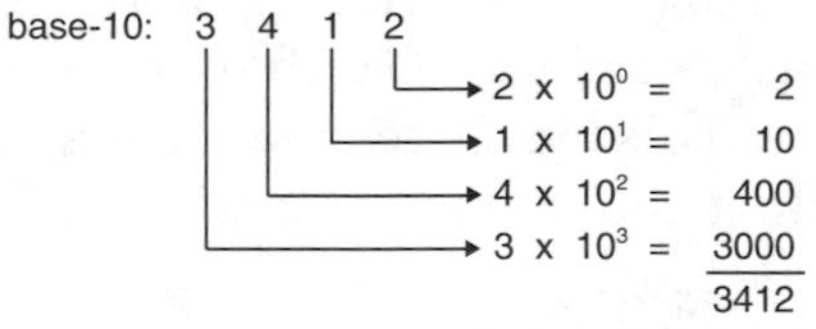

Figure B.1.
The base-10
breakdown of the
number 3412.

$$
\begin{array}{lrr}
\text{base-10:} & 3\ 4\ 1\ 2 & \\
& 2 \times 10^0 = & 2 \\
& 1 \times 10^1 = & 10 \\
& 4 \times 10^2 = & 400 \\
& 3 \times 10^3 = & \underline{3000} \\
& & 3412
\end{array}
$$

This same concept applies when you work in a base-2 numbering system. The power of 2 is just as common to your computer as the power of 10 is to you. The only difference is that the digits in a base-2 number represent powers of 2 and not powers of 10. Figure B.2 shows you what the binary numbers 101 and 100110 are in base-10. This is how you convert any binary number to its base-10 equivalent.

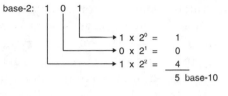

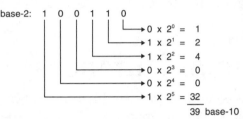

Figure B.2.
The base-2
breakdown of the
numbers 101 and
100110.

A base-2 number contains only 1s and 0s. To convert any base-2 number to base-10, add each power of 2 everywhere a 1 appears in the number. The base-2 number 110 represents the base-10 number 6. (There are two 1s in the number, one in the 2 to the first power, which equals 2, and one in the 2 to the second power, which equals 4.)

> **NOTE:** The largest binary number that a byte can hold is all 1s, or 11111111. If you add the first eight powers of 2, you get 255.

A binary number is not limited to a byte, as an ASCII character is. Sixteen or 32 bits at a time can represent a binary number (and usually do). There are more powers of 2 to add when converting that number to a base-10 number, but the process is the same. By now you should be able to figure out that 1010101010101010 is 43,690 in the base-10 numbering system (although it might take a little time to calculate).

Converting from decimal to binary takes a little more effort, and it is not covered here. Luckily, you rarely need to convert in that direction.

Most numbers are 16 bits long. That is, 2-byte words are used to store most integers. This is not always the case for all computers, but it is true for most PCs.

In the C++ programming language, you can designate numbers as either signed integers or unsigned integers (they are signed by default if you do not specify otherwise). If you designate a variable as a signed integer, the computer uses one bit to represent the sign (negative or

positive). If the sign bit is on (1), the number is negative. If the sign bit is off (0), the number is positive. If, however, you designate a variable as an unsigned integer, the computer uses the bit as just another power of 2. That is why the range of unsigned integer variables goes higher (generally from 0 to 65535, but it depends on the computer) than that for signed integer variables (generally from –32768 to +32767).

Hexadecimal Numbers

If it were up to your computer, you would enter *everything* as 1s and 0s! Because people don't like to program in 1s and 0s, a *hexadecimal* numbering system (sometimes called *hex*) was devised. The hexadecimal numbering system is based on base-16 numbers. As with other bases, there are 16 unique digits in the base-16 numbering system. Here are the first 19 hexadecimal numbers:

0 1 2 3 4 5 6 7 8 9 A B C D E F 10 11 12

Because there are only 10 unique digits (0 through 9), the letters A through F represent the remaining six digits. (Anything could have been used, but the designers of the hexadecimal numbering system decided to use the first six letters of the alphabet.)

To understand base-16 numbers, you should know how to convert them to base-10 so that they represent numbers with which people are familiar. Perform the conversion to base-10 from base-16 the same way you did with base-2, but instead of using powers of 2, represent each hexadecimal digit with powers of 16. Figure B.3 shows how to convert the number 4D8 to decimal.

Figure B.3. Converting hexadecimal 4D8 to its decimal equivalent.

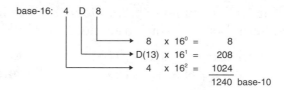

$$
\begin{array}{rll}
\text{base-16:} \quad 4 \quad D \quad 8 & & \\
8 \times 16^0 = & 8 \\
D(13) \times 16^1 = & 208 \\
4 \times 16^2 = & 1024 \\
\hline
& 1240 \text{ base-10}
\end{array}
$$

> **TIP:** There are calculators available that convert numbers between base-16, base-10, and base-2.

You should be able to convert 2B to its decimal 43 equivalent and E1 to decimal 225 in the same manner. Table B.1 shows the first 20 decimal, binary, and hexadecimal numbers.

Table B.1. The first 20 base-10, base-2 (binary), and base-16 (hexadecimal) numbers.

Base-10	Base-2	Base-16	Base-10	Base-2	Base-16
1	1	1	11	1011	B
2	10	2	12	1100	C
3	11	3	13	1101	D
4	100	4	14	1110	E
5	101	5	15	1111	F
6	110	6	16	10000	10
7	111	7	17	10001	11
8	1000	8	18	10010	12
9	1001	9	19	10011	13
10	1010	A	20	10100	14

Why Learn Hexadecimal?

Because of its close association with the binary numbers your computer uses, hexadecimal notation is extremely efficient for describing memory locations and values. It is much easier for you (and more important at this level, for your computer) to convert from base-16 to base-2 than from base-10 to base-2. Therefore, you sometimes want to represent data at the bit level, but using hexadecimal notation is easier (and requires less typing) than using binary numbers.

To convert from hexadecimal to binary, convert each hex digit to its four-bit binary number. You can use Table B.1 as a guide for this. For example, the following hexadecimal number

5B75

can be converted to binary by taking each digit and converting it to four binary numbers. If you need leading zeros to "pad" the four digits, use them. The number becomes

0101 1011 0111 0101

It turns out that the binary number 0101101101110101 is exactly equal to the hexadecimal number 5B75. This is much easier than converting them both to decimal first.

To convert from binary to hexadecimal, reverse this process. If you were given the following binary number

1101000011110111111010

you could convert it to hexadecimal by grouping the bits into groups of four, starting with the bit on the far right. Because there is not an even number of groups of four, pad the one on the far left with zeros. You then have the following:

0011 0100 0011 1101 1111 1010

Now you only have to convert each group of four binary digits into their hexadecimal number equivalent. You can use Table B.1 to help. You then get the following base-16 number:

343DFA

NOTE: The C++ programming language also supports the base-8 *octal* representation of numbers. Because octal numbers are rarely used with today's computers, they are not covered in this appendix.

How Binary and Addressing Relate to C++

Many C++ programmers learn C++ before delving into binary and hexadecimal representation. For those programmers, much about the C++ language seems strange, but it could be explained very easily if they understood the basic concepts.

The ASCII table (see Appendix C) should make more sense to you after this discussion. The ASCII character set is an integral part of your computer. Characters are not actually stored in memory and variables; rather, their ASCII bit patterns are. That is why C++ can move easily between characters and integers. The following two C++ statements are allowed, whereas you could not mix integers and characters in other programming languages:

```
char c = 65;    // Places the ASCII letter A in c

int ci = 'A';    // Places the number 65 in ci
```

The hexadecimal notation also makes much more sense if you truly understand base-16 numbers. For example, if you saw the following line in a C++ program

```
char a = '\x041';
```

you could convert the hex 41 to decimal (65 decimal) if you wanted to know what is being assigned. Also, C++ systems programmers find that they can better interface with assembly-language programs when they understand the concepts presented in this appendix.

ASCII Table

Dec X_{10}	Hex X_{16}	Binary X_2	ASCII Character
000	00	0000 0000	null
001	01	0000 0001	☺
002	02	0000 0010	☻
003	03	0000 0011	♥
004	04	0000 0100	◆
005	05	0000 0101	♣
006	06	0000 0110	♠
007	07	0000 0111	●
008	08	0000 1000	■
009	09	0000 1001	○
010	0A	0000 1010	■
011	0B	0000 1011	♂
012	0C	0000 1100	♀
013	0D	0000 1101	♪
014	0E	0000 1110	♪♪
015	0F	0000 1111	☼
016	10	0001 0000	►

Dec X_{10}	Hex X_{16}	Binary X_2	ASCII Character
017	11	0001 0001	◄
018	12	0001 0010	↕
019	13	0001 0011	‼
020	14	0001 0100	¶
021	15	0001 0101	§
022	16	0001 0110	▬
023	17	0001 0111	↨
024	18	0001 1000	↑
025	19	0001 1001	↓
026	1A	0001 1010	→
027	1B	0001 1011	←
028	1C	0001 1100	FS
029	1D	0001 1101	GS
030	1E	0001 1110	RS
031	1F	0001 1111	US
032	20	0010 0000	SP
033	21	0010 0001	!
034	22	0010 0010	"
035	23	0010 0011	#
036	24	0010 0100	$
037	25	0010 0101	%
038	26	0010 0110	&
039	27	0010 0111	'
040	28	0010 1000	(
041	29	0010 1001	)
042	2A	0010 1010	*
043	2B	0010 1011	+
044	2C	0010 1100	,
045	2D	0010 1101	-
046	2E	0010 1110	.
047	2F	0010 1111	/

Dec X_{10}	Hex X_{16}	Binary X_2	ASCII Character
048	30	0011 0000	0
049	31	0011 0001	1
050	32	0011 0010	2
051	33	0011 0011	3
052	34	0011 0100	4
053	35	0011 0101	5
054	36	0011 0110	6
055	37	0011 0111	7
056	38	0011 1000	8
057	39	0011 1001	9
058	3A	0011 1010	:
059	3B	0011 1011	;
060	3C	0011 1100	<
061	3D	0011 1101	=
062	3E	0011 1110	>
063	3F	0011 1111	?
064	40	0100 0000	@
065	41	0100 0001	A
066	42	0100 0010	B
067	43	0100 0011	C
068	44	0100 0100	D
069	45	0100 0101	E
070	46	0100 0110	F
071	47	0100 0111	G
072	48	0100 1000	H
073	49	0100 1001	I
074	4A	0100 1010	J
075	4B	0100 1011	K
076	4C	0100 1100	L
077	4D	0100 1101	M
078	4E	0100 1110	N

Dec X_{10}	Hex X_{16}	Binary X_2	ASCII Character
079	4F	0100 1111	O
080	50	0101 0000	P
081	51	0101 0001	Q
082	52	0101 0010	R
083	53	0101 0011	S
084	54	0101 0100	T
085	55	0101 0101	U
086	56	0101 0110	V
087	57	0101 0111	W
088	58	0101 1000	X
089	59	0101 1001	Y
090	5A	0101 1010	Z
091	5B	0101 1011	[
092	5C	0101 1100	\
093	5D	0101 1101	]
094	5E	0101 1110	^
095	5F	0101 1111	–
096	60	0110 0000	`
097	61	0110 0001	a
098	62	0110 0010	b
099	63	0110 0011	c
100	64	0110 0100	d
101	65	0110 0101	e
102	66	0110 0110	f
103	67	0110 0111	g
104	68	0110 1000	h
105	69	0110 1001	i
106	6A	0110 1010	j
107	6B	0110 1011	k
108	6C	0110 1100	l
109	6D	0110 1101	m

Dec X_{10}	Hex X_{16}	Binary X_2	ASCII Character
110	6E	0110 1110	n
111	6F	0110 1111	o
112	70	0111 0000	p
113	71	0111 0001	q
114	72	0111 0010	r
115	73	0111 0011	s
116	74	0111 0100	t
117	75	0111 0101	u
118	76	0111 0110	v
119	77	0111 0111	w
120	78	0111 1000	x
121	79	0111 1001	y
122	7A	0111 1010	z
123	7B	0111 1011	{
124	7C	0111 1100	¦
125	7D	0111 1101	}
126	7E	0111 1110	~
127	7F	0111 1111	DEL
128	80	1000 0000	Ç
129	81	1000 0001	ü
130	82	1000 0010	é
131	83	1000 0011	â
132	84	1000 0100	ä
133	85	1000 0101	à
134	86	1000 0110	å
135	87	1000 0111	ç
136	88	1000 1000	ê
137	89	1000 1001	ë
138	8A	1000 1010	è
139	8B	1000 1011	ï
140	8C	1000 1100	î

Dec X_{10}	Hex X_{16}	Binary X_2	ASCII Character
141	8D	1000 1101	ì
142	8E	1000 1110	Ä
143	8F	1000 1111	Å
144	90	1001 0000	É
145	91	1001 0001	æ
146	92	1001 0010	Æ
147	93	1001 0011	ô
148	94	1001 0100	ö
149	95	1001 0101	ò
150	96	1001 0110	û
151	97	1001 0111	ù
152	98	1001 1000	ÿ
153	99	1001 1001	Ö
154	9A	1001 1010	Ü
155	9B	1001 1011	¢
156	9C	1001 1100	£
157	9D	1001 1101	¥
158	9E	1001 1110	P$_t$
159	9F	1001 1111	ƒ
160	A0	1010 0000	á
161	A1	1010 0001	í
162	A2	1010 0010	ó
163	A3	1010 0011	ú
164	A4	1010 0100	ñ
165	A5	1010 0101	Ñ
166	A6	1010 0110	a
167	A7	1010 0111	o
168	A8	1010 1000	¿
169	A9	1010 1001	⌐
170	AA	1010 1010	¬
171	AB	1010 1011	½

Dec X_{10}	Hex X_{16}	Binary X_2	ASCII Character
172	AC	1010 1100	¼
173	AD	1010 1101	¡
174	AE	1010 1110	«
175	AF	1010 1111	»
176	B0	1011 0000	░
177	B1	1011 0001	▒
178	B2	1011 0010	▓
179	B3	1011 0011	│
180	B4	1011 0100	┤
181	B5	1011 0101	╡
182	B6	1011 0110	╢
183	B7	1011 0111	╖
184	B8	1011 1000	╕
185	B9	1011 1001	╣
186	BA	1011 1010	║
187	BB	1011 1011	╗
188	BC	1011 1100	╝
189	BD	1011 1101	╜
190	BE	1011 1110	╛
191	BF	1011 1111	┐
192	C0	1100 0000	└
193	C1	1100 0001	┴
194	C2	1100 0010	┬
195	C3	1100 0011	├
196	C4	1100 0100	─
197	C5	1100 0101	+
198	C6	1100 0110	╞
199	C7	1100 0111	╟
200	C8	1100 1000	╚
201	C9	1100 1001	╔
202	CA	1100 1010	╩

Dec X_{10}	Hex X_{16}	Binary X_2	ASCII Character
203	CB	1100 1011	╦
204	CC	1100 1100	╠
205	CD	1100 1101	═
206	CE	1100 1110	╬
207	CF	1100 1111	╧
208	D0	1101 0000	╨
209	D1	1101 0001	╤
210	D2	1101 0010	╥
211	D3	1101 0011	╙
212	D4	1101 0100	╘
213	D5	1101 0101	╒
214	D6	1101 0110	╓
215	D7	1101 0111	╫
216	D8	1101 1000	╪
217	D9	1101 1001	┘
218	DA	1101 1010	┌
219	DB	1101 1011	█
220	DC	1101 1100	▄
221	DD	1101 1101	▌
222	DE	1101 1110	▐
223	DF	1101 1111	▀
224	E0	1110 0000	α
225	E1	1110 0001	β
226	E2	1110 0010	Γ
227	E3	1110 0011	π
228	E4	1110 0100	Σ
229	E5	1110 0101	σ
230	E6	1110 0110	μ
231	E7	1110 0111	τ
232	E8	1110 1000	Φ
233	E9	1110 1001	θ

Dec X_{10}	Hex X_{16}	Binary X_2	ASCII Character
234	EA	1110 1010	Ω
235	EB	1110 1011	δ
236	EC	1110 1100	∞
237	ED	1110 1101	ø
238	EE	1110 1110	∈
239	EF	1110 1111	∩
240	F0	1111 0000	≡
241	F1	1111 0001	±
242	F2	1111 0010	≥
243	F3	1111 0011	≤
244	F4	1111 0100	⌠
245	F5	1111 0101	⌡
246	F6	1111 0110	÷
247	F7	1111 0111	≈
248	F8	1111 1000	°
249	F9	1111 1001	•
250	FA	1111 1010	·
251	FB	1111 1011	√
252	FC	1111 1100	η
253	FD	1111 1101	²
254	FE	1111 1110	■
255	FF	1111 1111	

NOTE: The last 128 ASCII codes listed in this table, numbers 128 through 255, are specific to IBM PCs and IBM compatibles.

C++
Precedence
Table

Precedence Level	Symbol	Description	Associativity
1	::	C++ scope access/resolution	Left to right
2	() [ ] -> .	Function call Array subscript C++ indirect component selector C++ direct component selector	Left to right
3 Unary	! ~ +	Logical negation Bitwise (1's) complement Unary plus	Right to left

Precedence Level	Symbol	Description	Associativity
	-	Unary minus	
	&	Addresss of	
	*	Indirection	
	sizeof	Returns size of operand in bytes.	
	new	Dynamically allocates C++ storage.	
	delete	Dynamically deallocates C++ storage.	
	type	Typecast	
4 Member Access	.*	C++ dereference	Left to right
	->*	C++ dereference	
	()	Expression parentheses	
5 Multiplicative	*	Multiply	Left to right
	/	Divide	
	%	Remainder (modulus)	
6 Additive	+	Binary plus	Left to right
	-	Binary minus	
7 Shift	<<	Shift left	Left to right
	>>	Shift right	
8 Relational	<	Less than	Left to right
	<=	Less than or equal to	
	>	Greater than	
	>=	Greater than or equal to	

Precedence Level	Symbol	Description	Associativity
9 Equality	==	Equal to	Left to right
	!=	Not equal to	
10	&	Bitwise AND	Left to right
11	^	Bitwise XOR	Left to right
12	¦	Bitwise OR	Left to right
13	&&	Logical AND	Left to right
14	¦¦	Logical OR	Left to right
15 Ternary	?:	Conditional	Right to left
16 Assignment	=	Simple assignment	Right to left
	*=	Assign product	
	/=	Assign quotient	
	%=	Assign remainder	
	+=	Assign sum	
	-=	Assign difference	
	&=	Assign bitwise AND	
	^=	Assign bitwise XOR	
	¦=	Assign bitwise OR	
	<<=	Assign left shift	
	>>=	Assign right shift	
17 Comma	,	Sequence point	Left to right

NOTE: Because of the confusion in most precedence tables, the postfix ++ and - - and the prefix ++ and - - do not appear here. Their precedence works the same in C++ as it does in C. The postfix operators usually appear in level 2, and the prefix operators appear in level 3. In practice, perform prefix before all other operators except for the scope resolution operator, and perform postfix right before the statement continues to the next executable statement in the program. C++ purists will cringe at this description, but it works 99.9 percent of the time, while the "technically correct" placements of these operators simply confuse programmers 99.9 percent of the time.

Index

J–K

L

N

P

Q–R

What's on the Disk

The disk contains the following:

All source code listings from the book, including programs that teach you all the basics of learning the C++ language.

Selected answers to questions and exercises.

Bonus questions and exercises to help further your understanding of C++.

Installing the Disk

Each lesson has a separate subdirectory on the disk. Within each subdirectory are the program listings, which have the .CPP file extension. The selected answers are found in a file named ANSWERS.TXT, and the extra questions and exercises are in a file named EXTRAQS.TXT.

To copy the files onto your hard drive, follow these steps:

1. Insert your companion disk into drive B.

2. Create a subdirectory called 101 on your hard drive.

   ```
   md 101
   ```

3. Change to that directory.

   ```
   cd\101
   ```

4. Copy the subdirectories and their contents to your 101 directory.

   ```
   xcopy b:*.* /s
   ```

License Agreement